THE SHI'A WORLDS AND IRAN

The Shi'a Worlds and Iran

Edited by
Sabrina Mervin

SAQI

in association with
Institut Français du Proche-Orient

*I wish to express my gratitude to Franck Mermier for his kind support,
and to Shikha Sethi and Alice Waugh for their attention to detail.*

ISBN: 978-0-86356-406-2

First published in French as *Les mondes chiites et l'Iran* by Éditions Karthala and IFPO, 2007

Printed and bound by CPI Mackays, Chatham, ME5 8TD

SAQI
26 Westbourne Grove, London W2 5RH, UK
2398 Doswell Avenue, Saint Paul, Minnesota, 55108, USA
Verdun, Beirut, Lebanon
www.saqibooks.com

in association with

www.ifporient.org

Contents

A Note on Transliteration

This book includes contributions from different cultural and linguistic areas, which have different systems of transliteration. In order to facilitate reading and for the coherence of the book, we have tried to harmonise spellings, when possible, around Arabic and Persian.

In the article about Turkey, we chose to keep the Turkish alphabet.

In Arabic, the long vowels are noted (â, î, û).

When a word or a proper name exists in Arabic and in Persian, it is transliterated according to the context. For example, we write *hawza* for Najaf (from the Arabic) and *hozeh* for Qom (from the Persian). In the same way, we write Khû'î when the name is mentioned in an Arabic context, Kho'i when it is mentioned in a Persian contextand Khoei when it appears in English (as it appears in official usage, see for example the Khoei Foundation).

Finally, spellings of frequently used proper nouns (such as Khomeini, Karbala, etc.) reflect common Western usage.

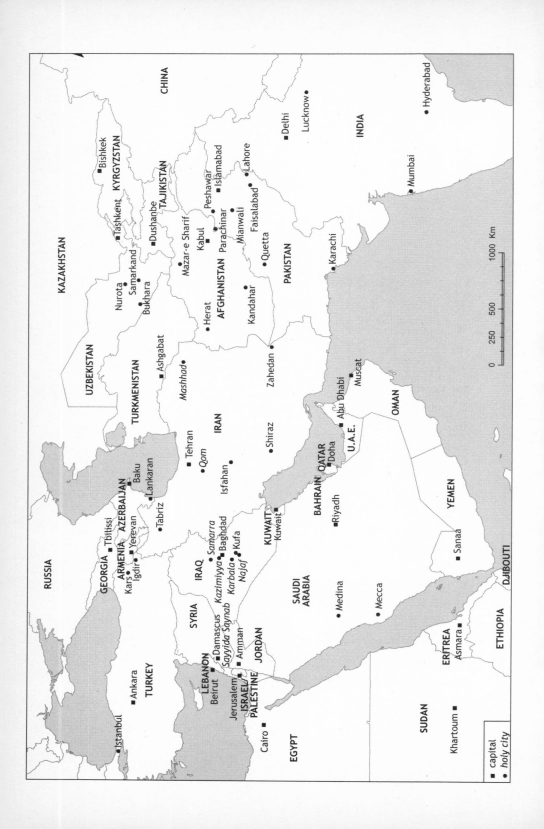

SABRINA MERVIN

Introduction

We may assume that the expression "Shiʿa worlds" will gain ground in the future. The "Shiʿa crescent", an easy and appealing construction, has made plenty of ink flow – probably too much – but it does not account for a complex and changing reality. Neither a crescent nor an arch form a homogeneous block under the direction of the Islamic Republic of Iran; there is rather a non-contiguous collection of spaces distributed over an area that is far wider than just the Middle East. There are zones hosting minorities and sometimes majorities of Twelver Shiʿa from Africa to China, without counting the diaspora in Europe, the United States and elsewhere. Hence we prefer to speak here of Shiʿa worlds, just as it is common to speak of Muslim worlds in plural,[1] because these worlds belong to different sociolinguistic spheres and are embedded in different local cultures. The researchers who have contributed to the present project specialize in the different regions that concern us, but they are also experts on contemporary Shiʿa Islam or on Islamic movements in general. The "crescent" is easily forgotten when we take a closer look at the subject and internalize the idea that "the Shiʿa factor" – another fashionable expression these days – has become an issue that needs to be taken into consideration.

It is useful to remember that the expression "the Shiʿa crescent" was born

---

1. With all necessary precaution, since the aim is not to essentialize but rather to contextualize and account for interrelations. On this subject, see Denoix, 2004, pp. 7–26.

out of fear of the resurgence or rise of Shi'a Islam following the American invasion of Iraq and the fall of Saddam Hussein in April 2003. In Iraq, but also in the Gulf, Shi'a started demanding that their demographic weight play its proper role in the political balance, which provoked reactions from Arab leaders as well as American neo-conservatives.[1] Mahmud Ahmadinejad's rise to power, bringing along his renewed revolutionary and millenarist enthusiasm, populist domestic policies, anti-American foreign outlook, and his firm position on nuclear power, has increased fear of a revival of Iranian influence. While the struggle to export the Islamic Revolution seemed to have ended in a relative defeat for Iran, a new era of strife was beginning between the major powers in the region – of which Iran claimed to be one. Later, the July 2006 war between the Lebanese Hezbollah and Israel reinforced the Tehran-Damascus-Hezbollah axis; this alliance on a new front of refusal was more political than Shi'a.[2]

Against the backdrop of a cold war between Iran and Saudi Arabia, the Jordanian king's complaints in 2004 about the "Shi'a crescent" were followed by repeated fulminations by the Egyptian president Husni Mubarak against what he called the "Iran-Hezbollah coalition" and its plots. The peak of the crisis came in spring 2009 when the Egyptians arrested a group of people and accused them of being linked with Hezbollah and plotting terrorist attacks in the country. At the same time, Morocco cut its diplomatic relations with Iran, accusing the Iranian mission of seeking to spread Shi'ism in the kingdom and to interfere in its internal affairs.

The idea for this book predates all these events; even before 2003, Shi'a Islam was becoming more visible, due to its rituals and institutions in various locations, and research on non-Iranian Shi'ism was starting to expand. Several publications had already carried contributions on various

---

1. The subject of Sunni-Shi'a conflicts, which have contributed to reshaping the Middle East, is treated by Vali Nasr in Nasr, 2006.

2. Among other factors, this political alliance is underpinned by religion, as some of the Alawis have moved closer to the Twelver Shi'ites in order to integrate more into the *umma*. This doctrinal overture started in the early twentieth century, developed in the 1950s and continued under the presidency of Hafez al-Assad. Lebanese as well as Iraqi Shi'a participated in this movement through the foundation of places of worship and *hawzas*. Cf. Mervin, 2002, pp. 281–288; and Mervin 2006, pp. 343–358.

Shi'a communities in different countries.[1] Researchers specializing in the subject began to expand their fields, collaborating around different themes, comparing and relating these geographically remote Shi'a worlds in an endeavor to account for their similarities and differences via a heuristical approach.[2]

In this collection of essays, we aim to continue in the same direction as well as exploring other paths by focusing on the tenuous relations, if any, between these Shi'a worlds and Iran, where Shi'ism is both the faith of the majority and the state religion. What is the place of Iran, a country that is routinely claimed to occupy a central position among these Shi'a worlds? Can we envisage its role without reducing it to the export of the revolution? To what extent can we speak of an Iranian model? The present book provides answers to these questions, broadening our knowledge of little-known communities such as the Ironi Shi'a of Uzbekistan and refining our understanding of groups that have been studied more extensively, like those in Iraq. Yet we do not want to close the debate or propose a theory: firstly, because the ties between Iran and the Shi'a worlds need to be considered in the long term;[3] and secondly, because many communities are not dealt with here, most importantly the Indian Shi'a – important for their vast numbers as much as their history – but also the community in Bangladesh, the diaspora, the small groups found in the Caribbean and the even less numerous and lesser known Shi'a of Thailand.[4]

The Shi'a dealt with here are Twelver or Imami Shi'a; it is to this group that most contributors refer when they use the term without further specification.[5] The Ismaili, Zaydi and other groups remotely or

1. Cf. Scarcia-Amoretti, 1994; and Fuller and Francke 2001.
2. Two colloquia were organised, one in Freiburg, the other in Geneva, and their proceedings published. Cf. Brunner and Ende, 2001; and Monsutti, Naef and Sabahi, 2007.
3. This would be easier in a monograph. See for example Chehabi, 2006, which transcends clichés and commonplaces about the relatively recent relations between Iran and Lebanon. See also Cole 2002, for a collection of essays on both the modern and contemporary periods.
4. Research on India and the Caribbean has concentrated on rituals. See among others Pinault 2001, and Korom 2003.
5. Among specialists, this distinction is clear, but in vulgarising publications and

closely related to branches of Shi'ism are not discussed here.[1] The dogma of Twelver Shi'ism acknowledges a succession of twelve Imams from the *ahl al-bayt* (people of the house) of Muhammad, who are his successors as leaders of the community. First among these is 'Alî b. Abî Tâlib, cousin and son-in-law of Muhammad, followed by his two sons Hasan and then Husayn, the martyr of Karbala. The twelfth and last successor is the Mahdî, the hidden Imam who, according to doctrine, has been in Major Occultation since 941 and will reappear before the end of times to restore justice on earth; the faithful await him.

Specifically Twelver rituals derive from the doctrine of the imamate, which, contrary to its Sunni counterpart the caliphate, is an integral part of the principles of the religion (*usûl al-dîn*). They are also related to the specific place occupied by the *ahl al-bayt* and their history. These practices consist mostly of *ziyâra* (pious visits) throughout the year to the tombs of the *ahl al-bayt*, pilgrimages that mark and punctuate the space of the Shi'a worlds. A special place is occupied by the shrines of the Imams 'Alî in Najaf, Husayn in Karbala and Ridâ/Rezâ in Mashhad.[2] Added to this cult of holy figures are the rituals of the month of Muharram in commemoration of the battle of Karbala in 680. These celebrations culminate on the tenth day of the month, the day of Ashura, when devotees relive the martyrdom of Husayn through public rites, processions and theatrical representations, sometimes accompanied by spectacular practices of mortification. Satellite channels broadcast the images, as if to illustrate the slogan "Every day is Ashura and the whole world is Karbala." On that day, after attending or participating in the rituals of their neighborhood, devotees watch their fellow believers in Shi'a worlds all over the globe perform the same movements and pronounce the same words. Despite local particularities, the mirroring effect is evident. The other is acknowledged as an individual belonging to a community much larger than that of everyday life, through a common expression of devotion to Husayn and the other imams and

---

in the media there is often confusion, and erroneous definitions circulate.

1. On the different branches of Shi'ism, see Halm 2004; and Mervin 2010, chapters VI and VII.
2. Other Imams, as well as Fatima, had their mausoleums in Medina until the Wahhabis relegated them to simple tombs after occupying the city in December 1925.

through the recitation of a shared history that began with the epos of the "people of the house".

This common history continues throughout successive *tabaqât* (layers) of religious scholars, who elaborated the doctrine and progressively assumed more of the prerogatives of the Imams, thus positioning themselves as guides to the community; spiritual guides who occasionally extended their authority to the political sphere.[1] This began in Kufa, the city where 'Alî exercised his imamate, and later branched out to other cities as well as modest villages, which for a while became places of Shi'a scholarship, until it reached Safavid Iran in the sixteenth century. When the Iranians adopted Shi'a Islam, their ambition was to become its center: becoming a "fluid field of interactions", undergoing influence from abroad and in turn exporting its influence to the Arab regions as well as Central and South Asia.[2] The number of Persian *ulemas* grew at the expense of Arabic *ulemas*.

Najaf and Qom: competing for centrality

The ancient *hawza* of Najaf soon became an important centre of Shi'ism, attracting students and clerics from Iran and elsewhere who came to gain and share knowledge of the religious sciences. This knowledge did not remain unchanged; little by little, it became more rational as the *usulî* current gained the upper hand over the more literal *akhbârî* approach. But although the former prevailed, in part through the use of violence in the eighteenth century, polemics and doctrinal divisions between clerics continued to guarantee a degree of plurality in doctrinal approaches. The incessant mingling of populations from the remote regions where Shi'a identities developed, anchored in local cultures and formed through processes specific to each culture, added another level of diversity to this plurality. Thus Najaf and the other *'atabât* (sacred thresholds) of Shi'ism, such as Karbala, Samarra and Kazimiyya, developed a degree of cosmopolitanism that left considerable space for the expression of

---

1. For an overview of the development of this doctrine, see Amir-Moezzi and Jambet, 2004, pp. 181–220; or for a shorter account, Mervin, 2001, chapter VII.
2. Cole, 2002, p. 2.

local particularities and linguistic identities, strengthening ties among those who shared a common origin. Nevertheless, solidarity networks also developed between Shi'a worlds, creating the embryo of a "Shi'a international"[1] even as animosities between Arabs, Turks and Persians,[2] to mention just a few, were beginning to appear. Moreover, there was an increasing rivalry between cities (such as Najaf and Karbala), while some city quarters were controlled by gangs linked to certain *ulemas* (such as the Zugurt and Shumurt in Najaf) and clerical families eager to increase their control over the management of sacred affairs. Indeed, there was no uniformity in this society of turbaned men in perpetual negotiation, divided by internal discord but nevertheless presenting a united front towards the outside world. The centre – made up of Najaf and her sisters, the other *'atabât* – expanded its influence to the very limits of the Shi'a worlds in order to attract new candidates to perpetuate the group.

From the mid-nineteenth century onwards, Najaf positioned itself as the seat of the *marja'iyya*, which provided Shi'ism with religious authority in the person of the *marja'*, a grand cleric and an institution who certainly made informal appearances but also organized clerical hierarchies and the relationship between believers and the top ranks of this hierarchy. In the early twentieth century, when the advent of the telegraph intensified communications between the centre and the periphery, Najaf flourished not only on a doctrinal but also on a political level. The Iranian constitutionalist movement (1906–11) was endorsed by leading Persian clerics living in the holy city, such as Mohammad Kâzem Khorasâni (d. 1911). The *ulemas* also played a decisive role in the fight against the British mandate and the formation of modern Iraq.[3] However, the political defeat which they suffered weakened them, and some were exiled to Iran where they participated in the "re-foundation" of the school of Qom in the 1920s.[4] This marked the beginning of the rivalry between the two centers of Qom and Najaf, which continue to this day to compete for primacy as

---

1. Cf. Litvak, 1998, p. 31, who took the expression from Chibli Mallat.
2. The Turks concerned here are in fact Azeris. Cf. *Ibid.*, p. 201, footnote 38.
3. On this subject, see Luizard 1991.
4. Qom derives its legitimacy as a holy city from the presence of the mausoleum of Fâtima, sister of the eighth Imam.

the sacred source, home of knowledge, centre for the formation of clerics and seat of religious authority "ruling" over all the Shi'a worlds.

Already before the Iranian revolution, the efforts of Ayatollah Borujerdi (d. 1961), a *marja'* who was recognized by all, to modernize the *hozeh* of Qom had notably undermined the prestige of Najaf and attracted many students. The establishment of the Islamic Republic led to new reforms in Qom, as the objective now became to train clerics who would also be government officials, and to attract foreigners liable to support the Islamic project upon their return to their home countries. Qom had the necessary means to develop a religious education system that was modern and efficient while simultaneously claiming a tradition that attested to the depth of the studies. The city's influence grew, to the detriment of Najaf and the holy cities in Iraq, which were also under attack by Saddam Hussein's Ba'athist regime. Today Qom has around 30,000 students, while Najaf has barely a few thousand. The renewal of the Iraqi *hawza* expected after the fall of Saddam Hussein in 2003 seems to have been postponed *sine die* due to the chaos submerging the country, which does not allow even for a normal functioning of the schools, even if ambitious new projects are being prepared.

Nevertheless, Najaf remains Qom's rival, particularly as the city hosts four *marja'*, including 'Ali Sistani, to whom the majority of believers not just in Iraq but throughout the Shi'a worlds refer.[1] Sayyida Zaynab, a suburb of Damascus named after the sister of Imam Husayn whose shrine is located there, is a minor centre but it has been compensating for the failure of Najaf since the 1980s. Although it is a popular pilgrimage site (notably for Iranians who visit there on organized tours) and a place where Shi'a populations mix, no famous *marja'* resides there. Only the Lebanese Muhammad Husayn Fadlallâh maintains a regular presence, often visiting for lectures. Najaf and Qom both have their own networks of interaction, which may overlap, with places that function as relay stations as well as local centers with their own characteristics, such as Mashhad in Iran, the southern suburbs of Beirut in Lebanon or Lucknow in India.[2]

1. The other three are Muhammad Sa'îd al-Hakîm, Ishâq Fayyâd and Bashîr Najafî Pakistanî.
2. The southern suburbs of Beirut are a recent centre, created by Shi'a migrating from South Lebanon and the Bekaa valley to the capital. It benefits from

Marjaʻiyya and Hawza, the pillars of religious authority

The centrality of the holy cities relies first and foremost on the sacred nature of the locations and their appeal as pilgrimage destinations which entails the movement of populations and the circulation of goods. Mash-had, for example – a phenomenon which unfortunately has not yet received the in-depth study it merits – welcomes over ten million visitors per year. Their centrality is further based on the two interdependent institutions around which the clergy is structured, the *hawza* and the *marjaʻiyya*. These constitute the pillars of religious authority in contemporary Shiʻism, and an understanding of their functioning is indispensable for the study of the religion.[1]

The term *hawza* refers to a system of teaching, to a religious school where clerics are educated, to a group of schools situated in one city, and to the clerics who make up its students and teachers. Two systems coexist today and tend to complement each other: the classic system, and the system of the "reformed" schools, usually called *maʻhad* (institutes). The former is also called the "free" system, as students can choose the courses they wish to follow and the masters with whom they desire to study. The studies take many years and are divided into three cycles: the first, *muqaddimât*, aims at acquiring the basics; the second, *sutûth*, at assimilating the classic works of each discipline; and the third, *khârij*, trains the students to the practice of *ijtihâd*. The subjects studied are the classical Islamic religious sciences.[2]

In the institutes of the reformed system, students enroll after their secondary education and take four years to complete the first two cycles. In addition to the classical courses, they take new religious sciences (Islamic economy as laid out by Muhammad Bâqir al-Sadr, comparative *fiqh*,

---

taking over the role formerly played by Jabal ʻÂmil in Shiʻa history. Lucknow has been a Shiʻa centre since the beginning of the eighteenth century.

1. There are many books and articles about these institutions in Arabic and Persian that cannot be referred to here. For the sources available in English and French, the reader can consult Fischer, 1980; Litvak, 1998; Walbridge 2001; Abdul-Jabar 2002; Khalaji 2006; and references in articles by Sabrina Mervin: Mervin 1995, 2003 and 2004.

2. Arabic language, rhetoric, logic, *fiqh* and *usûl al-fiqh*, Qurʼanic exegesis, *hadîth* and theology, to which can be added Islamic philosophy and gnosis (*ʻirfân*).

history and philosophy of *fiqh*); history (of religions and of Islam); and introductory courses in social sciences (sociology and psychology.). If the students wish to continue their studies, they are required to attend *khârij* courses, which are always "free" and are taught by a renowned *mujtahid* or even a *marja'*. Very few *hawzas* are capable of providing *khârij* courses, so most students go to Qom or Najaf to complete this cycle, hence these two cities are the breeding-ground of Shi'a clergy. They are also the places where religious intellectuals and militants are educated who wish to acquire a religious formation in parallel to their university studies. Moreover, most of the books and journals documenting the doctrinal debates engaging the *hawza* circles are published here.

Qom, with its leading masters in classical *fiqh* and its modern Islamic universities, offers a wide choice to Iranian students. Foreigners are directed to the International Centre of Islamic Sciences (Markaz jahâni-ye 'olum-e eslâmi) which, after intensive courses of Persian, takes them through the various stages of their education which may last up to fourteen years. Modern methods and techniques as well as reformed sciences are taught there. Around one hundred nationalities are represented in the centre: Arabs, Pakistanis, Afghans, Azeris and Indians, but also Chinese – the latter including Sunnis – come to merge in the melting pot of Qom and partake of the spirit that pervades its atmosphere. In addition, an organization based in Tehran takes care of the founding and the functioning of schools abroad.

What does this "spirit" of Qom that spreads through the Shi'a worlds consist of? It is not just a revolutionary spirit, but also a certain concept of Islamic modernity which all can adapt and apply after returning to their own societies. It means being informed on the debates that scholars engage in, profiting from the cosmopolitan ambience to open up to the world and develop networks, as well as acquainting oneself with Persian language and culture. Qom is moreover home to a dozen *marja'*,[1] all with different opinions concerning the Khomenist theory of *velâyat-e*

---

1.   It is difficult to find an exhaustive, accurate up-to-date list in the sources available. We could refer for example to the list made by Mehdi Khalaji (Khalaji 2006), which mentions Javâd Tabrizi *marja'* who deceased in 2006, but omits two important figures, 'Ali Montazeri, who died in 2009, and Kâzem Hâ'eri..

faqih and the way it has been implemented since the birth of the Islamic Republic of Iran. This is an element of the particular "spirit" of Qom; no other place offers such a concentration of grand clerics, although most of them exert only a limited local and national influence.

The *marja'* is formed in the *hawza* and generally goes on to teach there. Some basic rules determine the qualities he is required to possess – the first of which is to be the most knowledgeable among his peers – and govern his relationship with his adepts, i.e. the modalities of *taqlîd* (imitation) and the right way to follow his religious precepts. In addition to these few rules, the *marja'iyya* is organized according to unwritten manners and customs rather than explicit rules that can be freely consulted; it therefore does not permit external control, while guaranteeing the flexibility of an institution that has been subject to continuous redefinition since its creation.

The process of the emergence of a *marja'* is very subtle, as he is not designated or elected by any organ or institution. He is required to rise above the pool of *mujtahid* and succeed in being recognized as the best among them by the clergy, the *hawza* masters and advanced students, as well as by the financial circles on whose support he will depend. When he has in addition written a *risâla 'amaliyya* (practical treaty) of *fiqh*, offering religious precepts for his adepts to follow, believers are free to adopt him as their *marja'* and pay religious taxes (*khums* and *zakât*) to him. This system ensures the plurality of the *marja'iyya*.

Although it continues to function elsewhere, in Iran the system was disrupted in 1989 over the choice of a successor to Khomeini as *marja'* and *rahbar* (guide) of the state. As *marja'*, Khomeini was the rival of the grand master of the *hawza* of Najaf, Abu al-Qâsem Kho'i (d. 1992), who had more followers in Iraq and in the Shi'a worlds than Khomeini. But Khomeini was also the Guide of the Republic and before his death, he designated 'Ali Khamenei as his successor in this double role. Khamenei, a cleric, was not even recognized as *mujtahid* at that time. This maneuver provoked resistance in Iran, where clerics refused to acknowledge Khamenei's *marja'iyya*. He suffered a second setback in the mid-1990s, when he tried to impose himself as *marja'* of all the Shi'a worlds. Believers preferred other *marja's* to him, notably those who defined themselves as successors of Kho'i, that is to say non-political clerics from the school of Najaf, such as 'Ali Sistani.[1] In Lebanon, during the 1990s, Muhammad Husayn Fadlallâh distanced himself from Iran – and from Hezbollah – to emerge as a *marja'* who would resist Iran's hegemonic claims.[2] His relations with them gradually warmed up and he came back as a political ally during the 2006 Israeli war against Lebanon, but he still claims his intellectual, religious and financial independence.[3]

   'Ali Khamenei's attempt to monopolize the *marja'iyya*, which would have resulted in the creation of an Iranian *marja'iyya* related to the Islamic Republic, thus failed. Over the years, he has succeeded in obtaining followers outside Iran, positioning himself as a sage and a charismatic arbitrator, especially after the rise to power of Ahmadinejad, who has played the role of "revolutionary" and "extremist". But his support of Ahmedinejad during the political crisis that occurred after the presidential elections of June 2009 weakened him. The *marja'iyya* remains plural, divided between Qom, Najaf and other possible poles like Mashhad or Beirut. 'Ali Sistani remains the most widely followed *marja'*.

Nationalisms and transnationalism

The *marja'iyya* is essentially supra-statal and transnational, largely because of its economic independence: it is financed by the believers themselves through *khums* money rather than by any state. Its function is to redistribute these funds through charitable institutions and religious schools, which heighten its prestige and ensure the continuity of the group of clerics. Each *marja'*, therefore, stands at the head of a religious enterprise that sometimes handles enormous sums of money, as Kho'i did in the past and Sistani does today. The *marja'iyya* thus implies managing not just matters of spiritual salvation but also very mundane and worldly affairs,

---

1. Cf. Martin, 1993; Buchta, 1995; Buchta, 2000, chapter V; Gieling 1994; and Roy 1999.
2. Sankari, 2005, p. 256–260; Shaery-Eisenlohr, 2008, p. 123 ff, which argues that Fâdlallâh wanted to construct an Arabic *marja'iyya* by distinguishing himself through a modernist reformist project.
3. According to Khalaji, 2006, p. 10, he manages a fortune of 500 to 700 billion dollars.

which goes some way towards explaining the stakes of the competition hidden beneath the velvet appearances of clerical circles.

Each *marja'* has *wakîl* (agents) to represent him in places where he has a following. The agents are charged with the task of, on the one hand, divulging his precepts and on the other, collecting religious taxes, to be used locally or to be transferred to the seat of the *marja'iyya*. We are in effect talking about a widespread organization with tentacles stretching across the Shi'a worlds. In any place with a strong Shi'a presence, especially in the holy cities, *marja's* offices abound, one next to the other, sometimes several in the same street, as if to mark their territories. Furthermore, nowadays every *marja'* runs his own website, or even several of them, which eliminates distances and implies a new type of communication between the *marja'* and his followers.[1] Some even offer the possibility of paying religious taxes online.[2]

Shi'a transnationalism thus relies on the networks formed by clerical circles and resulting from a long history of population movements, especially the migrations of *ulemas*, and marital bonds between different clerical families. While these are not recent phenomena, they are still being perpetuated, re-negotiated or recreated. Certain families thus have anchor-points in different countries, which they maintain and renew through alliances and intellectual affinities. The Sadr family is an example in point. Descendants of a lineage from Jabal 'Âmil (now South Lebanon) and present in Lebanon under the name Sharaf al-Dîn, the family has branches in Iraq and Iran that continue to intermarry, thus ensuring group cohesion. Moreover, this family, like many others, has allied itself with political figures and leading clerics.[3] This practice unites the ranks, increasing everyone's political options. It is interesting to note, for example, the Iranian origins of certain families in Bahrain or Iraq, such as the Shirâzi, who are known as a family from Karbala but who, as

---

1. On this subject, see Rosiny 2003–04.
2. The sites of 'Ali Sistani as well as those of the Kho'i foundation: www.al-khoei. org
3. The Iranian Mûsâ Sadr and the Iraqi Muhammad Bâqir al-Sadr, two figureheads of Islamic movements, were cousins and brothers-in-law, while Muqtadâ al-Sadr married a daughter of Muhammad Bâqir. Cf. Mervin, 2000, p. 437; and Chehabi, 2006, p. 140, fig. 6.1. This table shows the relationships established with Mohammad Khatami and Ahmad Khomeini.

their name indicates, originated in Iran. The identitary representations resulting from this can be astonishing when viewed from the outside: Kho'i and Sistani are in the first place perceived as *marja's* embodying the school of Najaf, even if they are Iranian. Indeed, Sistani, who even speaks with a Persian accent, is seen as "more Arabic than Iranian" and appeals to Arab nationalists.

This transnationalism neither prevents Shi'a communities from constructing national identities, nor stops them from integrating into the states they reside in. While this phenomenon may leave observers perplexed, the players themselves see no contradiction in it. Returning to the example cited above, Mûsa Sadr, born in Iran, whose mother tongue is Persian and culture is Iranian, worked for the integration of the Shi'a in Lebanon where he established himself in 1959 to ensure the continuity of the *magistere* of a remote cousin, 'Abd al-Husayn Sharaf al-Dîn. In 1963, President Fuad Shihab accorded him Lebanese nationality; ten years later, he conflicted with the Shah of Iran, and then lost his Iranian nationality. As if he had lived two lives, two very different images of Mûsa Sadr now exist in Iran and in Lebanon.[1]

Without calling it actual contradiction, we nevertheless observe a certain tension between local or national Shi'a identities involved in a process of definition and redefinition, and Shi'a transnationalism, on which Iran's claim of hegemony over the Shi'a worlds has grafted itself. This claim dates back to the foundation of Iranian Shi'ism under the Safavids and could also be observed under the reign of Reza Shah, even though the latter implemented a policy of secularization. With the arrival of the Islamic Republic, the claim began to be used in a different way.[2] The question of the export of the revolution has been dealt with

---

1. Two research centres are dedicated to him, one in Lebanon and one in Iran. On Mûsa Sadr in Iran, an aspect until now rather neglected in the available publications, we want to mention the excellent article of Houchang E. Chehabi and Majid Tafreshi, 'Mûsa Sadr and Iran' in *ibid*.
2. It must be noted that it is difficult to speak of an action taken by 'Iran' as if it is emerging from one entity. The politics of the Islamic Republic are developed through different institutions and organisations, many of which are connected to its Guide, but others to ministers and foundations that are more or less independent – such as the very powerful Astan-e Qods of Mashhad – or even to individuals. On this point Buchta, 2000, is very useful.

exhaustively in research published during the 1990s.[1] The historiography of the construction of local identities is currently being undertaken and reveals the particularities of each Shi'a community.[2] However, little attention has been paid to this tension, which is precisely what the five articles opening this volume propose to do, under the title "The Export of the Revolution and National Integrations". After a general overview by Olivier Roy, Alessandro Monsutti presents the case of Afghanistan, while Laurence Louër treats the Gulf states. Two articles deal with the Lebanese Hezbollah: Joseph Alagha studies the evolution of the notion of the Islamic state as developed by the party, while Kinda Chaib approaches the link with Iran through the iconography of martyrs in the Shi'a regions and quarters of Lebanon.

The second part, "Constructing Shi'isms", presents analyses of identitary inscription processes through particular case studies, showing how the Shi'a emerge and invent themselves as a group. This part also focuses on the role Iran plays in this process, whether through broadcasting religious rituals, scattering "Shi'a culture" via its institutions (cultural centers, religious schools), or political activism. Thierry Zarcone writes the contemporary history of the Shi'a communities of Turkey and discusses the place Iranians occupy in this history and, more recently, the role played in it by Iran. Next we move to Central Asia: Bayram Balci relates the renaissance of Azerbaijani Shi'ism and demonstrates how Iran contributed to this process, while Boris Pétric deals with the Shi'a of Uzbekistan, known as the Ironis. Still further afield, in Africa, the Shi'a of Senegal consist of two groups, Lebanese and local converts, presented here by Mara Leichtman.

Which "Iranian model" is transmitted and how? Is it possible to understand this model while transcending established ideas of direct Iranian influence on this or that contesting party? Part Three attempts to shed light on this matter. Two articles on Muqtadâ Sadr, the insurgent cleric, one by Pierre-Jean Luizard and the other by Peter Harling and Hamid Yassin Nasser, explain a phenomenon that is still poorly understood, despite its omnipresence in the media. The authors illustrate the complex

---

1. Referring, for example, to Esposito, 1990; Menashri, 1990 and 1997; Amirah-madi and Entessar, 1993. To see how the research questions change later, see Keddie and Mathee, 2002
2. Cf. notably Nakash, 2006.

relationship between the revolutionary Iraqi and his Iranian neighbor. What is this Iranian model that no longer consists exclusively of the political model of revolutionary Islam? Mariam Abou Zahab reveals certain aspects (Islamic feminism, rationalism and the modernity of an education that permits social mobility) by following the voyage of Pakistani women who go and study at the *hozeh* of Qom. Other elements are discussed by Sabrina Mervin, who endeavors to define the influence exerted on intellectual and Islamic Arab circles by the laboratory of religious ideas that is Iran.

Because it is continually shifting, it is difficult to measure the impact on the Shi'a worlds of the internal political crisis into which Iran sank after the presidential elections of June 2009, just as the Obama administration reduced the pressure on Iran. There is a deep divide between an increasingly autocratic power and an educated civil society that is demanding a return to republican political practices. Debates about the Khomeinist theory of *velâyat-e faqih* restarted, up until now more inside Iran than outside. Ahmedinejad's plan to impose a new Cultural Revolution (with a systematic Islamization of social sciences in the universities) would provoke a variety of reactions, as well as informing other debates.

On a strictly political level, Iran's neighbors, especially concerned by the maintenance of safety and order in the region, considered this turmoil as an internal question. The same applies to its ally Hezbollah, whose deputy secretary-general Sheikh Naim Qassem said during the dramatic events that occurred after the poll: "The disagreements between the parties in Iran are affairs that concern essentially the Iranians." On the other hand, the party claims wide independence in the conduct of its own affairs inside Lebanon. Towards its allies and the Shi'a worlds, Iran has implemented a politics of cultural diplomacy and soft power: a long-term, patient work of developing deep cultural ties.

Bibliography

Abdul-Jabar, Faleh, ed., *Ayatollahs, Sufis and Ideologues. State, Religion and Social Movements in Iraq*, London 2002, Saqi Books.

Abdul-Jabar, Faleh ed., *The Shiʿite Movement* in Iraq, London 2003, Saqi Books.

Adelkhah, Fariba, "Économie morale du pèlerinage et société civile en Iran: les voyages religieux, commerciaux et touristiques à Damas", in *Politix*, n°77, 2007/1, pp. 39–54.

Amirahmadi, Hooshang, and Entessar, Nader, eds, *Iran and the Arab World*, New York 1993, St. Martin's Press.

Amir-Moezzi, Mohammad-Ali and Jambet, Christian, *Quest-ce que le shiʿisme ?*, Paris 2004, Fayard.

Bontems, Nathalie, "Iran-Liban, le Hezbollah fait le dos rond", on slate.fr. http://www.slate.fr/story/7485/iran-liban-hezbollah-syrie-israel-nasrallah-ahmadinejad

Brunner, Rainer, and Ende, Werner, eds, *The Twelver Shiʿa in Modern Times. Religious Culture and Political History,* Leiden 2001, Brill.

Buchta, Wilfried, "Die Islamische Republik Iran und die religiös-politische Kontroverse um die marjaʿiyat", in *Orient*, 36, 1995, pp. 449–74.

Buchta, Wilfried, *Who rules Iran? The Structure of Power in the Islamic Republic,* Washington 2000, Washington Institute for Near East Policy-Konrad Adenauer Stifting.

Chehabi, Houchang E., ed., *Distant relations. Iran and Lebanon in the last 500 years*, London 2006, I. B. Tauris and Centre for Lebanese Studies.

Chehabi, Houchang E., and Majid, Tafreshi, "Musa Sadr and Iran", in *Distant relations. Iran and Lebanon in the last 500 years*, New York 2006, I. B. Tauris, pp. 137–161.

Cole, Juan, *Sacred Space and Holy War. The Politics, Culture and History of Shiʿite Islam*, London and New York 2002, I.B. Tauris.

Denoix, Sylvie, "Des culs-de-sac heuristiques aux garde-fous épistémologiques ou comment aborder l'aire culturelle du 'monde musulman'", in *REMMM*, 103–104, 2004, pp. 7–26.

Esposito, John L., and Voll, John, *Makers of Contemporary Islam*, Oxford 2001, Oxford University Press.

Esposito, John L., ed., *The Iranian Revolution: its Global Impact,* Miami 1990, Florida international University Press.

Fischer, Michael M.J., *Iran from Religious Dispute to Revolution,* Cambridge and London 1980, Harvard University Press.

Fuller, Graham E., and Francke, Rend Rahim, *The Arab Shiʿa. The Forgotten Muslims,* New York 2001, Palgrave.

Gieling, Saskia, "The *marjaʿiya* in Iran and the Nomination of Khamenei in December 1994", in *Middle Eastern Studies*, 33, 1997, pp. 777–87.

Goodarzi, Jubin M., *Syria and Iran. Diplomatic alliance and power politics in the Middle East*, London and New York 2009, I. B. Tauris.

Halm, Heinz, *Shi'ism*, New York 2004, Columbia University Press.

Harb, Mona, "La Dâhiyya de Beyrouth : parcours d'une stigmatisation urbaine, consolidation d'un territoire politique", in *Genèses*, 51, 2003, pp. 70–91.

International Crisis Group, "Yemen: Defusing the Saada time bomb", in *Middle East Repor*t n°86, 27 May 2009.

Keddie, Nikki R., and Matthee, Rudi, eds., *Iran and the surrounding world. Interactions in culture and cultural politics*, Seattle and London 2002, University of Washington Press.

Khalaji, Mehdi, "The last Marja: Sistani and the end of the traditional religious authority in Shi'ism", in *Policy Focus* 59, The Washington Institute for Near East Policy, September 2006.

Korom, Frank J., *Hosay Trinidad: Muharram performances in an Indo-Caribbean Diaspora*, Philadelphia 2003, University of Pennsylvania Press.

Litvak, Meir, *Shi'i Scholars of nineteenth-century Iraq. The 'Ulama' of Najaf and Karbala,* New York 1998, Cambridge University Press.

Louër, Laurence, *Transnational Shi'a Politics. Political and Religious Networks in the Gulf,* London and New York 2008, Hurst and Columbia University Press.

Luizard, Pierre-Jean, *La formation de l'Irak contemporain. Le rôle politique des ulémas chiites à la fin de la domination ottomane et au moment de la création de l'État irakien*, Paris 1991, CNRS éditions.

Martin, Pierre, (alias Luizard, Pierre-Jean), "La direction religieuse chiite dans une zone de turbulences", *Peuples Méditerranéens, Statégies II,* nr 64–65, July-December, 1993, pp. 241–264.

Menashri, David, ed., *The Iranian Revolution and the Muslim World*, Boulder Colorado 1990, Westview Press.

Menashri, David, ed., *Revolution at a Crossroad: Iran's Domestic Policy and Regional Ambitions,* Washington 1997, Washington Institute for Near East Policy.

Mervin, Sabrina, "La quête du savoir à Najaf. Les études religieuses chez les chi'ites imâmites de la fin du XIXe siècle à 1960", in *Studia Islamica,* 81, 1995, pp. 165–185.

Mervin, Sabrina, "Sayyida Zaynab: banlieue de Damas ou nouvelle ville sainte chiite?", in *CEMOTI*, 22, *Arabes et Iraniens*, 1996, pp. 149–162.

Mervin, Sabrina, *Un réformisme chiite. Ulémas et lettrés du Jabal 'Âmil (actuel Liban-Sud) de la fin de l'Empire ottoman à l'indépendance du Liban,* Paris 2000, Karthala-CERMOC-IFEAD.

Mervin, Sabrina, "Quelques jalons pour une histoire du rapprochement (*taqrîb*) des alaouites vers le chiisme", in *Islamstudien ohne Ende, Festschrift für Werner Ende,* Deutsche Morgenländische Gesellschaft, Würzburg 2002, Ergon Verlag, 2002, pp. 281–288.

Mervin, Sabrina, "La *hawza* à l'épreuve du siècle: la réforme de l'enseignement religieux supérieur chiite de 1909 à nos jours", in al-Charif, Maher, and al-Kawakibi, Salam, eds., *Le courant réformiste musulman et sa réception dans les sociétés arabes,* Damascus 2003, IFPO, pp. 69–84.

Mervin, Sabrina, "Les autorités religieuses dans le chiisme duodécimain contemporain", in *Archives de sciences sociales des religions,* nr.125, January-March, 2004, pp. 63–77.

Mervin, Sabrina, "'L'entité alaouite', une création française" in Pierre-Jean Luizard ed., *Le choc colonial et l'islam. Les politiques religieuses des puissances coloniales en terre d'islam,* Paris 2006, La Découverte, pp. 343–358.

Mervin, Sabrina, "Muhammad Husayn Fadlallâh, du 'guide spirituel' au marja' réformiste", in Mervin, S. ed., *Le Hezbollah, état des lieux,* Paris: Actes Sud, 2008, pp. 277–285.

Mervin, Sabrina, *Histoire de l'islam. Fondements et doctrines*, Paris 2010, Flammarion/Champs.

Monsutti, Alessandro, Naef, Silvia, and Sabahi, Farian, eds, *The Other Shiites: From the Mediterranean to Central Asia,* Bern 2007, Peter Lang.

Mottahedeh, Roy, *The Mantle of the Prophet : learning and power in Modern Iran,* London 1985, Chatto & Windus.

Nakash, Yitzhak, *Reaching for Power. The Shi'a in the Modern Arab World,* Princeton 2006, Princeton University Press.

Nasr, Vali, *The Shi'a Revival. How Conflicts within Islam will Shape the Future*, New York 2006, W.W. Norton.

Pinault, David, *Horse of Karbala: Muslim Devotional Life in India*, London 2001, Palgrave.

Pinto, Paulo G., "Pilgrimage, commodities and Religious Objectivation: The Making of Transnational Shi'ism between Iran and Syria", in *Comparative Studies of South Asia, Africa and the Middle East,* 27/1, 2007, pp. 109–125.

Rosiny, Stephan, "Internet et la *marja'iyya*. L'autorité religieuse au défi des nouveaux medias", in *Maghreb-Machrek,* 178, winter, 2003–2004, pp. 59–74.

Roy, Olivier, "The Crisis of Religious Legitimacy in Iran", in *The Middle East Journal*, n°. 53, 1999, pp. 201–216.

Sankari, Jamal, *Fadlallah. The Making of a Radical Shi'ite Leader,* London 2005, Saqi Books.

Scarcia-Amoretti, Biancamaria *Sciiti nel mondo*, Rome 1994, Jouvence.

Shaery-Eisenlohr, Roschanack, "Iran, The Vatican of Shi'ism?" on *Merip Report online,* 233, Winter, 2004. www.merip.org/mer/mer233/shaery-eisenlohr.html

Shaery-Eisenlohr, Roschanack, *Shi'ite Lebanon: Transnational Religion and the Making of National Identities*, New York 2008, Columbia University Press.

Von Maltzahn, Nadia, "The Case of Iranian Cultural Diplomacy in Syria", *Middle East Journal of Culture and Communication,* 2, 2009, pp. 33–50.

Walbridge, Linda, ed., *The most Learned of the Shi'a. The Institution of the Marja' Taqlid,* New York 2001, Oxford University Press.

PART ONE

The Export of the Revolution and National Integrations

OLIVIER ROY

The Impact of the Iranian Revolution on the Middle East

The Islamic revolution of Iran was never intended to be a "Shi'a" revolution: it has always defined itself as the vanguard of the *umma* (nation) of all Muslims. Yet the networks that carried the revolution into Iran, as well as those that have exported it abroad, have mainly been Shi'a. Furthermore, its ideology – millenarianism, the role of the Imam, the concept of *velâyat-e faqih*, or Guardianship of the Jurists – is equally profoundly marked by Shi'ism. This ambiguity is also found in the Iranian constitution, which defines Twelver Shi'ism as the state religion yet pronounces the Guide of the revolution to be the Guide of the entire *umma* without distinguishing between religious schools. Implicitly, therefore, Shi'ism is presented as the most perfect form of Islam, something which obviously offends many Sunnis, including those who welcomed the revolution.

The failure of the revolution to export itself in any durable fashion beyond Iran's borders can be attributed to two causes. Firstly, the revolution was unable to transcend the Shi'a-Sunni divide to any substantial degree. On the contrary, by giving Shi'ism a new universalist and radical dimension, mobilizing parts of the Shi'a communities abroad and rejecting any structural alliance with the larger Sunni Islamist movements such as the Muslim Brotherhood (itself not necessarily eager to form an alliance), it revived the rift between the two schools. Of course, this has more often been instrumentalized by political and religious leaders than risen spontaneously among the populations concerned. But the paradox remains that the Shi'a-Sunni divide, which had seemed to be fading since 1959 when a *fatwa* of al-Azhar acknowledged Shi'ism as the fifth Islamic school, was abruptly exacerbated by the revolution; this led to armed confrontation in several countries (Pakistan in the first place, but also Lebanon, Afghanistan and Iraq). Secondly, the revolution was not carried unanimously by all Shi'a, even if the majority of non-Iranian Shi'a did feel solidarity. Iran tried to impose a single leadership based on *rahbariat* (a political principle embodied in the theory of *velâyat-e faqih*) at the expense of *marjayat* (religious and clerical traditions). The conflict between *velâyat* and *marjayat* was clearly tied in with the "nationalization" of Shi'ism in Iran and Tehran's instrumentalization of non-Iranian Shi'a communities in its foreign policy.

The end of the revolutionary dynamic in Iran after Khomeini's death in 1989 and the emergence of a Shi'a power in Iraq since 2003 have brought the problem of political relations between Shi'ism and Sunnism to the forefront again and created new controversies over the relationship between the spiritual and political leadership within the Shi'a community.

Initially the revolution attracted many Sunni supporters, but they never formed autonomous and consistent militant movements in the Sunni countries. We note the apparition of the Kurdistan Islam Partisi in Turkey in December 1980, whose militants later joined the Turkish Hezbollah under the direction of Husayn Velioglu. Similarly, in Iraqi Kurdistan the Ansâr al-Islâm movement, which appeared much later, had ties with Tehran before joining the al-Qa'ida network. However, we mostly see isolated Sunnis such as the Tunisian Fouad 'Ali Saleh (responsible for the attacks in France in 1986) taking Iran's side. These individuals were recruited by the Iranian secret services without any broad dynamic of political mobilization among the Sunni populations.

After a few months of enthusiasm in the wake of the Iranian revolution, the larger Sunni Islamist movements soon distanced themselves from the Iranian regime in a split that was consolidated when the war between Iran and Iraq took off in September 1980. While this disaffection did not automatically translate into support for Saddam Hussein, it did lead to their refusal to side with Iran. Two vectors interacted here: for the Arabs, Arab and Sunni solidarity; for all Sunni Islamists (including the Jama'at-e eslami in Pakistan), condemnation of millenarist Shi'a theories and the role of the Imam – and as such, of Khomeini.[1] Sunni Islamism insisted on its own orthodoxy, a tendency that would increase as the Salafist and Wahhabi influence emanating from Saudi Arabia grew. This divide, which was originally political, took a religious turn as the Salafist and Wahhabi movements increasingly denounced the Shi'a as heretics from the mid-1980s on.

Thus the Iranian revolution rapidly retreated into the ghetto of Shi'a minorities, without becoming hegemonic within these communities. Yet the most radical actors, such as the Pasdaran (Islamic Revolutionary Guard Corps) and President Ahmedinejad (elected in 2005), have never renounced the mobilization of Arab Sunnis, and were able to revitalize the anti-Israeli "rejection front" on the occasion of the Lebanese war in 2006.

The Sunni-Shi'a divide

Since 1980 the Iranian revolution has increased sectarian tensions between Shi'a and Sunnis in the Muslim world. Confessional belonging became increasingly politicized and was often perceived as a geo-strategic factor ("Persians" against "Arabs", for example). The Gulf monarchies feared a rallying of the oil regions, with their majority Shi'a populations, under the leadership of Iran. In other words, the polarization was not so much brought about by choices made by the players as it was imposed by the dominant interpretation of the regimes in power.

It is of course true that from 1979 onwards Saddam Hussein unleashed a vehement repression on the Iraqi Shi'a elites, who were seen as inclined to support the Iranian revolution, a campaign which culminated in the assassination of Ayatollah Muhammad Bâqir al-Sadr and the deportation of several hundreds of thousands of Shi'a to Iran on the pretext of their

---

1. Sheikh Talmasani, then guide of the Egyptian Muslim Brotherhood, explained in January 1982 that Shi'ism and Sunnism are fundamentally different, while still avoiding a polemic with the Iranian regime. Cf. Matthee, 1986.

presumed Iranian origins. But this hostility emanated from the state and was not carried by a mass Sunni movement. In Pakistan, however, the radical Sunni movements that emerged during the 1980s were explicitly anti-Shi'a, some focusing almost exclusively on fighting the Shi'a. Some of these movements had ties to the state, in particular with the ISI (Inter-Services Intelligence). This was the case for the SSP (Sepâh-e Sahebân), founded in 1985 in Jhang, a party which called for a law to criminalize offending the names of the companions of the prophet and of his wife A'isha – explicitly targeting the Shi'a. A division of the Lashkar-e Jhangwi party was responsible for killing Iranian diplomats in Pakistan in the 1990s. Since 1985 Pakistan has seen violent sectarian confrontation taking the form of the assassinations of leaders or, in the case of Shi'a victims, members of the social elite (doctors, lawyers and the like) as well as attacks against mosques. These attacks often provoked retaliations, driving the Shi'a to form paramilitary forces of their own, such as the Jaysh-e Mohammad. The large political Shi'a movement that was founded in 1980, Tehrik-e Nefâz-e Fiqh-e Ja'fariyya (TNFJ – Movement for the Conservation of Ja'fari Law, i.e. Shi'a law), is, as its name indicates, also a reaction to the politics of Islamization implemented from 1977 on by General Zia ul-Haqq, which were effectively a "Sunnitization" of the law.

In Afghanistan, the majority of Shi'a are part of the Hazara ethnic group (although there are also Persian-speaking Shi'a in Kabul and Herat who are not Hazara, and Pashtun speakers in Kandahar) and the Shi'a-Sunni divide is often used to accentuate ethnic rifts. During the Soviet invasion, political affiliations followed religious lines: Shi'a parties had their offices in Iran while their Sunni counterparts were based in Afghanistan. The tensions between the two religious communities were muted during the war, but returned with a vengeance after 1992. That year, Kabul fell to a non-Pashtun coalition from the north of the country under the command of Massoud and many Shi'a were massacred in Kabul, mainly by Salafist groups.[1] The rise to power of the Taliban resulted in a real war against the Shi'a, in which villages were destroyed and massacres committed, waged with the support of radical Pakistani Sunni groups such as the SSP. When

---

1. Notably the *Ettehad-e eslami* led by Rasul Sayyaf.

the Taliban conquered Mazar-e Sharif in August 1988, thousands of Shi'a, including the Iranian consulate staff, were killed.

As for Syria, Shi'a leaders have shown willingness to include the Alawis in the *umma*. Ayatollah Hasan Shirazi created the first Twelver Shi'ism *hawza* (seminary) in Sayyida Zaynab, a suburb of Damascus and a pilgrimage destination for Iranians. On the other hand, the Syrian Muslim Brotherhood developed an anti-Shi'a attitude and therefore received no support from Iran, although their position on the Islamic state is clearly closer to that of Khomeini than to Hafez al-Assad's vision, proving again that strategic political factors outweigh religious considerations. Iran did not support the Muslim Brotherhood's 1982 uprising in Hama. Repression in Syria took a sectarian turn with Alawis repressing Sunnis (even if the Ba'athist movement also had Sunni cadres).

In Kuwait and Bahrain in the late 1980s, Shi'a were involved in actions against the regimes of the Sunni emirs who subsequently subjected them to varying degrees of repression. The riots during the annual pilgrimage to Mecca in 1987 were also clearly sectarian: only Shi'a joined the movement initiated by Iranian pilgrims. To counter the Iranian threat, conservative regimes, with Saudi Arabia and Pakistan at the forefront, encouraged the development of radical Sunni movements whose inspiration was Salafist. Saudi *ulemas* (scholars) issued *fatwas* declaring the Shi'a heretics and calling them *râfida*.[1] While this maneuver succeeded in isolating Iran, it also put in place an integral radical structure that would later become a part of al-Qa'eda's networks.

The Iranian response to the alliance between Arab Sunni governments and Sunni Islamist movements was to seek out pro-Iranian Sunnis of any color, with the result that they often ended up supporting radical and marginal figures. At some point, Tehran recruited the leaders of small Sunni movements; these were either isolated in their own countries or the result of internal divisions, such as the Harakat-e Enqelâb faction led by Mawlawi Mansur in Afghanistan or Sheikh Sha'bân's Islamic Movement of Tripoli in Lebanon. The Afghan Gulbuddin Hekmatyar equally found refuge in Tehran after being rejected by the Pakistanis and

---

1. The noun *râfidî* (plural *arfâd* or *râfida*), literally "refuser", is a derogatory term applied to the Shi'a.

the Taliban in 1999. But these were opportunist and isolated connections, never involving mass movements. Their only value for Iran lay in their leaders' participation in the many conferences on the problems in the region held in Tehran.

Most importantly, Tehran has never ceased to uphold the Palestinian cause in order to position itself as the vanguard defending the Muslim world, as opposed to the "treasonous" Arab governments. Tehran's incessant criticism of Arafat contrasted sharply with its justification of Hamas. However, without the Lebanese Hezbollah, Tehran would hardly have any influence. What is particular to this case is not the position of Tehran, but the political and ideological position of Hezbollah, which remains the only Shiʻa mass movement to engage in alliances with non-Shiʻa and even non-Muslim groups on an equal footing, in a combination of Lebanese nationalism, pan-Islamism and Shiʻa identity.

Transnational Shiʻism

In its endeavor to expand its influence among non-Iranian Shiʻa, Iran was able to rely on two main structures: the traditional expansive network of the clergy, and the more recent network of radical Shiʻa movements, often initiated by younger mullahs. The relationship between the two is complex: many clerics are reluctant to accept the very principle of *velâyat*; while the more radical movements, operating within their particular national settings, have often been instrumentalized by Iran to the detriment of their local implantation.[1]

Shiʻa political networks

The political radicalization of the non-Iranian Shiʻa is not simply a consequence of the Islamic revolution: it had begun earlier, under the influence of local players, usually religious figures. The conditions that contributed to the outbreak of the Iranian revolution were present elsewhere too: the politicization of young mullahs; the pressure of social problems (in

---

1. Mention should also be made of the commercial networks of Shiʻa of Lebanese origin who settled throughout West Africa and Latin America, some of which may serve as intermediaries or relays in the transmission of Iranian activities.

Lebanon, Afghanistan and Pakistan, large landowners were no longer perceived as the natural representatives of the community and their authority
was challenged by an emerging leadership of a new type); and finally a
demand for participation in civil society, i.e. the refusal to be treated any
longer as second-class citizens – a refusal that also drove many Shiʻa to
join radical secular parties in Lebanon, Iraq and Afghanistan.

The Amal movement in Lebanon, al-Daʻwa in Iraq, Nasr in Afghanistan
and the Organization for the Islamic Revolution in the Gulf all emerged
before the Islamic revolution of 1979. Later, many of their members,
already active and politicized, would refuse to be used by Tehran,
considering themselves to be promoters of the movement of revival and
politicization of Shiʻism. In Pakistan, however, as we have seen, the political
Shiʻa movements developed as a reaction to and in defense against the
emergence of radical Sunnism rather than as the basis of a revolutionary
political project or even a Shiʻa project. There had been no movement
before the Tehrik-e Nefâz-e Fiqh-e Jaʻfariyya was founded after the Iranian
revolution in 1979. Its founder was Allama Arif Huseyni, a Pashtun from
Parachinar who had studied with Imam Musa Sadr and was assassinated in
Peshawar in 1988. Led by highly educated Sayyids (doctors and agricultural
engineers), the movement became a political party in 1987. In Pakistan, as
elsewhere, the cadres of these movements were players of a new type, often
clerics who were not part of the traditional Shiʻa elites. Three dimensions
of these movements immediately stand out:

1. An ideological dimension: they promoted the idea of an Islamic state
   or at least the idea of a re-Islamization perceived as "progressive" and
   not simply based on the reintroduction of Sharia using political and
   economic slogans, although the movement is not only made up of
   revolutionaries;

2. A supranational dimension: they insisted on the bonds linking all
   Shiʻa, on the role of an international clergy, and on the *hozeh* (religious academies) as meeting places and educational institutions that
   transcend borders, with Persian and Arabic as shared languages;

3. A national dimension: they did not demand separate states (although
   that idea would gain ground in some countries later on) but rather

the integration of the Shi'a as citizens in their respective states; this obviously differs from the situation in Iran, where the Shi'a make up a demographic and political majority.

The Iranian revolution allowed these movements to put forward their demands more forcefully, while in addition offering them a supportive "home base" in Iran; but it also gave them a model to emulate as well as Iranian sponsorship, which they used to consolidate their domestic positions – at the risk of being seen as an Iranian fifth column. The revolution has without a doubt contributed to the radicalization of these movements; both through the participation of Iranian nationals and through a systematic push for total allegiance to Tehran, which encouraged the most radical elements. At times, the various national paradigms have thus been pushed aside by the hegemonic ambitions of the Iranian authorities, who thereby helped to exacerbate tensions within the movements while also giving suspicious Sunni regimes some reason to portray the movements as "pro-Iranian".

In all cases, these movements have positioned themselves on their national scenes as Islamo-nationalists, demanding political integration into the national framework, even as they were simultaneously enjoying the strategic benefits of Iranian support and integration within transnational clerical networks.

1980–9: Keeping political conflicts under control

While the difference between religious and quietist movements on the one hand and supporters of the Islamic revolution on the other was not initially very clear-cut, the 1980s were a turning point in the polarization of the Shi'a world, which was caused by the Iranian authorities' endeavor to control and make use of Shi'a movements abroad. Total adherence to Tehran became the criterion for receiving support and being designated a real Islamism movement. This policy has had ambiguous results, as it divided Shi'a communities virtually everywhere, to the point of armed conflict in the case of Afghanistan, without ensuring complete Iranian control.

Multiple fault lines now appeared: the first divided the traditional secular Shi'a elites and the radical Islamist movements. This predates the revolution and was obviously restricted to places such as Lebanon and Afghanistan where there was a class of large Shiʻa landowners, who were called *arbâb* and generally belonged to the group of Sayyids. Musa Sadr broke the power of the Shiʻa elites in South Lebanon, while the Nasr party in Afghanistan opposed itself to a Shura controlled by the *arbâb* and the Sayyids; this gave rise to a full-scale civil war that ended with the abolition of the Shura.

Secondly, although they were the most influential Shiʻa organizations, the traditional clerical networks were unable or unwilling to become political movements. For example, Grand Ayatollah al-Khoʼi, who was based in Najaf, probably had a larger following than Khomeini in 1980 but many of his disciples joined pro-Iranian organizations because he refused to take part in politics. The divide between the political and religious paradigms was thus present from the outset.

The third fissure emerged between 1982 and 1988 from within the Islamist Shiʻa tendency, separating those who aligned themselves completely with Tehran from those who preferred to remain autonomous. This division was inspired by Tehran. In Lebanon, Husayn Mûsawî created Islamic Amal as a successor to the Amal party founded by Musa Sadr, who disappeared in 1978; other young clerics, among them Hasan Nasrallah, founded Hezbollah in the Bekaa valley. Hezbollah became the dominant organization on the militant level and was directly supported by Iran, with Iranian Pasdaran present in Lebanon. On the religious level, Sheikh Shams al-Dîn, President of the Supreme Shiʻa Council, kept his distance from Iran while Muhammad Husayn Fadlallâh became the highest in rank to support Tehran. His support, however, has always been complex: unequivocal on the political level, but less so religiously, since he rejects *velâyat*. The Daʻwa party in Iraq, founded in the late 1950s, was another radical movement. In the eyes of Tehran it presented the double inconvenience of being too autonomous and rejecting *velâyat*. Iranian leaders therefore encouraged the development of the Supreme Council of the Islamic Revolution, directed by Muhammad Bâqir al-Hakîm, a former member of al-Daʻwa and the son of Grand Ayatollah al-Hakîm. The Organization for Islamic Action in the Gulf was founded by Ayatollah Muhammad Shirâzi, who was born in Karbala and died in Qom in 2001. The Shirâzi movement, which is led today by his nephews Muhammad Taqî and Hâdî Mudarrisî, only developed its Gulf network fairly recently.

The dividing lines in Pakistan are less related to Iran and instead have local, often ethnic, causes. The Tehrik split after the Iranian elections of 1997; the party was left in the hands of students, and Pashtuns from Parachinar along with Shi'a from southern Punjab abandoned it in droves at this time. It was never a revolutionary movement but worked first and foremost to defend the rights of the Shi'a on a sectarian basis. However, the anti-Shi'a violence by Sunni movements that started in 1985 led to the creation of more radical branches; the Imamiyya Students' Organization and especially the Sepâh-e Mohammad (Army of Muhammad), which responded to the wave of assassinations targeting Shi'a notables with assassinations of their own.

Further complicating this picture is the role played in the division and radicalization of Shi'a movements outside Iran by the complex networks connected to the Iranian state apparatus: the Pasdaran, the secret services and the different *hozeh* of Qom (and in the cases of Mashhad and Afghanistan, the powerful foundation of Astan-e Qods). Each of those has its own clientele and network, enabling any Afghan or Pakistani cleric sidelined by the Pasdaran to maintain some support from the *hozeh* where he studied and to rely on its connections and interventions.

Conflicts within the Shi'a clergy: rahbariat, marjayat *and* velayat

The Shi'a clergy is transnational and multi-ethnic. Great Ayatollah families such as the Tabâtabâ'i, which produced Grand Ayatollah Muhsin al-Hakîm, whose sons would lead SCIRI, the Supreme Council of the Islamic Revolution in Iraq, the Shirazi and the Sadr are Arab as much as they are Iranian and have representatives and disciples among all the Shi'a populations. Imam Mûsâ Sadr is a good example of this supranationality. Ayatollah Sistani, the most important religious leader in Iraq in the 1990s, was also born in Iran.

These transnational links have had ambiguous effects on the Iranian revolution, as many of the important ayatollahs rejected either the idea of the revolution itself, and thus the *rahbariat* (political leadership of the Guide), or the concept of the *velâyat-e faqih*, or even Khamenei's *marjayat* after Khomeini's death. Almost everywhere, "quietist" branches emerged – in Lebanon with Sheikh Shams al-Dîn, in Afghanistan with 'Ali Beheshti, in Iraq with al-Kho'i – which refused to pledge allegiance to Iran on either the religious or political level.

The concept of *velâyat-e faqih* constituted a clear rupture with Shi'a tradition and was met with reluctance and even overt opposition from several religious personalities. For Khomeini, the religious paradigm, whether judicial (Sharia) or institutional (*marjayat*), must be subject to the political paradigm of the state – on condition that the state is Islamic. In the Iranian constitution, the Guide is not necessarily the highest representative of the religious hierarchy, but the one who is *agah be zamân* ("conscious of his time"), which marks his participation in history and politics.[1] Khomeini explicitly reiterated this primacy of politics over religious law in his letter of February 1988 to president Khamenei, in which he states that it is legitimate to suspend a religious obligation (in this case the pilgrimage) if a compelling reason of State demands it (on condition of the State being Islamic, of course).[2] At the time of Khomeini's death, when a new Guide had to be elected, a political successor – Khamenei, who was not even an ayatollah – was preferred to the grand ayatollahs. When in an effort to harmonize political and religious orders, Islamists tried to bestow upon him the religious titles that the political leader of the revolution lacked, this was rejected by all the grand ayatollahs, including those favorably disposed towards the regime.

The Islamic revolution, therefore, entailed the marginalization of the quietist grand ayatollahs, although their following outnumbered by far the support base of more radical figures such as Khomeini. Without any doubt, the largest number of believers throughout the Shi'a world

---

1. For further details, see Khosrokavar and Roy, Paris 1999.
2. This places religious law in a relative rather than an absolute position. The automatic assignment of children to the father's family in the event of his death and the lack of alimony for the wife in the event of divorce – two principles of Islamic law contested by Islamist women – have been rejected in official Iranian legislation because they created insurmountable social problems (war widows would have lost custody of their children, for example).

recognized the authority of Ayatollah Kho'i from Najaf. The paradox here is that the centre of quietism thus moved to Najaf, because of both the political marginalization of quietists in Iran and because of the elimination of Islamists in Iraq under Saddam Hussein. In this fashion, the Iranian revolution has systematically promoted a younger generation of religious figures, many of them more revolutionary than properly speaking Islamic.

It would of course be a simplification to paint a picture where the grand ayatollahs, quietist with the exception of Khomeini, were opposed across the board to the younger, more militant mullahs (mostly *hujjat al-islâm*) who built the state apparatus in Iran and the radical political movements abroad (such as Nasrallah in Lebanon). Many of the grand ayatollahs approved of the revolution and supported the Iranian regime even if they did not participate directly in the political management of the revolution – and even if they rejected the *velâyat-e faqih*. We could mention Golpayegani, Ma'rashi-Najafi and Azari-Qomi – although the latter opposed the election of Khamenei as the Guide because he was not a grand ayatollah. Others have opposed the revolution from the start, for example Taleqani – although his criticism was based on a leftist point of view – and Shari'at-Madari, who was literally "defrocked" by Khomeini.

The revolution nevertheless led to the dissociation of *marjayat* and *rahbariat* in the sense that political and religious choices could differ. In Afghanistan, many young men who followed Kho'i on the religious level joined the Nasr and later the Wahdat parties in their opposition to local Shi'a elites. In Lebanon, Muhammad Husayn Fadlallâh has always declared his support for the Islamic revolution in Iran but never accepted the principle of *velayât*. The death of Khomeini accentuated the divide, with many local ayatollahs who accepted Khomeini as *marja'* refusing to consider Khamenei as such. The Shirazi group opposed the theory of *velayât* after the death of Khomeini and Fadlallâh refused to recognize Khamenei as a grand ayatollah.

A final fault line appeared when many non-Iranian Shi'a militants who supported the concept of *velayât* refused to become mere tools of Tehran and wanted to maintain a national line, even when they were in favor of a struggle within the framework of the *umma*. This was the case of many SCIRI cadres and older militants of the Organization for the Iranian Revolution in the Gulf who wished to integrate themselves into their respective national political frameworks. The overthrow of Saddam Hussein and the timid openings made by the Gulf monarchies have offered these militants the opportunity to distance themselves from Tehran.

Although the revolution did not create unanimity, it did produce at least two results: a change in the hierarchies, forms of legitimacy and power divisions within the clergy; and an "Iranization" of Shi'ism.

The burnout of revolutionary fervor

While Tehran's policy of radicalizing Shi'a movements was relatively successful and led to the establishment of politico-military groups, it also emphasized the isolation of the Shi'a and increased the influence of the Salafist and Wahhabi currents among radical Sunnis to such an extent that by the late 1980s Tehran had not only lost all hope to reach out to the Sunnis, but was facing the emergence of a Sunni religious movement that was both radical and anti-Shi'a.

1989 saw the turning point: the death of Imam Khomeini marked the end of the expansion of the revolution, as the newly elected president Rafsanjani adopted a more pragmatic and less sectarian policy. The retreat of Soviet troops from Afghanistan left the country in the hands of a radical Sunni coalition supported by Pakistan and Saudi Arabia. In the same year, the Taif Agreement made Hezbollah into a central force in Lebanese politics and revealed the foreign policy shift of Iran, which strove for rapprochement with the conservative Arab states during Rafsanjani's presidency. The idea was no longer to export the revolution but instead to build the Shi'a movements in Iran's neighboring states into political factors that would no longer be ignored – or even into fully fledged political alternatives. This would clearly increase Iran's weight in the regional power balance; henceforward the policy would be to try to unify the various Shi'a movements rather than impose the dominance of radical elements. Tehran, in other words, accepts the nationalist aspects of non-Iranian Shi'a. Secondly, political alliances with Sunni groups must be negotiated. This was a realistic choice: the revolution had failed, the

Shi'a were divided and the weakening and subsequent disappearance of the USSR as a player in the region increased the influence of the United States. The new policy produced swift results: in Afghanistan, nine Shi'a parties joined forces in 1989 to form what later developed into the Hezb-e Wahdat, an ethnical Hazara party transcending ideological divisions and uniting former opponents. In Lebanon, Iran supported the Taif Agreement; in Iraq, it kept a very low profile during the western coalition's military intervention and refrained from supporting the 1991 Shi'a uprising.

President Khatami, elected in 1997, formed his foreign policy around an attempt at overture towards the West and the conservative Arab regimes. He had no wish to play the radicalization card, be it Shi'a or Sunni. Yet the supranational Shi'a militant networks were still present, directed by the office of the Guide, the Pasdaran and the secret services, while the purely clerical and family connections had no problem in surviving any political vagaries.

Ahmadinejad: the return of revolutionary fervor or a new factor?

September 11, 2001 overturned the entire equation once again. US military interventions freed Iran of its two Sunni enemies and rapidly alienated the Sunni population, all the while weakening the conservative Arab regimes. A large part of the Iranian program was thus implemented and Iran was able to dust off its old revolutionary dream of enlisting the Shi'a axis into the service of the "rejection front" (or vice versa) and presenting itself as the champion of anti-imperialism and anti-Zionism in order to become the Great Power of the Middle East.

Hamas's election victory and the 2006 Lebanon war temporarily turned Hezbollah into the new hero of the Arab masses, who have also taken great satisfaction in seeing Iran evolve into a nuclear power (something that continues to arouse great fear among conservative Arab regimes). Iran has, probably temporarily, emerged from its Shi'a ghetto and is trying to impose itself as the main player in the Middle East, especially in view of the imminent American retreat from Iraq. But the two paradigms involved could turn out to be mutually contradictory. The exacerbation of Sunni-Shi'a tensions in Iraq today is resurrecting the alliance between the Ba'athist nationalists and Sunni Salafists who opposed Iran in the 1980s, while at the same time a Sunni-Shi'a alliance is growing around the Palestinian conflict. This explains the extremely ambiguous attitude displayed by the conservative Arab regimes towards Hezbollah during the July 2006 war. They initially condemned Hezbollah's adventurism and only later switched to supporting the party in the name of its resistance against Israel.

Since the invasion of Iraq in 2003, different battles are being fought on ever-shifting frontlines. In Afghanistan, the Americans are fighting the Taliban, who are the enemies of Iran and are supported by Pakistan, which itself is an American ally. The Salafists and Arab nationalists are fighting the Shi'a in Iraq while supporting them (at least vocally) in Lebanon. The Americans have brought Iran's allies to power in Iraq, while simultaneously trying to set up an international and regional coalition against Iran. The conservative Sunni states in the region are very hostile towards Iran but cannot officially endorse the American alliance on account of public opinion in their countries. Any attempt to disconnect Iran from the Israeli-Palestinian conflict requires the Americans and Israelis to negotiate with Hezbollah, Hamas and Syria, which they refuse to do in the name of the war on terror. The US, moreover, lumps Shi'a radicals and al-Qa'ida groups together under the heading of "global terrorism", even while these groups are fighting each other to the death in Iraq. Finally, the US is forced to maintain close relations with a Pakistan that shelters Bin Laden and the Taliban, and a Saudi Arabia whose *ulemas* sustain the fiercely anti-American Salafist movement that more or less overtly supports groups close to al-Qa'ida.

Ahmadinejad plays skillfully on all these contradictions, but tensions within the coalition of the rejection front are high. The question is whether or not the Iranian and Shi'a successes in the Gulf will in the long term conflict with the Sunni-Shi'a front fighting in Israel and Palestine. The Shi'a axis and the rejection front are based on contradictory paradigms with conflicting views on the place of Arab nationalism and Sunni Salafism. The key factor now is the choice that the Lebanese Hezbollah will make between solidarity with Iran or Lebanese nationalism, especially in a perspective where a boycott of Iran or even a western attack on its nuclear installations would cause a latent war between Iran and the United States.

Bibliography

Khosrokhavar and Roy, *Iran, comment sortir d'une révolution religieuse,* Paris 1999.

Matthee, R., "Egyptian Opposition and Iranian Revolution", in J. Cole and N. Keddie (ed), *Shiʻism and Social Protest*, Yale 1986.

ALESSANDRO MONSUTTI

Islamism among the Shi'a of Afghanistan: from Social Revolution to Identity-Building[1]

Social recomposition and political demands

Religious labels are very prominent in Afghanistan and often overlap with ethnic designations. The correlation between ethnic and religious identities is particularly strong in the case of the Hazaras,[2] an ethnonym that refers mainly to the Persian-speaking Shi'a groups who used to inhabit the high plateaus and mountains of central Afghanistan but have long since migrated to the towns or to other countries. Their religion sets them apart from the Sunni majority without drawing them closer to their fellow-Shi'a.[3] In fact, the Shi'a of Afghanistan are subdivided into quite different groups in respect of their history, social-economic conditions, religious traditions and identity referents, and they can never really be

---

1. This paper is a revised version of the original French. It has been translated by Patrick Camiller.
2. Canfield, 1973, pp. 4–5, 12.
3. In the absence of a reliable census, the most recent and most credible figures for Afghanistan derive from the US State Department, which puts the size of the population at somewhat more than 20 million for a surface area of 647,500 km². The main ethnic groups are the Pashtuns (38%), the Tadjiks (25%), the Hazaras (19%) and the Uzbeks (6%). The same source mentions a religious breakdown of 84% Sunni and 15% Shi'a (a count in which certain Ismaili and Sunni population groups were considered to be Hazaras). See www.adfa. oz.au.

said to have formed a single political and cultural entity.[1] Although the Hazaras make up the majority of Shi'a, mention should also be made of other groups – sometimes called *Farsiwan* (literally "Persian-speaking") in Western literature – who are present near the western frontier with Iran, in Herat and Kandahar, as well as the Qizilbash, who settled especially in Kabul when they arrived there in the eighteenth century with the armies of Nâder Shâh. These are prosperous communities, but so unobtrusive and small in size that the terms "Shi'a" and "Hazara" are mostly interchangeable in the popular parlance and imagery of Afghan Sunnis.[2] The label carries heavy negative connotations of religious heterodoxy, political marginality, geographical remoteness, cultural backwardness and material poverty.

The late-nineteenth-century subjugation of the Hazaras by the central Afghan state marked the beginning of a long period of political and economic marginalization. Paradoxically, however, the recent wars opened up new spaces of freedom for the Hazaras, and more generally for the Shi'a of Afghanistan. Their role in the post-Taliban government was greater than any they had had before, and they have refused to accept a return to the old Pashtun hegemony.

The political discourse of Hazara leaders has been shaped partly by the Islamic revolution in Iran, but it was given a different interpretation by various forces on the ground. Moreover, the ideological struggles have often masked social conflicts. In the 1980s, events in Iran influenced the young clerics, often from a modest background, who took power by ousting the traditional elites. In the course of the following decade, the various factions developed a formal, though partial, agreement around an ethnicist discourse.

In 1979 the first local revolts were organized around tribal chiefs. Internal conflicts soon broke out, however, leading to a polarization between secular and religious forces. In a second period between 1982 and 1984 the most radical Islamist currents inspired by the Iranian revolution took control of the greatest part of Hazarajat; there was thus a pronounced Islamization of the resistance. At the end of the 1980s, when the Soviets

1. Edwards, 1986.
2. Tapper, 1988, p. 28.

pulled out and new issues came to the fore in the national arena, Hazara leaders understood that they had to move beyond their antagonism and unite with one another: this led to the birth of a new political formation, the Hezb-e wahdat (Unity Party), whose leaders developed a series of ethnic demands and adopted a compromise between the secular and religious poles. Although Islamism played an essential role in the politicization of the Shi'a of Afghanistan, this new turn signaled the end of the revolutionary process in favor of more pragmatic policies.[1]

Islam, politics and modernity

The relations between religion and politics in the Islamic world are the subject of much debate among specialists. In his reflections on the Afghan case, Olivier Roy has helped to clarify this relationship by distinguishing between traditionalism, fundamentalism and Islamism. He defines traditionalism as: "the desire to freeze society so that it conforms to the memory of what it once was ... In this vision history and tradition are merged; the historical development of society is effaced in favor of an imaginary timeless realm under attack from pernicious modernity."[2] For fundamentalism, on the other hand: "it is of paramount importance to get back to the scriptures, clearing away the obfuscation of tradition. ... The enemy is not modernity but tradition ... In itself fundamentalism sits uneasily within the political spectrum, for the "return to first things" may take many different forms."[3] Finally, in Roy's analysis, Islamism is a political ideology that may be traced back to the emergence of the Muslim Brotherhood movement in Egypt in the 1930s; its ambition is to construct the state and society on the principles of Islam.[4]

A complementary grid may be proposed for the interpretation of three tendencies within Islam, over and above its different branches: legalism; quietism and mysticism; and millenarianism. Legalism represents a form of orthodoxy organized around the practice of law. Quietism embodies the mystical dimension, which mostly goes together with a withdrawal

---

1. This evolution has been well described in Harpviken, 1996.
2. Roy, 1990, p. 3.
3. Ibid.
4. Roy, 1994, pp. 1–3.

from social life. In this analytical grid, millenarianism is the revolutionary and messianic pole. Strictly speaking, it may be defined as the forecast that the end of the world is nigh, though of uncertain date, and that a time of happiness will then follow for the just. More generally, it refers to the numerous movements that have repeatedly developed in response to situations of marked injustice, which have challenged the legitimacy of the established powers and sought to bring about a more equitable society.

These two typologies (traditionalism-fundamentalism-Islamism and legalism-quietism-millenarianism) should not be conceived of separately from each other; there are many possible overlaps between them. In Afghanistan, for instance, Olivier Roy remarks that individuals who have followed higher religious studies – the *ulemas* and specialists in Islamic law – as well as the organizing cadre in mystical fraternities have a rather fundamentalist sensibility. Thus, the anti-colonial struggle drew upon the Sufi movements, fundamentalist references and millenarian discourses so often found in tribal milieus.[1]

Millenarian hopes inspired a number of politico-religious movements and many of the revolts that have punctuated the history of both Sunni and Shi'a Islam, from the rebellion of Abû Islâm (which brought the Abbassids to power in the middle of the eighth century) through the Qarmatians (late ninth to early tenth century) to the sect of the Assassins, or even the Safavids. These movements invariably referred to the original era of Islam and Muhammad's opposition to the Mecca aristocracy as the ideal model of struggle against illegitimate and iniquitous rulers. In Shi'ism the figure of the Hidden Imam has played a crucial role: he remains alive, though concealed, and might reappear at any moment, no one knows where or when. Beyond their differences (the Qarmatians representing a form of millenarian anarchism and the Assassins a form of millenarian theocracy), all these movements have had charismatic leaders with a messianic message. Claiming to be the Mahdi, or to be directly inspired by him, they have all proclaimed that their power comes from God himself: "God has chosen me ... Recognize the sacred character of my mission and follow me!" In claiming to bring back social justice and to save men from sin, they have

---

1. Roy, 1990, pp. 6–7.

often had temporary success in constituting a community of believers based upon equality and solidarity.

In Shiʿism, in the absence of the Hidden Imam, any form of rule may be called into question. In Iran, the clergy was already an economic and political force, a veritable counter-power, in the Safavid period. In contrast to the Ottoman world, numerous oppositional movements were led by religious figures. In his westernization drive, Mohammad Reza Shah conducted severe repression against the Shiʿite clergy; this was the context in which Ayatollah Khomeini came to prominence as theologian and mystic, jurist and poet, revolutionary and statesman, militant third-worldist and rigorist thinker. A charismatic leader, he knew how to mobilize a long intellectual and doctrinal tradition while giving new life to the fervor and messianic spirit of Shiʿism. Through his political activism he overturned the attitude of political withdrawal that characterized large minorities of the clergy. His declared goal was to restore the divine order destroyed by the rule of the infidels; they would be defeated, and their defeat would usher in an era of peace and justice. At the same time, he defended the rights of the *mustadʿafûn* (deprived masses). Opponents of the Shah were compared to the martyrs of Karbala, and the Shah himself to Yazid, the impious caliph and murderer of Imam Husayn. The *ulemas* were the legitimate successors of the Prophet Muhammad, of ʿAli and the Imams; their task was to regain the power that secular governments had usurped over the centuries. It was necessary to unite the temporal and spiritual powers and to establish a theocracy that sacralized the political order. Power should be held by the *vali-ye faqih* (Supreme Jurisprudent) – hence the theory of governance or guidance by the jurist, the expert in *velâyat-e faqih* (Islamic law).[1]

This Shiʿa absolutism was largely based on Khomeini's personal prestige and charisma and on the popular support he enjoyed. Upon his death in 1989, the second-ranking cleric ʿAli Khamenei was appointed to succeed him. The title "Guide of the Islamic Revolution" was changed to "Guide of the Islamic Republic"; this marked a resizing of the regime's political and religious ambitions and a retreat into a conservative model of society.

---

1. On the uses to which the Karbala events and the figure of the Imâm Husayn were put during the Islamic revolution, see Fischer, 1980. More generally, on Shiʿa reform currents and movements, see Richard, 1991.

The very principle of a sanctified government came under criticism from eminent members of the clergy, and many were those who preferred to withdraw from politics. Although the regime remained in clerical hands, the surge of revolutionary messianism had come to an end.

Like any revolutionary movement, millenarianism occupies an ambiguous position. On the one hand, it has a great capacity to mobilize people against social injustice and offers a sacred, unchallengeable mandate to justify the seizure of power. On the other, it raises popular expectations to a degree that cannot easily be fulfilled; succession problems become insoluble, as the regime rests upon popular recognition of one individual's charisma, not on established rules for the transmission of power. A series of questions present themselves. How can one be sure that individuals who claim their authority to be sacred are not driven by personal interests? What guarantees that the source of their authority really is transcendent? What can be done about the huge expectations that this kind of legitimacy arouses? The claim to a sacred form of power inevitably leads to bitter disappointments. Indeed, contradictions within the modes of regime legitimacy are one of the reasons for the failure of political Islam predicted by Olivier Roy.[1]

The Hazaras from one war to another[2]

The role of Shi'ism in defining Hazara identity, the openness of Hazaras to Iranian influences, the gradual strengthening of ethnic references and the echo that these have in the population are the result of a socio-historical process bound up with two conflicts: the war that ravaged Afghanistan towards the end of the twentieth century, and the campaigns to subdue Hazarajat waged by the emir of Kabul between 1891 and 1893. The latter episode has left its mark on people's minds: it added a dramatic edge to the distinction between Sunnis and Shi'a by providing the latter, especially the Hazaras, with a whole register of symbols associated with suffering.

Identity is a construct that is constantly renewed and renegotiated, a political process rather than a cultural fact. More specifically, an ethnic

---

1. Roy, 1994.
2. This section summarises and factually updates, in a different perspective, a number of considerations developed in Monsutti, 1999.

group should not be defined by a set of objective cultural traits: it is a form of social organization, in which the determining element is not objective differences but what the actors themselves regard as significant. As Barth put it, "ethnic groups are categories of ascription and identification by the actors themselves, and thus have the characteristic of organizing interaction between people."[1] Group boundaries are maintained by a number of emblems, or even stereotypes, which display belonging and exclusion and draw upon the registers of religious affiliation, social-occupational category, physical appearance, dress, diet, and so on. Conflict situations are the main setting for the emergence and reinforcement of ethnic distinctions; the old social-economic complementarities have grown less marked, and confrontational dynamics over the control of natural and economic resources have been acquiring a predominant role. The division of labor, together with distinct ecological and economic niches, is dying out.

The term *hazâra* was used by Babur, founder of the Mogul dynasty in India, in the sixteenth century, when it served to designate any non-subjugated mountain tribe.[2] Only later did its meaning narrow to apply specifically to the group now known as the Hazaras. The origins of this group are the subject of controversy,[3] as are the conditions under which it converted to Shi'ism. Even the etymology of the name continues to be debated. As *hazâra* signifies "thousand" in Persian, it is generally believed that it alludes to the Mongol word *minggan*, which has the same meaning. In the age of Genghis Khan, *minggan* was used to denote the basic thousand-warrior unit of the Mongol armies, and by extension it could also have the sense of "tribe". Most probably, Mongol groups that were pushed back into the Hindu Kush between the thirteenth and fifteenth centuries (from Central Asia in the north and Iran in the west) mingled with local Iranian inhabitants and eventually adopted

---

1. Barth, 1981, p. 199.
2. This connotation has not disappeared, and *hazara* still serves to designate populations in north-eastern Afghanistan that share with the Hazaras proper only their situation of geographical and political marginality. Cf. Centlivres and Centlivres -Demont, 1988, pp. 50–51.
3. Bacon, 1951; Schurmann, 1962; Poladi, 1989; Mousavi, 1998.

their language. At the end of this process, *hazara* replaced *minggan* and became an ethnic designation.

Afghanistan took shape as a modern state in the eighteenth century (through the action of Pashtun warrior tribesmen) and developed in the nineteenth century as a buffer state between the Russian and British empires. Pashtun monarchs gradually took control of the territory assigned to them by the great powers of the time. Hazarajat was then a long way from being unified; it was a segmented society, with a low degree of horizontal solidarity. Each of its zones was controlled by powerful tribal chiefs, the *mirs*, who kept up a latent state of war with one another.[1] It was only to confront gradual encroachment by the central government that the first inter-tribal coalitions came into being. During the campaigns waged by Emir 'Abdur Rahmân between 1891 and 1893, there was a clear polarization between the Shi'a population and the Sunni conquerors. Faced with strong resistance, 'Abdur Rahmân obtained the support of the Sunni religious authorities, who issued a *fatwa* declaring the Shi'a to be infidels. He then proclaimed a holy war or *jihâd* against them.[2] The Hazaras held out for a long time before they were finally crushed and lost their old autonomy.

Although 'Abdur Rahmân's subjugation of Hazarajat helped to consolidate the central power, it confirmed the Afghan state as a Sunni institution and sharpened the fusion of religious and political identities by creating a Sunni bloc on the side of orthodoxy against a Shi'a bloc on the side of dissidence.[3] The twentieth century was a difficult period for the Hazaras, who were considered second-class citizens by a state apparatus gradually extending its hold to the local level.[4] The tribal chiefs kept a dominant position by virtue of their wealth and social connections; they functioned as representatives of the population before officials of mostly Pashtun origin. Although serving as intermediaries in political affairs,

---

1. Social inequalities appear to have been very marked. The *mirs*, being large landowners, controlled the means of production. See Canfield, 1971; Roy, 1990, pp. 140–1; Mousavi, 1998, p. 91.
2. Kakar, 1971; Kakar 1973.
3. Canfield, 1973, p. 109.
4. Canfield, 1971.

they nevertheless lost any real decision-making power.[1] The Pashtun grip was evident in other parts of the country too,[2] but it seems to have been especially pronounced and intolerant in Hazarajat.

On the eve of the Communist coup of April 1978, it was possible to identify four socio-political categories among the Hazara elites of Afghanistan:[3] the *mirs* and the *khâns* (tribal leaders, large landowners); the *sayyids* (descendants of the Prophet forming a kind of largely endogamous religious aristocracy); the *sheikhs* (individuals with a higher religious education, almost equally known as *ruhâni* or *âkhund*); and the *roshanfekr* (lay intellectuals, often Maoist-inspired).[4] These players stood out because of their relationship to the religious domain and the pitch of their discourse of political legitimization (local groups, ethnic emancipation, the Islamic community as a whole). As Harpviken has shown, they could be situated along two axes: secular–religious and local–regional–global. The legitimizing sources of the *mirs'* power were tribal, secular and local (a group of villages, a valley or at most a district); the intellectuals engaged in a Marxist-style anti-religious discourse, stressing the need for power-sharing among ethnic groups and advocating an end to social inequalities; the *sayyids*, for their part, based themselves on regional networks with a religious complexion that grouped together their congregation (which might come from large areas of Hazarajat); and the *sheikhs*, with their supranational religious sensibility, thought of politics in terms of the *umma* and were oriented towards the great Shi'a intellectual centres of Iran and Iraq.[5] Whereas many *sheikhs* were *sayyids*, it was very rare for a *sheikh* or a *sayyid* to be a *mir*. On the other hand, lay intellectuals often came from the lines of tribal chiefs.[6] There was thus a separation between those who were invested with religious prestige (*sheikhs* and *sayyids*) and

---

1. Grevemeyer, 1988, p. 212; Harpviken, 1996, pp. 28, 55. .
2. Centlivres and Centlivres -Demont, 1988, pp. 229–45.
3. Roy, 1990; Harpviken,1996.
4. In fact, except in Kabul, very few Hazara intellectuals turned to the Communist Party, which was dominated by Pashtuns and Tajiks. The great majority preferred to join Maoist-inspired movements such as *Sho'la-e melli* ("Eternal Flame") or *Setam-e melli* ("National Oppression'), which echoed the demands of minority groups in the population.
5. Harpviken, 1996, pp. 28–31.
6. Roy, 1990, pp. 140–2.

those who held the political authority and the major economic resources (*mirs* and intellectuals).

The war was the setting for a profound restructuring of power, locally, regionally and nationally, and for a reconstruction of politics and identity. In April 1978 the Communists of the PDPA (People's Democratic Party of Afghanistan) took power. Very soon they began to implement their program of reforms: land redistribution, women's rights, provision of schooling, and so on. They attacked existing privileges but failed to attract the support of the poor peasantry. Indeed, through their repressive methods and their overt atheism, they rapidly lost the sympathy of rural layers. Hazarajat became one of the first regions to experience local uprisings, in the spring of 1979, and freed itself from the government's grip the following summer. In September 1979, a large meeting led to the creation of the Shurâ-ye enqelâbi-ye ettefâq-e eslâmi-ye Afghanistân (Revolutionary Council of the Islamic Alliance of Afghanistan). A religious dignitary, Sayyed 'Ali Beheshti, was elected as its leader.

This apparent unity concealed grave tensions, which came to light as soon as the external military threat declined. Incapable of holding the area, government troops and then the Red Army lost interest in Hazarajat, which was anyway not a strategic priority; they were content to maintain a post at Bamyan which they used for occasional expeditions. The Shurâ was divided into three antagonistic tendencies: a secular pole made up of the *mirs* and left-wing intellectuals; an Islamist pole, with the *sheikhs* influenced by the newly developing Iranian revolution;[1] and a traditionalist centre controlled by the *sayyids*.[2] The *mirs* took the initiative for the first revolts, but the *sayyids*, in alliance with the Islamists, soon took charge of operations. *Mirs* and secular intellectuals were violently eliminated.

Several factors account for this evolution. First, the religious reference had a great capacity to mobilize people against an openly atheistic regime. Second, as we have seen, the *mirs* drew some of their influence from their role as intermediaries between the rural population and the state apparatus, and so their power base dwindled as the state withdrew from sight. Lastly,

---

1. The upheavals in the two countries were actually concurrent, as the fall of the imperial regime in Iran occurred in February 1979.
2. Roy, 1990, p. 142.

the *sayyids* could rely on larger and more established networks than the *mirs*, whose authority was confined to tribal segments.[1]

Dominated by the *sayyids*, the Shura put in place a system modeled on a government. The administrative and fiscal burden of this structure exhausted the people's goodwill and left it open to the activity of the Islamists,[2] who by 1982 were playing their own political and military cards with support from Iran. The Islamists eventually won out and in the spring of 1984 took control of the greatest part of Hazarajat. In fact, this initiated a process of political modernization, as the victors, often from modest origins, were champions of a reformed Islam, in contrast to the traditional practices of the *sayyids*. Whereas the *mirs* and *sayyids* evolved into a clientelist network, tribal and local for the former, religious and regional for the latter, the *sheikhs* insisted that all believers had to make a free choice of a spiritual guide. Horizontal relations took the place of the vertical links formerly predominant. This conception offered the framework for a restructuring of social relations, for an expansion of solidarity and the basis of recruitment: it was thus more suited to the needs of modern warfare, which go well beyond the codified logic of tribal confrontations.[3] Furthermore, the *sheikhs'* religious considerations were coupled with a social reform project;[4] their aim was to fight inequality in a language intelligible to the whole of the Hazara population. Religious figures thus managed to break the power of the old elites, thanks to a discourse that combined references to religion with the liberation of the oppressed masses.

Two quite distinct movements shared the stage, often in competition with each other: the Sâzman-e nasr (Victory Organization) and the Sepâh-e pâsdâran (Army of Guardians). The divisions between them were a reflection of the factional struggles then shaking Iran. The first seemed to be linked to the Ministry of Foreign Affairs and the entourage around Ayatollah Montazeri (a close associate of Khomeini, who would disown him shortly before he died); the second was directly controlled by the Iranian Pasdaran, an elite corps whose activity was as much political as

---

1. Canfield, 1986; Harpviken, 1996, pp. 55f., 69, 76–7.
2. Roy, 1990, p. 142f.
3. See Roy, 1992, pp. 185–207; Centlivres, 1997.
4. Grevemeyer, 1988, p. 215.

military. Under the influence of Islamic radicalism, it was not long before ever deeper ideological nuances began to emerge: the Nasr movement stuck more to its independence of the great Shi‘a patron and was more sensitive to the issue of ethnic discrimination;[1] the Sepah remained more attached to the establishment of an Islamist state in line with the Khomeini model.

In 1989, when the Red Army pulled out of Afghanistan, it was expected that the President Najibullah's Communist regime would swiftly founder. Yet it maintained itself until April 1992 by taking advantage of the discord among various factions of the resistance. Although the ethnic character of recruitment into the main parties did not show in their explicit ideology, it played a stronger role as they all tried to grab power by linking up with Communist elites in the same ethnic group. The peace talks were faltering, but they all had something in common: held under Pakistani sponsorship, they disregarded the Shi‘a component of the Afghan population. Threatened with exclusion, Shi‘a political leaders realized that they urgently needed to stop dwelling on their differences. With the active support of Iran – released from the war with Iraq by the ceasefire in 1988 and seeking to assert itself as a regional power and counterbalance to Pakistan – the principal Shi‘a factions agreed to form a single broad movement, the Hezb-e wahdat-e eslâmi-ye Afghanistân (Islamic Unity Party of Afghanistan). Its foremost figure, ‘Abdul ‘Ali Mazari, was aware of the need to overcome recent rifts, and the party's discourse of political legitimization swung towards the new ideological terrain of Hazara identity. The reins of power remained in the hands of the *ruhâni*,[2] but the Hezb-e wahdat also incorporated numerous lay intellectuals – including former Marxists and Maoists (military men, engineers, doctors, teachers, etc.) as well as nationalists.[3] On the margins

---

1. Harpviken, 1996, p. 88.

2. As Harpviken puts it: "the new unity party was not the result of a change in elites, rather it was a strategic decision taken by established elites in a changed situation ... the Hazara nationality formed the core of Wahdat, and it was that, not Islamism, that gave the partners to the unity a common platform ... Wahdat accommodated formerly conflicting groups around a common core of ethnicity, dominated by the Islamic leaders." Cf. Harpviken 1996, pp. 99–100.

3. They tried to make themselves indispensable by founding NGOs responsible

of this now dominant current were the Islamists (particularly those in the Sepah) who remained faithful to the Khomeinist state model and rejected the ethnic turn, and the non-Hazara Shi'a grouped together in the Harakat-e eslami (Islamic Movement).

As at the beginning of the war, the majority of Hazaras had formed into a single movement. But sociological, political and economic conditions had changed quite fundamentally. The old tribal and religious elites had been eliminated and the issues at stake were no longer the same: it was a question of gaining recognition for the Hazaras at the national level and securing their political participation on an equitable basis. Although mostly coming from the Islamist parties – especially the Nasr – the Wahdat leaders adopted a resolutely ethnic discourse, although they did not abandon references to religion, as in their persistent demand for Shi'ism (the Ja'fari school of law) to be given equal recognition by the state as Sunnism (the Hanafi school of law).

After the fall of the Najibullah government in 1992, Afghanistan underwent a lasting fragmentation and it is difficult to analyze the constant and unpredictable shifts of alliances that followed. The complex, fissiparous character of the Afghan socio-political fabric stands in the way of true ethnic polarization. The appearance of the Taliban in the winter of 1994–5 and their spectacular advance towards Kabul in spring 1995 followed by their capture of Herat in autumn 1995 and of the capital in September 1996 changed the balance of forces. They mainly recruited Pashtuns and their idea of Islam was marked both by their tribal and rural origins and by the time they had spent in the refugee camps in Pakistan. Their leaders' discourse did not emphasize the ethnic dimension, but their conceptions instilled fear in the urban elites and minorities. For the first time, there really was an ethnic polarization: on the one side Pashtuns; on the other a fragile coalition of minority groups within the heterogeneous Northern Alliance.[1] The Taliban took Mazar-e Sharif in August and Bamyan in September 1998; thereafter only the US intervention in response to the 9/11 attacks would reverse the balance of forces. But the sharp tensions surrounding the discussion of a new constitution in the

---

for public health, education, road construction, and so on. Roy, 1998, pp. 206–7.

1. Maley, 1998.

winter of 2003 indicate that common reference to Islam scarcely provides the terrain for agreement on the reconstruction of the country. The issue of power-sharing (between different ethnic and religious groups, the urban and rural population, émigré elites and commanders who fought inside Afghanistan, etc.), as well as numerous other questions, such as the role of women in politics or the choice between a centralized and a federal system, are far from settled.

From Islamist revolution to pragmatic politics

Internal conflicts resulted in the victory of the Islamists in Hazarajat. One determining factor was the logic of battle itself, which made it necessary to go beyond the local sphere; transverse networks came into being as the parties sought new clients and the resistance commanders scoured around for weapons. The belligerents had to expand their recruitment base if they were to operate more effectively.[1] By virtue of their ideological references, their mode of organization and their contacts with the outside world, the *sheikhs* were best equipped to meet these developing requirements. The circumstances were such, however, that their discourse gradually swung away from Islamism towards a projection of Hazara identity beyond mere ethnicism:[2] that is, it went beyond the cultural domain by demanding real political and territorial autonomy and by forming the skeleton of a state.[3]

The population of central Afghanistan, which had for a long time been independent and split up in the relative isolation of the mountains, was forcibly subjugated by the government in Kabul at the end of the nineteenth century. This conflict brought about the formation of large antagonistic blocs hinging on the religious opposition between Sunnis and Shi'a. After their defeat, the Shi'a suffered systematic social and

---

1. Roy, 1993.
2. The meaning of this term as used here is "the attachment of high philosophical, ideological or other value to ethnic identity, the (more or less theorized) representation of the ethnic group as the source of values and the guiding principle of action" (Gossiaux, 1996, p. 191).
3. In official speeches, this program was expressed in the abandonment of the term Hazarajat in favor of Hazaristan, which was deemed worthier because of its resemblance to the names of major countries in the region.

economic exclusion throughout the twentieth century. The war that has ravaged Afghanistan since 1978 gave the Hazaras the opportunity to regain their lost independence – a development that has gone together with a spectacular modification of the balance of forces and a profound reconstruction of their identity.

We have seen that in 1979 the first revolts were organized at the local level around the *mirs*. It did not take long for internal conflicts to emerge, however, as the *sayyids*, supported by the *sheikhs*, rose up against the power of the *mirs*. A polarization between secular and religious forces ensued, and the most radical Islamist forces gained the upper hand, drawing inspiration from the Iranian revolution. The resistance was Islamized while members of the clergy were transformed into political leaders at the expense of the old elites. By the end of the 1980s, Hazara leaders had understood that it was necessary to unite and to silence their mutual hostility: this led to the birth of a new formation, the Hezb-e wahdat. This turn marked the end of the Islamist revolutionary process to the benefit of a more pragmatic politics. After a long period of division, the Hazaras seemed to have achieved the greatest political cohesion of any ethnic group in Afghanistan: theirs was the only force to have an explicitly ethnic set of demands, although it did not go so far as to advocate partition of the country.[1]

We have also seen that ethnicization was the outcome of a long process.[2] Several factors explain why this was especially advanced among the Hazaras and generated a veritable political project. First, the congruence between the specifically ethnic dimension and the religious dimension facilitated the drawing of ethnic boundaries. Next, the Hazaras were irredeemably confined in their position as a minority, and so long as they were split they could not hope to play a political role. Ethnicist demands enabled their leaders to constitute a relatively united political group beyond ideological divisions, but also – in a changing political context – to free themselves from Iranian, Shi'a and Islamist tutelage. Lastly, the war made it possible to challenge the social barriers; there were spectacular instances of ascent or

---

1. Glatzer, 1998.
2. As Olivier Roy wrote: "ethnicity is an achievement, not a given fact; it is one of the levels of identity, not the identity; but it increasingly came to be the relevant reference pertaining to political alignment." Cf. Roy, 1998, p. 206.)

loss of status, and the old elites lost their predominance. The disappearance of these intermediate powers opened the way for an enlargement of identity references and spheres of action. As the local, national and international context changed, the Hazara leaders waged a fierce struggle with one another before they found a formal, if imperfect, agreement around a discourse of ethnicity – one formulated and presented through a vast symbolic apparatus, in which the evocation of past sufferings occupied a premier position. Involving a process of political mobilization and legitimization, this discourse also corresponded to the aspirations of a people weary of the humiliations of past history. Power strategy and popular sentiment thus came together to lend undeniable weight and efficacy to the construction of a new identity referent. No lasting settlement of the Afghan conflict can leave it out of account.

The Hazaras – who form the great majority of the Shi'a of Afghanistan – had always been a marginal population. All the conditions for the emergence of a protest movement with millenarian overtones seemed to be met: political exclusion, poverty, social injustice, war, and so on. Largely inspired by the Islamic revolution in Iran, many leaders challenged the established order both within Hazarajat society and among the different components of the Afghan nation as a whole. They drew on religious references to legitimize their discourse of social justice and political equality. Once they had taken control of most of Hazarajat, their reform impetus gradually faded in the wider political and military context. This helped to freeze the positions of power achieved in the course of war.

The political evolution of the Hazaras after the Communist coup of 1978 cannot be explained without mention of Iran. It was marked by the triumph of Islamism, a revolutionary pole in opposition to more traditional, legalist or quietist forms of Shi'ism. In an early phase, the old religious leaders who had been the main intercessors between the faithful and the transcendental realm were ousted by young Khomeinists with a highly politicized vision of Islam, who were bent on leading a social revolution against the old property-owners. In a second phase, these same leaders gradually modified their discourse and tended towards an ideology that was more ethnicist than Islamist. The 1990s were thus characterized by the elaboration of a new discourse, which expressed a relative weakening of Iranian influence and marked the switch from revolutionary demands and militant Islamism to a more pragmatic politics.

Islamism was thus the vehicle of a certain political modernization among the Hazaras and, more generally, the Shi'a of Afghanistan. But it seems to have gradually given way to ethnic demands that crystallized the expectations of large and historically marginalized swathes of the Afghan population. Unfortunately, the political expression of these particularisms involved numerous dangers and carried the seeds of future explosions.

Bibliography

Bacon, E. E., "The Inquiry into the History of the Hazara Mongols of Afghanistan", in *Southwestern Journal of Anthropology*, 7/3 (1951), pp. 230–47.

Barth, F., "Ethnic Groups and Boundaries", in F. Barth, *Process and Form in social Life: Selected Essays of Fredrik Barth*, London, Boston & Henley 1981, Routledge & Kegan Paul, pp. 198–227 [1ˢᵗ edn.: 1969].

Canfield, R. L., *Hazara Integration into the Afghan Nation: Some Changing Relations between Hazaras and Afghan Officials*, New York, Afghanistan Council of the Asia Society, Occasional Paper 3, 1971.

Canfield, R. L., *Faction and Conversion in a Plural Society: Religious Alignments in the Hindu Kush*, Ann Arbor, University of Michigan, Anthropological Papers 50, 1973.

Canfield, R. L., "Ethnic, Regional, and Sectarian Alignments in Afghanistan", in A. Banuazizi and M. Weiner (eds.), *The State, Religion, and Ethnic Politics: Afghanistan, Iran, and Pakistan*, Syracuse 1986, Syracuse University Press, pp. 75–103.

Centlivres, P., "Violence légitime et violence illégitime: à propos des pratiques et des représentations dans la crise afghane", in *L'Homme*, 144 (1997), pp. 51–67.

Centlivres, P., and Centlivres-Demont, M., *Et si on parlait de l'Afghanistan? Terrain et textes 1964–1980*, Neuchâtel and Paris, 1988, Institut d'ethnologie and Maison des sciences de l'homme.

Edwards, D. B., "The Evolution of Shi'i Political Dissent in Afghanistan", in Cole, J., and Keddie, N. R., eds., *Shi'ism and Social Protest*, New Haven 1986, Yale University Press, pp. 201–29.

Fischer, M. M. J., *Iran: From Religious Dispute to Revolution*, Cambridge and London 1980, Harvard University Press.

Glatzer, B., "Is Afghanistan on the Brink of Ethnic and Tribal Disintegration?", in Maley, W., ed., *Fundamentalism Reborn ? Afghanistan and the Taliban*, London 1998, Hurst & Co., pp. 167–81.

Gossiaux, J.-F., "Un ethnicisme transnational: la résurgence de l'identité valaque dans les Balkans", in Fabre, D., ed., *L'Europe entre cultures et nations*, Paris 1996, Maison des sciences de l'homme, pp. 191–8.

Grevemeyer, J.-H., "Ethnicity and National Liberation: the Afghan Hazara between Resistance and Civil War", in J.-P. Digard (ed.), *Le fait ethnique en Iran et en Afghanistan*, Paris 1988, Éditions du CNRS, pp. 211–18.

Harpviken, K. B., *Political Mobilization among the Hazara of Afghanistan: 1978–1992*, Oslo 1996, Department of Sociology/University of Oslo, Report 9.

Kakar, M. H., *Afghanistan: A Study in Internal Political Developments, 1880–1896*, Lahore 1971, Panjab Educational Press.

Kakar, M. H., *The Pacification of the Hazaras of Afghanistan*, New York 1973, Afghanistan Council of the Asia Society, Occasional Paper 6.

Maley. W., ed., *Fundamentalism Reborn? Afghanistan and the Taliban*, London 1998, Hurst & Co.

Monsutti, A., "Guerre et ethnicité en Afghanistan", in *Tsantsa: Revue de la Société suisse d'ethnologie*, 4 (1999), pp. 63–73.

Mousavi, S. A., *The Hazaras of Afghanistan: An Historical, Cultural, Economic and Political Study*, Richmond 1998, Curzon Press.

Poladi, H., *The Hazâras*, Stockton 1989, Mughal Publishing Co.

Richard, Y., *L'islam chiite: Croyances et idéologies*, Paris 1991, Fayard.

Roy, O., *Islam and Resistance in Afghanistan*, Cambridge 1990, Cambridge University Press [1st French edn.: 1985].

Roy, O., *L'échec de l'Islam politique*, Paris 1992, Seuil.

Roy, O., "La guerre d'Afghanistan: de la guerre idéologique à la guerre ethnique", *L'Homme et la Société*, 17 (1993), pp. 85–92.

Roy, O., *The Failure of Political Islam*, London 1994, I. B. Tauris.

Roy, O., "Has Islamism a Future in Afghanistan?", in W. Maley (ed.), *Fundamentalism Reborn? Afghanistan and the Taliban*, London 1998, Hurst & Co., pp. 199–211.

Schurmann, H. F., *The Mongols of Afghanistan*, The Hague 1962, Mouton.

Tapper, R. L., "Ethnicity, Order and Meaning in the Anthropology of Iran and Afghanistan", in Digard, J.P., ed., *Le fait ethnique en Iran et en Afghanistan*, Paris 1988, Éditions du CNRS, pp. 21–34.

LAURENCE LOUËR

The Rise and Fall of Revolutionary Utopias in the Gulf Monarchies

During the 1980s, Iran's "Islamic diplomacy",[1] which declared its intention to export the revolution abroad, suddenly brought the Shi'a populations of the western Gulf coast to the forefront.[2] Countries like Saudi Arabia, Bahrain and Kuwait found themselves faced with protests from Shi'a Islamic movements, which appropriated the message of the Iranian revolution and waged often violent action in an effort to bring it about locally. Our understanding of this phenomenon is marred to this day by our lack of knowledge of the history of Shi'ism in Eastern Arabia,[3] with the result that many prejudices continue to surround the nature of the Shi'a presence in this region, as well as Iran's influence. Thus, although a large part of the Shi'a population living on the western Gulf coast claims

1. i.e. priority is given to solidarity among Muslims and export of the Islamic revolution. Cf. Djalili, 1989.
2. In the absence of census taking into account the category "Shi'a", the proportion of Shi'a on the Arabian coast can only be estimated. They are predominantly situated in Bahrain (70% of the population), Kuwait (25 %) and Saudi Arabia, where credible estimates range from 6% to 15%. It is important to keep in mind that they are concentrated in the Eastern Province (the oases of al-Qatif and al-Hasa) where the oil resources of the country are situated, and where they make up between 33% and 50% of the population. Shi'a are estimated to make up 10% of the population of the United Arab Emirates, 15% in Qatar and 3% in Oman.
3. Cf. Cole, 2002, p. 31.

indigenous Arab descent and employs Shi'ism as a nativist ideology, the Shi'a presence on the Arabian coast of the Gulf is often considered the result either of migratory movements from the eastern Gulf coast[1] or of proselytizing activities undertaken by the Iranian state. In this perspective, the Shi'a of the western coast are commonly perceived to be tied to Iran by quasi-organic bonds of solidarity that would make them natural exponents of that state's hegemonic ambitions. Understanding the origins of the Shi'a Islamic movements in the Gulf[2] and the evolution of their various political projects necessitates a departure from this approach, which fails to explain the current decline of the Iranian political model in the opinions of those who used to be its main proponents. Understanding this phenomenon requires a reassessment of the role Iran plays in the larger geopolitical context and a greater emphasis on the interaction between the foreign policy of the Islamic Republic on the one hand, and the domestic political issues of the Arab Gulf states on the other.

The Iraqi connection

The marja'iyya networks

Iranian influence on the Shi'a movements of the Gulf passed mostly through the filter of Iraqi *marja'iyya*, so that its internal struggles, as well as its ambiguous and evolving relations with the Islamic Republic, have profoundly influenced the Shi'a political landscape in the Gulf monarchies. Indeed, Iraq-based clerical networks often lie at the origin of these movements. The first propagandists of political Shi'ism in the Gulf monarchies were religious students who sympathized with the ideas of the Iraqi al-Da'wa ("The Call") party.

Founded in Najaf in the late 1950s in opposition to the Iraqi regime and inspired by the ideas of the Muslim Brotherhood, al-Da'wa recruited its members among religious students and the lower and middle ranks of the

---

1. Cf. al-Naqeeb, 1990, p.3 who attributes the Shi'a presence on the Arab coast of the Gulf to the Iranian immigration.
2. "Gulf" is used in this essay to translate the Arabic "*khaliji*", used more and more by the local population to refer to a common identity among the citizens of the states of the Gulf Cooperation Council (GCC), based on a shared history and way of life.

clergy.[1] Its ideas spread rapidly among Gulf students at Najaf seminaries, particularly those who attended the lectures of Sayyid Muhammad Bâqir al-Sadr, the principal founder and main source of inspiration of al-Da'wa. While the party's influence has remained relatively marginal in Saudi Arabia, it took root in Kuwait through two foreign *ulemas*: Sheikh Muhammad Mahdî al-Âsifî, an Iraqi who served for a long time as one of the party's main leaders, and Sheikh 'Alî al-Kûrânî, a Lebanese who trained at the *hawza* of Najaf. Both men spent several years in Kuwait between the late 1960s and the mid-1970s. The party was also influential in the United Arab Emirates, where Sayyid Mahdî al-Hakîm, one of its founders and the son of Sayyid Muhsin al-Hakîm, the most important *marja'* at the time, took up residence in the early 1970s. He established and for a long time managed the Ja'farite *waqf* (religious endowment) in Dubai and Sharja. During the same period, al-Da'wa's ideas found acceptance in Bahrain through influential local *ulemas* who had studied with Muhammad Bâqir al-Sadr; namely Sheikh 'Abd al-Amîr al-Jamrî (d. 2006), sheikh 'Isâ Qâsim and Sayyid 'Abdallah al-Ghurayfî. At the time of writing, Qâsim and al-Ghurayfî were considered the spiritual leaders of al-Wifâq, currently the main Shi'a movement in Bahrain. While al-Da'wa in Iraq was a real opposition party, in the Gulf monarchies it initially presented itself as a loosely defined militant group that used cultural and charitable organizations (the Islamic Enlightenment Society[2] in Bahrain, the Social Society for Culture in Kuwait) to raise popular awareness. Only after the Iranian revolution did political parties in the strict sense of the word emerge from these circles.

In the early 1970s, the Gulf monarchies became the preferred field of action for the Message Movement (*al-haraka al-risâliyya*), another Iraqi Shi'a movement, which changed its name to the Organization for Islamic Action after the revolution. The movement was founded in the late 1960s in the city of Karbala by a clerical family of Iranian origin, who had settled in Iraq in the mid-nineteenth century. Its central rallying figure was the controversial Sayyid Muhammad al-Shîrâzî.

Al-Shîrâzî had proclaimed his *marja'iyya* some years earlier, while

---

1. Cf. Jabar, 2003, pp. 85–87.
2. This is their own English translation of their name as found on their website www.Islam.org.bh

still in his thirties; this aroused the anger of the grand *mujtahid* of Najaf, who have denounced his presumption ever since. He set out to change some of the tacit rules governing the *marja'iyya*, which determine among other things that the status of *marja'* can only be obtained at an advanced age. He aimed to impose a reform on the religious leadership in order to bring it more in line with the expectations of the younger generations, who were abandoning the religious authorities and turning to secular parties – mainly communist ones – instead. While al-Da'wa courted the grand ayatollahs of Najaf to the point where it could be considered their political tool, al-Shîrâzî and the Message Movement presented themselves as an alternative, and, for that purpose, played without restraint on the regionalist sentiments and popular religiosity of the inhabitants of Karbala, who traditionally resented the domination of Najaf.

The export of factional strife

It was the failure of the Iraqi project that led al-Shîrâzî and his followers to relocate their activities to the Gulf monarchies. The movement had not only failed to impose al-Shîrâzî's legitimacy on the *mujtahid* of Najaf, but additionally faced the repression of the Iraqi regime. Over time, all al-Shîrâzî's family left Iraq for Syria, Lebanon and later Kuwait, where he settled in 1971. Based in the old Shi'a quarter of Bneid al-Gar, he succeeded in mobilizing the rich Shi'a merchants for projects such as the construction of mosques and libraries and the founding of religious and charitable organizations. Most importantly, he founded the *hawzat al-rasûl al-a'zam* (Hawza of the Supreme Prophet), which attracted students from all over the Gulf monarchies. In the space of a few years, he managed to train a network of cadres for local political Shi'a groups, of which he became the spiritual leader, and which for that reason are known today under the generic name of the Shîrâziyyîn. Actively assisted by his nephews, Sayyid Muhammad Taqî al-Mudarrisî and Sayyid Hâdî al-Mudarrisî, who took charge of the purely political aspects of the Shîrâziyyîn's activities, al-Shîrâzî moreover sent his followers out to spread his message to the neighboring countries.

After a short stay in the United Arab Emirates, where he obtained citizenship, Hâdî al-Mudarrisî settled in Bahrain, in a Shi'a quarter of the capital Manama. The authorities initially welcomed his presence, probably because in this young outsider they saw an opportunity to counterbalance the influence of local clerics connected to al-Da'wa. The sheikh was offered a regular platform on local television and even obtained Bahraini citizenship. In this small emirate, where the Shi'a population – a 70 per cent majority – feels excluded from the power wielded by the Al-Khalifas and their Sunni allies, he rapidly managed to surround himself with a group of young activists.

He continued to visit the United Arab Emirates on a regular basis. Although the Shi'a constituted only a small minority in that country, there was a class of rich Shi'a merchants who were close to the ruling families and whose support he sought. The Gulf was not only important because it had no previous history of Shi'a Islamic activism, but also because the average income of its inhabitants was far higher than that of any other Middle Eastern state, enabling them to contribute significantly to various awareness-raising activities. As for Oman, al-Shîrâzî sent one of his young Saudi students, Sheikh Hasan al-Saffâr, to the country; he frequently returned to his native town of al-Qatîf to spread the ideas of his mentor, encouraging young men to take up a religious vocation and sending them to study at the *hawza* in Kuwait. He was often assisted in this task by Sheikh Murtadâ al-Qazwînî, an Iraqi cleric who had followed al-Shîrâzî to Kuwait and regularly led religious ceremonies in al-Qatîf. Marginalized on the Iraqi scene, the Shîrâziyyîn rapidly became an essentially Gulf phenomenon.

But the conflicts of Iraq were also transposed to the Gulf; the grand ayatollahs of Najaf, particularly Abû al-Qâsim al-Khû'î, pursued al-Shîrâzî with religious edicts denouncing his *marja'iyya* as illegitimate and his activities as suspect. Their local representatives vilified the Shîrâziyyîn, describing them as a populist political movement disregarding the interests of the religion and showing little respect for the authority of Najaf. The rivalry between the Message Movement and al-Da'wa, which also had a number of cadres in Kuwait, grew to proportions it had never reached in Iraq. In Kuwait and Bahrain, each movement denounced the activities of the other in the mosques and *husayniyyas* under their control, while forming small groups of radical followers ready to fight physically. In

Bahrain, where religious rituals, most importantly the Ashura procession, were held in the streets of the capital, these celebrations led to mutual provocations in which the two camps gauged their respective strength and following.[1] In Kuwait, where regular student elections were held, al-Da'wa and the Shîrâziyyîn presented rival lists.

The Islamic revolution: who was mobilized?

The limits of popular mobilization

For the Shi'a in the Gulf monarchies, the Islamic revolution of February 1979 functioned as a catalyst for a sense of community and, especially in Bahrain and Saudi Arabia, for the frustrations of a population barred from power and subjected to numerous forms of discrimination.[2] In both countries, the Shi'a find themselves in an essentially conflictual relationship with the state, which they see as an entity co-opted by the Sunni tribes of the central Arabian peninsula (the *Najd*) and imposed *manu militari* on the local communities. The Shi'a-Sunni divide fits into an array of antagonisms opposing the conquered to the conquerors, the indigenous to the newcomers, and the *hadâra* (civilized people) to the *badâwa* (Bedouin tribes). In Saudi Arabia, the close links between the Al-Saud family and the followers of Muhammad Ibn 'Abd Al-Wahhâb, who preach a particularly rigid version of Sunni orthodoxy, further complicate the situation, as Shi'a beliefs, although tolerated up to a point, are considered impure. In Bahrain, the 1970s saw the failure of the first experiment with parliamentary democracy when the Emir dissolved the parliament in 1975 and declared a state of emergency.

For the Shi'a of Saudi Arabia and Bahrain, the revolution in Iran was thus logically perceived as a mobilizing call, even more so because the young republic quickly announced its intention to propagate the revolutionary dynamic of overturning oppressive regimes. In November 1979 the Ashura rituals gave rise to large popular demonstrations in both countries, with

---

1. In Kuwait, in order to avoid public order problems, Shi'a religious rituals are obligatorily performed within the *husayniyya*.
2. Cf. Bahry, 2000; and Fuller and Francke, 2001, pp. 119–154 and 179–201.

the masses carrying portraits of Imam Khomeini and shouting slogans hostile to the regimes. In both countries, the demonstrations were violently repressed, resulting in the deaths of dozens of youths and the arrests of hundreds more. In Saudi Arabia, this event, which was the culmination – up to now – of popular mobilization, is remembered as the Intifada of *muharram* 1400.

In Kuwait and the other Gulf monarchies, the relationship between the Shi'a and the state has never been conflictual to the same degree. In Kuwait, the important Shi'a merchant families arrived simultaneously with the ruling Al-Sabah family, in the first half of the eighteenth century.[1] They originated mostly from Iran, Bahrain and Hasâ, although some also came from Jabal 'Âmil (South Lebanon), or even from Iraq. They fall within the category of so-called "original Kuwaitis" *(aslî)*, those who arrived before 1920 and enjoy all social and political rights including the right to vote in national elections. Another part of the Shi'a population arrived from Iran more recently, in the late nineteenth and early twentieth centuries, and is made up of poor families attracted by the economic boom enjoyed by Kuwait in the wake of the development of the pearl trade and later the oil industry.[2] Some hold Kuwaiti nationality, but their naturalization does not entitle them to all political rights; specifically, they do not have the right to vote.[3] Because of the extremely restrictive conditions for obtaining nationality others, although often born in Kuwait, officially remain Iranian citizens. Others yet are *bidûn* (stateless) and while enjoying some social rights are deprived of any political rights.

What all this means is that the Shi'a of Kuwait are in no position to claim they are the country's only native inhabitants. Contrary to what happened in Saudi Arabia and Bahrain, therefore, Shi'a political mobilization has never thrived on a nativist language. The merchant families who participated in the founding and the prosperity of the country have always been on good terms with the Al-Sabah family, to the point where the political history of the Shi'a of Kuwait has been profoundly

1. Cf. Al-Khâlidî, 1999, p. 91.
2. Ibid., p. 92.
3. Naturalized Kuwaitis have to wait twenty years before being allowed to vote in national elections and don't have the right to put themselves forward as candidates.

marked by a tacit pact between the religious and commercial elites and the ruling family, and directed against the Sunni Arab merchant oligarchy who are wedded to the ideals of the Arab nationalists. The latter, organized in an opposition movement against the regime and well represented in the various assemblies elected between the 1930s and the 1970s, were in fact hostile to the presence of Iranian immigrants, who they considered to be a threat to the Arab character of Kuwait.[1] Until the 1970s, when they were heavily criticized by the first generation of Islamic activists, these Shi'a notables, who were close to the authorities, acted as intermediaries between the rulers and the Shi'a, whether naturalized, foreigners or stateless.

Living in a different socio-historical context from their Saudi and Bahraini fellow believers, the Shi'a of Kuwait thus saw the Islamic revolution in a different light. There were no spontaneous popular demonstrations in support of the revolution evolving into demonstrations of hostility towards the regime. A single solemn procession, organized in February 1979 by Sayyid 'Abbâs al-Muhrî, Khomeini's main representative, was the only instance which came close to the mass movements of Bahrain and Saudi Arabia. The objective of the procession was to congratulate the new regime. In 1980, after giving a series of lectures in which his son Ahmed argued for a more equal distribution of powers and resources in Kuwait, Ayatollah al-Muhrî was stripped of his Kuwaiti nationality and exiled to Iran with his entire family. The political violence that did take place in Kuwait has never taken the form of a popular uprising, or any attempt at such. Instead, it was perpetrated by small groups pursuing limited political objectives. The country thus witnessed several terrorist attacks during the 1980s, including one in 1985 that targeted the Emir in person, and which resulted in a wave of expulsions of Shi'a to Iran and purges of Shi'a from sensitive government sectors. The assassination attempt was ascribed to al-Da'wa, whose main objective was to convince the Al-Sabah family to retract its support for Iraq in its war on Iran.[2]

---

1. Cf. Al-Mudayris, 1999, pp.19–21.
2. Cf. Marschall, 2003, p. 37.

Iranian ethnicity

This brief juxtaposition of the case of Kuwait and those of Saudi Arabia and Bahrain allows us to formulate a first conclusion regarding the channels of political influence from Islamic Iran on the Shi'a of the Gulf monarchies: these channels are not of an ethnic nature. In other words, Iran's political influence is not primarily exercised through Iranian minorities living on the Arab coast of the Gulf. Indeed, in Kuwait, where Shi'a are predominantly of Iranian origin, in some cases even official Iranian citizens, popular mobilization has been weak. In Saudi Arabia and Bahrain, where the Shi'a population is respectively completely and predominantly Arab,[1] revolutionary fervor was widespread.

The case of Bahrain is a particularly significant illustration of the difference in mobilization between Arab and Iranian Shi'a. In fact, there is widespread agreement among the Arab Shi'a in the *Bahârna* (archipelago) that the *'Ajam* (their Iranian fellow citizens)[2] were relatively indifferent to the Iranian revolution. The *Bahârna* feel resentment over this until today, many of them convinced that the *'Ajam* seized the opportunity offered by the revolutionary enthusiasm of the *Bahârna* to forge closer ties with the authorities. While the Arab Shi'a were marching in the streets carrying portraits of Imam Khomeini, the Iranian Shi'a kept a low profile, reasserting their allegiance to the ruling Al-Khalîfa family. It is generally thought that the reason that the Iranians of Bahrain did not agitate in favor of the revolution was their precarious situation. Iran has long claimed Bahrain as a part of its territory, a claim it has never completely given up,

---

1. According to the local population, some 10% of Bahrain's 'Shi'a are estimated to be Iranians. Other sources offer a hypothesis of 22%: cf. Fuller and Francke, 2001, p. 120. In Saudi Arabia, there are virtually no Shi'a of Iranian origin. On the other hand, there are numerous Sunnis of Iranian origin, who are well represented among the merchant oligarchy.

2. The very derogatory Arabic term 'ajam literally means 'those whose language is incomprehensible'. By extension, it designates non-Arabs. In the Gulf monarchies and in the Arab world more generally, it is used to designate Iranians who live there as members of the diaspora. Because of the spontaneous association made between Shi'ism and Iranian ethnicity, the term can also be used by Sunni Arabs to mean all Shi'a. Arab Shi'a, on the contrary, will only use it to mean Iranians or those perceived as such, whether they are Sunni or Shi'a.

which made the Iranian Bahrainis prime candidates for a suspected fifth column of Iranian expansionism. On the other hand – and for the same reason – many didn't have Bahraini citizenship and either carried old Iranian passports or were stateless. Nevertheless, it is untrue to claim that the Iranian revolution has served as an occasion for them to strengthen their ties to the ruling family, as is indicated precisely by the issue of the mostly Iranian stateless Bahrainis. They were only granted citizenship in 2001 in the framework of a set of political reforms enacted as part of the process of national reconciliation initiated by Emir Hamad at the occasion of his accession to power in 1999.[1]

One of our Bahraini interviewees summed up the mechanisms of Iranian political influence in the revolutionary period thus:[2]

> The Iranians in Bahrain, they felt no sympathy for the revolution in Iran. We [Arabs] had a problem: we wanted to get rid of some people [in power], so we were receptive to these slogans ... We sympathized with Iran on a political and religious level. But them, they didn't sympathize. They stayed out of it. They said: Bahrain is our country and 'Isâ[3] is our Emir.

In other words, the Islamic revolution has had a domino effect only among populations involved in a conflictual relationship with the ruling powers, to whom it represented both an idiom in which to frame their conflict and the hope of assistance from a foreign power.

The role of local elites

The essentially political character of the influence exerted by the Islamic revolution in the Gulf monarchies is confirmed by an analysis of the socio-economic profiles of its activists. In Bahrain and Saudi Arabia, al-Da'wa as well as the Shîrâziyyîn found followers among the local elites. In Bahrain, al-Da'wa recruited local clerics who were part of the establishment, such as 'Abd al-Amîr al-Jamrî, who held the function of Ja'farite *qadi* for some time, before becoming the leader of the Shi'a protests in the 1990s until health problems forced him to retire from public life. Al-Da'wa also found

---

1. Cf. Louër, 2003.
2. Interview, Bahrain, August 2002.
3. The previous Emir of Bahrain, deceased in 1999.

some resonance among the great clerical families, such as the al-Ghurayfî. Like most of the Bahraini clergy since the seventeenth century, the al-Ghurayfî were *akhbârîs*,[1] but in the first half of the twentieth century they turned to Usûlism, a doctrine to which one of their most illustrious descendants, Allâwî al-Ghurayfî, converted numerous Bahraini Shi'a in the 1960s. Sayyid 'Abdallah al-Ghurayfî, one of the most eminent living members of the family, has espoused al-Da'wa's ideas and is now the main representative of Muhammad Hussayn Fadlallâh in Bahrain. While the Shîrâziyyîn recruited among the younger generations, they enrolled the sons of established families. A good example in this respect is the al-'Alawî family, which has supplied at least two important figures of the Shîrâziyyîn, including its local leader, Sayyid Muhammad al-'Alawî. As a family of Sayyids, they sponsored one of the most important *husayniyyas* of Manama, which to this day is the main bastion of the Shîrâziyyîn. Its members are rich merchants and businessmen who have long played a central role in the organization of Ashura processions in the capital. In Saudi Arabia, the Shîrâziyyîn has been recruiting among the al-Bû Khamsîns, one of the most important families of Hasâ, which has produced a long line of famous men of religion and *qadis*.[2] Mûsâ al-Bû Khamsîn, a figurehead of the Shîrâziyyîn in Hasâ, is the grandson of the Mûsâ al-Bû Khamsîn who, together with other great *ulemas* of the region, negotiated an agreement with King 'Abd al-Aziz Ibn Saud in 1913 when the latter conquered Hasâ, stipulating that the Shi'a agreed to pay allegiance to al-Saud in exchange for their religious freedom.[3]

In Saudi Arabia and Bahrain, the symbiosis between the Islamic opposition and at least part of the elite shows how the message of the Islamic revolution could transcend social divides in those countries where the organization of power was deeply segregated and where even notables co-opted by the regime were profoundly dissatisfied. The case of Kuwait confirms this by showing the opposite mechanism in action: here, the elites distanced themselves from the Shi'a movements. The cadres of al-Da'wa and the Shîrâziyyîn included none of the names of the great merchant families that have traditionally been close to the authorities, whom they

---

1. Cf. Cole, 2002, pp.52–56.
2. Cf. Al-Hasan, 1993, part I, p. 23.
3. Cf. Al-Hasan, 1993, part II, p. 12; Steinberg, 2001, p. 243.

served as bankers before the petrol boom and as political allies during the entire era of Arab nationalist militancy. Since Kuwait has never been known for great lines of men of religion, names of notable clerics are also absent. In reality, the relationship between the state and the Shiʻa elites was satisfactory enough for the latter to have no desire to contest it in any fundamental way. Consequently, local Islamic activists, whether from al-Daʻwa or the Shîrâziyyîn, were generally outsiders who used the revolutionary ideology to contest the authority of the merchant elites, as is clear from the history of the Social Society for Culture. Created by notables in the early 1960s to promote Shiʻa interests, it was partly financed by public funds. During the 1970s, it became the theatre of a struggle between these notables and a young generation not dependent on traditional Shiʻa patronage networks and influenced by the ideas of al-Daʻwa, which eventually succeeded in drawing the Society into its orbit. In Kuwait, the revolution was essentially a catalyst for a classic internal rivalry between Shiʻa elites and Shiʻa outsiders.

The vagaries of co-optation

A (brief) moment of unity

For the Iraqi leadership of al-Daʻwa and the Shîrâziyyîn, the Islamic revolution followed by the Iran-Iraq war clearly changed the picture. The increased repression made the situation for those remaining on Iraqi territory untenable. In Kuwait, the Baʻathist regime was putting pressure on the local authorities to intensify their cooperation and chase out Iraqi opposition figures, who quickly realized they had no other choice but to move on to Iran. This was in any case an evident choice for the leaders of al-Daʻwa and the Shîrâziyyîn, who had unambiguously declared their support for the revolution. Muhammad al-Shîrâzî, who had a personal relationship with Khomeini since the 1960s, left Kuwait for Iran shortly after the foundation of the Islamic Republic, leaving his younger brother Sâdiq in charge of his Kuwaiti affairs. The latter in turn left after being threatened by thugs of the Iraqi regime when the Iran-Iraq war broke out. The Hawza of the Supreme Prophet was closed shortly afterwards, putting a temporary end to the Shîrâziyyîn's public activity in Kuwait and the beginning of its clandestine phase. In Bahrain, Hâdî al-Mudarrisî, implicated in actions in support of the revolution, was stripped of his Bahraini citizenship and deported.

In Iran, the Iraqi Shîrâziyyîn leadership was actively involved in the policy of exporting the revolution. Al-Shîrâzî's nephews Muhammad Taqî and Hâdî al-Mudarrisî were close to Mohammad Montazeri and Mahdi Hâshemi,[1] the successive heads of the Office of Liberation Movements (the organ of the Revolutionary Guards charged with supervising the actions of movements abroad). Some claim that Muhammad Taqî al-Mudarrisî had actually been involved in the creation of the Revolutionary Guards.[2] Several sources confirm that for some time he headed an umbrella organization supervising all movements abroad.[3] In any case, the two brothers used their connections with the regime to consolidate their hold on the Gulf movements, who were now turned from rather loose groups into structured organizations officially announcing their existence in press communiqués. The Organization of the Islamic Revolution in the Arabian Peninsula was led by Hasan al-Saffâr. In Bahrain, the Islamic Front for the Liberation of Bahrain had as its leader Muhammad al-'Alawî. Both movements were formally headed by Muhammad Taqî al-Mudarrisî who, besides leading the Islamic Action Organization,[4] saw himself as the supreme chief of a grand regional pan-Shi'a movement. The Kuwaitis, who had no revolutionary project in their own country, prudently limited themselves to publishing propaganda material.

In a general way, therefore, the Shîrâzî Gulf activists were linked with the apparatus for the export of the revolution, even if it was through the intermediary of their Iraqi mentors rather than directly. While this

---

1. Cf. Ra'ûf, 2000, pp. 263, 286, 289.
2. Ibid., p. 286.
3. Which is said to have been called the Supreme Council for Islamic Revolution in the World. Cf. Dunn, 1987, pp. 43–51. Marschall, 2003 (p. 31) reprints Dunn's information, while asserting that she has been unable to confirm it through her own sources. Richard, 1990 (p. 172) also mentions Muhammad Taqî al-Mudarrisî's role in the coordination of Shi'a movements, but without naming his sources. Muhammad Taqî al-Mudarrisî himself, in an interview in Iran in July 2005, only admitted to an advisory role in all of these organs.
4. The name taken on by the Message Movement after the Islamic Revolution. Cf. *supra*.

involvement allowed for an intensification of their activities, it also cut them off – partially or completely, depending on the case – from local communities. Even where they were not in obvious breach of a legal prohibition, the activists found themselves in a precarious relationship with the authorities of their country. In the case of Kuwait, a number of activists followed al-Shîrâzî and his entourage to Iran, while others traveled to the United States for university studies. Only a few opted for permanent exile; most returned home on a regular basis. In Saudi Arabia, a large number of Shîrâzi activists had to flee the country immediately after the Intifada of November 1979. While some left to resume their studies in Great Britain or the United States, many settled in Tehran, where they founded the Hawza of the Awaited Imam (*al-Qâ'im*), which was to play a more or less similar role of incubator for Islamic activists as the Hawza of the Supreme Prophet in Kuwait. They too returned regularly to Saudi Arabia from their Iranian exile. Almost all of them spent time in prison there, but they also managed to maintain their contacts with local society. A different scenario played out in Bahrain, where Hâdî al-Mudarrisî, from his base in Tehran, involved local activists in an attempted coup in 1981. The coup was thwarted by the authorities, however, which forced the militants to move to Iran, Western Europe and the United States. Contrary to Kuwait and Saudi Arabia, the break with local society was almost complete here, leaving the field open for al-Da'wa, which, by persisting in peaceful awareness-raising activities, managed to survive and even consolidate its presence. The movement would not get involved in violent protests until the 1990s.

The return to realpolitik

The symbiosis between the Gulf Shi'a movements and the Islamic Republic was short lived. Many factors played a role in this but most important was the fact that Iran entered a phase of "routinization of the revolutionary process",[1] which, from the first half of the 1980s onwards, saw the pragmatists within the regime rise to power with Hâshemi Rafsanjani as their figurehead and in 1989, after the death of Khomeini, take over. Faced with the isolation of their country on the international political

---

1. Cf. Adelkhah, Bayart and Roy, 1993, p. 16

scene, they pushed for a less ideologized diplomacy, which more or less resumed the policy of national interest followed by the preceding regimes.[1] In the Gulf priority was given to appeasement, the regime sending multiple goodwill signals to the petro-monarchies who, faced with the Iranian threat, had buried their longstanding feuds and united in the Gulf Cooperation Council (GCC) in 1981. This organization offered material and logistic support to Iraq and served moreover as the main operating base for the United States in the region. Within the GCC, Saudi Arabia claimed a Sunni leadership role that aimed to re-encapsulate Iran in its Shi'a particularism.

The rapprochement with the Gulf monarchies – a laborious process that only acquired real consistency after the Gulf war of 1991 – inevitably involved putting an end to the activities of the revolutionary Gulf movements, an operation that in its turn entailed reining in the Iraqi sponsors of these movements, as well as their supporters within the Iranian regime. Since 1982 Iran had been trying to reduce the autonomy of the Iraqi groups through the creation of the Supreme Council for the Islamic Revolution in Iraq (SCIRI), which was to serve both to federate the Iraqi opposition forces and to place their actions under direct Iranian control. In 1986 the leadership was reshuffled to place SCIRI firmly in the hands of the al-Hakîm clerics,[2] who had no networks in the Gulf monarchies. The al-Da'wa cadres and the Islamic Action Organization, now marginalized, split into rival groups who disagreed on the way to deal with Iran's hold on the organization.[3]

Muhammad al-Shîrâzî, who had settled in Qom to continue his didactic activities while Muhammad Taqî al-Mudarrisî handled the political activities of the Shîrâziyyîn from Tehran, had already repeatedly uttered his reservations about certain aspects of the Iranian government's policies, including its mishandling of the war, its blocking of a multiparty system and its lack of real support for the Islamic and Shi'a causes. A rupture became unavoidable and in the mid-1980s al-Shîrâzî was placed under house arrest and forced to end most of his activities. Until his death in December 2001 he would suffer constant harassment by the Iranian

1. Adelkhah, Bayart and Roy, 1993, pp. 115–122; Marschall, 2003, p. 149.
2. Ibid., p. 241.
3. Cf. Jabar, 2003, pp. 256–259.

security services. The precise causes of the conflict remain unclear, but while it is safe to assume that disagreements on Iranian domestic and foreign policies played an important role, the fact that al-Shîrâzî saw himself as a transnational political *marja'iyya* independent of any state power was certainly an additional factor. Indeed, in this he placed himself in direct competition with Khomeini. The conflict between the two men dealt a serious blow to the Shîrâziyyîn, who did not weather the change in Iranian policy as well as al-Da'wa. 1986 was also the year of Irangate, which offered an opportunity to the pragmatists to rid themselves of a number of radicals, most of all Mahdi Hâshemi, who was executed in 1987 for revealing the American sale of arms to Iran in the Lebanese media.[1]

The autonomization of the Gulf movements

The deterioration of relations between Iraqi opposition groups and the Iranian regime played a central role in the formation of the current Shi'a political scene in the Gulf monarchies. While the Shîrâziyyîn fell into disgrace, a faction of al-Da'wa's Gulf activists continued to support the Iranian regime and to advocate its ideology, eventually becoming known under the generic name "Hezbollah". Contrary to their Lebanese name-sake, while the name "Hezbollah" is even now used in the Gulf monarchies to refer to pro-Iranian Shi'a movements, it mostly designates a collection of loosely defined tendencies and with the notable exception of Kuwait, does not refer to structured organizations. Because the term carries negative connotations among the general population, the activists of this tendency prefer the label "Imam's Line", designating those who present themselves as the guardians of Khomeini's heritage in Iran.[2] The designation refers to a number of religious and charitable organizations as well as semi-official political movements, such as the National Islamic Alliance in Kuwait and the Hijazi Hezbollah in Saudi Arabia. Since the death of Khomeini in 1989 and the ensuing polemics, the labels "Hezbollah" and "Imam's Line" also designate those who recognize the political and religious legitimacy of Ali Khamenei, Khomeini's widely contested successor.

---

1.   Fuller and Francke, 2001, p. 135.
2.   Students of the Imam's Line participated in the hostage-taking in the American embassy in Iran in November 1979.

In the Gulf, the Hezbollah tendency caused uproar in 1996 when it was held responsible for an attempted coup in Bahrain and a bombing in the Saudi city of al-Khobar. In Bahrain, however, observers have been doubtful of the existence of a structured group named Hezbollah and are also skeptical about the reality of the attempted coup of 1996. The mutation of parts of al-Daʿwa into Hezbollah should not be allowed to obscure the far more significant process of autonomization of the Gulf movements. The clearest example of this is precisely Bahrain. Between 1994 and 1998, the activists of al-Daʿwa played a central role in the so-called Intifada. Labeled "Hezbollah" by the regime, which refused to see this uprising of disadvantaged Shiʿa youths as a symptomatic expression of their economic situation and lack of political prospects, the protesters were more significantly united in the Bahrain (Islamic) Freedom Movement, based in London[1] and led by personalities such as Mansûr al-Jamrî, a son of ʿAbd al-Amîr al-Jamrî. By opting for exile in London, the movement was able to develop a political strategy independent from Iran based on international pressure on the Bahraini regime through mobilizing British MPs, the media and human rights organizations. In Bahrain, Iran's pragmatic turn also cleared the road for the al-Daʿwa tendency to mature by rallying the population behind a national political project.

Under the leadership of Muhammad Taqî and Hâdî al-Mudarrisî, the Gulf militants of the Shîrâziyyîn left Iran and moved to Syria at the end of the 1980s, transferring their activities to Sayyida Zaynab, a small Shiʿa pilgrimage town where Sayyid Hasan al-Shîrâzî, a brother of Muhammad al-Shîrâzî, had founded the first *hawza* in the 1970s. The reasons for their move to Syria are complex. First, their settling there has certainly benefited the Syrian state on various levels. On the one hand, Hafez al-Asad and his regime, denounced by the opposition as a heretical minority sect, have always been keen to demonstrate that they are a branch of Shiʿa Islam and therefore favor connections with the Shiʿa world. On the other hand, Syria was engaged in a power struggle with Saudi Arabia and the Gulf monarchies and therefore had a direct interest in offering refuge to their opposition movements. As for the Gulf movements, their Syrian home

---

1. Where they run an English and Arabic website called *Voice of Bahrain*: www. vob.org.

allowed them to gain autonomy from Iran, but also to free themselves from the grip of the al-Mudarrisî brothers. It was not just the legitimacy of an Iraqi leadership whose strategy of integration into the Iranian apparatus for exporting the revolution had failed and who, deprived of Iranian support, had ever fewer means to provide for the basic material needs of their activists that was questioned; it was more generally the pretension of the brothers' pan-Shi'a dream that was criticized. For the Shîrâziyyîn in the Gulf, the objective henceforward would be to formulate their own political projects adapted to the reality of local playing fields, and to replace the revolutionary perspective with case-by-case negotiations with the respective regimes.

The 1991 Gulf war consolidated these efforts at autonomy. At first, it clearly prioritized the Iraqi question over the Gulf causes. At one point, the Iraqi opposition held the legitimate belief that the Americans would either themselves defeat Saddam Hussein or support the Intifada of the Shi'a south. During this brief window of hope, the Iraqi cadres of the Shîrâziyyîn asked their partners in the Gulf to tone down their diatribes against the ruling families. Their objective was a rapprochement with the GCC regimes, allies of the United States and future neighbors whose support would be crucial after a takeover of power in Iraq. To put it briefly, the al-Mudarrisî brothers were in their turn confronted with the principle of reality.

Whereas the hope for a rapid fall of the Ba'athist regime quickly vanished, the episode did reinforce the Gulf movements' desire for independence, particularly since the Gulf war opened a window of opportunity for negotiations with the ruling families. The invasion of Kuwait, followed by its liberation by foreign troops, had indeed exposed the fragility of these regimes, whose survival was largely assured by American military protection. Opposition movements of all shapes and colors grasped the opportunity to regroup.

In Saudi Arabia, dissidence against the Al-Saud family manifested itself in the heart of Sunni orthodoxy itself. The Shi'a Islamic activists, weakened by the Iranian turnaround, saw this as an opportunity to get closer to the regime. While stressing the intrinsically tolerant nature of Shi'a Islam, they also played on the threat of creating a sacred union with the Salafist opposition. This bet paid off in 1993, when the leadership of the Shîrâziyyîn signed an agreement with the regime allowing them to return to Saudi territory. The scenario in Kuwait was similar. Here, moreover, Shiʿa movements including Hezbollah and Shîrâziyyîn could boast of their resistance against the Iraqi invasion[1] and – this time in total agreement with the pragmatic orientation of Iran's foreign policy – mobilize their Iranian support in defense of the Al-Sabah family. They were rehabilitated immediately following the liberation of the land and are today represented in Parliament. Only in Bahrain was the reconciliation of the Shiʿa movements with the regime yet to take place. In an extremely deteriorated economic context, the country faced a revolt of disadvantaged Shiʿa youths which resulted in dozens of deaths and hundreds of imprisonments between 1994 and 1998.[2] It was not until the death of Emir ʿIsâ and the succession of his son Hamad in March 1999 that the time for change arrived; this was consolidated in 2001 by a general amnesty for the opposition followed by municipal and legislative elections in 2002.[3]

Redefining the relationship with Iran

The reinterpretation of factionalism

Thus at the onset of the twenty-first century, the Shiʿa movements in the Gulf succeeded in finding spaces in which to express themselves and participate in the local political arenas, which were now more open to them. In this context, the factional antagonism between the Shîrâziyyîn and the various avatars of al-Daʿwa took on a new meaning. While earlier this rivalry had mainly reflected the factionalism of the Iraqi *marjaʿiyya*, it now assumed political significance, expressed as follows by a Kuwaiti Shîrâzi figure speaking about his rivals of Hezbollah:

> Politically, they follow the line of Iran, 100%, without any reserva-
> tions. We, on the political level, follow the *watanî* (national line),
> [...] that of the Kuwait's interests, without being concerned with the

1. Cf. Mudayris, 1999, p. 39 and Al-Khâlidî, 1999, pp. 124–125.
2. Cf. Fakhro, 1997.
3. Cf. Louër, 2003.

position of Iran. The position of Iran, that's not our business. But they, no. Their position reflects the Iranian position. [...] They are the voice of Iranian politics in Kuwait.[1]

After its initial phase of espousing revolutionary and pan-Shi'a ideals, the Shîrâziyyîn in the Gulf today presents itself as the representative of a nationalist Shi'ism in line with the national interests of states. In this context, their dispute with the Islamic Republic is framed as the expression of an independent spirit and as a rejection of foreign instrumentalization. This line offers the advantage of following the agendas of the regimes themselves. Threatened by a weakening of their redistributive capacity, the regimes want to promote a more ideological version of the political pact, one in which the sense of national belonging rather than the redistribution of the oil rent is at the basis of the bond between governors and governed.

The nationalist mutation of the Shîrâziyyîn seems most advanced and most promising in Kuwait, partly because the Shi'a have always been in a better position there, but partly because in general the sense of national belonging predates the nationalist discourse. In this country, the Shîrâziyyîn seems able to marginalize its Hezbollah rivals. The movement not only succeeded in uniting the other currents of Kuwaiti Shi'ism in a kind of community league (the Gathering for Justice and Peace) against the Hezbollah old guard; it has also pushed Hezbollah in a minority position among the five Shi'a deputies elected to Parliament in 2003. The Saudi Shîrâziyyîn has taken the same road, albeit less successfully, under the leadership of Hasan al-Saffâr, who is a prolific producer of publications celebrating the virtues of national belonging.[2] In this country, the movement is hindered by the lack of any sense of belonging among the Shi'a of the Eastern Province, who for the most part find it an utterly absurd notion that they should feel a connection with the rest of the country, particularly with the Najd, other than through an unfortunate historic event. The regime, however, favors the project, as it is keen to

---

1. Interview, Kuwait, June 2003.
2. Found partly on his website www.saffar.org, specifically in the small volume titled *The nation and citizenship. Rights and duties*, published in 1996 in Beirut (Dâr al-Safwâ).

support any initiative which proposes the idea of a national bond among its subjects. In both Kuwait and Saudi Arabia, the regime seems to be the Shîrâziyyîn's preferred ally in the struggle with Hezbollah. After all, far from expressing a contestatory nationalism, the movement contributes to the formulation of a state nationalism that presents the ruling families as the very embodiment of national unity. The enemy here is no longer the regime but the Sunni Islamic activists – and particularly the Salafists – whose religious intransigence is presented as the main obstacle to a mutual understanding between all elements of society. At the same time, nationalist Shi'ism contributes to a resurgence of communal tensions, which is of course perfectly in line with its real project of promoting equality between communities, not individuals.[1]

Another criticism the Shîrâziyyîn launches against the Iranian model concerns the interpretation of the conflict they have with the Islamic Republic as the manifestation of a profound ideological disagreement over the nature of political power and its relation to the clerics. The Shîrâziyyîn have a longstanding theory on the matter of Islamic government centered on the concept of *shûrâ al-fuqahâ'* (Council of Doctors in Islamic Law). They hold this principle to be diametrically opposed to the khomeinist concept of *wilâyat al-faqîh*: the Islamic state is to be led by a college of grand *ulemas* rather than by a single one. This idea, hardly an original concept in circles of Shi'a Islamic activists,[2] has never really been elaborated in detail by al-Shîrâzî himself, and is today subject to competing interpretations by various actors within the movement. For the laymen cadres, who stand in competition to the clerics who they believe to carry too much political weight, the *shûrâ al-fuqahâ'* is both a democratic form of Islamic government and an advisory rather than a governing organ. They readily present the Shîrâziyyîn more generally as incarnating a liberal Islam working towards a synthesis with the West. The *ulemas*, on the other hand, offer a different view. They see the *shûrâ al-fuqahâ'* as resembling a kind of democracy among the grand *ulemas*, whose governing role must remain preeminent. To them, the *shûrâ al-fuqahâ'* is not so much a concept of Islamic government that is radically different from the *wilâyat al-faqîh*

1. Cf. Louër, 2004, pp. 197–201.
2. The idea of a council was also proposed, for example, by Muhammad Bâqir al-Sadr, the Iraqi leader of al-Da'wa.

as it is a means to affirm the political role of the clergy while at the same time supporting the idea of a constitutional pluralism rather than a mere contingent of the *marja'iyya*.

The forms of Iranian influence

While the emergence of an anti-Iranian current among Shi'a Islamic activists in the Gulf monarchies is a sign that the political model of the Islamic Republic is losing its appeal, it should not be interpreted as a cut-off of the manifold cultural, religious, economic and family ties between the two Gulf coasts. On the contrary, these ties seem in actuality to be strengthened by the various pacification processes that we have dwelled on above. The Shîrâziyyîn are a typical case in this respect. The family of Muhammad al-Shîrâzî, and specifically his younger brother Sâdiq who succeeded him as *marja'* in 2001, still resides in Qom in Iran and entertains no plans to resettle in Iraq in the short term. Despite its difficult relationship with the Iranian regime, the family feels that there is currently no more appropriate place than Qom from which to carry out its task of spreading Islam. The coming to power of Khatami in 1997 has in fact resulted in the lifting of most obstacles to its activities, as well as those of other dissident grand ayatollahs. Muhammad al-Shîrâzî's brothers, grandsons and cousins, almost all living in Qom[1] and all wearing the turban, teach in freedom; openly receive visitors from the four corners of the Shi'a world; manage numerous cultural and charitable organizations; sponsor several *husayniyyas*; run an Arabic website;[2] and record programs that are broadcast on their satellite channel al-Anwâr, which was founded at the end of 2003, its headquarters currently based in Kuwait. While there has been no official reconciliation with the Islamic Republic, the Shîrâziyyîn, like others, have benefited from the relaxing of the regime's

---

1. Two of Muhammad al-Shîrâzî's brothers are still alive: Sâdiq and Mujtabâ. The latter currently resides in London. Muhammad has six sons, all living in Qom except two: Murtadâ, who lives in Washington in the United States, where he manages the Global Foundation of Imam al-Shîrâzî, and Muhammad 'Alî, who returned to Karbala after the fall of Saddam Hussein's regime. Sâdiq al-Shîrâzî has four sons, one of whom, Ahmad, lives in Kuwait.
2. www.s-alshirazi.com

grip on the activities of the clergy, which has allowed Qom to regain a certain measure of independence.

The al-Shîrâzî family moreover enjoys financial independence due to its great capacity for deterritorialization and its good relations with the Shiʿa merchant oligarchy in the Gulf. It has therefore chosen to stay in Iran, which is after all the place where a *marjaʿ* enjoys a large degree of political stability and the greatest concentration of students and men of religion, as well as an unequalled capacity to rally the Shiʿa masses, who flock every summer to the holy places of Qom and Mashhad and visit the grand ayatollahs as well as celebrated preachers. Throughout the summer, Sâdiq al-Shîrâzî's house teems with people: groups of Gulf tourists armed with the latest in cameras and video cameras, Iraqis coming to meet their spiritual guide or see their companions in exile who stayed on in Iran, Islamic intellectuals eager to debate points of doctrine with the master, and clerics of all origins coming to report to the *marjaʿ* on the activities they finance in his name in their home countries.

In the Gulf monarchies, even those cadres of the Shîrâziyyîn who are most virulent in their denunciation of Iranian instrumentalization are far removed from a total rupture with Iran. Some, particularly in Kuwait, maintain ancient family relations in the country, which they would not give up for anything in the world. Often of Iranian origin, many Kuwaitis continue not only to speak Farsi in family situations, but also to marry Iranian wives. Some of their children who are born in Iran even enjoy Iranian nationality. Together with the social networks built up during their exile in Iran, these family networks have also proved to be very useful in the economic sphere. As bilateral relations between Iran and the Gulf monarchies are today mostly peaceful, at a time when economic uncertainty is driving the GCC countries to look for ways to diversify their economies the Iranian market represents an important source of expansion – and the same holds true for Iran.[1]

In this context, all initiatives of economic cooperation between the two Gulf coasts are encouraged by the GCC. Here too, the cadres of the Shîrâziyyîn are not about to be outdone: ʿAbd al-Husayn al-Sultân, who manages the movement's newspaper in Kuwait, *al-Hayât*, also runs a small

---

1. Cf. Marschall, 2003.

office offering Kuwaiti men – and, more to the point, women – plastic surgery operations at reduced prices in Iran, combined upon request with a trip around the country's main tourist sites.

The political position taken, therefore, seems unconnected to influences of this nature, which in any case have ancient origins. Cultural, religious, economic and family ties linking Iran with the western Gulf coast are several hundred years old and persist beyond their necessary and permanent redefinition. While politics sometimes appropriate these means of communication, as is shown by the spread of Shi'a Islamic activism through these clerical networks, it also follows its own logic. Thus, while the Islamic revolution has not followed ethnic lines and only really mobilized those Shi'a populations already involved in predating conflictual relationships with their governments, Iran's political influence could make itself felt again in case of a resurgence of conflicts, as the issues opposing the regimes and their Shi'a populations are in reality far from solved everywhere. This is specifically true of Bahrain and Saudi Arabia, where political liberalization currently seems to have reached its limits. In Bahrain, the Shi'a movements have all boycotted the parliamentary elections of 2002 which were meant to seal the reconciliation. They decided to participate in 2006 but have been disappointed by their inability to influence political decision-making. Youth unemployment among the Shi'a remains high, and is made harder to accept because confessional discrimination persists in the job market, particularly in sensitive public sectors such as the army, police and oil industry. In Saudi Arabia, Hasan al-Saffâr's nationalist strategy is currently facing criticism as many think it has produced limited results. Some cadres of the Shîrâziyyîn are skeptical and remain convinced that only external pressure can persuade the regime to really change its policy. They place their hopes on American support, without however excluding the possibility of having recourse to Tehran's assistance when appropriate.

While these crisis scenarios remain vague, to say the least, in the minds of those who formulate them, their mere existence proves that Iran still has some space of intervention as long as local political conflicts remain unsolved, even more so as the promised return to prominence of Najaf – and indeed Iraq in general – as the religious and political reference point for the Shi'a proves to be a more long-term project than foreseen. Until the security situation in Iraq is better controlled, Iraqi Shi'ism will remain of little geopolitical consequence. Muqtadâ al-Sadr cannot project his influence abroad today the way al-Da'wa and the Shîrâziyyîn were able to do in the past. Everything in the current regional geopolitical reality works, on the contrary, for a return to power for Iran, which, while not in actual control of the Iraqi Shi'a movements, excels in manipulating the most wayward among them. Indeed, it is exactly the example of Muqtadâ al-Sadr that should give the proponents of anti-Iranian and nationalist discourses plenty to think about in terms of facing the principle of reality. After having built his power base in part on stigmatizing Iranian influence and celebrating Iraqi and Arab nationalism, he ended up seeking – and receiving – Tehran's support in his struggle for hegemony over the Shi'a population. While today the export of the revolution is not the issue anymore, Iran still remains uncontestable as a regional power, and as such plays the traditional game of power politics, trying to influence the political situation of its neighbors in its favor.

Bibliography

Adelkhah, F., Bayart, J.F., and Roy, O., *Thermidor en Iran*, Paris 1993, Complexe.

Bahry, L., "The Socioeconomic Foundations of the Shiite Opposition in Bahrain", in *Mediterranean Quarterly*, 11/ 3, (2000).

Cole, J., *Sacred Space and Holy War. The Politics, Culture and History of Shiite Islam*, London 2002, I.B. Tauris.

Djalili, M. R., *Diplomatie islamique. Stratégie internationale du Khomeinisme*, Paris 1989, PUF.

Dunn, M., "When the Imam Comes : Iran Exports its Revolution", in *Defense and Foreign Affairs*, vol. 15, July-August 1987.

Fakhro, M.A., "The Uprising in Bahrain: An Assessment" in Potter, L.G., and Sick, G., ed., *The Persian Gulf at the Millenium: Essays in Politics, Economy, Security and Religion*, New York 1997, Saint Martin Press.

Fuller, G. E., and Francke, R. R., *The Arab Shi'a. The Forgotten Muslims*, New York 2001, Palgrave.

Al-Hasan, H., *Al-Shi'a fî al-mamlaka al-'arabiyya al-sa'ûdiyya* (Shi'ism in Saudi Arabia), London 1993, Mu"assasat al-baqî li-ihyâ al-turâth (two volumes).

Jabar, F. A., *The Shi'ite Movement in Iraq*, London 2003, Saqi Books.

Al-Khâlidî, S. N., *Al-Ahzâb al-islâmiyya fî al-kûwayt : al-shi'a, al-ikhwân al-muslimîn, al-salafiyya* (Islamic Parties in Kuwait: Shiʻism, the Muslim Brothers, Salafism), Kuwait 1999, Dâr al-naba li-l-nashra wa al tawzîʻ.

L. Louër, "Les aléas du compromis des élites au Bahreïn", in *Maghreb-Machrek*, 177, 2003, pp. 59–76.

Louër, L., "Les reconfigurations du chiisme politique au Moyen-Orient", in Leveau, R., ed., *Afrique du Nord et Moyen-Orient. Espaces et conflits, les études de la documentation française*, Paris 2004, Broche, pp. 187–201.

Marschall, C., *Iran's Persian Gulf Policy. From Khomeini to Khatami*, London/ New York 2003, Routledge Curzon.

Al-Mudayris, F. A., *Al-haraka al-shîʻiyya fî al-kûwayt* (The Shiʻite movement in Kuwait) Kuwait 1999, Dâr al-Qurtâs.

al-Naqeeb, Kh., *Society and State in the Gulf and Arab Peninsula. A Different Perspective*, London 1990, Routledge.

Raʼûf, A., *Al-ʻamal al-islamî fî al-Iraq. Bayn al-marjaʻiyya wa al-hizbiyya. Qirâʼa naqdiyya li-sira nisf qarn (1950–2000)* (Islamic actions in Iraq. Between *marjaʻiyya* and partisanism), Damascus 2000, al-Markaz al-ʻiraqî li-l-iʻlâm wa al-dirâsât.

Richard, Y., *L'islam chiite*, Paris 1990, Fayard.

Steinberg, S., "The Shiites in the Eastern Province of Saudi Arabia (Al-Ahsaʻ), 1913–", in Brunner, R., and Ende, W., eds., *The Twelver Shia in Modern Times. Religious Culture and Political History*, Cologne 2001, Brill.

JOSEPH ALAGHA

Hezbollah's Conception of the Islamic State

Introduction

Hezbollah, the Lebanese Shi'a resistance movement, did not come into being fully formed. Its evolution was a sequence of gradual stages, each developing from its predecessor. In fact, many of the foundations of Hezbollah's thought, doctrines, and policies – especially its *infitâh* (opening up) policy – were laid down by Imam Mûsâ Sadr and the 1969 program[1] of the Islamic Shi'a Higher Council. Hezbollah considers Mûsâ Sadr as one of its ideologues.

Mûsâ Sadr, a charismatic and distinguished leader, mobilized the Lebanese Shi'a in the 1960s and 1970s and was able to channel their grievances into political participation. Although Sadr built on Shi'a popular heritage and religious history, he perceived his mission in Lebanon predominantly in secular and integrative terms, through a search for

---

1. The seven-point political program could be outlined as such: (1) To organise the affairs of the Shi'a community and to improve its socio-economic conditions. (2) To implement a holistic vision of Islam with regard to thought, practice, and jihad. (3) To strive for total unity among Muslims without any discrimination. (4) *Infitâh* ("opening up"): to cooperate with all Lebanese sects and communities and safeguard national unity. (5) To fulfill patriotic and national duties, and to protect Lebanon's independence, sovereignty, and territorial integrity. (6) To combate ignorance, poverty, backwardness, social injustice, and moral degeneration. (7) To support the Palestinian resistance and to effectively take part in the liberation of Palestinian "raped" land with the brotherly Arab countries. *Al-Shirâ'*, 1984, pp. 33–34.

Shi'a identity and its mobilization for political, social, and economic advancement. Thus, building on his religious knowledge and charisma, Sadr was a pioneering figure in promoting religion as an idiom of opposition in modern Lebanese history.[1] He never called for an Islamic state, but rather for equality and social justice among the various denominations within the multi-confessional Lebanese system.

In 1978, Israel launched its first invasion of Lebanon; in that same year, Imam Sadr disappeared under mysterious circumstances in Libya. A year later, Imam Khomeini announced the victory of the Islamic Revolution and the creation of the Islamic Republic of Iran, while 'Abbâs Al-Mûsawî, along with his students and other leading *ulemas*, officially founded "The Hezbollah of Lebanon".[2] These catalysts were compounded by the second Israeli invasion in 1982, which resulted in the occupation of a third of Lebanon's territory, including Beirut. The invasion, with all of its appalling multi-faceted consequences for the Lebanese population and its various ramifications, acted as a direct accelerator for the emergence of Hezbollah, a new resistance movement with a religious background, Islam serving as the backbone of its ideology and principles, against the occupation. Many existing Shi'a Islamist groups, as well as independent Islamist activists and clerics, joined the ranks to establish Hezbollah as an Islamic *jihâdî* (struggle) movement. These groups came together to fight the Israeli occupation and built the backbone of the party, most importantly its "resistance identity".

Their unprecedented accomplishments in landing several severe blows to the Israelis gained these groups a solid reputation in their constituencies and gave them serious credibility as a party renowned for fighting Israel and aggression against the Lebanese. Their later achievements in addressing the socio-economic grievances resulting from the Israeli aggression gained the party a solid grassroots following. This prompted its leadership to publish its political constitution, manifesto, or *Open Letter*, in 1985; in it, it declared its political ideology, thus engaging directly in Lebanese political life after operating clandestinely for some years.[3]

---

1. *Al-Shirâ'*, 1984, pp. 14–78; Mervin, 2002, pp. 285–300.
2. Al-Madînî , 1999, p. 172. As far as I know, this is the only book that affirms this as a fact and offers primary sources to substantiate this claim.
3. 'Alî Al-Kûrânî, a Hezbollah middle-rank cadre, was the first to expose the

However, Hezbollah's reputation as an Islamic resistance movement has been marred by Western accusations of "terrorist" operations, the majority of which were claimed by Islamic Jihad. Some of the attacks that brought Hezbollah global attention were the suicide attacks on the US embassy of 18 April 1983[1] and 20 September 1984; the 23 October 1983 double suicide attack that led to the death of 241 US marines[2] and 58 French paratroopers; the Buenos Aires bombing of the Israeli embassy on 17 March 1992;[3] and the taking of Western hostages. The Israeli government and the US administration claim that Hezbollah's Islamic Resistance constitutes a semi-clandestine organization, while Islamic Jihad makes up its clandestine wing.[4] In an endeavor to ward off the charges of terrorism, the party systematically and constantly denies any connection or link to Islamic Jihad and the actions it has claimed responsibility for.

From 1985 to 1990, Hezbollah emerged as an internally strong organization with a limited following. Subhî Al-Tufaylî's[5] firm, uncompromising political discourse and his repeated references to the establishment of an Islamic state in Lebanon – unprecedented in Lebanese political discourse – backfired domestically, alienating other political and social movements from the party and to a large extent excluding it from the Lebanese public sphere. Thus, Hezbollah's policies were counterproductive, failing to integrate it into Lebanese political life,

social movement's mobilization strategies in his book: Al-Kûrânî, 1985, pp. 183–203.

1. According to US political analysts, this incident served as a blueprint for the Marines' bombing six months latter. On this basis, it ought to have served as an omen to the CIA to try to prevent the Marines' bombing. (Brent Sadler, CNN, 11 GMT News, 23 October 2003). The death toll of the US Embassy in West Beirut was sixty-three people, of whom seventeen were Americans, including the entire Middle East contingent of the CIA. Cf. Byers, 2003, pp. 26–35.

2. The same sources claim that the 12,000-ton explosion was the largest non-nuclear device that resulted, in one instance, in the largest number of US casualties since the Second World War. Till now, the US holds Iran and Hezbollah responsible for the incident. Ibid., pp. 28–33.

3. In retaliation to Israel's assassination of Sayyîd 'Abbâs al-Mûsawî, Hezbollah's second secretary general, on 16 February, 1992.

4. Shay, 2005, pp. 89–100; Byers, 2003, pp. 36–49; Karmon, 2003, pp. 1–29.

5. Hezbollah's first secretary general.

especially after the party's vehement criticism of the Taif Agreement,[1] Lebanon's new Constitution.

Since the end of the Civil War in 1990,[2] Hezbollah has been confronting major developments in Lebanon: notably the emergence of a pluralist public sphere and increasing openness toward the myriad other communities, political parties, and interest groups in the Lebanese arena. This resulted in a change in discourse and priorities; the mixed confessional space in Lebanon led Hezbollah to move from marginalization to *infitâh*, through which the party has become a major player in the Lebanese public sphere, altering its stance and changing its policy from Islamization to "Lebanonization"[3] by propagating a down-to-earth political program. Thus, from the early 1990s, Hezbollah followed the pragmatic approach of its leader Sayyid Hasan Nasrallâh,[4] gradually evolving into a mainstream political party with an extensive network of social services (offered to Christians as well as Muslims). It entered the arena of electoral politics and decided to take an active part in Lebanese public life by participating in the parliamentary elections of 1992, 1996, 2000 and 2005, as well as the municipal elections of 1998 and 2005. After the Syrian withdrawal in the summer of 2005, Hezbollah joined the Lebanese cabinet with two ministers. Hezbollah's participation in the elections, as well as its work in

---

1. The "Document of National Accord", known as the Taif Agreement, was negotiated by fifty-eight members of the Lebanese parliament in Taif, Saudi Arabia, between the 30 September and 22 October 1989. The bulk and parcel of the agreement dealt with textual changes to the Constitution; the rest handled procedural matters such as ending the state of war, dissolving the militias and integrating their members in the Lebanese Army, Lebanese-Syrian relation, etc. The proposed changes in the Taif Agreement were officially written into the Constitution in August and September 1990. The final document is known as "The Constitution of Lebanon after the Amendments of 21 August 1990". In short, the Taif Agreement is a "bill of rights" or a blueprint for national reconciliation and reform aimed towards a more equitable political system for all sectarian-confessional groups. Salem, 1991, pp. 119–172.

2. See Hezbollah's political declaration of 3 January, 1991.

3. According to Hezbollah's discourse, Lebanonization refers to the party's integration in the Lebanese public sphere, including the political system and state structures.

4. Nasrallâh was elected on February 17, 1992, one day after an Israeli helicopter assassinated Sayyîd 'Abbâs Al-Mûsawî, Hezbollah's second secretary general.

the cabinet, can be considered crucial events shaping its current identity.[1] In short, since the early 1990s the party has promoted its Islamic identity and agenda by following a pragmatic political program, mainly to lull Christians and other Muslims who were opposed to the Islamic state. In the meantime, it has remained faithful to its Shi'a constituency by employing a bottom-up Islamization process, working within the state's political and administrative structures, whilst at the same time establishing Islamic institutions in civil society.

As such, the stereotyped notion of Hezbollah's advocacy of an Islamic state seems to hamper or at least obscure the party's political program of *infitâh* or integration into the Lebanese public sphere. In other words, the claim to an Islamic state seems to boost Hezbollah's religious credentials at the expense of its political credentials. It will be argued that, in its first (1978–85) and second (1985–91) stages, Hezbollah pursued the establishment of an Islamic state from the perspective of a political ideology and a political program respectively. However, as will be highlighted, in the third stage (1992 to the present), Hezbollah's Islamic state has remained a political ideology, rather than a political program.

First stage (1978–85)

Wilâyat al-faqîh (*Guardianship of the jurisprudent or jurisconsult*)

Hezbollah views the principle of *wilâyat al-faqîh* as its true Islamic cultural identity, and recognized Imam Khomeini as the official *marja' al-taqlîd*[2] (religious-legal authority) of the Islamic Republic and the first *faqîh* after *al-ghayba al-kubrâ* (Great Occultation)[3] in contemporary history

---

1. Alagha, 2005, pp. 34–39.
2. *Marja' al-taqlîd* is the religious authority who is acclaimed by a significantly large number of believers as being their model in religious practices. Traditionally, there has been more than one *marja'* to be emulated by the faithful at the same time, and even in the same place. This multiplicity is negated by the theory of *wilâyat al-faqîh* as introduced by Khomeini. However, *wilâyat al-faqîh* is not universally acknowledged by Shi'a all over the world.
3. The Great Occultation is the time during which the twelfth Shi'a Imam remains hidden before reappearing at the end of times to establish justice in the world. According to Shi'a beliefs, the Great Occultation started in 941.

to assume the title of deputy of the Imâm al-Mahdî and to establish an Islamic state. The party followed the religious authority of Iran, paid homage and allegiance to Khomeini as the political and religious leader of the *umma,* and abided by his *wilâyat al-faqîh* as a major pillar in its religious-political ideology.

In the early 1980s, Imam Khomeini instructed Khamenei, at that time Deputy Minister of Defense, to take full responsibility for the Lebanese Hezbollah: since then, Khamenei has been Hezbollah's godfather. (This is why since its inception, and on religious and ideological grounds, the party has fully abided by the ideas and opinions of Imam Khomeini as communicated by Khamenei.[1]) The religious and ideological bond between the Islamic Republic of Iran and Lebanon during that period can be analyzed through the declarations made by Hezbollah and Iranian officials. Sheikh Hasan Trâd: "Iran and Lebanon are one people in one country"; Sayyid Ibrâhîm Amîn Al-Sayyid: "We do not say that we are part of Iran, we are Iran in Lebanon and Lebanon in Iran"; 'Ali Akbar Mohtashemi: "We are going to support Lebanon politically and militarily as we buttress one of our own Iranian districts"; Sheikh Hasan Surûr: "We declare to the whole world that the Islamic Republic of Iran is our mother, our religion, our *ka'ba*, and our veins."[2]

Views on nizâm islâmî *(the Islamic order) in relation to the* wilâyat al-faqîh

To denote the Islamic order, Hezbollah uses the terms *al-dawla al-islâmi-yya* (Islamic state), *al-hukûma al-islâmiyya* (Islamic government), and *al-jumhûriyya al-islâmiyya* (Islamic Republic) interchangeably. Sayyid Sâdiq al-Mûsawî is a religious scholar (*'âlim*) of Iranian origin, who has compiled 1,300 pages of declarations and opinions that support the immediate establishment of an Islamic republic in Lebanon without delay. In line

During the period of occultation, the body of *marja'*, which form the highest ranking clerics, are considered deputies of the Hidden Imam and thus fulfill the public duties of the Imam himself such as collecting the *khums* (the 20% share of the imam of the capital of believers) and managing social affairs.

1. Alagha, 2006a, pp. 99, 340.
2. *Al-'Ahd* 8 (21 *Dhul-Qadah* 1404/17 August 1984), p. 6 [about *Al-'Ahd*, see p. 99, footnote 2].

with the *wilâyat al-faqîh* that prescribes the establishment of an Islamic order under the guardianship of the jurisconsult, Imâm al-Mahdî's deputy Sâdiq al-Mûsawî argued that the Qur'an is the eternal divine constitution of Muslims, who must abide by it and act according to its injunctions because it is the revealed word of God. He added that Muslims should obey God and his Prophet, execute their *wâjib shar'î* (religious duty or obligation), and destroy every unjust ruler in order to establish the Islamic government, which will establish justice and equality and ward off evil and discord among Muslims. According to him, *hâkîmiyya* (absolutist governorship) and sovereignty only belong to God (12:40). God's divine law prescribes the precepts of human behavior and the ordinances of government on a global scale. He stressed that Islam executes the injunctions through a just government in the person of the Prophet, the Imams, and the *ulemas*, the heirs of the prophets (4:58). In line with Imam Khomeini, al-Mûsawî affirmed that God commanded the Muslims to anathematize and regard as infidel every authority or government that does not rule by God's revelations. God has prohibited governance by tyrants, deeming it hypocrisy and vice, in this world and in the next (4:60–1 and 4:51). Also under the influence of Imam Khomeini, al-Mûsawî argued that abiding by *al-qawânîn al-wâd'iyya* (positive or man-made laws and legislations) instead of by the Islamic sharia is totally un-Islamic.[1]

Sayyid Husayn Al-Mûsawî[2] stressed that Hezbollah's religious ideology dictated that the party establish an Islamic order based on Khomeini's *wilâyat al-faqîh*, justifying the choice of the religious-ideological slogan of the Islamic republic as it is used in Iran and arguing for the feasibility of its application in Lebanon. Al-Mûsawî argued that, in general terms, Islamic government is based on divine principles mentioned in the Qur'an, the *hadîth* (Traditions), and the jurisprudential deductions or stipulations derived from them, which deal with man's social, economic and political concerns. He contended that the contemporary concept of the "Islamic Republic" is an extension of the efforts of the Prophet and imams, and is a living incarnation of the long experience of divine messages, and further argued that the system of governance that was in existence during

---

1. *Al-Shirâ'*, 1984, pp. 323–336. Cf. Khomeini, 1996, p. 60.
2. Amal's deputy president; in 1982 he defected and founded Islamic Amal, which later became part of Hezbollah.

the Prophet's time did not bear a specific name. However, with the complexities of modern life, Muslims started using different words such as "caliphate", "emirate", or "state" to denote the Islamic order. He took this to imply that the door is open for Muslims to choose the label they deem fit to express the concept of Islamic order and governance depending on the context. According to al-Mûsawî, this explains why Muslims feel comfortable choosing the name of the system that makes it incumbent upon itself to implement Islamic sharia, even if that name is different from those used by the early Muslims. Since "republic" implies a political system based on the will of the population, and "Islamic" means that the opinions of the people lose their credibility if they are not in conformity with the Islamic *thawâbit* (immutable set of values or principles), Hezbollah uses the slogan "The Islamic Republic in Lebanon" to denote a system that enforces Islamic laws in Lebanon based upon God's injunctions in the Qur'an as laid down by the *wilâyat al-faqîh*: "Whoever does not judge according to what Allah has revealed – those are the unbelievers [*kâfirûn*], evildoers [*zâlimûn*], and transgressors [*fâsiqûn*]" (5:44–6).[1]

Second stage (1985–91)

Wilâyat al-faqîh

During its first two stages, Hezbollah argued that in its early formative years, it needed a unifying religious-political ideology rather than an elaborate political program. It therefore based itself on the *wilâyat al-faqîh* and regarded Imam Khomeini as the jurisconsult of the Muslims.[2] In stage one, Hezbollah was ideologically completely dependent on Khomeini. In stage two, this dependency started to give way in the sense that the party did not blindly follow the Iranian regime anymore; rather it had some *khusûsiyya* (specificity), since in his capacity as the *Rahbar* (Supreme Leader) Khomeini was endowed only with the right to determine the legitimacy of Hezbollah. Khomeini highlighted certain precepts within which they could move freely – but he left their implementation to the leadership's discretion. Thus, although Hezbollah was ideologically

---

1. Interview conducted on 26 October 1983. *Al-Shirâ'*, 1984, pp. 219–233.
2. Sayyid Hasan Nasrallâh, NBN, 21 July 2002.

dependent on the Iranian regime, it had some room to maneuver in its decisions on certain Lebanese domestic issues. Although the multiplicity of *marja'* among the Shi'a continued after Imam Khomeini's death, in Hezbollah's case the issue of *marja'iyya* has been determined on the doctrinal-ideological basis of following the official *marja' al-taqlîd* in Iran, who is recognized by the Islamic Republic. Thus, Hezbollah's religious authority was and will continue to be the Iranian *al-walî al-faqîh*. This made the transition after Khomeini's death smoother while Hezbollah entered its third phase, especially since Khamenei had been appointed by Khomeini as Hezbollah's godfather since its early inception. That being said, from a religious and an ideological point of view, Hezbollah used to fully abide by the ideas and opinions of Imam Khomeini as communicated by Khamenei. Hezbollah regarded Imam Khomeini with high esteem, and after his death, the same allegiance and respect was accorded to Khamenei.

The Islamic state

The *Open Letter*, inter alia, classified Hezbollah as a social movement that called for the establishment of an Islamic state in Lebanon modeled on Iran's Islamic Republic. Hezbollah's political ideology advocated an end to political Maronism and rejected any participation in Lebanon's sectarian-confessional political system. Nevertheless, it also stressed that it would not impose an Islamic state in Lebanon by coercion – rather the party would establish an Islamic state if and only if the majority of the Lebanese populace demand it and consent to it, since in Lebanon it is necessary that the political system is mutually agreed on by Muslims and Christians. Thus, Hezbollah was inviting others to become part of an Islamic state in Lebanon, while refusing to submit to the governance of, or to co-operate with, the un-Islamic Lebanese regime.

Hezbollah conveyed its dedication to the rule of Islam, calling upon the population to opt for the *al-nizâm al-islâmî* (Islamic system) as the only system capable of warranting justice, liberty and security. The party portrayed its discourse in political-ideological terms by affirming that only the Islamic system is capable of halting any new colonialist-imperialist intervention in Lebanon.[1] In line with Imam Khomeini, it argued that abiding by *al-qawânin al-wâd'iyya*[2] instead of Islamic sharia is the second of four ways in which colonialism seeks to distort Islam.[3]

According to the *Open Letter*[4] and Hezbollah's political declarations, one of Hezbollah's objectives is to grant the Lebanese population (both Christians and Muslims) the right to self-determination by freely letting them choose the form or system of government they deem fit based on mutual agreement:[5] "There is no compulsion in religion; true guidance has become distinct from error. Thus he who disbelieves in the Devil and believes in Allah grasps the firmest handle [bond] that will never break ..." (2:256). However, Hezbollah anticipated the result by contending that "they would definitely choose Islam". That is why it calls for the implementation of the Islamic system. Indeed, it emphasizes in the *Open Letter* and its political declarations that it does not want Islam to reign in Lebanon by force like the "oppressive system" of political Maronism.[67]

Sheikh Na'îm Qâsim[8] commented on the above that the *Open Letter* is clear in its call to establish the Islamic state in Lebanon based on the free will and free choice of the population. He added that Hezbollah is totally in harmony with its convictions and with the practical-objective

1. *Open Letter*, section 7: "Our objectives in Lebanon".
2. See p. 93.
3. Khomeini, 1996, p. 60 ff.
4. *Open Letter*, section 7: "Our objectives in Lebanon".
5. See Hezbollah's political declaration on the third anniversary of the annulment of the 17 May 1983 agreement with Israel. *Al-'Ahd* 100 (15 *Ramadan* 1406/ 23 May 1986), p. 11.
6. By political Maronism Hezbollah means the leading Maronite notables and their retinue, which constitute the symbols of the Lebanese political system. Their retinue included the Sunni Prime Minister and the Shi'a speaker who were completely under their command, blindly exercising their every political whim and will. The late Prime Minister Sâmî al-Solh said that the prime minister is only "ketchup" in the hands of the president. Thus, from 1943 until 1990, Muslims in general and Shi'a in particular had been politically marginalized as the Maronites wielded the economic and political power and had absolute control over the country's resources and riches.
7. See section 9: "We are committed to Islam, but we do not impose it by force".
8. Member of Hezbollah's *Shûrâ* Council, and the current Deputy Secretary General.

circumstances in which it operates (i.e. the Lebanese milieu). Thus as long as these circumstances preclude Hezbollah from establishing an Islamic state because the choice of the people is otherwise, then the population should bear the responsibility for the political system they chose: "Had your Lord willed, everybody on earth would have believed. Will you then compel people to become believers?" (10:99).[1]

In al-'Ahd,[2] Hezbollah stressed that the Muslims have no right whatsoever even to entertain the idea of a Muslim canton (a mini-Islamic state)[3] or a Shi'a canton, or a Sunni canton ... Talking about cantons annihilates the Muslims, destroys their potential power, and leads them from one internal war to another. Only the Islamic state upholds their unity.[4]

The *Open Letter* explains that Islam[5] or the Islamic order is characterized by ideology, doctrine, political order and mode of governance,[6] without specifying the components or contents of these terms. Muhammad Z'aytir,[7] however, did specify them, arguing that based on strict religious criteria, Islamic government takes its decisions, undertakes its projects, wages wars, ratifies or rejects treaties, and deals with the international situation from the point of view of reform and Islamization. He added that Islamic government constitutes a practical embodiment of Islamic laws and injunctions. It is stipulated that the governor should be knowledgeable of Islamic laws and injunctions, and just in applying them, because an

1. Qâsim, 2002, p. 39.
2. *Al-Intiqâd* is Hezbollah's current mouthpiece and weekly newspaper. It was established on 18 June 1984 as *al-'Ahd*, but changed its name and orientation in 2001, thus conveying a "secular" image by dropping the Qur'ânic substantiation (5:56) on the right side of the front page, and removing the portrait of Khomeini and Khamenei on the left. The last issue of *al-'Ahd* was number 896, dated 6 April 2001 or 12 *muharram* 1422 AH; the first issue of *al-Intiqâd* was number 897, dated 20 April 2001 or 26 *muharram* 1422 AH.
3. Unlike the Progressive Socialist Party and The Lebanese Forces, Hezbollah neither established a mini-state – with its own ports, airports, and civil administration – within the Lebanese state, nor did Hezbollah call for federalism.
4. Sayyid Hasan Nasrallâh, *al-'Ahd* 95 (9 *sha'bân* 1406/18 April 1986), p. 11.
5. This mirrors Khomeini who argued that Islam is a state, sharia, and a just government that upholds the rule of law and accords people serenity. Khomeini, 1996, pp. 86–88.
6. See section 9.
7. He was a Hezbollah cadre at the time.

ignorant governor would lead the people astray, and the unjust would steal their money, take away their rights and destroy the *umma*: "My covenant does not apply to the evil-doers" (2:124). Z'aytir emphasized that Hezbollah seeks the realization of two important objectives in establishing an Islamic Republic in Lebanon: (1) to prevent any ruler from becoming a tyrant abusing the people in their security and freedom; and (2) to consolidate the Islamic content of the system. The concept of the Islamic state means that Hezbollah ought to build its Islamic republic, establish its Qur'anic government, and found an Islamic community based on the foundation of an Islamic understanding of the universe and human life, which is the best system for humanity.[1]

Z'aytir concretely outlined the components of the Islamic order, arguing that authority in Islam is a means to take care of people's rights, and to improve their daily lives and dealings. He affirmed that the system of Islamic governance, in addition to the application of *hudûd* (penal law), orders social, political, economic and monetary relations, and coordinates and balances between rights and duties. It is based upon the following: social solidarity and social justice; righteousness, fear of God, confidence in Him, and obedience to the Qur'an and Sunna; rendering people their rights and giving them security, justice, fairness, equity and compassion; liaising between the people; and establishing mutual trust. In short, the system of Islamic governance prepares the ground for raising free and noble human beings through holistic social programs, execution of the sharia, encouraging education and progress, and treating everyone on an equal footing before the law.[2]

Z'aytir's views on the Islamic state were expressed in stronger terms than the *Open Letter* and other cadres in that he underlined the forceful application of God's governance and sovereignty. Overall, he seemed much more radical in his political-ideological views than the party establishment; this might suggest that he represented a certain militant camp that advocated the establishment of the Islamic state by force, including the annihilation the political Maronites. He appeared to be against the overly conciliatory and compromising attitude of the Hezbollah

1. Z'aytir, 1988, pp. 57–60.
2. Ibid., pp. 52–57.

establishment. His criticism of *al-hâla al-islâmiyya* (the Islamic Milieu) might be interpreted as an indirect attack on Ayatollah Fadlallâh,[1] who was not forceful enough in his Islamization project. Z'aytir did not accept Fadlallâh's Qur'anic logic of *hudna* or *muhâdana* (truce or ceasefire)[2] and gradual Islamization through a bottom-up process, but rather called for a violent and radical overthrow of the regime through a top-down process, even where the power balance does not favor the Islamists.[3] Hezbollah was heavily influenced by Imam Khomeini's views on the *wilâyat al-faqîh* and indeed, its anathematizing of the Lebanese political system might also be attributed to Khomeini.[4] However, in practice, the establishment did not agree with Z'aytir.

The place of Christians in the Islamic state

Conforming with the *Open Letter*, in one of its political declarations Hezbollah states that in the presence of peace-loving Christians who reside in the areas under its control, it sees the credibility of its *infitâh* and the tolerance of Islam. The *dhimmis* or *ahl al-dhimma*[5] share with the Muslims the social values of overt and purposeful tolerance such as love, fraternity and solidarity. However, Hezbollah clarified in its declaration that political Maronism is excluded from such tolerance and regarded as

1. Sayyid Muhammad Husayn Fadlallâh is considered by many to be the godfather of the Islamic movement in Lebanon.
2. Fadlallâh, 1985, p. 258
3. Z'aytir was a strong advocate of establishing an Islamic State in Lebanon according to the Khomeinist ideology, but as far as I know he did not occupy a prominent role in Hezbollah's leadership. His other book, which contains 1,136 pages of severe political-ideological Maronite-bashing, is officially banned in Lebanon. (The book's cover portrays a blue map of Lebanon with a black cross in the center). See Z'aytir, 1986.
4. Imam Khomeini issued a *fatwa* (religious edict) stressing that the Lebanese system is illegitimate and criminal. In 1986, Khamenei clarified Khomeini's *fatwa*, arguing for the need for Muslims to rule Lebanon since they comprise the majority of the population. al-Madînî, 1999, pp. 162–163; Sharâra, 1997, p. 342. The chief of staff of the Iranian Revolutionary Guard Corps in Lebanon stressed that Hezbollah and the Revolutionary Guards were going to bring down the Maronite regime just like the Iranians brought down the Shah. *Al-Anwar*, 9 February 1988.
5. Non-Muslim "people of the book" living under Islamic protection.

hypocritical (63:1).[1] 'Alî Kûrânî stated that the freedom accorded to the *ahl al-dhimma* in the Islamic state is within the confines of the safeguards of Islamic sharia.[2] He clarified that the Christian minorities who live under Muslim governance are accorded all their civil and religious rights but not their political rights, since they are governed and not ruling anymore, as was the case in political Maronism.[3] Thus, contrary to the Prophetic tradition that granted non-Muslims partnership in the political structure, Hezbollah's tolerance or inclusiveness clearly excluded Christians from political life. Hezbollah seems to imply that tolerance is the responsibility of the "majority" and integration is the responsibility of the "minority".

According to Z'aytir, the Islamic republic that the Muslims are striving to install in Lebanon will not force Christians in general and the political Maronites in particular to convert to Islam, because Islam does not need them in its ranks, rather it is *they* who need Islam. He warned that governance and administration of the *umma* should be the prerogative of Muslims, and that Muslims must not allow others to interfere in their affairs:

> O believers, do not take as close friends other than your own people [co-religionists]; they will spare no effort to corrupt you and wish to see you suffer. Hatred has already been manifested in what they utter, but what their hearts conceal is greater still. We have made clear Our signs to you if only you understand" (3:118).

Based on this verse, Z'aytir posed the rhetorical question: since it is a religious imperative not to allow Christians to participate in government, then how could Muslims accept to be ruled by them?[4]

In this respect, Sayyid 'Abbâs al-Mûsawî said that compulsion in religion is forbidden, otherwise Prophet Muhammad would not have revealed the Constitution of Medina. Sayyid 'Abbâs considered the Prophet as the inter-religious arbitrator among the Muslims, the *ahl*

---

1. See Hezbollah's Political Declaration of 31 May 1986.
2. Al-Kûrânî, 1985, p. 181.
3. Al-Kûrânî added that neither Israel nor the US care about the Lebanese Christians, since they have cost them too much and offered very few benefits in return. Ibid., p. 191.
4. Z'aytir, 1988, p. 106.

al-dhimma, and others. Although the city was made up of many religious communities, Medina was a monolithic political community headed by the Prophet Muhammad. Thus, non-Muslims conferred legitimacy to the Prophet as the political leader and final arbitrator. Since the Prophet's religious authority over non-Muslims was restricted, the Constitution of Medina granted each religious community full rights to follow its own religion and to practice its own internal affairs as it deems fit. In Sayyid 'Abbâs's opinion, this is how Hezbollah treats the People of the Book.[1]

Hezbollah's treatment of Christians as *dhimmis* is most likely a specific interpretation of the Prophet's political Constitution of Medina, although it is undoubtedly also inspired by the Islamic Republic's Constitution. In addition, Hezbollah may also have been influenced by Sayyid Muhammad Husayn Fadlallâh who, basing his argument on the Qur'an, argued that the Muslim stance toward the Christians is anchored in a horizon of mutual co-existence, cooperation and dialogue, which should be based on points of convergence and common grounds that all parties agree upon.[2]

Relations with Christians

Hezbollah's political ideology has always been selective in its treatment of Lebanese Christians. Although when taken at face value, Hezbollah's call seemed addressed to all Christians, in reality the party shunned any contact with political Maronism, Maronites and anyone collaborating with Israel. Although there was some low-level contact with Christians living in its constituencies, no substantial or high-level dialogue materialized between Hezbollah and the Christians. Despite Hezbollah's exhortation to Christians to convert to Islam, it did not impose this conversion by force; rather the party applied its theory of tolerance to those Christians living in the areas that it controlled as well as to other Christians, so long as they were not treacherous or aggressive.

Waddâh Sharâra claims that Hezbollah's political ideology was in fact intolerant towards Christians. He also accuses Hezbollah of imposing its will on all Lebanese of all denominations, sects, and religions.[3] There

---

1. *Al-Safir*, 7 September 1985.
2. Fadlallâh, 1987.
3. Sharâra, 1997, p. 348.

is surely a certain tension between Hezbollah's propositions; between the stated intention not to impose Islam but instead to persuade the Christians to adhere to its call; and the mission of establishing an Islamic order. Maybe the confusion has to do with Zʿaytir's denial of the need to convert Christians and the Hezbollah establishment's call for conversion through peaceful means. Nevertheless, both Zʿaytir and the Hezbollah establishment have always agreed that there should be "no compulsion in religion" (2:256) and that an "equitable world" or common grounds (3:64) should guide the relationship between Muslims and Christians.

Third stage (1992 to the present)

Wilâyat al-faqîh

The year 1992 may be considered pivotal in the shaping of Hezbollah's identity. The party had difficulty deciding whether to participate in the parliamentary elections or not. In the end, after much heated internal debate, the twelve member committee took a positive decision. Since *al-walî al-faqîh* determines "legitimacy" even in practical political matters, Khamenei had to intercede and grant legitimacy to political participation. This caused a considerable schism in the party, as al-Tufaylî[1] contested the decision and pursued a confrontational course with both the party and the Lebanese state.

The committee recommended that participation in the elections was both beneficial and necessary, in harmony with Hezbollah's *holistic* vision, which favors fulfilling the expectations of the people by serving their socio-economic and political needs. Hezbollah's greater jihad and dedication to addressing the plight of the people does not contradict its priority of the smaller military jihad for the sake of the liberation of occupied land. Participating in the elections would lead to tangible political results, and was also regarded as an important step towards interaction with others. This was a novel experience in the *infitâh* of a young Islamic party,

---

1. Al-Tufaylî held a high post in the leadership of Hezbollah in the early 1980s, but later created minor dissent in the party for reasons that appear to be social but in fact involved a fight for control over the Baalbek region. Al-Tufaylî today represents the faction within Hezbollah that still upholds the Iranian revolutionary ideology of the 1980s.

but the committee stressed that it was in accordance with Lebanese specificities as well as the nature of the proposed elections, which allowed for considerable freedom of choice. In short, the pros outweighed the cons by far; participation in Parliament was deemed worthwhile, as it was another way of working for change and making Hezbollah's voice heard, not just domestically but regionally and internationally.[1] Thus Hezbollah seems to have been forced by political circumstances, the Taif Agreement and the end of the civil war to enter a new phase in its history by propagating a matter-of-fact political program and co-operating with the Lebanese system.

A further shift occurred when, in its third stage, Hezbollah argued that it did not consider the Iranian regime to be the jurisconsult of *all* Muslims, and that in consequence, not all Islamic movements must abide by its orders and directives.[2] Another shift occurred in May 1995, when Khamenei nominated Sayyid Hasan Nasrallâh as Hezbollah's Secretary General and Sheikh Muhammad Yazbik, a member of the Shûrâ Council, as his representative for religious and legal affairs in Lebanon. This led to increased "Lebanonization", in line with the specificities of Lebanese society, rather than blind adherence to Iran. Thus, Hezbollah has moved from complete ideological dependency on Khomeini in the first stage, to lessened dependency after his death in the second stage, finally gaining some independence in decision-making in the third stage.

This manifested itself not only in practical politics but also in doctrinal matters, to the extent that, at least in some cases, Hezbollah seems to make almost entirely independent decisions. For instance, after the Syrian withdrawal in the summer of 2005, the party secured the legitimacy to participate in the Lebanese cabinet for the first time in its history; this was apparently granted by Sheikh 'Afîf al-Nâbulsî,[3] the head of the Association of Shi'a Religious Scholars of Jabal 'Âmil in South Lebanon.

---

1. Qâsim, 2002, pp. 267–273.
2. Nasrallâh, NBN, 4 August 2002.
3. Nâbulsî is not a Hezbollah member, but rather an influential local cleric revered by Hezbollah. It is worth mentioning that later, when the five Shi'a ministers – including the two from Hezbollah – boycotted the Lebanese cabinet from 12 December 2005, Nâbulsî issued a *fatwa* barring any other Shi'aShi'a from joining the cabinet in their absence. (See the Lebanese newspapers of 21 December 2005.)

It can thus be seen that Hezbollah heeds Lebanese religious authority in addition to Iranian edicts. Participation in the Lebanese cabinet, which ideologically requires the implementation of the *shar'i* and the legitimization of the *faqîh*, was thus relegated to an administrative matter, on which Hezbollah's leadership is capable of taking an autonomous decision. As soon as this freedom had been attained, Hezbollah joined the cabinet; when President Mahmud Ahmadinejad came to power in Iran, it had already began to proliferate in Lebanese state institutions and administrative departments.

It has been contended by some analysts that since the death of Imam Khomeini, a discernible change in Hezbollah's political relationship with Iran seems to have occurred. They believe that the liberalization process in Iran may have influenced Hezbollah's policies towards moderation.[1] However, there is no evidence that the reformers in Iran drastically affected Hezbollah's external and internal policies. This is explained by the fact that Hezbollah's relationship with Iran is limited, to a large extent, to the official *marja'* and Iranian state institutions. For this reason, the passing of the presidency from the reformist Khatami to the conservative non-*'âlim* (non-cleric)[2] Mahmud Ahmadinejad does not alter Hezbollah's relationship with Iran. Hezbollah's leaders clarified during their August 2005 visit to Tehran that, contrary to the common perception that categorizes Iran as torn between reformists and conservatives, they regard Iran as a monolithic order. Indeed, the previous presentation points to a shift in Hezbollah's relations with Iran, arguably moving towards increasing independence; autonomy in decision-making; strengthened Lebanese identity; and greater emphasis on Lebanese specificities and interests, irrespective of the person of the *faqîh* or the president.

It is worth mentioning that Hezbollah's religious ideology continues to play a significant role even now, simply because it is difficult to separate the party from religious concerns. However, religion no longer constitutes the sole ideological justification and legitimization of Hezbollah's behavior, since it is nominally based upon the moral claims of Shi'a Islam, rather than on an uncompromising dogmatic basis as it was in

---

1. For instance see Buchta, 2000.
2. Which also had not happened since 1981.

the first stage of its formation. Based on inside sources and fieldwork observations by the author, it is fair to state that the majority of the cadres consider disagreements in religious and political opinions and viewpoints among the leaders to be a phenomenon that represents a healthy "democratic" atmosphere. However, strict obedience and discipline prevent disagreements from festering into discord, al-Tufaylî's case being an exception.

Views on the Islamic state

None of Hezbollah's parliamentary and municipal election programs state anything about establishing an Islamic order in Lebanon. Nevertheless, Hezbollah's views on the Islamic state in the era of the political program are addressed by the discourse of its leaders and cadres, most notably Nasrallâh and Qâsim.

The leadership argues that every Islamic movement advocates the establishment of an Islamic state in its own country;[1] that no committed Muslim who supports Islamic doctrine and believes in its legitimacy does not endorse the project of establishing an Islamic state, since it conveys and stands for the (social) justice that man aspires for.[2] However, as we have seen, Hezbollah has rejected recourse to force in order to establish an Islamic state, arguing that it would need massive popular backing. If the population rejected the Islamic state, then it would not impose it in fifty or even one hundred years.[3]

In its 1998 "Statement of Purpose", Hezbollah clarified that its objective is a presentation of Islam that addresses people's minds. It later stated in its 2004 "Identity and Goals" – its latest self-description, which includes aspects of its political ideology and political program – that one of its strategic *ideals* is the establishment of an Islamic republic. This should not be achieved by force or violence but rather through peaceful political action, which offers the opportunity for the majority in any society to adopt or reject it. Islam rejects violence as a means to

---

1. Nasrallâh, *al-ʿAhd*, 26 August 1994.
2. Qâsim, 2002, p. 38.
3. Nasrallâh, LBC, 24 September 1995.

gain power, exhorting non-Islamists not to have recourse to force in order to implement their agendas.[1]

Thus it seems that, for practical purposes, Hezbollah has put to rest once and for all the issue of the establishment or implementation of an Islamic state in Lebanon. This accounts for Hezbollah's participation in electoral politics, and its decision to take an active part in the Lebanese public sphere. The party seems to have become down to earth and pragmatic in its political programs, most probably because it realized that it is counter-productive and politically unwise to mention its earlier commitment to an Islamic order. However, there is a discrepancy between these programs and the discourse of its leaders, who continue to perform lip service to the old ideological commitment of establishing an Islamic order. Thus, it is most likely that Hezbollah was guided by political expediency.

Hezbollah's dialogue with the Lebanese Christians

Conforming with Sayyid 'Abbâs' political program, which called for a process of Lebanonization, *infitâh* and dialogue, most notably with the Christians, in 1992 Hezbollah leaders took the initiative to visit the Maronite Patriarch. Talks centered mostly on Christian-Muslim dialogue and Hezbollah's gradual integration in the Lebanese public sphere. However, with the passage of time, dialogue has been extended to the other Christian groups that make up the Lebanese mosaic. As to the content, Hezbollah tried to avoid engaging in theological or religious discussions, concentrating instead on political, socio-economic and sociological issues.

In its political program, Hezbollah blamed political sectarianism for Lebanon's malaise, calling for its abolition in line with the 1990 Constitution, and embarking on an open, peaceful, and constructive dialogue with all sects, political parties and civilian organizations in order to tackle the source or origin of cultural, political, theoretical and practical differences. The 2006 national dialogue sessions among the fourteen leading politicians in Lebanon dealt with such issues, including

---

1. "Identity and Goals"; Nasrallâh expressed similar views in *al-'Ahd*, 16 February 1998.

taboos such as Hezbollah's weapons and its defense strategy. Nasrallâh in person conveyed the party's position.

Hezbollah tried to portray itself as an important promoter of Muslim-Christian co-existence, stressing the importance of pluralism through multi-confessional representation. It incorporated Christians, including Maronites, on its parliamentary election lists and granted them the right to speak in its name as long as they did not deflect from the party's established doctrines. Moreover, it shared municipal council seats with Christians. This garnered the party support in its resistance against Israel and its *infitâh* policies, especially among Christians. By adopting what many observers would consider a "Christian discourse", namely the abolition of political sectarianism, Hezbollah displays a progressive-liberal, pragmatic view on the abolition of political sectarianism, which conforms to the position of the Maronite Church and the Papal Guidance. The late Pope's call for fraternity and the inculcation of dialogue and tolerance among the Lebanese struck a responsive cord in party circles, for much of it was reminiscent of Imam Mûsâ Sadr's discourse on Christian-Muslim understanding, mutual coexistence, and open and permanent dialogue. Thus Hezbollah based its political program of dialogue with Lebanese Christians on the Papal Guidance.

Conclusion

In the first and second stages, Hezbollah's Islamic current affirmed that the Qur'an is the Constitution of the Islamic *umma*, and Islam is both a religious and a governmental order. Hezbollah urged Muslims, wherever they are, to strive with all legitimate means to implement the Islamic order. The party based its argument, in the Lebanese context, on demographic realities (the fact that Muslims constitute the majority of the population) and proposed that Lebanon become part of the all-encompassing Islamic state. The cadres argued the necessity to establish an Islamic order, stressing that social change must begin by changing the political system and annihilating the ruling elite through a top-down revolutionary process.

During these phases, Hezbollah considered the Lebanese political system, which was dominated by the political Maronites, as a *jâhiliyya* (pre-Islamic paganist) system. The same consideration applies to any non-Islamic system, be it patriotic, democratic or nationalist, even if governed by Muslims. The religious ideology behind this policy was to instate God's sovereignty and divine governance on earth through *hâkîmiyya* and the execution of God's law by instituting an Islamic order as a *taklîf shar'î* (religious and legal obligation).[1] In contrast, the political ideology was not to impose the Islamic order by force. This should not be taken at face value, since Hezbollah's rhetoric in stages one and two was different from what it was actually doing, in that it was actively engaged in preparing the ground for establishing an Islamic order, at least in the areas where it wielded power.

In the third stage, Hezbollah's pragmatic and realistic approach dominated, as the leadership conceded that the majority of the Lebanese would refuse its Islamic order. Hezbollah did not blast political Maronism but rather its current political equivalent, "political sectarianism", in which both Sunnis and Shi'a participate. Based on its demographic strength, Hezbollah called for changing the electoral system to proportional representation, which the party believed would give the eighteen ethno-confessional communities more equitable representation. Thus, the shift from blasting "political Maronism" in stages one and two to censuring "political sectarianism" can be seen as a rhetorical shift rather than a genuine policy shift.

Now in stage three, Hezbollah argues that it benefits from its jurisprudential vision that believes in the doctrine of *wilâyat al-faqîh*, which gives it the legitimacy of having a political program in a multi-cultural, multi-religious country characterized by pluralist groupings and forces, without encroaching upon its doctrinal convictions.[2] Employing this logic, Hezbollah reformulated its definition of an Islamic state by making a categorical distinction between *al-fikr al-siyâsî* (political ideology), which it maintained, and *al-barnâmaj al-siyâsî* (political program), which it promoted. From an ideological perspective, Hezbollah is committed to an Islamic state, and this will not be dropped as a legal abstraction. However, Hezbollah's political program must take the political status quo

---

1. One should keep in mind that the concepts of *jâhiliyya* and *hakîmiyya* constitute a common denominator among Islamic movements, and, as such, are not exclusive Hezbollah notions.

2. 'Izzeddine, 2001, p. 6; *al-Safîr*, 12 November 2001.

and the overall functioning of the Lebanese political system into account. Since the general will of the Lebanese people is against the establishment of an Islamic state, it is not feasible to establish one.[1]

Thus, Hezbollah moved from Islamization in the narrow sense to Lebanonization and *infitâh* policy. It seems that the party is moving ever closer to being a full participant in "normal" Lebanese politics – with the limitations that implies – and merging into the Lebanese sectarian-confessional system that it abhorred and defined as corrupt in stages one and two.

A final note

As a mainstream political party, Hezbollah operates according to *Realpolitik* calculations of political expediency, benefit and *maslaha* (interest). The party's gradual incorporation into "normal" Lebanese politics – by joining Parliament, municipal councils, and the cabinet – begs the question of how much it is willing to be co-opted into the Lebanese political system and state institutions. The political victories of 2005 and its acclaimed military victory in 2006[2] illustrate the patriotic and nationalist character of a party that is supported not only by its major Shi'a constituency, but also by a fairly considerable number of Sunnis, Druze and Christians. If popular support allows, Hezbollah aims to become the biggest political force in Lebanon. Although the party leadership denies it, its success in balancing its nationalist political commitments on the one hand, and its Islamic background on the other came at the price of compromise, even on some doctrinal issues.

Through arguing for civil peace, social freedoms and a functioning civil society, Hezbollah attempted to preserve its Islamic identity while working

1. Nasrallâh, *al-Jazeera* TV, 24 September 1998; Qasim, 2002, p. 38; and 'Alî Fayyâd, member of the Political Council and director of Hezbollah's think tank CCSD, as cited in Abun-Nasr, 2003, p. 127.

2. The 34-day war, from 12 July to 14 August 2006, between Israel and Hezbollah led to the death of around 1,200 Lebanese, a third of them children under the age of twelve; wounded and handicapped 4,000; displaced more than one million; and cost around 20 billion dollars in damage and lost revenues. According to Israeli media sources, more than two-thirds of the 159 Israeli dead were soldiers: 118 soldiers and 41 civilians. *Daily Star* and *AFP*. See http://www.dailystar.com.lb/july_War06.asp. See also Alagha, 2006b, p. 36.

within the domain of the Lebanese state's sovereignty and inside the confines of a non-Islamic state and a multi-confessional polity. On these grounds, Hezbollah conferred de facto recognition upon the Lebanese state. Thus, Hezbollah ended up being unable to surpass the limitations of an "ordinary" political party. Rather than calling for an Islamic state or forming a "state within a state" as a political remuneration for its acclaimed "divine victory" in the 34 day war with Israel, Hezbollah asked for the formation of a national unity government, where the party and its Christian allies[1] wield the one-third veto power. In addition to integrating more into the Lebanese public sphere and political system, it may be argued that Hezbollah emerged from the war enjoying more popularity than ever before.

Bibliography

Abun-Nasr, F.M., *Hezbollah: haqâ'iq wa ab'âd* (Hezbollah: Facts and Dimensions), Beirut 2003, World Book Publishing.

Alagha, Joseph, *The Shifts in Hezbollah's Ideology*, Amsterdam 2006a, Amsterdam University Press.

Alagha, Joseph, "Hezbollah's Promise" in *ISIM Review*, 18, Autumn 2006b, p. 36.
http://www.isim.nl/files/Review_18/Review_18-36.pdf

Alagha, Joseph, "Hezbollah After the Syrian Withdrawal", *Middle East Report* 237, Winter 2005, pp. 34–39.

Alagha, Joseph, "Hezbollah and Martyrdom", *ORIENT: German Journal for Politics and Economics of the Middle East* 45/1, March 2004, pp. 47–74.

Alagha, Joseph, "Hezbollah, Terrorism, and Sept. 11", *ORIENT: German Journal for Politics and Economics of the Middle East* 44/3, September 2003, pp. 385–412.

Alagha, Joseph, "Hezbollah's Gradual Integration in the Lebanese Public Sphere", in *Sharqiyyat: Journal of the Dutch Association for Middle Eastern and Islamic Studies* 13/1, 2001, pp. 34–59.

Asadullahi, M., *Al-Islamiyyûn fî mujtama' ta'âdudî: Hizbullâh fî Lubnân namudhajan* (The Islamists in a Pluralist Society: The Lebanese Hezbollah as a Case Study), Beirut 2004, Markaz al-istishârât wa al-buhûth.

'Atrisî, Ja'far, *Hizbullâh: al-khiyar al-as'ab wa damanât al-watan al-kubrâ* (Hezbollah: The most Difficult Choice and Lebanon's Greatest Guarantee), Beirut 2005, Dâr al-mahajja al-baydâ'.

---

1. Mainly the "Free Patriotic Movement" led by ex-General Michel 'Aûn. See http://www.tayyar.org.

Buchta, Wilfried, *Who Rules Iran? The Structure of Power in the Islamic Republic*, Washington DC 2000, The Washington Institute for Near East Policy and the Konrad Adenaueur Stiftung.

Byers, Ann, *Lebanon's Hezbollah (Inside the World's Most Infamous Terrorist Organizations)*, London 2003, Rosen Publishing Group.

Fadlallâh, Muhammad Husayn, "Reflections on the Muslim-Christian Dialogue", A lecture delivered at the American University of Beirut, 22 December 1987.

Fadlallâh, Muhammad Husayn, *al-Islâm wa mantiq al-quwwa* (Islam and the Logic of Power), Beirut 1985, Dar al-mu'assasa al-jami'iyya lil-dirâsât wa al-nashr (3rd edition).

'Izzeddine, H., "How is Hezbollah looked upon and how does it introduce itself?", Paper delivered as a contribution to an LAU (Lebanese American University) conference on "Arab Stereotyping", 6-9 November 2001.

Hezbollah's Politburo, The Committee of Analysis and Studies, *Wathiqât al-Tâ'if: dirâsât fî al-madmûn* (The Taef Document: textual studies), Beirut 1989.

Al-Husaynî, Sh., "Hizbullâh: haraka 'askariyya am siyâsiyya am dîniyya?" (Hezbollah: A Military, Political or Religious Movement?), *al-Shirâ'*, 17 March 1986.

Al-Jazeera TV, 24 September "Hezbollah: Identity and Role", in *Nuqta Sâkhina* ("Hot Spot"), 1998.

Karmon, Ely, "Fight on all Fronts: Hizballah, the War on Terror, and the War on Iraq', in *Policy Focus* 46, December 2003, Washington, DC: The Washington Institute for Near East Policy.

Khomeini, Ruhollah, *al-Hukuma al-islâmiyya* (The Islamic Government), Tehran 1996, The Institute of Coordinating and Publishing Imam Khomeini's Heritage.

Al-Kûrânî, A., *Tarîqat Hizbullâh fi al-'amal al-Islamî* (Hezbollah's Method of Islamic Mobilization), Tehran 1985, Maktab al-i'lâm al-Islamî, al-mu'assasa al-'âlamiyya.

Al-Madînî, T., *Amal wa Hizbullâh fi halabat al-mujâbahât al-mahalliyya wa al-iqlîmiyya* (Amal and Hezbollah in the Arena of Domestic and Regional Struggles), Damascus 1999, al-Ahli.

Mervin, Sabrina, "Les yeux de Mûsâ al-Sadr", in Mayeur, Catherine, ed., *Saints et héros du Moyen-Orient contemporain*, Paris 2002, Maisonneuve et Larose, pp. 285–300.

NBN, 21, 28 July and 4 August 2002, *Ahzâb Lubnân: Hizbullâh* (Lebanese Parties: Hezbollah, Parts I, II, III) (3 Videotapes).

Qâsim, Na'im, *Hezbollah: The Story from Within*, London 2005, Saqi Books (English translation of his Arabic book below), 2005.

Qâsim, Na'im, *Hizbullâh: al-manhaj, al-tajriba, al-mustaqbal* (Hezbollah: The Curriculum, the Experience, the Future), Beirut 2002, Dâr al-hâdî.

Sayyid, Ahmad R., *Hasan Nasrallâh: thâ'ir min al-janûb* (Hasan Nasrallah: A Rebel from the South), Cairo 2006, Dar al-kitab al-'arabî.

Sharara, Waddâh, *Dawlat Hizbullâh: Lubnan mujtama'an islamiyyân* (The State of Hezbollah: Lebanon as an Islamic Society), Beirut 1997, al-Nahâr (2nd edition).

Shay Shaul, *The Axis of Evil: Iran, Hizballah, and the Palestinian Terror*, London 2005, Transaction Publishers.

Salem, Paul, *The Beirut Review* 1/1, Spring 1991, Beirut, Lebanese Centre for Policy Studies (LCPS), pp. 119–172.

Al-Shirâ, al-harakât al-islâmiyya fi Lubnân (Islamic Movements in Lebanon), Beirut 1984.

Tawfiq, Fadî, *Bilâd Allâh al-dayyiqa: al-dâhiya ahlân wa hizbân* (God's Small Country: al-Dahiya, People and Party), Beirut 2005, Dâr al-jadîd.

Z'aytir, M., *Nazra 'ala tarh al-jumhûriyya al-islâmiyya fi Lubnân* (An Outlook at the Proposal of the Islamic Republic in Lebanon), Beirut 1988, al-wikalâ' al-sharqiyya lil-tawzî'.

Z'aytir, M., *al-mashrû' al-marûnî fi Lubnan: juzûruhu wa tatawwurâtuhu* (The Maronite Project in Lebanon: Roots and Developments), Beirut 1986, al-wikalâ' al-'âlamiyya li-l-tawzî'. (This book is banned in Lebanon).

KINDA CHAIB

Hezbollah Seen through its Images:
the Representation of the Martyr

In February 2002,[1] a woman[2] allowed me to view a half-hour documentary about her husband, who died in a military operation. The film was made in 1988 in a South Lebanese village that today sports the colors of Hezbollah. A funeral takes up most of its running time. Iranian flags fly over the *husayniyya* and the public square. In the funeral procession, children proudly carry portraits of Khomeini and more Iranian flags. The bodies of the martyrs are wrapped in Iranian flags too. According to my interpreter, the absence of the Lebanese flag is explained by the fact that this was a "military march", and since the Lebanese state did not support Hezbollah in the 1980s, its flag had no right of presence. This does not surprise her fourteen-year-old daughter, who asserts that Iran "was the only one to help the resistance" – that is, the Islamic Resistance, the armed branch of Hezbollah.

Today there are no Iranian flags in the Lebanese villages, only portraits of Khomeini and Khamenei, even on the bicycles of the youngest kids. What has changed between the end of the 1980s and 2004? How does the iconography produced by Hezbollah – itself presented as an emanation

1. That is to say during my first stay in the field. This essay is based on studies conducted between 2002 and 2004 in South Lebanon and the southern suburbs of Beirut. The interviews at the artistic design office of Nabatiyeh date from March 2004.
2. The word "widow" is generally rejected by the players.

of Iran – show an evolution in the connection the party maintains with that country? How did the visual landscape set up by the party evolve from references to Iran to other references, and what are these other references?

In order to explain the context and the way it affects Hezbollah, we must first recall the history of the movement. The rise to prominence of the intellectual current from which Hezbollah would sprout started at the end of the 1970s,[1] when three major events affected the Shi'a community in Lebanon. In 1978, one of the leaders, if not *the* leader, of the community, Mûsâ Sadr,[2] disappeared during a visit to Libya; in 1979, the Iranian revolution succeeded in establishing the Islamic Republic; and on 14 March 1978, Israel invaded Lebanon the first time. The second Israeli invasion of 1982 turned the budding Hezbollah into a reality. The reservoir from which the party selected its militants was the Amal movement founded by Mûsâ Sadr, some of whose members left the movement in 1982. On 16 February 1985, on the first anniversary of the death of Sheikh Râghib Harb,[3] the emblematic face of the resistance to the occupation, a manifesto was read out and distributed to the press:[4] this is the party's official birth certificate.

At that time, the movement was supported by Iran, its fighters trained by the Pasdaran in camps in the Bekaa valley. Not only did the financing come from Iran, Hezbollah's very structure led it to allegiance with the Iranian Republic, as it recognized the authority of the *walî al-faqîh*, the theory of "guardianship of the jurisconsult" developed by Khomeini.

The Taif Agreement of 1989 left Hezbollah as the only movement authorized to keep its weapons within the framework of the fight against the Israeli occupation of the south of the country. In 1992, the party entered the election process, although it refused to participate in the successive governments,[5] preferring not to be forced to support policies it

---

1. Alagha, 2001a.
2. Mervin, 2002.
3. After being imprisoned numerous times, he was finally killed by the Israelis in his village of Jibshit.
4. Palmer Harik, 2004.
5. In 2005, Hezbollah agreed for the first time to enter the government of Fuad Siniora. The Hezbollah ministers subsequently resigned in November 2006.

condemned. Hezbollah accepted the principles of the Lebanese political system and the rules of its game. Many voters supported it regardless of religious or sectarian adherence because of its commitment to resistance. Today, Hezbollah presents itself as a Lebanese party like any other, while continuing to claim credit for the actions of the resistance,[1] which confer legitimacy on the party within and without its natural recruitment basin of the Shi'a community.

For several years, Hezbollah has been producing an iconography in many widely varying forms, which it displays on the roads and in the villages. To understand the nature of its links to Iran, we will study the codes, forms and design modes used. The subjects represented are equally varied, most notably in their widespread origins. This permits us to study the mobilizing function of this iconography, which is so abundantly present in Shi'a majority zones.

A framed freedom

The artistic design office is responsible for the creation of Hezbollah's portraits and its giant billboards, as well as for the production of recurring and occasional ceremonies. It has three branches: one in the South, one in the Bekaa valley and one in Beirut. According to the employees in the Nabatiyeh center (in the south of the country), the three regional structures are supervised by one organ, whose members are not artists but politicians. At the regional level, each centre is run by two representatives, respectively responsible for the artistic side and the informational aspects, who oversee a number of employees – three in the case of Nabatiyeh.

They follow an annually fixed agenda that includes commemorations (Jerusalem Day, Ashura, Resistance Week, Martyr's Day), various anniversaries as well as unscheduled events as they occur (the martyrdom of a combatant, international events or, in 2003, the prisoner exchange with Israel). The main policy lines are fixed in advance at the top level and implemented locally, on both the artistic and the communications level, in close cooperation between the design centers and regional

---

1. The parliamentary bloc that it forms with its allies was called "Support for the Resistance"; this has recently been changed to "The Resistance and Development Bloc".

party representatives. As Ahmad Tîrânî, the artistic representative at Nabatiyeh, tells us, the administrative agent supervises both the artistic and communications aspects of the work. The artists, however, work in perfect independence and with total freedom to choose the lines along which they create their productions, although always following the concepts set out by the art director. He adds that the party imposes no restrictions on the graphic designers. The artist is considered to be a specialist; nobody will give him orders on matters pertaining to his field of competence.

Tîrânî further explains that the office produces two types of works: those commissioned by the party, which remain unsigned and feature only the party logo; and those commissioned by municipalities and institutions closely or remotely connected to the party, which are signed by the commissioning actors without the name of the party appearing.

A fine arts graduate of the Lebanese University, Ahmad Tîrânî works in an office filled with a diverse collection of art books and CD-ROMS containing reproductions of pictures and sketches – mostly his own productions, but also models of speaking stands or parade floats. His references, as displayed on the shelves of his library, are more European than Arab or oriental in origin: the Louvre CD-ROM is prominently displayed next to that of Quai d'Orsay and books on Lebanese or European contemporary painters. But while he insists on western influences, a claim that seems to be corroborated by the number of works on the subject, it should not be forgotten that oriental references, both Arab and Muslim, are part of his mental and cultural world – the world of everyday life that is assimilated and therefore does not require systematic bibliographic researches.

Tîrânî admits that the tools used at the centre are primarily digital, a fact that he regrets, maintaining that for an artist it rapidly becomes "boring"[1] to work on martyrs' portraits, as their production is essentially a repetitive process. Recurrent themes dominate (the party, the land, God) and templates are created using software. The creator's only task is to handle the layout of the different elements. These templates can be reproduced at will, which can become "boring" but on the other hand

---

1.   He uses the word *mummil* here.

allows the employees to concentrate on the creative aspects of their work. For Tîrânî, creativity is at work during the ceremonies, which must be visualized. We may therefore assume that two types of works are produced in these workshops: mass productions and unique artists' works.

On a more anecdotal level, our visits to the offices and conversations with the employees reveal a different source of raw material from what is displayed on the shelves of the art director's library. This alternate source is found in the computers, stacked with all sorts of images ranging from the tackiest sunsets on desert islands to the works of contemporary Iranian painters such as Mahmud Farshchiyân or Mostafâ Godarzi. Flowers, leaders of the movement, mountains, landscapes, birds, friezes and arabesques allow the composition of images and templates. As mentioned before, the employees of the centre mainly work digitally, with Paint Shop Pro as their preferred software. The art director is the only one with a formal fine arts education, but all employees have enjoyed a digital graphic design training financed by Hezbollah.

The professionals thus work to spread the image of Hezbollah, but they are not the only ones. Youngsters who died fighting for Hezbollah – martyrs – often left interesting graphic design work behind too. This work is preserved by Hezbollah's Martyr's Institute, which features a section specifically devoted to keeping the memory of the martyrs alive. This section has expanded considerably over the past three years. It is now employing more workers, occupying new and more spacious offices and has collected a dedicated library. Drawings by martyrs are progressively sent out to be framed and some now decorate the white walls of the institute's offices. As an inevitable corollary, the institute is also in charge of selecting the photographs[1] that serve as the basis for the portraits to be displayed in the villages and on the roads.

What I propose to do here is give a macro-outline of the graphic productions of Hezbollah, as the format of this article does not allow for the micro-analysis of individual iconographic documents. The selection of a broad corpus of representations permits a discussion of wide-ranging aspects of this multiform iconography. Traveling through

---

1. I learned this during an interview with the managers of the "Memory of the Martyrs" section, April 2002.

the archives, as well as on the roads of Lebanon, gives access to different types of documents of widely varying nature. Some, designed by the party itself, reflect an ideology, others show a graphic production outside the frame.

The party produces giant billboards, which are displayed on the main roads. They are at the same time martyrs' portraits and propaganda or advertising billboards glorifying the movement. Through its institutions, Hezbollah also fulfills the role of "movie director" for the testaments of the party's fighters; preserving the testaments, publishing them and physically validating them through aesthetic and ideological choices, which we will discuss later. Institutions connected to Hezbollah include a bewildering number of publishing companies of varying sizes. They publish works connected to the party – although that is not what interests us here – and make visual choices displayed on book covers, in shop windows and on booksellers' stands in the markets.

A more freeform graphic art is produced in the margins of the official circuit. Some of it is the result of freelance activities by employees of Hezbollah's design offices, but some is also produced by the party's fighters. To study these works is certainly a choice, but also a result of the reality on the ground, which often imposes unexpected bifurcations on us. The analysis of the giant billboards, of course, was intrinsically limited, if only by the factors of space and time.

The martyr today constitutes one of Hezbollah's commercial bases, a source of legitimacy that is beyond criticism. They enjoy the unwavering attention of the graphic design centers and are the object of a policy that validates their image – or the image of the party through them. Billboards of gigantic size are on display on numerous Lebanese roads and represent above all emblematic martyrs, authors of operations of voluntary martyrdom, religious or political leaders or, in the case that interests us here, founding martyrs of Hezbollah.

The testament books, in different sizes, are in fact templates for the testaments the fighters are required to write – although in reality this rule is not systematically observed. Besides religiously "compulsory" clauses, they contain pages that have remained empty but for the title of the clause. In the archives of the institute, a category of testaments of a different design can be found. Some were reproduced by employees of the institute and contain decorations – different illustrations and slogans. On some of the original handwritten testaments,[1] illustrations, sketches and some slogans can also be found.

Graphic works produced by the larger Hezbollah movement can be commissioned, for example for Ashura. A small sound and light show as well as a thematic bookshop was set up on the fringe of an exhibition of some fifteen paintings by a painter from Khiyâm in 2003, Ahmad 'Abdallâh, in a big tent erected for the occasion in the center of Nabatiyeh.

Drawings and paintings of the "amateur" painters among the martyrs of Hezbollah are classified in archives with their testaments and other memorabilia. A sample of twenty-seven works, constituting about two thirds of those held in the archives of the institute in 2004, serves as an overview of the recurrent themes that structure the universe of these often young fighters.

Flowers, land and blood

In the martyrs' drawings, the land is frequently represented by cracked soil, stones or trees. It represents the nation in the religious sense of the Muslim *umma,* or in the more secular sense of the people or the fatherland. The cracked soil may be a realistic representation of the nature of South Lebanon in the summer, but more probably it is the allegoric meaning that predominates: a land drained by the occupation which awaits only the blood of the martyr to be revived.

We very frequently find representations of the martyr himself in these drawings, in the form of symbols and colors. Red flowers personify the martyr. Growing on arid soil, they become the symbol of the martyr, who, through his struggle, nourishes the land and makes it come alive again. These flowers illustrate the capacity of the fighters to bring life back to the nation through their sacrifice; in whichever sense the term "nation" is used. In the case of Hezbollah militants, this sense is the Muslim *umma*

---

1. These are few since the families often prefer to keep them. However, there are photocopies – hardly legible and kept alongside their typed out or copied version.

– although that is a very categorical statement, and conversations with activists and families allow us to mitigate it: the term *watan* (fatherland) is used in all cases. Reading the testaments confirms this: the *umma* is certainly prominently present, but the fatherland is mentioned in a quasi-systematic way in the texts. Let us not forget that the fighters are often very young. They follow the cause, the party and the movement, but without giving up their hopes and expectations. These can differ from the guidelines, which, until the early 1990s, went in the direction of a struggle for the Muslim nation in varying versions according to the integration of Hezbollah in Lebanese political life and the abandonment of its original political program which demanded the establishment of an Islamic republic in Lebanon.

Blood, too, is often represented. Besides representing all the symbolism of the color red, it flows from a flower or, in a rare case of explicit representation, from the wounds of a martyr. One drawing is rather striking by its originality: while no wounds are visible, we see a fighter blending in with – becoming entangled in – the land onto which his blood flows. He holds his weapon in his right hand and the words "*al-janûb*" (the South) are written in the puddle of red blood, heavily symbolically charged in an otherwise black and white drawing. In general, however, red flowers are preferred to blood. This marks a difference with the young Iranian fighters in the war against Iraq, who possessed vignettes representing the martyr – often unflatteringly – after his death.[1]

In Hezbollah's regular publications of the late 1980s, tulips can be found illustrating pages that tell the martyrs' stories. They are imported from Iran – or from Afghanistan via Iran[2] – as tulips are not among the flowers growing in Lebanese fields. Martyr images from abroad were around for years in Lebanon, and what could be more natural, when one draws one's religious references from a specific country, than to draw artistic inspiration from that country's symbols? These publications were after all produced directly by party institutions. From the 1990s onwards, we see that on the whole, the foreign flowers disappear: today, painters

1. Butel, 2000 and 2002.
2. Centlivres, 1988.

draw roses or poppies – the actual flower not being that important anyway, provided it is red.

Lebanese landscapes are often depicted on martyrs' portraits: mountains, rivers or creeks. Sheaves of wheat, symbols of the generosity of nature, are sometimes also present. It is worth noting that, with the exception of paintings set in summertime, these landscapes are not dry and arid. The rivers, the densely wooded mountains and intensely green hills, are an idealized vision of the local environment. The above-mentioned exception concerns hills reminiscent of those of South Lebanon, parched by the sun, with stunted vegetation. This billboard dates from some years back, and the new ones are very different (cf. *infra*). The recurrence of local references in texts and images can be analyzed as a nationalist posture, with the fighters struggling for Lebanon and for its land.

In the Bekaa valley, the portraits of martyrs and of party officials feature the famous columns of Baalbek. If, as Ahmad Tîrânî asserts, "Lebanon *is* the cedars and Baalbek", their depiction is a way of asserting, once again, the party's Lebanese anchoring. In the south, however, these columns are not included, as they are not a local reality: regional references such as hills and streams are preferred here. Every centre deploys its own references, those it estimates best qualified to represent the land and to mark the regional belonging of its martyrs.

In a quasi-systematic way, depictions of symbolic places, the holy places of Islam, are included in the portraits of leaders. One could be forgiven to expect depictions of Mecca or the mausoleums of 'Alî and Husayn, but such is not the case: the only place with a right of presence seems to be the al-Aqsâ mosque of Jerusalem. On martyrs' portraits, we can observe the same phenomenon: very often – in more than two thirds of cases – the al-Aqsâ mosque is present. Nonetheless, while informed persons can identify this powerful symbol without a problem, when interrogating inhabitants of Nabatiyeh, for example, one is surprised to hear statements such as: "this is the *husayniyya* of Nabatiyeh, the old one, not the new one"; or even: "this is the mosque of Bir 'Abed, in Dahiyeh (a southern suburb of Beirut)". Even where one might expect a symbol to be universally known, this is not always the case!

Until the late 1980s, illustrations on testaments were extremely rare.

Later, testament books become more frequent and occasionally feature depictions of the al-Aqsâ mosque. In these documents, allusions to Lebanon appear only in the words of the fighters. Over the years, as if under the influence of the testament books, the frequency of illustrations on other types of testaments increases. Other religious symbols are also present. On a testament written by a martyr in 1984 we see above the text a drawing of a parchment with a Qur'anic verse, held in a closed fist and changing into a feather. This design seems to testify to the role of "transmitter" that the fighter plays, notably through his testament. The text, on the other hand, is not religious: it does not contain the required prayers. This is a militant testament intended for the fighter's "brothers in the faith"; he is, in a way, passing on the baton. He asks to continue the struggle for "our land". His drawing is meant to be a clear illustration of the text since both transmit the idea of battle and struggle. In the classical conception of the martyr, this role is important, as the martyr can act as an intercessor between man and God.

There is another element in these images which should not be overlooked: the legend, always expected, which explains them. There is true interactivity between text and image, with the typography of the text itself creating an image to direct the reader. So it goes with calligraphy, which can be considered simultaneously as text and image. The calligraphy on the banners of Ashura is virtually always done in the *farsî* style. *Farsî* is the Arab name for the *nastaliq* style, which was created in Persia in the fourteenth century and rapidly became widespread in the Arab world. The banners are designed by the Hezbollah centre, sometimes commissioned by municipalities or local branches of the party. The banners exert a strong influence and their aesthetics have been adopted by other movements (parties, district committees, etc.) who produce these types of "images".

Beside the allegoric representations of struggle, the martyrs – the source of legitimacy for Hezbollah and other parties – are the centerpiece of these pictures. Hamit Bozarslan[1] has created a typology of Kurdish martyrs which can also be applied to Lebanon. The term for martyr – *shahîd* – is polysemous and can refer to different types of deceased. According to the category in which they fall and the importance this

---

1. Bozarslan, 2002.

confers on them, the institutions referring to them will apply a specific code, which includes the decision of whether they will be represented anonymously or as individuals. Non-combatant victims are "massified" and remain anonymous. This is the case for the victims of the Israeli bombing of the UNIFIL camp in Qana (South Lebanon) in 1996, who are never represented as individuals but instead depicted as a collective. The place of their suffering has become a memorial space, with a museum built there.

Combatant martyrs, through their individual commitment and sacrifice, confer legitimacy on their organization by working for the survival of the fatherland in its entirety. Their death is the consequence of their individual commitment within an organizational structure. In the Kurdish case, they do not enjoy an individualized representation; in Lebanon they do, but their number prevents their transformation into emblems or symbols.

Emblematic martyrs form a limited number of faces, which occupy the symbolic world and structure the militant space through visual art. They are the "heroes" among the martyrs; leaders or founders of organizations who, through their exceptional individual careers or their extraordinary deaths, rose above the ranks and gave sense to the concept of commitment to the party. This category includes the leaders and founding martyrs of Hezbollah, but also martyrs who took exceptional actions through their commitment or their death, such as the authors of what are commonly called "suicide operations".

The civil war martyrs seem to be part of a past that is to be forgotten. They do not have status outside their party, which, perhaps out of a concern for national unity, does not assign them an overly conspicuous place in the memory under construction.

Let us take a look at the way the martyrs are visualized. The large majority have a determined but by no means hard look – the beginning of a smile can often be discerned. Determination and softness illustrate the righteousness of the defended cause. They look into the distance. Those who have never had their portrait drawn by a professional, especially a Lebanese professional, may be unaware of what we are talking about. Let us not forget that these portraits, designed by the party, are based on photographs provided by the family after the death of the martyr. So where do these pictures come from? Simply from the photo albums and collections that we all have at home: ID pictures, family portraits, and so on. In France, we tend to smile for ID pictures, but in Lebanon it is no laughing matter; it is a very serious occasion, and the photographer makes the model sit in a very slight profile, head raised and looking into the distance. Perhaps this is the origin of these looks that seem to contemplate an afterlife full of promise. It is certain that Hezbollah makes the most of these poses, which agree well with the meaning the designers want to convey with the portraits.

As for the portraits of leaders, they attest to a generational conflict of kinds. The old (Ruhollâh Khomeini and 'Abbâs al-Mûsawî[1]) look very serious, while their successors ('Ali Khamenei and Hasan Nasrallâh) are smiling. They are very often represented together, the "young" appearing under the benevolent patronage of their elders, thus asserting religious and political continuity.

It is certain that the fixed look of the deceased evokes an afterlife, as we have said. This impression is enhanced by the added halo of white light encircling the head. Other sources of light, such as a rising sun or a white full moon, fulfill the same function. The light can also emanate from a source outside the image from which a beam of light seems to be directed at the martyr. This may indicate that he is illuminated, assisted in his struggle by an undetermined guide.

The employees of the foundation possess different photographs of the same martyr, taken at different ages. The correlation between the martyr's age on the picture selected and his age at the time of his martyrdom carries little weight: he is very often represented as young. This results in the image of a movement carried by young men who sacrifice themselves for the cause while they still have their futures before them. The photograph used for the billboard depicting Ahmad Qasîr[2] dates back many years before his operation, lending strength to the cause and adding to its relevance.

About two years ago, the portraits decorating the roads and squares of South Lebanon have presented martyrs proudly wearing military uniforms

---

1. Secretary-General of Hezbollah until his assassination in 1992.
2. See photographs of Ahmad Qasîr in *al-'amaliyyât al-istishhâdiyya, wathâ' iq wa suwar,* Beirut 1985, al-markaz al-'arabî li-l-ma'lûmât, pp. 31–32.

and sometimes also a checkered black scarf – the symbol of the resistance. It does not take a genius to guess that this is the efficient digital work of specialists at the graphic design office. According to the art director, it allows us to identify the depicted person's organization and cause of death immediately: he was a fighter, and a fighter for the resistance.

The new templates for billboards, and specifically for portraits, no longer sport the previously omnipresent flags of Hezbollah: they are no longer necessary, as everybody is now able to identify the source of the billboard merely through elements such as the color yellow or the name, written in a calligraphic hand, of the military branch of the party, the "Islamic Resistance". Very often, even these are only partly visible, put up in the name of the martyr but partly hidden behind a pinkish red sheen. According to Ahmad Tîrânî, Hezbollah's logo resembles that of the Iranian Revolutionary Guards Corps, the common elements being the weapon and the clenched fist; although he says there are also differences, he seems unable to identify them. The logos do seem to be identical: the land represents the connection between liberation movements worldwide; the Qur'an is featured too, and a sheaf of wheat represents generosity.

On a rather more general note, the predominant colors of the different types of billboards have evolved as well, from the darker colors of the past to today's lighter shades such as yellow or sky blue. Like the themes, the framing and everything else connected to the design of these images, they are decided on by the artist according to his personal affinities and his interpretation of the subject matter. The importance of light colors is explained by what the martyrdom itself represents: it is not experienced as a sad event but on the contrary as a moment of rejoicing. Black is out of bounds, as it is a color "reserved for Ashura". The light colors seem to point to a transition towards a newly opened perspective.[1] Most of the south of Lebanon has now been liberated and as a result the legitimacy of the struggle of national liberation is not as relevant as it once was, which explains the necessity of seeking broader legitimacy.

Let us now concentrate on a specific point. Ahmad Tîrânî has created a picture which is strangely reminiscent of a painting by the Iranian

---

1. It is worth noting that in Arabic the words for "light" and "opened" share the same root (*f-t-h*).

Mostafâ Godarzi called *The Ascension*,[1] specifically in the way the martyr is represented. The artist admits being inspired by Godarzi's painting and copying part of it – the bust to be precise. The "Lebanese" painting, hung on a lamppost at the exit of Khiyâm, is a transposition of Godarzi's work. A dead young man is lying in a luscious green landscape, with a red cloth around his head and two red holes in his side. His face is serene and colored a pink red: the dead man seems to have fallen gently asleep. Another adaptation of Mostafâ Godarzi's painting was used by a publishing company to illustrate the biography of a Hezbollah martyr published in 2001. Contrary to a painting by Farshchiyân representing Husayn's horse returning to the camp without him – an image omnipresent during Ashura (on banners, frames, carpets, etc.) – Godarzi's painting has taken on a new life in Lebanon. Another publishing company from the array of those connected to Hezbollah used a portion of an anonymous Iranian painting[2] on the cover of a work on jihad published in 1999.

Nevertheless, maybe we should ask ourselves whether our sustained attempt to find the mark of an unfaltering allegiance with Iran behind these references and borrowings is not merely an obsessive concern for academic researchers. When the inhabitants of a village are asked about these flowers, arabesques or birds, they do not see there a mark of Iranian sponsorship, but simply nice images illustrating ideas and concepts. These tools of illustration are perceived as simple amenities. While there is a fringe of the population that immediately detects the Iranian imprint in these foreign motives, they remain a minority. If these references do not echo in the imagination, it is because they are not a part of known symbolic codes. The red flower is easily assimilated as symbolizing the martyr. As for assigning a more oriental origin to it, that is a step that even Ahmad Tîrânî, a man familiar with the importance of red roses in the texts of the great fifteenth-century Persian poet Hâfez, does not take. Perhaps the use of roses is merely a loan, like so many others, or maybe it is just the fruit of the active interaction among artistic circles.

The painters and designers at Hezbollah's centers have a marked tendency to prefer Iranian references in depicting concepts linked to

1. Butel, 2002
2. Butel, 2000, CD-ROM annex, anonymous painting, CD-ROM/martyr/ painting / P07 (without title)

Shi'ism, but the population as a whole does not read anything into this other than a very decorative way of illustrating themes close to their heart.

Advertising for mobilization

As we saw before, the changes observed in Hezbollah's graphic compositions over recent years seem to mark the transition from the perspective of an effective, even imminent liberation to a liberation transposed to the eschatological horizon. The reference to Jerusalem, the only element to have survived the modification, constitutes an element of this perspective. The transition from dark to light colors and the appearance of smiles in the portraits of the leaders both play the same role.

The giant billboards installed in places where operations of voluntary martyrdom have taken place have been revamped. Instead of images of explosions and destruction, we now see a preference for red flowers and light beams, as if the desire for physical destruction of a nearby enemy has been transformed into an overture towards something broader. Following the same logic, the martyrs' drawings express this change using representations that have become more and more positive over the years. In the 1980s – and specifically during the Iran-Iraq war – the enemy is clearly identified in most works: the Iraqi flag is trampled while the Iranian flag is held high. Later, the drawings become more allusive and conceptual, showing rather the battle, the struggle, the idea of martyrdom. This transition from the negative to the positive, from annihilation of the enemy to positive depiction of a purpose, opens the door towards a new horizon, which could be seen as the liberation of Palestine – in a sense more allegoric than real.

The artistic design office also developed a new design for the billboards representing the combatant martyrs when the representatives for the South, on their own initiative, decided on a policy of standardization for the portraits. No similar phenomenon was observed in the Bekaa valley at that time. When roaming the roads of the South, one becomes aware that, with very few exceptions, only a few templates prevail today – the centre offers three. It is the party that decides where to put the portraits of any particular martyr, but the choice of template is left to the families.

The predominant concern for the Nabatiyeh office is henceforth the implementation of this policy of uniformization. We could add that the use of templates permits reducing the interpretation of the image to an automatic reflex to the message on the side of the spectator. It also empowers the visual space.

There can be no doubt that Hezbollah devotes special attention to its image and that its image is made by its martyrs. The uniformization of representations therefore allows the party to present a more streamlined and homogeneous image of itself as a party that takes great care of its fighters who fell for Lebanon – which is what today's speeches stress – and through them of its own image as the party of the resistance, victorious over the powerful Israeli army.

It is not only the design of the billboards that has been transformed: they have also been repositioned. Indeed, until the summer of 2003, billboards, and specifically portraits, were omnipresent on all roads of the Bekaa valley, the southern suburbs of Beirut and South Lebanon. Later, in a concerted effort, many billboards were removed or transferred elsewhere. Their positioning was revised in a more targeted way, the preferred places becoming the places of origin of the martyrs and those where they carried out their operations. As a result of this policy, the road connecting Sidon and Nabatiyeh in the South found itself deprived of an important part of its scenery.

The declared purpose of this repositioning of the martyrs was a desire not to appear too ostentatious in the celebration of slain fighters who did not originate in the local population. We thus observe a reconstruction of the past through places and heroes. The billboards, omnipresent until that time, are now redeployed to places where their presence will mark the mind more deeply: the home villages of martyrs, where each and every one will feel concerned; and the theatres of operations, symbolic spaces *par excellence*. From now on, it is not mere quantity that is at stake, but the relevance of the positioning of the images and the search for an effectiveness that the previous billboards, too present in the visual landscape, could not offer. Rudolf Wittkover[1] has pointed out the disappearance of selectivity in a receiver confronted with permanent visual

---

1. Wittkover, 1987.

messages, and the way in which the receiver operates different attention modes according to his knowledge of the symbolic codes employed. Today, the design office, perhaps aware of the excess flood of images, helps the receiver in making his choice by constructing a controlled and selective memory. This redeployment policy points more generally to a transition from territorial marking for the aim of mobilization to the erection of memorial spaces,[1] which would imply that we have already entered the phase of commemoration.

An entire bureaucratic routine has been installed to transform the symbolic space with the aim of controlling the imagination. Through the graphic monuments that billboards are, the population is encouraged to identify with these their heroes and, beyond that, with the cause they fought for. This is political propaganda, the party using the tools of advertising to sell its product – the martyr and hero – by branding him with its logo, its name in calligraphy and its color – all this on posters the same size as the ones that extol the qualities of car rental companies and supermarkets to us. Propaganda is considered an essentially twentieth-century phenomenon, linked to the development of new information vectors for "the masses" and questioning the meaning of icons. Frederic C. Bartlett defines propaganda as "the attempt to influence social opinion and conduct in such a way that individuals will adopt a specific opinion and conduct".[2] Advertising and propaganda are governed by parallel mechanisms: in both cases, it is a matter of limiting the interpretation of the image to a reflex to the message in the spectator, which is obviously the case here.

As an illustration, let us return to the billboard depicting Ahmad Qasîr in Tyre, the very place where he performed his operation of voluntary martyrdom – the first of its kind in Lebanon – against the Israeli military tribunal. When we study the billboard closely, we observe, in watermark printing, nine framed portraits representing most of Hezbollah's voluntary martyrs.[3] These portraits mark the succession of voluntary martyrs as anchored in a battle which transcends them and linked in a chain of

1. Nora, 1984–1992
2. Bartlett, 1940.
3. Out of a total of thirteen, according to the archives of Hezbollah's Foundation of the Martyr.

"glorious" warriors. The chronology is also marked by a phrase written in both Arabic and English: "*fâtih 'ahd al-istishhâdiyyî*" – "the pioneer of the martyrdom fighters' era"; Hezbollah does not take its communications lightly. In the middle of the billboard, in large red Arabic characters, is the date, "11 November 1982", followed, in even bigger print, by the text: "Day of the Martyr of Hezbollah". Finally, Hezbollah's logo, recognizable to all, as well as some words in English, in the centre: "Islamic Resistance, Service of Military Information" – placed, like the brand name of some product, at the end of the text. The billboard, conceived as an advertisement for the glory of Hezbollah, seems to be telling us that, more than the individual history of Ahmad Qasîr, known to all, it is the start of the suicide operations that is the subject here. The conclusion imposing itself is that this young man was a member of Hezbollah on whom, logically, the merit of the action reflects. Underneath the portrait of the young man, taken some time before his death, the place of the operation is shown, surrounded by a halo of fire. The violence of this image clashes with the extremely soft portrait of the fighter. This left section of the billboard is thus reminiscent of posters of big Hollywood productions where the hero is presented through a photo and the depiction of an explosion – the idea being that this hero is going to save the world from disastern ... Ultimately, that is what Ahmad Qasîr did when, by initiating the fight through this type of operation, he began the elimination of the "absolute evil" represented, in Mûsâ Sadr's words, by Israel.

In short, Hezbollah runs a business in which many inhabitants of the regions concerned can recognize themselves. Like others before and after it, it has turned itself into the impresario of its martyrs for the aims of edification and exemplariness. Nevertheless, the liberation of the South was a turning point in the mobilizing force of its fighters. What, in a Lebanese Muslim community, can have as much force as the liberation of the land? The transition to a supreme struggle, a struggle for the Muslim nation in its entirety, through Jerusalem! This reference has a religious and timeless dimension, but also one that is anchored in the present, which lends it a very useful concreteness in terms of mobilization, with the fight of the Palestinians benefiting from the support of Iran as well as Hezbollah. Besides, it was Khomeini himself who instituted the celebration of Jerusalem Day, on the third Friday of Ramadan, and Hezbollah celebrates it every year during the fast. After the quasi-complete liberation of South Lebanon, Palestine offers a powerful stimulus to mobilization. The advantage of this orientation towards Palestine is that immediate results are much less likely. Palestine is today certainly a bigger seller than Iran. Examples of borrowings Hezbollah made from Iran are numerous, but let us not forget that this inspiration is perhaps in the nature of artistic creation.

Men everywhere have their references and their inheritances, often those of the group to which they feel closest, and grafted onto this historic cultural inheritance are references to a culture transported by satellites and the media. The giant billboards dedicated to suicide operations are clear examples of this, as the new templates have evolved into true advertising posters. They reveal a mental universe constructed through various influences, distant or close, conscious or unconscious, but all resonating in the mind of the spectator who, in his turn, was also raised on this heterogeneous mixture. The symbols are of various, sometimes overlapping origins and natures. Local references are there: the rivers of Lebanon, Mount Hermon in the south, rocks and vegetation, but also the cedar, ultimate symbol of Lebanon. Elements with a more religious connotation are grafted onto these.

Hezbollah's stated policy of playing for national and regional stakes is enacted on two fields. On the one hand, the party takes part in the domestic political game by deciding not to impose itself visually and advertise itself more as the Lebanese resistance. Logos are discreetly removed to make way for colors, still identifiable but less obtrusive. Nevertheless, there are real links with Iran. The creation of Hezbollah was encouraged and its institutions financed by Iran. A member of Hezbollah's Martyr's Institute states that while today the institute has independent finances, it depended on Iranian contributions for its functioning until 2004. The Iranian government actually included a specific clause in its national budget allocating support to Islamic movements in Lebanon[1] and

---

1.   Chelkowski and Dabashi, 2000, p. 294.

to "the righteous struggle of the weak [including the Palestinians] against the strong everywhere in the world,"[1] as part of Iran's stated mission.

Ultimately, Hezbollah uses the financial means provided by Iran to rally its supporters over geographically and religiously close issues they can identify with. The Lebanese Hezbollah was given the logistical tools needed for the renewal of its capacity for mobilization. References to Iran are limited to the religious field, but in a party centered around religion, this cannot be considered insignificant. The guide of the community is in Iran, and in spite of the strong political autonomy of the Lebanese party, he does orient a number of its general choices. The links, therefore, are tenuous, since the connection to Iran in a number of fields is probably experienced as being weaker today than before – an influence rather than a dependency. A Hezbollah militant's commitment is to a patriotic Lebanese vision and a larger religious vision, and this is also what shows through in the extremely varied images continuously produced by Hezbollah.

Bibliography

Alagha, Joseph, "Successen Hezbollah bij "kleine oorlog" om Shib'a" (Hizbul-lah's Successes in the "Small War" in Shib'a), in *Soera,* 9.2, Amsterdam, July 2001, pp. 34–38.

Alagha, Joseph, "Hizbullah's gradual Integration in the Lebanese Public Sphere", *Sharqiyyât*, 13/1, Leiden, 2001, pp. 33–59.

Alagha, Joseph, "Hizbullah, Iran and the Intifada", *ISIM Newsletter*, 9 January 2002, p. 35.

Alagha, Joseph, "Hizbullah, Terrorism and September 11", *Orient*, 44/3, September 2003, Hamburg, pp. 385–412.

Balaghi, Shiva and Gumpert, Lynn, eds., *Picturing Iran, Art, Society and Revolution*, London 2002, I. B. Tauris.

Bartlett, Frederic C., *Political Propaganda*, Cambridge 1940, Cambridge University Press.

Beaugé, Gilbert, and Clément, Jean-Freançois, eds., *L'image dans le monde arabe,* Paris 1995, IREMAM- CNRS, "Études de l'Annuaire de l'Afrique du Nord" collection.

Bozarslan, Hamit, "La figure du martyr chez les Kurdes", in Mayeur, Catherine, *Saints et héros du Moyen-Orient contemporain,* Paris 2002, Maisonneuve et Larose, pp. 335–348.

---

1. Article 154 of the Constitution of the Islamic Republic of Iran, *ibidem*.

Butel, Éric, *Le martyre dans les mémoires de guerre*, unpublished PhD dissertation, directed by Christophe Balaÿ, Paris 2000, Inalco.

Butel, Éric, "Martyre et sainteté dans la littérature de guerre Irak- Iran", in *Saints et héros du Moyen-Orient contemporain*, op. cit., pp. 301–318.

Centlivres, Pierre, "Les tulipes rouges d'Afghanistan. Ancêtres, maîtres spirituels et martyrs dans une société musulmane", in *Les ancêtres sont parmi nous*, Neuchâtel 1988, Musée d'ethnographie, pp. 45–64.

Centlivres, Pierre and Centlivres-Demont, Micheline, *Imageries populaires en islam*, Geneva 1997, Georg éd.

Centlivres, Pierre and Centlivres-Demont, Micheline, "Les martyrs afghans par le texte et l'image (1978-1992)", in *Saints et héros du Moyen-Orient contemporain,,* pp. 319–334.

Chelkowski, Peter, "The Art of Revolution and War : the Role of the Graphic Arts in Iran", in *Picturing Iran, Art, Society and Revolution*, pp. 127–142.

Chelkowski, Peter, and Dabashi, Hamid, *Staging a Revolution : the Art of Persuasion in the Islamic Republic of Iran*, London 2000, Booth-Clibborn.

Fischer, Michael J., and Abedi, Mehdi, *Debating Muslims. Cultural Dialogues in Postmodernity and Tradition*, Madison 1990, Wisconsin University Press.

Mervin, Sabrina, "Les yeux de Mûsâ Sadr (1928-1978)", in *Saints et héros du Moyen-Orient contemporain,*op. cit., pp. 285–301.

Nora, Pierre, ed., *Les lieux de mémoire*, 3 vol., Paris 1984–1992, Gallimard.

Palmer Harik, Judith, *Hezbollah, the Changing Face of Terrorism*, London 2004, I. B. Tauris.

Ram, Haggai, "Multiple Iconographies : Political Posters in the Iranian Revolution", in *Picturing Iran, Art, Society and Revolution*, pp. 89–103.

Wittkover, Rudolph, *Allegory of the Migration of Symbols*, London 1987, Thames and Hudson.

PART TWO

Constructing Shiʻism

THIERRY ZARCONE

Shi'isms under Construction:
the Shi'a community of Turkey in the
Contemporary Era

Geographically, the Turkish Shi'a are easy to situate: they live mainly in Istanbul and in Eastern Anatolia; in the border zones separating Turkey from Armenia and from the enclave province Nakhichevan (Azerbaijan); and in the cities of Kars, Iğdır, Arpaçay, Tuzluca and Aralık. The large majority are linguistically and culturally related to the Azerbaijani world.[1] The Shi'a native to this part of Turkey are therefore Azeris. Today, only the Ottoman-era history of the Shi'a of Istanbul, who did not appear as an active and organized community until the mid-nineteenth century, is known.[2] Their history since the creation of the Turkish Republic, on the other hand, has yet to be written. This more recent period has brought important changes in the physical make-up of the community, especially after the two major episodes of rural exodus of the 1950s and the 1980s, which brought a immigrant population from Kars and Iğdır that deeply affected the social composition of Istanbul. As might be expected, these immigrants were socially and culturally the antipodes of the city's original Shi'a population, which is also mostly composed of Azerbaijanis, but has lived a very different history. This circumstance created various problems.

---

1. Andrews, 1989, pp. 73–4, 294–8.
2. Zarcone and Zarrinebaf-Shahr, 1993; Zarcone, 1993a, pp. 57–83; Strauss, 2002.

Another factor that affected – and continues to affect – the contemporary history of the Shiʻa community in Istanbul is the 1979 Iranian revolution. Tehran's attempts to control and influence the Turkish Shiʻa, in particular the immigrants from Eastern Anatolia, through its embassy and consulates constitutes an important chapter in the recent history of Turkey's Shiʻa communities. The thousands of Iranian refugees who settled in Istanbul and Ankara in the 1980s, however, have not affected the functioning of Shiʻism in these cities very much at all; in any case most of them left the country for Europe or the United States or returned to Iran. Finally, it will be necessary to devote some space to clarifying a specific point that continues to be the subject even in academic writings of serious errors of judgment, namely the amalgamation of Shiʻism and Alevism.

A new geography of Shiʻism: the question of the Azerbaijanis of Turkey

The rich social, political and cultural history of the Iranian community in Istanbul ended during the first ten years of the republic, despite the fact that it had occupied a notable position in the Ottoman Empire in general and in Istanbul especially since the mid-nineteenth century. It was mostly composed of traders – generally Azerbaijani, to a lesser extent Iranian – who settled in Istanbul in the eighteenth and nineteenth centuries. Despite the overwhelming presence of Azerbaijanis, the community qualified itself as "Iranian" or "Persian", in reference to the country of origin of its members. The community later welcomed intellectuals opposed to the Qâjâr dynasty, exiled to or seeking refuge in Istanbul, who entertained a mutually beneficial relationship with the first Ottoman constitutionalists and later with the Young Turks. They were financially supported by the rich merchants who controlled a large part of the Caucasian and Iranian trade. On the religious level, Shiʻa ceremonies, initially prohibited, were gradually authorized to the point where, in the early twentieth century, the commemoration of Husayn's martyrdom on the tenth day of the month of *muharram* became a grand spectacle and an important date in the religious year for the Ottoman capital.[1]

---

1. And, 1979, pp. 238–54; Zarcone and Zarrinebaf-Shahr, 1993; Glassen, 1993, pp. 113–29.

From the late nineteenth century onwards, Istanbul's Shi'a community was in clear decline. The loss of its merchants' economic privileges, changes in trade agreements between Iran, the Ottoman Empire, Russia and Britain, and the opening of new trade routes[1] were all factors that considerably weakened the community. The re-establishment in Iran of the constitutional government, which had been abolished the year before, in 1909 and the subsequent return to the fatherland of many of the Persian and Azerbaijani elites living in Istanbul left an intellectual void that would never be filled again.

This general decline is clearly reflected by the *khân* (Valide Han) of the Persian traders of Istanbul, once a prosperous place and one of the main powerhouses of the economy of the Empire, where the cultural, political and religious life of the community was concentrated. In the 1930s, the security agent guarding the *khân* reported that the place was a mere shadow of itself; it was neglected, half in ruins and emptied of its Persian population.[2] According to a former occupant, there had once been 500 workshops headed by Persians, a publishing company, several foundations, a library and a political club. The Russian Orientalist Vladimir Gordlevski, who was among the last to witness a *muharram* celebration in the Valide Han, has left us a rich and detailed description of the lively animation centering on the *khân*.[3] Today, the houses, workshops and boutiques belong to Turkish traders and artisans; only an old inscription in Persian, dated 1907-1908,[4] recalls the Iranian presence in this place where there is still a mosque devoted to Shi'a worship, and the Iranlılar hayır derneği (Iranian Charity Foundation) unites the original members of the Persian community of this city with the newcomers.

Anti-religious measures taken by the young Turkish Republic between 1923 and 1946 limited Shi'a rituals as they constrained all of Islam in Turkey. According to Vladimir Gordlevski, under the pressure of Persian intellectuals in Istanbul, enactments of the tenth of *muharram* – considered too violent and unworthy of a civilized country – were already forbidden

---

1. Zarrinebaf-Shahr, 1993, pp. 207–8.
2. Koçu, 1961, pp. 3310–2.
3. Gordlevski, 1928, pp. 167–72; Gordlevski, 1993, p. 238.
4. Photograph published in Zarcone and Zarrinebaf-Shahr, 1993 (photo nr. 5).

in 1928.[1] In spite of its rich past, the Persian community of Istanbul sank slowly into decline and would ultimately be all but forgotten.

But the disappearance of their main religious celebration does not mean that the Persians of Istanbul assimilated and were integrated into the Sunni population of the city. We can observe today that several cultural and religious traditions are kept alive through the *Dabistân-e Irâni* (Persian school) located in the district of Sultanahmet, where members of the community as well as Iranian diplomats posted to the Consulate General send their children to be educated. Similar functions are fulfilled by the second historical Shi'a mosque of the city, in the Asian district of Üsküdar, as well as the nearby Iranian cemetery, where Persian families of Istanbul have buried their deceased since the eighteenth century.[2] In both places, especially the latter, it is still possible to come across descendants of this first Shi'a community of Istanbul. Its members, however, remain very discreet; their Shi'ism is more cultural than devotional and they refuse any assimilation with the newcomers.

Beside the slow erosion of this historical community, a new phenomenon occurred in the history of Turkish Shi'ism, namely the aforementioned arrival in Istanbul of Turkish Shi'a from Eastern Anatolia. Their arrival has affected the physical appearance of Shi'ism in this city in at least two ways: firstly by reinvigorating the existing Shi'a places of worship; and secondly – and more importantly – by establishing new, active centers of religious worship, some of which became hotbeds of Islamic radicalism and bridgeheads for Iranian propaganda. The study of the modern gravestones in the Iranian cemetery of Üsküdar neatly confirms the explosive expansion of the Shi'a community in Istanbul in the middle of the twentieth century. The places of birth of the deceased that are engraved on the modern gravestones provide a mine of information. The main provinces of origin of these immigrants are Kars and Iğdır; and the regions Arpaçay, Tazekent, Yılanlı, Büyükpirveli and Aralık.[3] Many of these Shi'a from East Turkey are refugees or the descendants of

1. Gordlevski, 1993, p. 169; Koçu, 1961, p. 3312. See also Glassen, 1993, p. 129.
2. On the Persian school, the Shi'a mosques and the Iranian cemetery, see Zarcone, 1992, pp. 10–12; 1993a, pp. 74–77; 1993b, pp. 99–101; 1996, pp. 217–21.
3. The geography of Shi'ism and of the Azeri settlements in Turkey can be found in Andrews, 1989, pp. 73–4.

refugees from the Caucasus and Russian Azerbaijan, as is indicated by the gravestone of the daughter of a (Sufi?) sheikh from the Caucasus: *Kafkaslı Şeyh Mehmet Oğullarından Samet Kızı Rukiye Yıldırım* (Samet Kızı Rukiye Yıldırım among the sons of the Caucasian Şeyh Mehmet).

Apart from Azerbaijanis of Turkish nationality, I also observed the presence of an "Iranian" from Erzurum:[1] *Garib Erzurum Iranlılarından Baba Şakazade, 1888–1957* (Baba Şakazade, 1888-1957, from the Persians of the Erzurum [region], [village of] Garib). The existence of a community of Persian traders in the city until the end of the Ottoman Empire and the presence of a Persian cemetery make it very likely that there should be more of these "Iranians".[2] On another note, the modern gravestones in the Iranian cemetery of Istanbul tell us that burials of Shi'a from Eastern Anatolia began after 1964[3] (this is by no means a definitive conclusion, as it is founded simply on the oldest gravestone of the immigrant community I could find). I have observed moreover that these gravestones differ from modern gravestones and tombs for descendants of the historical community, which are distinctly inspired by Iranian modern funeral art; among other characteristics are the use of Persian for epitaphs and an imposing and flashy decoration.[4]

Tensions rapidly grew between the historical community and that of the newcomers, which was different in every respect. The former had a longstanding bourgeois urban tradition, and was Shi'a by tradition and cultural identity. As for the newcomers, they came from a rural universe and were strongly attached to religious traditions but also aware of their Azeri identity. Is it a quarrel of this nature or a simple lack of space – the official explanation provided – that provoked the Direction of the Istanbul Cemeteries to decide in 1986, at the request of the Iranian Charity Foundation, to allow only the burial of "Iranians" in this cemetery?[5]

1. On the Persians of Erzurum, see Zarrinebaf-Shahr, 1993, p. 206.
2. Başar, 1973, p. 11.
3. Observations made in 1993.
4. For example, the tombs of the following Persian families: 'Abdulmuttalib Rafizâde, Akbarzâde, 'Ali Qurbanzâde, 'Ali Zakizâde, Bergi Shadi, Ibrâhim 'Ali, Kelanteri, Ramzi, etc; it is not impossible that the cemetery also contains Iranian families who settled in Turkey in the republican era.
5. Decision of the City Council of Istanbul, Direction of Cemeteries, of 25 March 1986.

Shi'a rituals in Eastern Anatolia and Istanbul

This brief overview of the current situation of Shi'ism in Istanbul and Turkey is by no means exhaustive and does not pretend to answer all the questions that could be raised. Rather, it is a first effort in the study of this phenomenon, which will demand more extensive field studies and an exhaustive analysis of the literature produced by the players of the movement.[1] The small amount of information presented here was gathered between 1995 and 2004 in the course of several research projects focusing on Shi'a Imams in Istanbul and the milieus surrounding the Shi'a mosques in the city. Additionally, part of the Turkish Shi'as' literary output and a number of press articles were studied.

The ban on *muharram* ceremonies and especially of the related flagellations that was imposed by the authorities in Ankara in 1928 put an end to public Shi'a ritual and spectacle in the former Ottoman capital. It is important to note, however, that the Shi'a of Eastern Anatolia, particularly those in Iğdır, never ceased to perform the ceremonies, including the flagellation ritual. Moreover, they reintroduced the *muharram* ceremony to Istanbul in the 1980s. As previously noted, there is little information on the history of the historical community of the Iranians and Azerbaijanis of Istanbul during the first decades of the republic. Perfectly integrated in the country, the community maintained its distinctive cultural and religious identity with great discretion, burying the deceased in the Iranian cemetery of Üsküdar, where an ancient *ghassâl-khâna* (washing facilities for the bodies prior to burial) is annexed to the mosque. The Iranian Charity Foundation, based in the Valide Han mosque, is charged with the administration of the cemetery and its mosque. Little is known of the history of the Valide Han mosque between 1928 and the 1950s, but we do know that the old mosque was destroyed in a fire in 1947 and rebuilt in 1951 with the support of the foundation. Its president at that time was Hacı Mehmet Naki Şefizade.[2] The mosque was officially inaugurated and opened to Ja'fari worship in 1953 by Turkish Prime minister Adnan Menderes. Likewise, little information is found about the Iranian cemetery

---

1. Capezzone, 1995, pp. 95–113.
2. According to two inscriptions inside the mosque, one in Turkish (Latin script); the other in Persian.

and its mosque; merely that the *mihrâb* was imported from Iran in 1933–4 with several other objects donated by that country, including the big floor carpet.[1] These few details indicate that the foundation was then on very good terms with the Pahlavi state.

The Kemalist state did not exercise the same tight control over distant Anatolia which it could impose in the big cities and the nearer provinces, which explains why Shi'a could continue to hold public demonstrations in remote regions. Middle-aged persons born in the region of Kars and Iğdır and now living in Istanbul have informed me that during the 1950s *muharram* processions with flagellations were organized in Kars. They also know that similar ceremonies took place in fifteen other villages in the regions of Arpaçay, Iğdır, Tuzluca and Aralık.[2] Today, nothing seems to have changed and the rituals are performed even more passionately. In 1992 *muharram* ceremonies in Kars and the neighboring cities of Iğdır, Tuzluca and Aralık are reported to have attracted an audience of 150,000. Daily life in the city of Kars was affected as a significant number of boutiques belonging to Shi'a traders were closed. The Shi'a, all dressed in black, gathered in the district of Yenimahalle, whipping their bare backs with chains and chanting "Ya Hüseyin, Ya Hüseyin". Others, dressed in white, slashed their foreheads until their faces were covered in blood.[3] These rituals were common in Iranian Azerbaijan and in Iran until Khamenei banned them in 1994, and have recently reappeared in ex-Soviet Azerbaijan.[4] In Iğdır, the main city of the Azerbaijanis in Turkey and the country's historical centre of Shi'ism, *muharram* is lived with a particularly intense fervor. A new mosque was constructed there in 1995; called Merkez Cami, it has joined older mosques such as Hacı Muhtar Cami (built in 1950) and Mava Cami. But today, Istanbul, with its extensive Shi'a diaspora, competes with Iğdır in terms of the practice of Shi'ism.

1. Zarcone, 1993a, pp. 76–7; 1993b, pp. 100–101.
2. Information given by Fahrettin Kirzioğlu to Metin And, in And, 1979, pp. 238–54.
3. Isleyen, 1992, p. 3.
4. Goltz, 1994, pp. 37–43. Pashazadä, 1991, pp. 89–102; Ähädov, 1991, pp. 93–138.

A story about mosques

The resurgence of Shi'ism in Istanbul dates back to the 1980s; the Zeynebiyye mosque, the most important in a series of new Shi'a mosques in the city, was built in 1979. It is located in a suburb of Istanbul, by the Küçükçekmece inlet in the district of Halkalı, on the European side of the Sea of Marmara. Is the building of this mosque in 1979 connected to the Iranian revolution or was the timing pure coincidence? Deeper analysis is needed to allow us to answer this question, but we can at any rate note that Tehran displays a rather intense interest in Turkish Islam in general, and in the Shi'a in particular.

At the end of the twentieth century, Istanbul counted about sixteen Shi'a mosques; today there are definitely more. The most important are the Zeynebiyye mosque, the Hüseyin mosque in Kay ışdağı on the Asiatic coast, and the Merkez mosque in Merter, in the Bakırköy quarter. Intense religious passion is displayed around these mosques, especially at the time of *muharram,* when processions of flagellants deliver spectacular demonstrations which Turkish journalists and even TV stations are more than happy to cover and film.[1] However, not all of Istanbul's Shi'a mosques are the scene of such ceremonies. The Valide Han mosque, for example, although frequented year-round by Azeri Turks, commemorates *muharram* in a more discreet way and differs from other mosques by the presence of Iranians, undoubtedly from the Consulate General. This is explained by the fact that this mosque is managed by the Iranian Charity Foundation – a direct link to the Islamic Republic that was also the origin of a number of problems that led to the closure of the mosque in 1992 and 1993. We will discuss this issue later. The mosque of the Iranian cemetery of Üsküdar, too, functions only when hosting funerals and does not commemorate the *muharram* like the others.

The Zeynebiyye mosque in Halkalı is located in the heart of the quarter where the Azeri of the eastern provinces live. It was abandoned after being damaged by the earthquake of 1999 and at the time of writing in 2004 the community was meeting in a provisional mosque nearby, awaiting construction of a new and bigger building. Several social and

---

1. A documentary was aired on Turkish television in 1994; the videotape is sold by Alemdar İletişim.

economic meeting places owned by members of the community exist in the immediate neighborhood: cafes, restaurants and a sports club, as well as various religious bookshops and travel agencies specializing in trips to Iran and Azerbaijan. The chief imam of the mosque, Selahettin Özgündüz, is the most important Shi'a leader in Istanbul. He holds the title of *hüccet ülislam (hujjat al-islâm)* (head of the Shi'i community in Turkey) and for years has had the honor of pronouncing the opening sermon for the religious ceremonies of *muharram*. This man holds the destiny of Shi'ism in Turkey in his hands.[1] He is accredited with the translation of a crucial religious text from Persian[2] and is often invited on television and local radio to express his views on Shi'a beliefs and on the question of Ja'farism and Alevism, both subject to intense public interest since the tragic events that divided Sunnis and Alevites in March 1995.[3]

Video and audio tapes of his sermons and pronouncements are sold by the company Temin Alemdar Iletişim, which also publishes the weekly Shi'a magazine *Alemdar*.[4] Selahettin Özgündüz is also said to have been at the origin of the publishing company Kevser, which publishes translations of religious works written by Iranians.[5] The second imam of the Zeynebiyye mosque, Hamit Turan, who authors articles in *Alemdar*, informed me that his mosque does not depend on the Ministry of Religious Affairs, but is managed by an association named Aytaş Mahallesi Cami ve Kuran Kursu Yaşatma Derneği (Foundation for the Creation and Functioning of the Mosque and Qur'an Studies of the Aytash Quarter). The Turkish Shi'a community is not recognized as a separate entity by the Ministry of Religious Affairs, which claims not to differentiate between the legal schools of Islam, but nevertheless remains dominated by Sunnism. Hamit Turan stresses the difference between the Zeynebiyye mosque and that of Valide Han; he is well aware of the problems which the latter has had with

1. Semavi, 1993; Albayrak , 1994.
2. See Shirazi, 1980.
3. These events took place in the Ghazi quarter of Istanbul and left nineteen dead.
4. I obtained the tape of his speech broadcast on radio Marmara FM: *Hüseyni Yol. Hüccet' ül-Islam Özgündüz' ün Akaid Konuşmas 1*, s.d.
5. Ilknur, 1993, pp. 42–5. I have reviewed the following works published by Kevser (names of the authors as they are written in Turkish): Muhaciri, 1992; Nakavi, 1992; Tabatabai, 1993; Caferiyan, 1994.

Turkish justice. For him, the Valide Han mosque is first of all the centre of the Foundation of the Iranians of Istanbul, which previously allowed Tehran to intervene in its management, a privilege it lost in 1995.

According to Hamit Turan, the main difference between the two resides in the fact that the Zeynebiyye mosque is not linked to Tehran and was never run by an Iranian imam, as was the case for the Valide Han mosque. He adds that the latter functions only partially, being accessible only for the noon prayer. The mosque of the Iranian cemetery, opened only for funerals, is in the same position. It is clear that Hamit Turan wants to minimize the position occupied by these two mosques in the functioning of Shi'ism in Istanbul. He is also concerned that the suspicions that rested on the mosque of the Valide Han – described at a certain moment as a bridgehead of the Islamic Republic of Iran and a hotbed of radical Islam – might attain other Shi'a mosques of Istanbul, and especially his own.[1]

But in 1993, journalists did draw attention to the Zeynebiyye mosque, insisting that the believers frequenting it were not insensitive to Tehran's propaganda. One journalist maintained that the mosque was a recruiting centre for the Turkish Hezbollah (an armed Islamic movement implicated in numerous assassination attempts); others saw it as a den of Iranian religious fanatics opposed to the secular Turkish state, which inspired fear in the people living in the quarter. Selahettin Özgündüz was even accused of being an agent of Tehran ...[2] There is certainly a lot of exaggeration at play here. The Azeri Turks who pray in this place seem deeply attached to Turkey and none of those I met, including Hamit Turan, appeared to me to be fanatical Muslims or to make themselves the interpreters of Tehran's politics. Nor does the presence in bookshops close to the mosque of works by Iranian theologians translated into Turkish constitute any proof, as these works are not propaganda texts but guides of morality, jurisdiction and religious practice.

On the other hand, it does seem that the Valide Han mosque was, for a time, controlled by the Islamic Republic through its consulate general in Istanbul, if a number of press articles published in 1993 are to

1.   Interview with Hamit Turan in April 1995.
2.   Ilknur, 1993.

be believed – and especially taking into account the fact that the mosque was closed for the better part of a year and the Iranian imams officiating there were deported from Turkey. Between 1992 and 1993, prayer there was conducted by imams holding Iranian nationality. However, this was not a new situation; I had observed on a visit in 1989 that the imam did not speak a word of Turkish.

One of the most recent and best-known imams at the mosque is Sabri Hamedani. Born in 1924 in Iran, he studied theology in Qom with several famous ayatollahs, including Khomeini himself, and subsequently held religious positions in many countries (India, Pakistan, Syria, Turkey, Egypt, Great Britain, Austria, Japan and China). Obviously, Hamedani knew Turkey well, having first visited before the Islamic revolution and again in 1983. He is the author of a work on Ja'fari jurisdiction that came out in its third edition in 1986,[1] and the Shi'a newspaper *Alemdar* has also published some of his texts.[2] The facts that led to the expulsion of Sabri Hamedani and another Iranian imam after him are not accurately known; it is necessary to turn to contemporary newspaper articles. According to these, Hamadani was appointed at the head of the Valide Han mosque following pressure from the Foundation of the Iranians of Istanbul. Later, suspected of spying – one journalist describes a parabolic antenna on the roof of the mosque – and having given sermons favorable to the Iranian regime, he was deported to Iran. The imam who succeeded him, Ismail Sabığı, was also imposed on the community by the foundation. He is the author of a guide to prayer and behavior based on Ja'fari jurisdiction, which he signed as "Imam of the mosque of the Iranians".[3] He, too, was deported, for the same reasons as Sabri Hamedani and in his place came an Azeri Turk, Bilgin Çoşkun, originally from the Caucasus, who was not appointed but elected by the community.[4]

Nonetheless, the Ministry of Religious Affairs ordered the closing of the mosque for several months in 1992 and 1993, with the intention – or such was the official explanation – of undertaking restoration works.

---

1. Hamedani, 1986.
2. For example, in issues 171 (10 April 1995, p. 2) and 172 (17 April 1995, p. 2).
3. Sabigi, n.d.
4. İşleyen, 1993, p. 12.

The consulate general of the Islamic Republic in Istanbul qualified this decision as "destructive".[1]

Bilgin Çoşkun complained that the ministry made him pay for the mistakes of his Iranian predecessors. He refused to admit that worshippers at the mosque could include "religious terrorists" and in 1993 declared to a journalist: "You will not find a single person among the Azeris visiting this mosque who would act against the state. It is wrong to think that terrorist activities could take place here. It saddens us to hear this."[2] Another journalist reports that Çoşkun told him: "The fact that we are Ja'fari does not make us supporters of Iran. Even assuming that we have a religious link with Iran, that does not make us supporters of Iran either ..."[3] Finally, at the end of 1993, the Ministry of Religious Affairs itself nominated a new imam, Mehmet Kıtay. He too is an Azeri Turk, from the city of Tuzluca (Iğdır), author of a book on history and theology, *Hakiki Islam Tarihi ve Ehlibeyt* ("The True History of Islam and the People of the House", 1994).[4]

Which Shi'a ulemas?

An interesting point to consider here is the training of Turkish Shi'a imams, and particularly the countries where they studied Ja'fari jurisprudence. The absence of Shi'a madrasas in Turkey leaves no choice to those among the Azeri Turks of Istanbul or the eastern provinces who want to dedicate themselves to religion. They are compelled, after having studied with local imams in the Shi'a mosques of their city or village, to continue their training outside the country, in either Iraq or Iran. In general, the Turkish Shi'a turned to Iraq and its holy cities, including Najaf. Mehmet Kıtay, a former imam of the Valide Han mosque, began his studies at the Hacı Muhtar mosque in Iğdır, then went to Tabriz in Iranian Azerbaijan in 1966, where he studied Persian, and finally took instruction at the Jâm'iat al-Najaf al-dîniyya madrasa in Najaf. After returning to Turkey, he held the position of imam of the Shi'a mosque of

1. *Hürriyet*, 17 March 1992.
2. Işleyen, 1993.
3. Ibid.
4. Kıtay, 1994.

Tuzluca for eighteen years. In 1993 he moved to Istanbul, where he was appointed to the Valide Han mosque.[1] Selahettin Özgündüz and Hamit Turan, the imams of the Zeynebiyye mosque, both studied in Iraq too, the first in Najaf, the second in Karbala. Özgündüz eventually became a close associate of Muqtadâ al-Sadr.

Later, as Hamit Turan confirms to me, the training of Shi'a imams was increasingly affected by the political situation in Iraq, by the police surveillance of which they became the object and finally by the first Gulf war, which forced the Turkish students of Shi'a religious sciences to turn to the Islamic Republic of Iran. Nevertheless, we should not ignore the fact that Iran had attracted Turkish students since the Islamic revolution. According to an imam in Iğdır, for example, the number of young people going to Iran for their religious studies had doubled since 1980. The city of preference was almost always Qom.[2] Some of these young clerics today live in Istanbul, where they are imams and work for Shi'a magazines. This privileged link to the Persian capital of Shi'ism persists today, indicated by the existence of a governmental publishing company, Ensariyya Yayinevi, which publishes works in Turkish that are intended for the Shi'a community of Turkey.[3]

In previous decades, the collapse of the Soviet Union and the creation of the CIS (Commonwealth of Independent States) have conferred a new importance on Turkey's eastern provinces. After the opening of the border at Sarp between Turkey and Georgia in 1989, another border crossing was created in 1993 in Dilucu, near Iğdır, between Turkey and the Azerbaijani enclave of Nakhichevan, which is today linked by a direct bus line to the Halkalı quarter of Istanbul. After several decades of separation, the Azerbaijanis of Turkey and those of Azerbaijan proper are finally able to meet again. Without doubt, the intense trade exchanges that have since developed between Nakhichevan and Turkey[4] are accompanied by full-scale cultural and religious exchanges. It has in any case been confirmed that the Shi'a mullahs of Istanbul and the region of Iğdır played an active

---

1. A short biography is featured on the cover of his book: Kitay, 1994.
2. Kaleli, 1990, pp. 215–6, 218–9.
3. For example Semavi, s.d.
4. 30,000 people per day crossed the Aras in Dilucu in the beginning of the 1990s.

role in the revival of Shiʻa Islam in Nakhichevan and perhaps in Azerbaijan too.[1] But they are no competition for the Ministry of Foreign Affairs and the non-governmental Turkish religious organizations (Fethullahcı, Süleymancı), which are well established across Azerbaijan but whose teaching is clearly marked by Sunnism.[2]

Turkish Shiʻism at the turn of the millennium: reforming, reclaiming, aspiring to unity

The participation of the Islamic Prosperity Party (Refah Partisi) in the coalition government of 1996–7 has had an indirect impact on the future of the Shiʻa community and the practice of Shiʻism in Turkey. In 1996, seeking the support of the main religious groups in the country (Sufi brotherhoods, Nurcus groups, etc.), Islamist prime minister Necmettin Erbakan tried to gather the main leaders of these groups at an *iftar* meal. Several refused the invitation, but others including Selahettin Özgündüz reacted favorably.[3] This commitment placed the Shiʻa community in a delicate position in February 1997, when the army forced the government to take measures against political Islam and all related currents. The Shiʻa were advised to stop the publication of a number of magazines, including *Alemdar*, which had been published since 1991 and was linked to Hamas and Tehran.[4] They were also pressured to lend their Ashura ceremonies a more human face, specifically by putting an end to the bloodshed and flagellations at the processions. The ban became effective around 1999 and was imposed across the Turkish territory, with the order coming from the Shiʻa imams themselves under pressure of the military.[5]

The pressure exercised by the military decreased in 2002 when the Party of Justice and Development came to power. This party had a background in political Islam, but defended a new project in which religion no longer occupied first place. Two new periodicals were then started: in 2002

1. This subject requires more study.
2. See Albayrak, 1998, pp. 135–47; Balci, 2004.
3. On this event, see Zarcone, 2004, p. 224.
4. Communication of Hidayet Koşaca, publishing adviser to the magazine *Erenler* (May 2004). On *Alemdar*, see Capezzone, 1995, pp. 105–13.
5. *Radikal*, 5 April, 2001; *Hürriyet*, 14 March 2003; *Sabah*, 14 March 2003.

Kıble, "a magazine for culture, literature and thought", eleven issues of which had appeared by spring 2004; and in 2003 *Erenler*, "a magazine for religion, thought and culture", with fifteen issues published by 2004. We also observe the appearance of websites run by members of the community.[1] Another important change was the return in Iğdır in 2002 of scenes of flagellation in the processions, while in Istanbul processions were still ordered to refrain from bloodshed. Selahettin Özgündüz's comments on the subject in 2003 and in 2004[2] and his reservations regarding the bodily acts of violence accompanying the ceremony are very interesting and show that he has adopted a reformist and critical discourse. This attitude was reminiscent of the negative attitude towards these ceremonies which the theologian Asadullâh Mâmaqâni adopted in the early twentieth century in Istanbul.[3]

Özgündüz initially insisted that he was not a reformer and was simply using *ijtihâd* to comment on the Qur'an according to the requirements of the era and the moment. He deemed it just to encourage his fellow believers to put an end to the bloody practices of *muharram* and consequently issued a revolutionary *fatwa* proposing to replace the chains used by the flagellants with straps of cloth and inviting them to donate their blood to the Red Crescent rather than waste it unnecessarily. This decision was an important step by the Shi'a leader to gather his community under the banner of Turkish modernity and lead it away from what was considered radicalism and religious fanaticism. However, Özgündüz was not followed by the Shi'a community at large and from 2002 onwards the imams of Iğdır chose, to return to the old practices. Kars, on the other hand, followed Istanbul's policy.[4] This disagreement betrayed the lack of unity in Turkish Shi'ism, which Özgündüz would try first of all to reconstruct – or more correctly, to *construct*.

An opportunity to call for unity and cohesion in the community came

1.   The main ones are: the site of the Shi'a Zeynebiyye mosque of Istanbul (www.zeynebiye.net), that of the publishing company Kevser (www.kevser.net) and the site of the Ja'faris of Turkey (Türkiye Caferiler Sitesi: www.caferilik.com). These sites in turn link to others.

2.   *Akşam*, 14 March 2003.

3.   Mâmaqâni, 1918 and 1956. For a summary of his ideas, see Glassen, 1993, pp. 124, 127–8.

4.   Bozkan, 2002.

in December 2003 when Shi'ism was denounced by a Sunni theologian (at the University of Marmara in Istanbul), who at the same time linked it to Wahhabism and Salafism. He moreover made the attack at a public conference and in the presence of the governor of Istanbul. He accused Shi'ism, among other reproaches, of being a "deviant current" of Islam and, indirectly, of inspiring religious radicalism and terrorism. The Shi'a of Istanbul, with Özgündüz at their head, reacted vigorously, demonstrating in large numbers in a square in Bakırköy, a popular quarter, and demanding the suspension of the theologian. The governor later declared that the author of the text did not represent the opinion of the government.[1]

Following this event Özgündüz traveled to Iğdır at the time of *muharram* in March 2004 to gather the Shi'a of Eastern Anatolia in an enormous meeting – the number three million has been mentioned – calling on them and their organizations to unite in a "Federation of the School of Ja'fari Law". He also used this meeting to attempt a reconciliation with the conservative Shi'a tendency. On 15 March, Özgündüz organised a similar meeting in Istanbul. Thousands of Shi'a were present, including delegates from mosques from all over the country as well as from the Turkish and Shi'a diaspora of Europe (such as an association of Turks from Kars established in Wezel, Germany). Ozgündüz openly criticized the policy of the Ministry of Religious Affairs but refrained from incriminating the government in any way. He declared above all that the Shi'a did not see themselves as a minority but as full citizens of the country, Turks first and foremost. "15 March 2004," he announced, "will be remembered as a historical day (...) A federation has been constituted (...)."[2]

The communiqué issued by the federation stressed the "right to a Shi'a identity" and rejected all qualifiers applied to Ja'faris considered to be incorrect or insulting: "the fifth school"; "without a school" *(Mezhepsiz)*; members of an Alevite sect ("kızılbaş"); and so on. The federation also denounced the exactions of the Ministry of Religious Affairs, the unsuccessful attempts to assimilate the Shi'a, the discrediting of their mosques and the humiliations suffered by their religious leaders. The campaign that the Shi'a intended to wage against the ministry, as specified

---

1. Bozkan: 'Caferiler Özgürlük Meydan 'nı Salladılar', 2004; 'Caferiler Kenetlendi', 2004.
2. Bozkan: 'Caferiler Kenetlendi', 2004.

in the communiqué, would be waged on the legal front and in the media, in Turkey and abroad.[1] 2004 thus promised a turning point in the history of Turkish Shi'ism and a true departure from its political history.

The commemoration of *muharram* of 2004 in the Halkalı quarter of Istanbul attracted thousands of believers (25,000 according to a journalist from *Özgür Politika*) and was an occasion of particular importance because of the preceding events. In accordance with tradition, groups of young men attached to different processions (*deste*) wore grand tunics in white, red or black colors and headbands displaying the name of Imam Husayn ("Yâ Hüseyin"). Young women, dressed in chadors with headbands carrying the names of Zahrâ and Zaynab, accompanied the decorated symbolic coffin of Husayn. All were beating their chests (*sine-dar*) in unison while marching. The place of celebration, a large empty field, was decorated with huge portraits of 'Alî, Husayn and Hasan; black flags and Turkish flags floated above the crowd. A large tent welcomed officials, representatives of the municipality of Istanbul and of the government. On a giant stage, one speaker after another addressed the crowd: Selahettin Özgündüz; Namık Kemal Zeybek, a former minister of culture; Hüseyin Hatemi, a Shi'a intellectual of Azeri origin; and Izzettin Dogan, the leader of an Alevite group. The atmosphere was much more feverish in Eastern Anatolia; the commemoration there was marked by a very ostentatious fervor in the presence of immense crowds; in Iğdır, for example, the whole city lived to the rhythm of waves of flagellants coming from the various mosques and to the uninterrupted sound of continuously chanted prayers and poems.[2] No blood flowed in Istanbul; more remarkably, no blood flowed in Iğdır either that year: a sign that the Shi'a conservatives of the province had joined Özgündüz. On the contrary, believers queued for the ambulances of the Red Crescent or visited hospitals to donate their blood.[3]

In Istanbul, Özgündüz insisted on giving the ceremony a political character, with guests from the government and the municipality. He had

1. Bozkan: 'Caferî Mezhebi Deklarasyonu', 2004.
2. CDs of the ceremonies in Istanbul and Iğdır containing the speeches are available: *Halkal 'da Aşura 2004 - VCD*, 2004, 3 VCD, Zeynebiye Cami, Alu' l-Beyt Yayıncılık; *Iğdır' da Aşura 2004 - VCD*, 2004, 1 VCD, Alu' l-Beyt Yayıncılık.
3. www.yonfm.com.tr (1 March 2004).

been repeating ceaselessly on radio and television that Turkey's Azeri Shi'a were born in the country and lived there and that he, as their leader, was "a defender of secularism, of democracy and of the constitutional state". He had always expressed his firm opposition to the idea of a theocracy and praised the religious freedom existing in Turkey, although he reproached the Ministry of Religious Affairs for not recognizing the Ja'fari school and turning a blind eye to publications hostile to the Shi'a.[1]

Having managed to create almost complete unity among the Turkish Shi'a, Özgündüz henceforth devoted himself to gaining respectability for his community in the eyes of the country by affirming his patriotism and challenging every amalgamation of the Shi'a with the Islamic Republic of Iran. But most of all, like the Alevis, he demanded that the Ministry of Religious Affairs differentiate between the Ja'fari school and the Sunni schools[2] and consequently assist it financially in training its mullahs, who, in the absence of a school for Shi'a imams, were forced to study in Iraq or Iran. Agreement on the status of the tenth of *muharram* as an official holiday was a part of this demand for the recognition of Ja'farism.

Autopsy of an error: the amalgamation of Shi'ism and Alevism

For several years, it has been possible to observe not exactly a rapprochement between the Shi'a and the Alevites in Turkey, but an enquiry into their own identity, especially on the Shi'a side. The Shi'a, who are generally not very well informed about what Alevism really means, regard the Alevites as "separated brothers", mainly because of a number of beliefs which the two communities hold in common. Some Alevites – a minority, it must be stressed – facing the hostility of Sunnism feel more comfortable aligning with the Shi'a and, in the name of the "beliefs" that connect them, are proponents of the idea of a common origin, some going to the point of adopting Shi'a rituals and visiting their mosques. This phenomenon certainly deserves our attention, but is not easy to study, above all because it requires a definition of Alevism and of its essential differences from Shi'ism.

---

1. *Milleyet*, 17 September 2003.
2. Sönmez, 2001.

Our knowledge of Alevism has considerably increased during the last forty years, notably through the pioneering work of Abdülbaki Gölpınarlı in Turkey and Irène Mélikoff in France,[1] and more recently through research carried out by Ahmed Yaşar Ocak, Krisztina Kehl-Bodrogi and Karin Vorhoff. Yet too many authors are still caught up in the unfortunate confusion which identifies Alevism with Shi'ism. The *Atlas des peuples d'Orient, Moyen-Orient, Caucase, Asie centrale* notes that Turkey has "a Shi'a minority of several million (...) Shi'a Turks whom the Sunnis call Alevis."[2] Elsewhere, a British sociologist attributes political positions of Alevism to the "Shi'a": "On the political and religious extremes, the far left was supported by Shi'ites (perhaps a quarter of the population)..."[3] The author is obviously unaware that there are Twelver Shi'a in Turkey and that their political positions are the antitheses of those espoused by Alevism. In a different field, geographer Xavier de Planhol, for practical reasons, makes an equally dangerous and unfortunate reduction when he understands "by Shi'ism, in a very broad definition, all forms of heterodoxy and Alevism, from the sedentary Kızılbaş to the nomadic Tahtacı."[4] On the other hand, we may commend the caution of some non-specialists of Turkey who are aware of the matter of the complexity of Shi'ism and therefore prefer not to make categorical statements on Alevism.[5]

This confusion springs from ignorance of the religious history of Turkey and of the history of Islam more generally. Nevertheless, some Turkish and French authors have for a long time emphasized the distinctiveness of Alevism and of the history of Shi'a ideas in Turkey. Indeed, the existence of Shi'a ideas among Muslims is not sufficient evidence to conclude that they are Shi'a, whether Twelver or otherwise. I refer here to an illuminating article by Claude Cahen, who mentions a "kind of internal shi'itization of Sunnism" in pre-Ottoman Anatolia and notes that "it is possible to be a convinced Sunni while still adhering to some Shi'a ideas."[6]

---

1. Gölpinarli, 1963; 1969; 1979; Mélikoff, 1992; Ocak, 1996; Kehl-Bodrogi, 1988; Vorhoff, 1995. See the bibliography in Vorhoff, 1998 for many other works on this subject.
2. Sellier, 1993, pp. 184–5.
3. Tapper, 1991, p. 8.
4. De Planhol, 1970, p. 103.
5. For example Richard, 1991, p. 17.
6. Cahen, 1970, pp. 115–29.

Before exploring in detail the points that make it inherently impossible to qualify the Alevites as Shi'a, we must highlight a Turkish author who has frequently and categorically pronounced himself on the subject. Abdülbaki Gölpınarlı first situates the "true" Shi'a of Turkey in the north-eastern regions of the country before expressing his opinion on the amalgamation of Shi'ism and Alevism.[1] He strongly insists on the fact that, "although they assert being *ja'farî-isnâ-asharî* (that is to say Twelver Shi'a or *ja'farî-ithnâ-'asharî*), (the Alevis) today present none of the characteristics of the Ja'fari sect."[2] Elsewhere, Mehmet Kıtay explains that the Shi'a and the Alevites certainly have a number of beliefs in common, but distinguish themselves very clearly in their religious rituals.[3]

In fact, except for a small but noteworthy number of beliefs – such as the veneration for the twelve Imams, the commemoration of the mourning of *muharram* and the practice of *taqiyya* (dissimulation) – that they share with the Shi'a (but also with some of Turkey's Sunnis[4]), in terms of religious rituals as well as social and political engagement, virtually everything distinguishes the Alevites from the Shi'a. History shows moreover that the Shi'a themes mentioned above did not feature in the early "Alevism" of the Safavid era, which originated in Turkmen and kızılbaş movements. No similar beliefs are discernible, for example, in the credo of the religious Turkmen leaders before that time, such as Hacı Bektash or Kaygusuz Abdal.[5] We must also note that the Alevites do not recognize the five pillars of Islam: not the daily prayer, nor the pilgrimage to Mecca (although they do visit the tombs of saints); not the Ramadan fast, nor the *zakât* (sharing of wealth); and not the *shahâdat* (confession of faith). Alevites do not visit mosques but gather in private houses called *cemevi* (meeting places). Moreover, they do not follow the Shi'a liturgy; in Istanbul, they do not bury their dead in the Shi'a cemetery. Their dead are instead buried in cemeteries that have belonged to them alone for a

1. Gölpinarli, 1979, p. 182; about Shi'a influence on Turkey, see pp. 189–92, and on the amalgamation of Shi'ism and Alevism, pp. 12–13.
2. Gölpinarli, 1969, p. 278.
3. Personal interview, Halkalı, 1995.
4. The commemoration of *muharram* is in fact observed by many Turkish Sunnis, especially by mystical brotherhoods such as as the Halvetiye and the Kadiriye; SMITH and İŞLI, 1983, pp. 403–6; Gordlevski, 1993, p. 236.
5. Mélikoff, 1975, pp. 52–3, 61.

long time (generally in Anatolia), or when they do not have the choice, as in Istanbul, in Sunni cemeteries, preferably close to Bektashi graves or mausoleums.[1] In Istanbul and in Anatolia, they do not commemorate the tenth of *muharram* together with the Shi'a, or only in exceptional cases. Habitually, they gather in their *cemevi* or around mausoleums of Bektashis, and they do not practice flagellation as the Shi'a do.[2] As a final observation on this subject, we must mention a sociological study, which showed that only a small minority of Alevites (7%) describe themselves as belonging to the Ja'fari school or as being Shi'a (2.8%); the majority define themselves as Alevite (57%), Bektashi-Alevite (13%) or kızılbaş (10%).[3]

In summary, on the religious and political levels, while the Shi'a in eastern Turkey and Istanbul are deeply respectful of the prescriptions of Islam, sometimes sensitive to the propaganda of Tehran and on occasion supportive of Islamist parties, the Alevites respect none of Islam's prescriptions, keep their distance from political Islam and support the Turkish left. These positions are related to their mistrust of Sunnism and to the specific characteristics of their credo. Since the 1990s, however, an attempt to "Shi'itize" Alevism led by "agents" of Tehran and the Turkish Shi'a has blurred distinctions and maintained the amalgamation of Shi'ism and Alevism. First, we must note that some Shi'a consider the Alevites to be "separated brothers", turned away from religious practice by persecution and the passing of time, and who therefore have to be redirected to the straight path.[4] This confusion is not a recent phenomenon. In 1986, for example, the Iranian imam of the Valide Han mosque dedicated his book on Ja'fari Law to his "Alevite Muslim brothers".[5] On the other hand, as early as the Ottoman era, Shi'a living in Istanbul and in other provinces of the empire where the Bektashi order – close to Alevism in its beliefs

1. Zarcone, 1991a, pp. 37–42; 1991b, pp. 69–75.
2. They meet, for example, in the *tekke* Sünbül Efendi of Kocamustafapaşa, or in the old Bektashi *tekkes* Karacaahmet in Selimiye, Seyyit Nizam in Zeytinburnu, Şahkulu in Merdivenköy or in the *cemevi* of the quarters of Ümraniye, Sarıgazi, Bağcılar, Gazi, etc.; Kehl-Bodrogi, 1994. See also Albayrak, 1994.
3. Aktaş, 1999.
4. Cf. for example Ilknur, 1993, and several articles in *Alemdar*. Selahettin Özgündüz also devoted a television program on Canal 7 to the subject (Alevilik, Caferilik).
5. Hamedani, 1986, pp. 3–4.

– was present tended to frequent their *tekkes* and often shared the meals of *muharram* with them.[1] Since the 1990s, the Shi'a have multiplied their contacts with Alevite groups. Some of the 1995 issues of *Alemdar* reflect this tendency. The objective of the magazine is to show that "true" Alevism complies with Ja'fari jurisprudence and is part of Shi'ism.

An attempt at rapprochement between the Shi'a and some Alevites has succeeded in Çorum in central Anatolia, where a newly built mosque led by a Shi'a imam is frequented by Alevites. Of course, only in-depth research in Çorum could adequately inform us on this phenomenon and determine accurately to which degree the two religious confessions interact in actual reality.[2] The Alevite community has besides also published, together with a number of Shi'a, a magazine called *Aşura*. The title of an article in this magazine is significant: "Caferi (Şia-Alevi) Mezhebinde Taklıd Anlayışı ve Temel Hükümler" (Explanation of the *Taklid* (Arabic: *taqlîd*) and Basic Prescriptions in the Shia-Alevite Ja'fari *Mazhab*).[3] One member of the magazine's editorial staff is Hasan Kanaatlı, a Shi'a from Kars who studied in Iraq and Iran and helped to open several Shi'a mosques in Turkey.[4] *Alemdar* (issues 171 and 172) also mentions contacts between the Alevite group of Çorum and the Zeynebiyye mosque. The basic conditions for a rapprochement are partly extolled in a voluminous work published in 1995 under the revealing title: *Alevilere Söylenen Yalanlar* (The Lies Told to the Alevites);[5] this discourse is clearly based on several instances of historical revisionism, as it attempts to establish scientifically the notion that Alevism is a diverted branch of Shi'ism. It is imperative to remember, however, that exchanges between Shi'a and Alevites remain a marginal phenomenon that preoccupies only a tiny fraction of this religious tendency, which, today as in the past, remains divided and diverse. Its trajectory has coincided with that of Shi'ism in the past, is coinciding with it today and will do so again in the future.

1. Zarcone, 1993b, pp. 107–11. On the common points and the differences between Alevism and Bektashism, see Zarcone, 2004, p. 298–301.
2. According to a report titled "Alevileri Şiileştirme Hareketleri" (Movements of Shi'itization of the Alevis), published in the Turkish weekly *Nokta* (28, 15 July 1990) and summarized in Kaleli, 1990, pp. 213–9.
3. Number 10, July 1991, p. 3.
4. Kaleli, 1990, pp. 213, 220–1.
5. Şahin, 1995.

On another level, for reasons of a purely political and strategic nature, the president of the Alevite foundation *Cem*, Izzettin Dogan, who actually considers Alevism to be a philosophical school rather than a religious current, has found in Selahettin Özgündüz an ally in his opposition to the Ministry of Religious Affairs. The two men have frequently issued joint statements on this point. In December 2003, the Cem foundation thus inaugurated a "Ministry of Religious Services for Alevite Islam", an informal organ estimated to represent a population of twenty-five million Alevites. Dogan demands that this be recognized by the Ministry of Religious Affairs, together with its right to benefit from a part of the grants which the state pays to the ministry. However, Cem is not representative of the broader Alevite community. Selahettin Özgündüz was present at the opening ceremony because the Shi'a have similar demands, but he was not invited to sit on the council of the organ, which represents only the Alevites. In return, Dogan is invited to speak on the occasion of the *muharram* ceremony in Halkalı in March, 2004, where he praises rapprochement between confessions and even mentions Christians.[1]

Conclusion

It is clear that today's Turkish Shi'a community is not the same as yesterday's. It is not even possible to say that there is a continuance. The only common point between past and present is the presence of Azerbaijanis, with the difference that in the last century, the Azerbaijanis – identified with the Iranians – came from Iranian Azerbaijan, while the Azerbaijanis who make up the current community come from "Turkish Azerbaijan", situated on the eastern borders of the country. To understand the Shi'a community better, it seems to me that next to its Shi'a specificity, emphasis should be placed on its Azeri identity. In this regard, the answer that Selahettin Özgündüz gave in 1993 to a journalist who asked him to describe himself is revelatory: "I am a Ja'fari, a Shi'a, and at the same time an Azeri Turk."[2]

---

1. *Zaman*, 28 December, 2003; *Halkalı'da Aşura 2004 - VCD*, 2004.
2. Ilknur, 1993.

This simultaneous membership of a religious community and a Turkish ethnic group constitutes what could be said to be the definition of the Shi'a community of Turkey. Indeed, all the Shi'a I have met in the course of my field studies stressed their Azeri identity – not to distinguish themselves from Turkish Turks, but rather to insist on a quality that characterizes them within the big family of Turkic peoples, specifically in an era in which the Turkish-speaking peoples of the Caucasus and Central Asia are finally meeting again. Their Shi'ism makes them no less Turkish: they are Shi'a precisely *because* they are Azeri. I am moreover convinced that, through their practice of Shi'ism and its ceremonies, the Shi'a of Turkey perpetuate what are above all Azeri cultural traditions. The way in which they commemorate the tragedy of *muharram* is characteristic. The religious fervor that the ceremony emanates has been interpreted as fanaticism – all the more dangerous because their attachment to Shi'ism made them *de facto* servants and "agents" of the Islamic Republic. But this conception betrays a lack of knowledge of the Azerbaijanis, who have always had their own way of commemorating *muharram*, more passionate and more ostentatious, which distinguished them from the rest of Iran.[1] This profound experiencing of their religion only proves that they are Azeris. Their Shi'ism is therefore neither more nor less than an identity marker. By reforming their rituals at the turn of the millennium and affirming their Turkish citizenship first and foremost before defining themselves as members of the Shi'a community, the members of the community distinguish themselves from their co-religionists across the Muslim world. But it does not make their position less difficult in the face of the disguised Sunnism practiced by the Turkish Ministry of Religious Affairs, which refuses to recognize their specificity.

---

1. Goltz, 1994, p. 37–43.

Bibliography

Newspapers and magazines

Dailies and weeklies: *Akşam; Cumhuriyet; Cumhuriyet Hafta; Hürriyet; Milliyet; Radikal; Sabah, Zaman.*

Magazines: *Alemdar; Aşura; Birikim, Kars Ardahan Iğdır' ın Sesi; Erenler; Kıble; Nokta.*

Books and articles

Ähädov, A., *Azärbayjanda Din vä Dini Mä'sisatlar* (Religion and religious institutions in Azerbaïdjan), Baky 1991, Azärbayjan Dövlät Näshrijatï.

Aktaş, A., "Kent Ortamında Alevilerin Kendilerini Tanımlama Biçimleri ve İnanç Ritüellerini Uygulama Sıklıklarının Sosyolojik Açıdan Değerlendirilmesi" (Sociological evaluation of the forms of auto identification of the Alevites and of their determination in the observance of rituals in the urban sphere), in *I. Türk Kültürü ve Hacı Bektaş Veli Sempozyumu Bildirileri (22–24 Ekim - 1998)*, Ankara 1999, pp. 449–82.

Albayrak, H., "Azerbaycan'da Din" (Religion in Azerbaijan), in *Türk Dünyasının Dinî Meseleleri*, Ankara 1998, Türk Diyanet Vakfı, pp. 131–47.

Albayrak, H., "Aleviler, Kerbela Şehitleri Anıyor", in *Cumhuriyet*, 20 June 1994.

And, Metin, "The Muharram Observances in Anatolian Turkey", in Chelkowski, Peter, ed., *Taziyeh: Ritual and Drama in Iran*, New York 1979, New York University Press, pp. 238–54.

Andrews, P. A., ed., *Ethnic Groups in the Republic of Turkey*, Wiesbaden 1989, Ludwig Reichert Verlag.

Balci, Bayram, "Islam et éducation islamique en Azerbaïdjan indépendant. Premiers résultats d'une recherche en cours", in *Études et Analyses*, 1, May 2004.

Başar, Z., *Erzurum'da Eski Mezarlıklar ve Resimli Mezar Taşları* (The old cemeteries and decorated gravestones of Erzurum), Ankara 1973.

Bozkan, I., "Caferiler Kan Ağladı"(The Ja'faris in Tears) *Akşam*, 25 March 2002.

Bozkan, I., "Caferiler Kenetlendi" (The Ja'faris are holding on), *Birikim, Kars Ardahan Iğdır'ın Sesi*, 7 March 2004.

Bozkan, I., "Caferî Mezhebi Deklarasyonu" (Declaration of the Ja'fari Law school), 2004, www.caferilik.com.

Bozkan, I., "Caferiler Özgürlük Meydanı'nı Salladılar" (The Ja'faris shake up Liberty Square), *Birikim, Kars Ardahan Iğdır'in Sesi*, 16 January 2004.

Bozkan, I., "Caferi (Şia-Alevi) Mezhebinde Taklıd Anlayışı ve Temel Hükümler" (Explanation of the *taklid* and basic commandments in the Ja'fari (Shi'a-alevi) school), *Aşura*, 10, July 1991, p. 3.

Caferiyan, H. R., *Masum İmamların Fikri ve Siyasî Hayatı* (Political thought and life of the infallible imams), Istanbul 1994, Kevser Y.

Cahen, Claude, "Le problème du shî'isme dans l'Asie Mineure turque préottomane", in *Le chi'isme imâmite*, Paris 1970, PUF, pp. 115–29.

Capezzone, Leonardo, "Note in margine ad alcune pubblicazioni sciite in Turchia", in *Lo Sciismo fuori d'Iran: Politiche Editoriali a confronto*, numero monografico *Oriente Moderno*, anno XIV (LXXV), 1–6, June-July 1995, pp. 95–113.

Glassen, E., "Muharram-Ceremonies ('Azâdârî) in Istanbul at the End of the XIXth and the Beginning of the XXth Century", in Zarcone, Thierry, and Zarrinebaf-Shahr, Fariba, eds., *Les Iraniens d'Istanbul*, pp. 113–29.

Goltz, Thomas C., "Ashura 94. Among the Reborn Shi'a of Post Soviet Azerbaijan" (unpublished), n.d.

Goltz, Thomas C., *Requiem for a Would-be Republic. The Rise and Demise of the Former Soviet Republic of Azerbaijan. A Personal Account of the Years 1991-1993*, Istanbul 1994, Isis Press.

Gölpinarli, A., *Alevi-Bektaşi Nefesleri* (Alevi-Bektachi poems), Istanbul 1963, Remzi Kitabevi.

Gölpinarli, A., *Türkiye'de Mezhepler ve Tarikatler* (*Mazhab* and religious orders in Turkey), Istanbul 1969, Gerçek Y.

Gölpinarli, A., *Tarih Boyunca İslam Mezhebleri ve Şiilik* (The schools of Islam and Shi'ism in history), Istanbul 1979, Der Y.

Gordlevski, Vladimir, "Dni Moharrema v Konstantinopole", in *Sbornik Museja Antropologii i Etnografii*, Moscou, vol. VII, 1928, pp. 167–72.

Gordlevski, Vladimir , "Les jours de Muharram à Constantinople", in *Les Iraniens d'Istanbul*, pp. 235–42.

Halkalı'da Aşura 2004 - VCD, 2004, 3 VCD, Zeynebiye Cami, Alu'l-Beyt Yayıncılık.

Hamedani, A.S., *İslamda Caferî Mezhebi ve İmâm Cafer Sadik Buyrukları* (The Ja'fari school in Islam and the commandments of Imam Ja'far Sadiq), Ankara 1986, Kadioğlu Matbaası. *Iğdır'da Aşura 2004 - VCD*, 2004, 1 VCD, Alu'l-Beyt Yayıncılık.

Ilknur, M., "Allahu Ekber, Hümeyni Rehber. İstanbul'da Bir Şii İbadethanesi" (Allah is great, Khomeini a guide. A Shi'i place of worship in Istanbul), in *Nokta*, 20 June 1993, pp. 42–5.

Işleyen, E., "Türkiye'de İran Dosyası" (The question of Iran and Turkey), in *Milliyet*, 4 February 1993.

Işleyen, E., "İstanbul'da 1352 Yıllık Acıyı Paylaştılar" (In Istanbul, people remember the sorrows of the year 1352), in *Cumhuriyet Hafta*, 17 July 1992.

Kaleli, L., *Kimliğini Haykıran Alevilik* (L'alévisme crie son identité), Istanbul 1990, Habora Kitabevi Y.

Kehl-Bodrogi, Kristina, *Die Kızılbaş/Aleviten. Untersuchungen über eine esoterische Glaubensgemeinschaft in Anatolien*, Berlin 1988, Klaus Schwarz Verlag.

Kehl-Bodrogi, Kristina, "Kerbela Şehitleri Kanlı Anıldı" (We remembered the martyrs of Karbala in blood), in *Cumhuriyet*, 21 June 1994.

Kitay, M., *Hakiki İslam Tarihi ve Ehlibeyt* (The history of true Islam and of people of the House), unpublished, 1994.

Koçu, R. E., "Büyük Valide Hanı" (The Valide Han), in R.E. Koçu ed., *Istanbul Ansiklopedisi*, Istanbul 1961, vol. VII, pp. 3307–13.

Mamaqani, A., *Din va Sho'un* (written in Istanbul in 1916), Tehran, 1956.

Mélikoff, Irène, "Le Problème Kızılbaş", in *Turcica*, VI, 1975, pp. 49–67.

Mélikoff, Irène, *Sur les traces du soufisme turc. Recherches sur l'Islam populaire en Anatolie*, Istanbul 1992, Isis.

Muhaciri, M., *Batının Batışı* (the collapse of the West), Istanbul 1992, Kevser.

Nakavi, M., *Batılılaşma Sosyologisi* (Sociology of Westernization), Istanbul 1992, Kevser Y.

Ocak, A. Y., *Türk Sufiliğine Bakışlar* (Glances on the Turkish Sufism), Istanbul 1996, İletişim Y.

Pashazadä, S. A., *Gafgazda Islam* (Islam in the Caucasus), Baky 1991, Azärbayjan Dövlät Näshrijatï.

De Planhol, Xavier, "La Répartition géographique du Chi'isme anatolien", in *Le chi'isme imâmite*, Paris 1970, PUF, pp. 103–8.

Richard, Yann, *L'islam chi'ite*, Paris 1991, Fayard.

Sabigi, I. S., *Caferi Fıkıhna Göre Dini Ameller ve Namaz* (Cult and Prayer According to the Ja'fari law), Istanbul, İranlılar Cami Imam Ismail Sabiki.

Şahin, T., *Alevilere Söyleyen Yalanlar* (Lies Told to the Alevites), Ankara 1995, Armağan Kitap ve Yayınevi.

Sellier, Jean and André, *Atlas des peuples d'Orient, Moyen-Orient, Caucase, Asie centrale*, Paris 1993, La Découverte.

Semavi, M. T., *Zikir Ehline Sorun* (Questions to people of the *dhikr*), Qom, İran İslam Cumhuriyeti, n.d.

Semavi, M. T., "Şiiler Hüseyin'e Ağladılar" (The Shi'a cried for Husain), *Cumhuriyet*, 1st July 1993.

Shirazi, *Özet İlmihal* (shortened catechism), Istanbul 1980, Zaman Y.

Smith, G. M., and Işli, N. , "Food Customs at the *Kaadirihane Dergah* in Istanbul", *Journal of Turkish Studies*, 7, 1983, pp. 403–6.

Sönmez, K., "Alevilik-Bektaşiligın Diyanet'te Temsili Problemi" (the problem of the recognition of Alevism-Bektachism at the Ministry of Religious Affairs), in *İslâmiyat*, Istanbul, IV, 1, 2001, pp. 41–9.

Strauss, J., "*Şii ne demektir?* Ein türkisches Traktat über die Schia aus dem Jahre 1925", in Brunner, R., Gronke, M., Laut, J. P., and Rebstock, U., eds, *Islamstudien ohne Ende*, Würzburg 2002, pp. 471–84.

Tabatabai, A., *İslamda Şia* (Shi'ism in Islam), Istanbul 1993, Kevser Y.

Tapper, R., *Islam in Modern Turkey. Religion, Politics and Literature in a Secular State*, London 1991, I. B. Tauris.

Vorhoff, K., *Zwischen Glaube, Nation und neuer Gemeinschaft: Alevitische Identität in der Türkei der Gegenwart*, Berlin 1995, Klaus Schwarz Verlag.

Vorhoff, "Academic and Journalistic Publications on the Alevite and Bektashi of Turkey", in Olsson, T., Özdalga, É., and Raudvere, C. , eds, *Alevite Identity. Cultural, Religious and Social Perspectives*, Istanbul/London 1998, Swedish Research Institute in Istanbul, pp. 23–50.

Zarcone, Thierry, "Merdivenköy et la géographie bektachie de l'Empire ottoman", in *Le* Tekke bektachi *de Merdivenköy, Anatolia Moderna/Yeni Anadolu, Derviches et cimetières ottomans*, Paris/ Istanbul 1991a, Jean Maisonneuve, vol. II, pp. 37–42.

Zarcone, Thierry, "Traditions concernant le tekke de Merdivenköy", in *Le* Tekke bektachi *de Merdivenköy, Anatolia Moderna / Yeni Anadolu, Derviches et cimetières ottomans*, vol. II, 1991b, pp. 69–75.

Zarcone, Thierry, "Un regard sur les lieux de culte chi'ites à Istanbul (fin d'Empire ottoman-époque contemporaine)", in *Lettre d'information de l'Observatoire urbain d'Istanbul*, 2, June 1992, pp. 10–12.

Zarcone, Thierry, "La Communauté iranienne d'Istanbul à la fin du XIXe siècle et au début du XXe siècle", in Scarcia-Amoretti, Biancamaria, ed., *La Shi'a nell'Impero Ottomano*, Rome 1993, Accademia Nazionale dei Lincei, pp. 57–83.

Zarcone, Thierry, "La Situation du chi'isme à Istanbul au XIXe et au début du XXe siècle", in *Les Iraniens d'Istanbul*, 1993, pp. 97–111.

Zarcone, Thierry, "The Persian Cemetery of Istanbul", in Bacqué- Grammont, Jean-Louis, and Tibet, Aksel, eds., *Cimetières et traditions funéraires dans le monde islamique*, Ankara 1996, Türk Tarih Kurumu, pp. 217–221.

Zarcone, Thierry, *La Turquie moderne et l'islam*, Paris 2004, Flammarion.

Zarcone, Thierry, and Zarrinebaf-Shahr, Fariba, eds., *Les Iraniens d'Istanbul*, Tehran/ Istanbul/ Paris 1993, IFEA-IFRI.

Zarrinebaf-Shahr, Fariba, "The Iranian (Azeri) Merchant Community in the Ottoman Empire and the Constitutional Revolution", in *Les Iraniens d'Istanbul*, pp. 203–12.

BAYRAM BALCI

Shi'ism in post-Soviet Azerbaijan: Between Iranian Influence and Internal Dynamics

Islam in post-Soviet Azerbaijan has gone through a period of profound transformation since the collapse of the Soviet Union. As in all ex-USSR states, the rupture inaugurated an era of relative freedom for all religions. Azerbaijan, however, occupies a special place in the Muslim ex-Soviet world, as about 60 per cent of its population adheres to Twelver Shi'ism. The Shi'a character of Azerbaijani Islam, its geographical proximity to Iran and the strong historical links that exist between the two countries explain the dynamic religious exchanges that have been taking place between both banks of the Aras river since the early 1990s. The present study proposes a synthetic analysis of the religious cooperation between Azerbaijan and Iran since that date.[1]

More precisely, we will present qualitative and quantitative research

---

1. The present paper is the result of several field studies carried out between November 2003 and May 2006 in all regions of Azerbaijan, among Azerbaijani students in Qom, the sizeable Azeri minority in the eastern provinces of Turkey and the Azeri-speaking provinces of Georgia. While preparing this article, I have greatly benefited from the assistance of two colleagues. Sabrina Mervin has always guided me in my quest for knowledge about Shi'ism. Her willingness to transport herself into "my" field has allowed me to refine the object of my research – any imperfections of which, of course, remain my responsibility. Likewise, my friend and colleague Altay Geyushov has generously introduced me to all the Islamic milieus of Azerbaijan. I would like to express my gratitude to both.

into the main Islamic influences on Azerbaijan from neighboring Iran. The central focus is on the means and channels by which this influence spreads and on the way these are perceived by the Azerbaijani state as well as by the different elements that make up Azerbaijani Islam. We will measure the impact of different Iranian Shi'a currents on the reinvention of Azerbaijani Islam. Do Shi'a discourses emanating from Iran succeed in integrating Azerbaijani Islam into Iranian Islam – as far as it is possible to speak about Iranian Islam and Azerbaijani Islam *stricto sensu*? In other words, do Iranian Shi'a influences not contribute more to integrating the Shi'a of Azerbaijan into their own country, rather than allying them to any exclusively Iranian Shi'a current?

Some elemental history

Islam has been implanted in what is currently the country of Azerbaijan since the earliest days of the Arab conquests, entering the southern Caucasus at the rhythm of the military advances of the different Iranian dynasties succeeding each other in the region. As a province of the Safavid Empire in 1501 – the year when Shâh Ismaïl elevated Shi'ism to the status of official state religion – Azerbaijan rapidly became part of Twelver Shi'ism's home ground. However, the Caucasus was also the terrain on which the confrontation between Shi'a Iran and the Sunni Ottoman Empire was played out, and as such it was never the exclusive domain of either doctrine. Both schools have always co-existed here, rather peacefully compared with elsewhere in the Muslim world. It is a part of the legacy of the Safavid Empire and its successors, who never maintained a strong military presence in the northern Caucasus, that the northern regions of Azerbaijan have remained more or less dominated by Sunnism. Although the religious map of the country has undergone many modifications over the course of the centuries, to this day the south remains more Shi'a than the north.

Iran and Russia signed the Turkmenchay treaty in 1828; this was a pivotal year in the history of Azerbaijan: until then an Iranian province, it was now partly annexed by the Russian Empire.[1] However, while a process

---

1. Swietochowski, 2004, pp. 1–84.

of identity differentiation between the Azeris remaining in the Persian Empire and those becoming subjects of the Tsar did take place, the cut-off between north and south was less radical in religious terms; the border formed by the Aras River remained porous until the arrival of Bolshevism in Azerbaijan, which then became a Socialist Soviet Republic. The permeability of this border allowed numerous religious exchanges between the Iranian Shi'a and those of Russia, who still enjoyed the right to go on pilgrimages to their holy cities of Mashhad, Najaf and Karbala.[1]

Nevertheless, while contacts between north and south were not immediately outlawed, a current of modernist thought influenced by Russian, Tatar and to a lesser extent Ottoman intellectual circles developed in the country and militated against the pervasive influence of religion on the population.[2] From the beginning of the nineteenth century newspapers like *Ekinçi* and *Molla Nasriddin* offered a forum to numerous secular Azeri intellectuals educated in Moscow, St Petersburg, Istanbul and sometimes even in Europe. Such was the case of 'Ali Merdan Topçubachi (1895–1981), who of all the intellectuals and politicians in Azerbaijani history has left the most important legacy. Other respected intellectuals such as 'Ali Bey Huseyinzade (1864–1941) and Ahmet Aghaev (1869–1939) also played a significant role in the struggle against certain Shi'a practices considered obscurantist and retrogressive. Through their intellectual activities and their specific denunciation of the rituals linked to Ashura, they contributed to the secularization of society and the weakening of Shi'a influence on the population.[3]

The end of the Tsarist Empire and the birth of the Soviet Union, which entailed the founding of the Socialist Soviet Republic of Azerbaijan, inaugurated a new and difficult period in Islam's survival. Research on this topic has long been dominated by the analytical grid developed by Alexander Bennigsen; this has, however, increasingly been invalidated by contemporary researchers of ex-Soviet Islam. Bennigsen's typology rests on the existence of two forms of Islam during this period, one official and the other underground, or as he puts it, "parallel".[4] While Islam was harshly

1. Geyushov, 2004, p. 10.
2. Adam, 2001.
3. Ibid.
4. Bennigsen, 1981.

suppressed and decimated all over the Soviet Union throughout the 1930s, from 1944 onwards the central authority started condoning the presence of an official Islam, creating four Spiritual Administrations (collectively known under the Russian acronym SADUM), which were put in charge of Muslim communities in the Soviet Union. Through SADUM, which was based on institutions that had existed under a different form in the Tsarist era, the Soviet regime attempted to control the part of Islam that ideological struggles had been unable to eliminate.[1] Beginning in the 1960s, this official Islam was also put to use in improving the USSR's image in the Muslim world. According to Bennigsen, the official religion co-existed with a parallel or popular Islam, which survived around pilgrimage sites and holy places. Sufi brotherhoods are supposed to have constituted the main ingredient of this Islam, especially in predominantly Sunni regions. But on the whole, according to Bennigsen and many other studies of Islam in this period, the attitude of the central authorities towards Islam was characterized by repression and the closing of places of worship.[2]

More recent research on Soviet Islam stresses the relative nature of the repression of Islam in the USSR. The work of Bakthiyor Babadjanov, for example, who has done new research on Muhammadjan Hindustani – one of the greatest Muslim scholars to have lived under the Soviet regime – presents a more nuanced attitude towards Islam's situation during the Soviet period.[3] In fact, the Soviets had a love-hate relationship with religion. On the one hand, Islam (like all religions) was almost completely expelled from the public space. Most mosques were closed, demolished or converted, religious education was banned, and public demonstrations of religious sentiment and rituals – such as the Ashura ceremonies in the case of the Shiʿa – were forbidden. On the other hand, however, Islam not only continued to exist in the private sphere, but managed to develop itself, with the full knowledge of the Soviet authorities. Showing one's religiosity and practicing one's rituals was in reality considered disreputable rather than being officially forbidden. Dozens of discussions with clerics who have lived under the regime made it clear to us that the repression was not particularly fierce, especially in remote provinces. We have met

1. Brower, 2003.
2. Roʿi, 2000.
3. Babadjanov & Kamilov, 2001.

several persons in the Azerbaijani countryside, notably in the southern regions of Lankaran and Massalli, as well as in Nakhitchevan, who were both exemplary members of the Communist Party – leaders of local party cells – and teachers of Qurʾanic recitation to the children in their district. Some peripheral regions of Azerbaijan have always continued to resist orders emanating from the center. This was the case, for example, in the cities of the south, but also – and especially – in Nardaran, a particularly religious city near Baku that houses an *imâmzâde*, namely the mausoleum of Rahime Hanim, daughter of the seventh imam.

Whatever the attitude of the authorities towards Islam may have been until the late 1980s, the relaxation of their control during the perestroika period and the subsequent decline and final collapse of the Soviet Union in 1991 left Islam free to come out of the private sphere and reoccupy the public space. The leaders of the newly created CIS states, often former apparatchiks of the Communist Party converted to nationalism, chose to rehabilitate Islam. President Heydar Aliyev had hardly come to power when he went on a pilgrimage to Mecca, opening the way for many Azerbaijanis, who had performed the *hajj* at a rate of less than ten persons per year during the Soviet era. Moreover, although the Azerbaijani constitution explicitly mentions the secular character of the country's institutions and refers nowhere to religion,[1] the general political and social climate of the era became more favorable to Islam. Religious literature enjoyed a relative bloom and mosques were constructed throughout the country, usually on local initiatives but occasionally supported by the political authorities.[2]

One of the main initiatives taken by the state that effectively favored the resurgence of Islam, and more specifically of Shiʿism, was the creation of the Islamic University of Baku. This university, the first public institution in Azerbaijan devoted to religion, was inaugurated in 1989 but only became operational following the declaration of independence. Endowed with two faculties, the university has the ambition to train religious cadres as well

---

1. The constitution of the Republic of Azerbaijan is very explicit on the secular character of the state (art. 17), the separation of politics and religion (art. 18) and religious freedom (art. 48).
2. On the resurgence of Islam in Azerbaijan in the early 1990s, see Motika, 2001.

as experts in Arabic and Iranian studies. Many graduates of the university have gone on to occupy religious positions, mostly in the countryside (as imam, *âkhund*[1] or mullah).[2] Although its rectorate does not advertise the fact, the university applies an educational policy that favors Shi'ism. Thus, the manuals used to teach *fiqh* (jurisprudence) are of the Shi'a school, and an abundance of Iranian literature is available in the classrooms and the library. Moreover, according to several teachers we interviewed in this establishment, *Nahj al-balâgha* is one of the first works studied by the students. Finally, most teachers of the establishment were trained in the first madrasas which were established by Iran throughout the country after 1990 – only to be closed again from the mid-1990s onward, when the government decided to counter Iran's religious influence.

But in reality the university has limited ambitions: accommodating students who have chosen it for want of anything better, and working with a professorial body that is trained on the job, its real objective is to train "technicians" of Islam: young people capable of explaining the rudiments of Shi'ism and spreading the official perception of Islam so as to ensure that the population remains loyal to the regime and its institutions.

The change of attitude towards religion on the part of the state also favored the birth of private Islamic initiatives. Representative of this current is the Center for Religious Research, directed until January 2006 by the young and dynamic Elçin Eskerov, which plays a key role in framing the public perception of religious phenomena. The Center describes itself as an independent NGO, but in reality the state exercises effective control over all of its activities, and especially editorial control over its publications. The Center runs two websites[3] and publishes a magazine called *Qutb* (Pole). All three focus on two themes of mobilization: the denunciation of Christian missionary movements (and Muslim movements such as Wahhabism) and the introduction of facultative religious

---

1. A Persian term that in post-Soviet Azerbaijan indicates the principal official in charge of a Shi'a mosque. The Sunni equivalent in Azerbaijan is imam. The mullah is for both Shi'a and Sunnis the person who takes care of menial chores such as washing the dead, running the daily business of the mosque, etc.
2. Discussions with Haji Sabir (rector) and Elchin Esenov (teacher), Islamic University of Baku, 19 May 2003.
3. The most active of the two is: www.islam.az

courses in secondary state schools. Another initiative worth mentioning – albeit a less dynamic enterprise – is the magazine *Kelam*, founded by one of the directors of the Islamic University, Qazi Haci Mireziz Seyid-zade, which regularly publishes general articles on Islam. Again, although the editorial staff does not mention it, the editorial line is pro-Shi'a and more precisely adheres to the current of 'Ali Khamenei, whose portraits decorate its offices. Finally, I must also mention the more recent launch of two magazines of Shi'a tendency, respectively called *Hikmet* (Wisdom) and *Deyerler* (Values). The latter aims to transcend the Sunni-Shi'a divide and was founded by Ilgar Ibrahimoglu, the extremely charismatic imam of the mosque of the old city, who we will meet again later.

The different aspects of the Shi'a resurgence

One of the first signs of the resurgence of Shi'ism in Azerbaijan, and the first embodiment of the religious encounter between Iran and Azerbaijan, was the return of some Azerbaijanis to Iran for theological studies. Religious studies were virtually non-existent in Azerbaijan during the Soviet period; except for the small informal circles animated by local religious authorities, they were only allowed (and therefore controlled) in Uzbekistan, in the madrasas of Miri Arab in Bukhara and al-Boukhari in Tashkent. Sunnism was the predominant school taught there. From 1991 onwards, therefore, hundreds of young Azerbaijanis rushed to study at Iranian religious establishments, notably in Qom and Mashhad, which has made it a policy to attract foreign students ever since the revolution created the Islamic Republic of Iran. Most students going to Qom were attracted by its *hozeh*.[1]

The massive numbers of Azerbaijani students frequenting the *hozeh* of Qom in the first years of independence have today come down to between 200 and 250. They are mostly concentrated in the two madrasas of imam Khomeini and Hojjatiyeh. Most of the Azerbaijani students come from Lankaran, Massalli, Lerik and Nakhitchevan – the border regions with Iran dominated by Shi'ism.[2] Azeris from Georgia and Turkey (the latter

---

1. Mervin, 1995.
2. Discussions with Azerbaijani students in Qom, April 2004 and February 2006.

mostly from Igdir and Kars) are also found among them. Since 1992, these students have been the main distributors of Iranian Shiʻa literature in Azerbaijan. Quick to learn Persian and Arabic, they have translated dozens of books into Azeri, distributing them to the main Islamic bookshops in Azerbaijan. Their role in the resurgence of Shiʻism in Azerbaijan, therefore, cannot be overestimated, given the influence which they exercise over their families and wider social environments. However, many of them have yet to return, because studies in the *hozeh* of Qom, as in others (Najaf for example), can easily last ten years and longer. The impact of their possible return will become clear over the coming years. Meanwhile, they do regularly travel between Iran and their country of origin, which contributes to the circulation of religious ideas.

To the influence exercised by this stream of students we must add Iranian initiatives, public or private, which have contributed widely to the resurgence of Shiʻism in Azerbaijan. The embassy of the Islamic Republic of Iran in Baku, through its cultural services, acted as a broadcasting relay. The embassy set up a cultural center endowed with a library, a conference room and even a *husayniyya* – most probably the only one in the country. The department of Persian studies in the Institute of Orientalism at the Academy of Sciences regularly receives important quantities of religious literature, promoting mainly the thought of the Imams Khomeini and Khamenei, the current Guide of the Islamic Revolution.

Finally, as part of the humanitarian assistance offered to the refugees and displaced of the Karabakh war, the charitable foundation *Imam Khomeini Imdad Komiteti* (Imam Khomeini Aid Committee) has also distributed abundant amounts of Shiʻa literature. The activism of these Iranian missionaries was particularly widespread during the first years of independence, when they benefited from the weakness and lack of organization of the young Azerbaijani state as well as popular demand and lively curiosity about Islam, which had become a subject of daily debate in the country towards the end of the Soviet era. However, after some years, the Iranians' activism diminished due to their disappointment when they realized that these "ex-soviets had been perverted too much by communist propaganda to be reconverted into good Muslims".[1]

---

1. Interview with the mullah of the great central mosque of Astara, an Iranian

Private organizations, although not under direct control of the Iranian state, also participated in the development of exchanges between various Islamic currents in Iran and Azerbaijan. Foremost was the Hodâ bookshop, based in Tehran, which has a very active subsidiary in Baku. Closed on several occasions by the Baku authorities, who accused it of working for the Iranian state and "importing into the country literature harmful to the national spirit", this bookshop nevertheless functioned without difficulties for some years. Its shelves are largely – although not exclusively – dedicated to religious literature. It is difficult to determine, however, whether it favors the thought of *mujtahid* or *marja'* over others, since it offers books and *risâla* by all the important religious leaders of the contemporary Shi'a world: Khamenei, Motahhari, Lankarâni, Sistâni, Sobhâni, Javâd Tabrizi and many more.[1]

Other networks, notably associations created by young clerics formed in Iran, in their own way distributed important quantities of Shi'a literature. One of these, *Manevi pakligha davet icmasi* (Association for the Promotion of Moral Purity), organizes regular courses and seminars allowing the young to acquire an Islamic education. Characteristic for this association is the importance it attaches to the education of girls, who are "future family mothers responsible for the education of their children" according to its representative, Elshan Mustafaev.[2]

This Iranian influence spread by Iranian and Azerbaijani initiatives encouraged Azerbaijani Islam to diversify, thereby giving birth to currents which had not existed in the Soviet period. A case in point is the Islamic Party of Azerbaijan, founded shortly after the country's independence, initially duly registered and recognized by the Ministry of Justice but banned shortly afterwards for its presumed activities in the service of Iran. Founded by activists from Nardaran, Islam's centre of survival under the Soviet regime, the party openly advertises its adherence to Khomeini's doctrines. At a conference on literary exchanges between Iran and Azerbaijan in April 2005, the former leader of the party proudly

---

city on the border with Azerbaijan.

1. Interview with Mirza Mir Aziz Ismayilov, manager of the Hodâ bookshop, Baku, January 2005.
2. Interviews with Elshan Mustafaev, representative of the Association for the Promotion of Moral Purity, Baku, April 2004 and March 2006.

claimed that the party's members had adhered to Khomeini's ideas even in the time of the Soviet Union. However, although it was created at the end of the Soviet era, the party clearly shows "soviet" characteristics, inherited by its senior cadres who were marked by the former regime's political culture. Yet these very cadres entertain regular contacts with Iranian religious circles and frequently spend time in Iran, which means that the party is submitted to direct Iranian influence and is moreover close to Iranian circles of power. This pro-Iranian commitment has nevertheless cost them dearly, as it has exasperated a number of cadres, who left to create their own political grouping, one that is less closely linked to the Iranian regime and aims instead to profit from the experience of the Party of Justice and Development in Turkey.[1]

Haji Ilgar Ibrahimoglu, until May 2004 the imam of the Friday mosque in the old city of Baku, and his entourage represent a new tendency and constitute a factor in the diversification of Azerbaijani Shi'ism. He is a young man (around thirty years old in 2005) and was imprisoned for his participation in "acts of vandalism" during the post-electoral demonstrations in October 2003. In recent years, he has been making the religious headlines because of an open conflict which opposed him to the State Committee for Religious Affairs and the Directorate of Spiritual Affairs of the Caucasus, organisms whose legitimacy he refuses to recognize. This open confrontation between the young leader and the state specifically centered on the status of the mosque whose imam he had been since 1993, and which the authorities wanted to transform into a museum. The conflict came to an end in July 2004 when the police removed him *manu militari* from the mosque.

Barely fifteen years old when the Soviet Union broke up, Ilgar Ibrahimoglu has enjoyed an independent Islamic education, contrary to most other religious cadres of the regime, notably those of the Directorate of Spiritual Affairs and of the Islamic Party of Azerbaijan, who are older and were educated in the only Islamic establishments authorized in the USSR, in Tashkent and Bukhara. Despite his youth and autodidactic education, Haji Ilgar is indeed an erudite person, at least in comparison

---

1. Interview with Kerbalai Tahir, originator of this schism and leader of the new Democratic Islam Party of Azerbaijan, Baku, March 2006.

with the experts preceding him. While most other religious leaders during the Soviet period and even afterwards acquired their knowledge on the job, he has had the privilege of spending eight years in Iran, where he studied theology and philosophy at the universities of Tehran and Qazvin. When asked about his studies in Iran, he proudly declares that he was influenced by the moderate teachings of Ayatollah Motahhari and by the philosopher Soroush.[1] Besides, most of his faithful, or at any rate his close advisers, also undertook consistent religious studies. The education he received in Iran – modest by Iranian standards, but impressive for Azerbaijan – confers on the imam a level of knowledge and theological rhetorical skills far superior to those of his rivals.

The way this leader and his community celebrate the annual ceremonies of Ashura, a practice that was frowned upon during the Soviet period but has experienced renewed interest since the early 1990s, is a perfect illustration of the movement's modernist character. While in other mosques the ceremony is the occasion for the traditional sessions of collective crying and self-flagellation, no such scenes take place in the mosque of Haji Ilgar's movement. In its desire to reconcile Islam, Ashura and modernity, the community has for several years now organized a blood collection to the benefit of children suffering from thalassemia, a genetic illness affecting hemoglobin that is common in Azerbaijan. According to Ilgar, blood must flow in accordance with religious precepts but there is no reason why it should not be put to good use. The pain that one inflicts on oneself must better serve the community. He feels Muslims should follow the precedent set by Imam Husayn, who sacrificed his own blood for the faithful, and give their blood to Muslims who need it on the occasion of Ashura.

On the other hand, Ilga's movement is clearly a product of the modern age: the young imam is very aware of current issues such as globalization, and he contributes to international religious debates. The dialectics of human rights and Islam, very fashionable in the Muslim world this last decade, are represented in Azerbaijan by this imam, who runs an Islamic association that is involved in the defense of human rights and more particularly the right of women to carry the veil on identity pictures.[2]

---

1. Discussions with Ilgar Ibrahimoglu, April 2005 and March 2006.
2. The website of his Islamic association for the Protection of Human Rights, in Russian and English: www.humanrights-az.org (consulted on 24/01/2007).

The imam entertains good relations with international bodies for the defense of religious freedom: he manages the Azerbaijani section of the International Religious Liberty Association, an American NGO known for its denunciations of attacks on religious freedom.[1] The Scandinavian Organization Forum 18 is another ally of the young imam in his struggle against the authorities.[2] During his overt confrontation with the authorities, the imam received substantial support from both organizations, which rallied several foreign embassies in Baku to his defense. This alliance with Christian organizations defending religious freedom allows him to project the image of a modern Muslim leader, open-minded and engaged in the dialogue between religions and civilizations. Whether he is sincere in this or merely uses it as a tactical ploy, the young imam thus occupies a unique position in the Islamic landscape of his country.

Another aspect of the transformation Azerbaijani Islam has been going through since the collapse of the Soviet Union concerns the *marja'iyya*, the fundamental institution of Shi'ism, and the rituals of Ashura, also a specifically Shi'a practice. An analysis of what the *marja'iyya* means in post-Soviet Islam in Azerbaijan, as well as a brief depiction of the rituals of Ashura during the last few years, tell us much about the country's Shi'ism and the relations it maintains with Iran.

Ashura

In Azerbaijan, which for centuries was a province of the Persian Empire, the month of *muharram* and its tenth day, Ashura, are important moments in the mourning commemorated annually by the Shi'a. Historical studies

---

1. The IRLA is an association founded shortly after World War II by Seventh Day Adventists who themselves experienced problems in civil service or in taking their day off on Saturday (they observe the Sabbath). But the causes they defend concern religious freedom in general, rather than specifically Adventist issues. They publish a magazine in French, *Conscience et Liberté*, and have an English website: www.irla.org (consulted on 24/01/2007).

2. Forum 18 was founded by several former employees of Keston News Service, a press agency known for providing information on religious persecution during the Soviet period. When KNS ended its activities for financial reasons (a Keston Institute still continues to provide news today), the employees proceeded to create a new agency named Forum 18 and based in Norway. See their website: www.forum18.org (consulted on 24/01/2007).

certify their importance across the centuries. Although suppressed by the Soviet authorities, the commemoration of Ashura by no means disappeared,[1] as is attested by a search through the archives and by many discussions we had with Muslims who lived under the Soviet regime. A particularity of Azerbaijan, where a tradition of understanding and cordiality between minority Sunnism and majority Shi'ism still prevails, is that the Sunnis in the country respect the Ashura ceremonies and the mourning during *muharram*. Russian and Soviet domination undoubtedly contributed to bringing the two schools closer to each other, with their leaders encouraging the faithful to make common cause against the oppression of the colonizer.[2] Under the communist regime, neither Shi'a nor Sunnis celebrated weddings or other ostentatious feasts during *muharram*; this is still the case today.

Since 1991, the rehabilitation of Islam and the closeness between religion and the new national ideology, which seeks to distance itself from its Soviet legacy, have both ensured that the observance of Ashura has become more widespread and especially more visible, as opposed to its former discreet or even clandestine nature. In Nardaran, a centre of militant Shi'ism which has often conflicted with the secular power since independence, the days of Ashura in March 2004, February 2005 and February 2006 attracted thousands of pilgrims who proceeded through the main arteries of the city to the mausoleum of Rahime Hanim at the crack of dawn; some even spent the night in this holy place.[3] After prostrating themselves before the saint's tomb, the crowd massed on the large esplanade between the mausoleum and the mosque. Loudspeakers at full volume broadcast Qur'anic recitations interspersed with the endlessly repeated stories of Husayn's martyrdom. In March 2004, the imam monopolizing the microphone, in spite of his accent, which left no doubt to his Iranian Azeri origin, made no comments demonstrating any hostility to the regime. In the centre of the esplanade, two rows had formed in different places, choreographing the spectacle in a way. In both groups, one of which was constituted by very young believers (between twelve and sixteen years of age), men were flagellating themselves with chains to

1. Adam, 2001.
2. Geyushov, 2004.
3. See *above*.

the rhythm of chants and cries. At times the demonstrators, caught in a trance of sorts, uttered words full of remorse for not having been able to rescue Husayn from assassination. Warlike slogans were shouted against Yazîd, the son of Mu'âwiya and Husayn's executioner, and his followers. In the periphery of this scene, small groups of women had gathered for the *mersiyye* rituals, singing funereal chants of extreme sadness. Among the crowd, some joined in the "chanting" while others beat their chests crying *"Shâh Husayn, Yâ Husayn!"* ("Lord Husayn, Ô Husayn!").

Another important place for Ashura commemorations is the courtyard of the Teze Pir mosque, seat of the Directorate of Spiritual Affairs, the symbol of official Islam. Here, more than around other places of commemoration, the streets adjacent to the mosque were pervaded by (often disabled or ill) beggars invoking the generosity of the faithful on this exceptional day. Failing alms, the beggars could at least benefit from the food and drink stands supplied by the faithful in memory of Husayn and his followers, who suffered thirst and hunger during their martyrdom. Compared with the public in Nardaran, the crowd in this central mosque was more random and varied. Women, children, working-class people and the rich all gathered here. However, contrary to what was seen in Nardaran, only grown-up men flagellated themselves, and in only two groups of five to six persons each. Children were kept away from these flagellations, which were in fact officially forbidden to all by the Directorate of Spiritual Affairs.

The marja'iyya

The second notion central to understanding the nature of Azerbaijani Shi'ism is the *marja'iyya*. In Azerbaijan, the institution of the *marja'iyya* is historically not very well known and has not been well established locally. Several causes lie at the root of this situation. First, as mentioned before, the Russian colonial presence between 1828 and the Bolshevik revolution, followed by the communist and atheist experience from the 1920s onwards, has more than elsewhere obstructed the penetration of the great Shi'a *marja'* and their ideas. During the Soviet period, communications between the Shi'a of Azerbaijan and the *mujtahids* of Qom and Najaf were almost completely interrupted. But the main reason for the lack of familiarity of Azerbaijani Shi'a with the reality of the *marja'iyya* is the fact that the concept was mostly developed in Iraq and Iran during the 1940s, a period when the Soviet regime was very restrictive. When one asks religious "professionals" in Azerbaijan today what the *marja'iyya* meant in their country during the Soviet period, they all answer that it has always existed and that from the 1970s and especially the 1980s onwards they had access to the theological works of Imam Khomeini. Without calling into question the good faith of our interlocutors, we think that few people had a well-defined idea of the principles of the *marja'iyya* during the Soviet period, in spite of the religious radio programs that were broadcast from Tabriz by the Islamic Republic of Iran starting in 1980. There is a widespread habit among religious professionals in the post-Soviet space at large that consists of stating that "we were here in the Soviet age too", indicating that they do not owe their faith and their Islamic knowledge to factors imported from abroad after the collapse of the Soviet Union. Yet it seems more probable that the notion of *marja'iyya* did not mean much in Azerbaijan until independence and that its spread through the country since then is not without connection to neighboring Iran.

Our field studies in all provinces of the country as well as the Azeri provinces of neighboring Georgia permit us to outline the balance of the influence of the *marja'* on Azerbaijan. Beginning at independence, when the opening of the border with Iran allowed students to go and study in Qom and Mashhad and believers to go on pilgrimages, the Iranian embassy's cultural activities caused several *mujtahids* to become well known in Azerbaijan. At present, the *risâla* and other essays on Islamic jurisdiction of most of the great *marja'* from across the Shi'a worlds are available in bookshops in Baku and the countryside. According to our observations in the main mosques, madrasas and Islamic bookshops of the country, it seems that the most widely read and followed are, in order of importance: Fazel Lankarâni, 'Ali Sistâni, Khamenei and Javâd Tabrizi. Khamenei benefits to a great extent from the support of the Iranian government. Sayyed 'Ali Akbar Ojaknejâd, manager of the very active Iranian cultural center is said to be Khamenei's *vakil* in Azerbaijan. Sistâni, who is the preferred *marja'* of the young students who have studied in Qom and Damascus, is appreciated for the accessibility of his teachings and the moderate nature of his ideas.[1] As for Fazel Lankarâni, a *marjaʿ* known in Iran for his radical ideas,[2] there are various reasons for his popularity. First, his presence in the *hozeh* of Qom puts him into direct contact with many Azeri students, for whom Qom is easier to reach than Najaf or Karbala. As a native of the Azerbaijani city of Lankaran and an ethnic Azeri, he moreover benefits from a goodwill among the Azerbaijanis that exceeds that of other *marjaʿ*.[3]

However, although they are now well known in Azerbaijan, the *marjaʿ* do not exercise a great deal of power and influence on the daily life of Muslims. Firstly, few Muslims in Azerbaijan frequent mosques and fewer still accept the pressures and prescripts of a *marjaʿ*. A recent study shows that few Azeris perform their daily prayers, although a greater number visits pilgrimage sites.[4] Besides, as we will see, governmental measures against foreign Islamic currents make it difficult for the *marjaʿ* to be very active in the country. For example, while all the *marjaʿ* named above have *daftar* (offices) in several Shiʿa regions of the world, none of them has obtained permission to open an official representation in Baku. When a *vakil* claims to represent a certain *marjaʿ*, he does so discreetly and unofficially. Lankarâni, to circumvent the Azerbaijani law which bans the official establishment of an office, opened a representation in Moscow, where an important expatriate community of Azeri Shiʿa lives. This difficulty of the *marjaʿ* to establish themselves in Azerbaijan is connected to state policies attempting to limit Iran's influence on the country.

---

1. Interview with a group of Azerbaijani students at the Hojjatiyeh school, Qom, April 2004.
2. Proof that Fazel Lankarâni is part of the "hard core" is that he is said to have approved *fatwas* legitimizing the assassination of opposition members, as well as the *fatwa* advocating the elimination of Salman Rushdie. See Buchta, 2000, p. 146–68.
3. Field studies in his home village of Erkivan have permitted us to measure to what extent he and his family are present in popular local consciousness.
4. See in this respect the very illuminating sociological study by Faradov, 2002.

The state's religious policies and their consequences for Azerbaijani Shi'ism

Like all ex-USSR states, Azerbaijan has made a *volte face* on religion, exhibiting tolerance and ensuring relative religious freedom from 1991 onwards, without abandoning all control over religious affairs. During the first ten years of independence this right of inspection was exercised in part by the Ministry of Justice, charged with the official registration of all new civil, political or religious organizations. But as under the communists, the new regime has mostly used the Directorate of Spiritual Affairs to ensure that religious developments in the country are in line with the policies of secularization and national independence pursued by the state. The highest official religious authority of the country, *sheikh al-islâm* Allahshukur Pachazade, who was already loyal to the Soviet regime, has shown the same enthusiastic loyalty to the post-Soviet regime. This relatively good understanding continues at present, although there has been a noticeable deterioration in relations between the state and the Directorate of Spiritual Affairs, to the extent that in 2001 the government created a new organ to control the religious sphere, namely the State Committee for the Coordination of Cooperation with Religious Organizations (*Dini Kurumlarla Ich Üzre Devlet Komiteti*), commonly known as the State Committee.

At present, it is still difficult to identify the motivations that drove the state to create a new body to control religious affairs, although it may be assumed that the main reason is found in the observation that the Directorate of Spiritual Affairs had became less efficient in its control of missionary activities originating from Iran. From its inception, the State Committee has displayed a particular fervor for the careful vetting of all foreign religious currents desiring to establish themselves in Azerbaijan. The committee, which is structured as a small ministry attached directly to the presidency, has as its credo the struggle against the missionary phenomenon, which "weakens the moral values" of the country. Since the committee was established, new religious organizations must be registered directly with the president's office, rather than with the Ministry of Justice.

In purely Shi'a matters, relations between the State Committee and Iran are extremely complex. It seems that the committee's main mission is to weaken the influence of Iran and of Shi'a leaders based in Iran on the reinvention of Azerbaijani Islam. As a tool of state control created to enforce the basic principles of the post-Soviet regime, the committee takes its cue in dealing with Iranian Shi'a currents from the state's relationship with Iran. In other words, the State Committee perceives Iranian religious currents as propaganda tools employed by the Islamic Republic, and feels that a Shi'a revival controlled by Iran poses a threat to the new Azerbaijani regime and its secular institutions. Since its creation the committee, headed by Rafig Aliyev, has been on bad terms with the Directorate of Spiritual Affairs, which displays a less critical attitude towards Iranian religious currents. Behind the suspicious attitude of the committee lies the Azerbaijani government's real fear of its neighbor, with which it has many disputes.

The first aspect to consider in explaining the tense relationship between the two countries is their shared historical legacy. Until 1828, both were part of the same empire. Moreover, Shâh Ismaïl, the founder of the Safavid dynasty that instituted Shi'ism as the official doctrine of the Safavid Empire (1501–1722), was himself an Azeri, as were most of the dynasties ruling Iran before the Pahlavis. It is interesting to note that after independence, as a part of its new ideological identity policies, the Republic of Azerbaijan erected a gigantic statue of Shâh Ismaïl on a wide avenue in Baku. One of the causes for the souring of relations between the two states is the fact that, for domestic and foreign policy reasons, they interpret their shared history and legacy in very different lights. In the north, it is feared that this legacy might arouse imperial aspirations in Iran, which in turn feels uncomfortable about a post-Soviet republic that might serve as a model for the twenty-five million ethnic Azeris living in Iran, with the possible emergence of secessionist tendencies as a result.

The latter question is indeed one of the crystallization points for the rivalry between both states. On both banks of the Aras, there is a fear that this important Azeri minority could be manipulated by the other side for foreign policy purposes. It is true that in Azerbaijan, the brothers to the south of the Aras are regarded with pride, notably in nationalist and pan-Turkist circles, and most pronouncedly during the first years of independence, when President Ebulfeyz Elçibey openly advocated the reunification of the ex-Soviet and Iranian Azerbaijans and made Tabriz the new capital. On the Iranian side, this Azeri community elicited great concern among the ruling elites, who witnessed the development of Azeri nationalism among youths and intellectuals and feared that Baku might become a model for them.[1] In reality, the question is much more complex and the political potential of Iranian Azeri nationalism is mystified and overestimated on both sides of the border.[2]

More fundamentally, tensions between both countries derive rather from the different cultural and ideological models they have chosen. Post-Soviet Azerbaijan has clearly opted for a rapprochement with the West, developing privileged partnerships with the United States and the Council of Europe, of which it became a member in 2001. Therefore, all influence from Iran, and especially religious influence, is perceived as a threat likely to cause this Western-type political development model to fail. This is the reason for the extremely strict – although in reality not very efficient – censorship applied to Islamic literature imported from Iran. In principle, the *risâla* of most *mujtahids* are banned in Azerbaijan, but this does not prevent them being sold in most Baku bookshops.

At the time of writing – June 2006 – relations between the two countries did not look set to improve in the short term, although Iranian president Mahmoud Ahmadinejad, engaged in an arm-wrestling match with the United States and the United Nations over his nuclear program, has been making multiple gestures of goodwill towards his northern neighbor in an effort to alleviate the country's diplomatic isolation.[3] Nonetheless, despite the government's professed neutrality, Baku seemed to lean more towards the American positions.

According to Rafig Aliyev, President of the State Committee for Religious Affairs, the authorities show a distinct preference for Turkey

---

1. Riaux, 2004
2. Field studies in February 2005 among Azeri nationalists in Tabriz and Erdebil show that they do not yet consider Baku as model to imitate, and are not very disposed to challenge the territorial integrity of Iran.
3. On the subject of Azerbaijan and the Iranian nuclear crisis, see the information provided by the Soros foundation www.eurasianet.org, specifically the articles by Rowshan Ismayilov: http://www.eurasianet.org/departments/insight/articles/eav050506a.shtml and Shahin Abbasov: http://www.eurasianet.org/deparments/insight/articles/eav041106b.shtml

over Iran in the matter of Islamic influences.[1] This honeymoon between Turkey and Azerbaijan has had consequences for the transformation of the religious landscape in the country. Thanks to privileged working conditions, Turkish religious currents are leaving a distinct mark on Azerbaijani Islam, spreading their Sunnism in the heart of the Shi'a community. A short analysis of these Turkish Sunni currents is therefore in order to better understand the current situation of Shi'ism in Azerbaijan.

The strong development of Turkish Sunnism in Shi'a Azerbaijan

The linguistic and cultural closeness that connects Turkey and Azerbaijan lies at the origin of the good relations between Ankara and Baku. Of all Turkic-speaking countries, these are the two states where Turkist currents have historically been strongest.[2] This Turkish solidarity has continued to bloom after independence. Romantic and chaotic until 1993, it became more rational when Heydar Aliyev, known for his pragmatism in foreign policy, came to power. Since October 2003, his son Ilham has continued the same policies. The linguistic closeness and even more the pro-Western commitment of both countries are the basic ingredients of their excellent relationship. In the regional political game, Turkey provides crucial support to Azerbaijan in its controversial relations with its other neighbors, notably Iran and Armenia.

Since the fall of the Eastern bloc, the *Diyanet* (the Directorate of Spiritual Affairs in Turkey), an official institution established to control and manage the religious sphere, has offered its services to all Muslim countries in the Balkans, the Caucasus and Central Asia.[3] We cannot here provide a detailed description of its activities, but we must nevertheless point out that the *Diyanet* has over the last fifteen years distributed abundant amounts of Islamic literature in all these states. It frequently

---

1. Discussions with Rafig Aliyev, President of the State Committee for Religious Affairs, Baku, April 2004 and February 2006.

2. Christopher, 1993, pp. 71–144.

3. The website of *Diyanet* provides some useful information on its cooperation with Muslim states of the ex-USSR: www.diyanet.gov.tr (consulted on 24/01/2007).

sends out cadres and civil servants who, through the Turkish embassies and their sections for religious cooperation, participate in spreading a Turkish brand of Sunnism. The most concrete – and undoubtedly the most efficient – activity it has deployed in Azerbaijan was the creation of a Turkish-financed faculty of theology in Baku in 1992, modeled on its counterpart at the University of Marmara in Istanbul. Although the constitutional document of the faculty stipulates that it must teach both Sunni and Shi'a schools, it is in fact Sunnism which is favored there.[1]

More efficient than the *Diyanet*'s activities are those of Turkish Islamic movements, which, in their turn, limit the impacts of Iranian Shi'a propaganda. Thus, the followers of Osman Nuri Topbach, one of the main *nakshibandi* leaders in Turkey, have created a foundation in Baku that plays a crucial role in establishing Turkish Sunnism in Azerbaijan. They organize Qur'anic recitation courses taught by personnel formed in Turkey. In the countryside, the foundation has founded madrasas in Sheki and Goychay as well as a faculty of theology in Zakatala. While these establishments are located in regions with a Sunni majority, children of Shi'a families study there too.

Two other Turkish movements, with a more "neo-Sufi" orientation, are known for their promotion of Sunnism in Azerbaijan. The first is the *Nurcu* movement, founded by Said Nursi (1876–1960) and developed in Turkey after his death by his numerous followers. Since the early 1990s, the decline of the USSR has allowed Nursi's heirs to reach the rest of the Turkic-speaking world. In Azerbaijan, the movement is well represented in the universities, where many Turkish students come to study. Additionally, many small Turkish companies established in Azerbaijan distribute Nursi's writings, especially his *Risale i Nur*, a Qur'anic exegesis that is widely available all over the territory of the former Soviet Union. The movement was imported into the country by Turkish expatriates who organized reading circles to discuss the *Risale i Nur*, and now boasts many Azerbaijani adherents, notably among the young.

Said Nursi in turn exercised a major influence on Fethullah Gülen, born in 1938 and currently in voluntary exile in the United States,

---

1. Discussions with teachers and students at this faculty of theology, Baku, June 2004 and March 2006.

who is without any doubt the most widely followed Turkish religious leader in the entire Turkic-speaking world.[1] His movement does not, however, present itself as a religious organization. His adherents, largely businessmen, teachers and students, have set up a large network of private schools that, while promoting a secular and modern education, spread the form of Islam advocated by Fethullah Gülen – a moderate Sunnism, marked by Turkish culture and entertaining good relations with local authorities. The movement's schools and companies, disseminated all over the country, form an ill-defined and discreet network. The good results of students graduating from these schools have provided the movement with respectability and support from the official authorities, who appreciate the educational services rendered by the Turks, who are nonetheless effectively Turkish Sunni missionaries in a majority Shi'a country.

Both the *Diyanet* and the private Turkish movements concentrate their religious activities mostly in the Sunni regions, notably in the north of the country where Shi'ism is not very widespread. But their preference for Sunni regions does not mean that they are entirely absent from Shi'a regions. They are notably present in the Baku agglomeration, where the Turkish religious presence is very strong. As a consequence of the anti-religious propaganda of the communist regime, by the end of the Soviet era many Azerbaijanis were unable to differentiate between Sunnism and Shi'ism. Azerbaijan is moreover known as a grey zone, where the differences between Sunnism and Shi'ism are at their most vague and imprecise. This situation was put to good use by the Turks who, supported by their country's positive image, used their activities to partly convert the Shi'a to Sunnism.

Conclusion

Shi'ism has been established in Azerbaijan since the sixteenth century and during much of its historical development there enjoyed a dominant position, which became relative during the Russian domination (1828–1918) and more isolated during the Soviet era (1920–90). During the latter

---

1.   On the movement's activities in all Turkic-speaking spheres of the ex-USSR, see Balci, 2003.

period, links between local Shi'ism and the intellectual centers of Iran were considerably weakened. By reopening the borders with Iran, independence established new religious bridges over the Aras, thus allowing various Iranian Shi'a currents to obtain a foothold in Azerbaijan.

However, while the influence of Iranian Shi'ism on Azerbaijan has shown a spectacular development in the beginning of the 1990s, it should not be exaggerated. During the first five years of independence, many Iranian missionaries did come to preach in Azerbaijan, but their influence has rapidly diminished for a multitude of reasons, not least of which is the secularist nature of Azerbaijani society. The long Russian and Soviet domination of the country has indeed secularized major parts of society, which complicated attempts of external Islamic currents to firmly establish themselves in Azerbaijan. Moreover, the competition of Turkish Sunni currents has also limited the impact of Iranian religious propaganda. But the main conclusion to be drawn from the development of religious relations between Iran and Azerbaijan is that Iran's image on the international stage, the nature of its activism and the political choices made by the authorities in Baku all conspire to favor the formation of an Azerbaijani Shi'ism that is very distinct from its Iranian counterpart. In other words, despite its leading position in the Shi'a world, Iran contributes – involuntarily, so to speak – to the integration of Azerbaijani Shi'ism into its own country, as it contributes likewise to the integration of the Shi'a in other countries where they are present in great numbers.

Bibliography

Abbasov, A., "Islam v Sovremennom Azerbaijane : Obrazhi I Realii", in Furman, D.E. , ed., *Azerbaijan I Rossia: Obshhestva I Gosudarstva,* Moscow 2001, Sakharov Foundation. http://www.sakharovcenter.ru/azrus/az_009.htm

Adam, Volker, "Why do They Cry ? Criticisms of Muharram Celebrations in Tsarist and Socialist Azerbaijan" in Brunner, R. and Ende (ed.), *The Twelver Shia in Modern Times. Religious Culture and Political History,* Leiden/Boston/Köln 2001, Brill, pp. 114–134.

Adams, Lawrence E. "The Reemergence of Islam in the Transcaucasus", *Religion, State & Society,* 24/2–3, 1996, pp. 221–31.

Algar, Hamid, *Wahhabism: a Critical Essay,* New York 2002, Islamic Publications Int.

Altstadt, Audrey, *The Azerbaijani Turks: Power and Identity under Russian Rule*, Stanford University 1992, Hoover Institution Press.

Babadjanov, B., and Kamilov, M., "Muhammadjan Hindustani (1892–1989) and the Beginning of the 'Great Schism' Among the Muslims of Uzbekistan", in Dudoignon, S., and Komatsu, H., eds., *Islam in Politics in Russia and Central Asia (Early Eighteenth to Late Twentieth Centuries)*, London, New York, Bahrain 2001, Kegan Paul, pp. 195–219.

Balci, Bayram, *Missionnaires de l'Islam en Asie centrale, les écoles turques de Fethullah Gülen*, Paris 2003, Maisonneuve et Larose.

Bastian, Jean-Pierre, Champion, Françoise, and Rousselet, Kathy, eds., *La globalisation du religieux*, Paris 2001, l'Harmattan.

Bennigsen, A., and Lemercier-Quelquejay, C., *Les musulmans oubliés. L'islam en Union Soviétique*, Paris 1981, Maspero.

Brower, Daniel, *Turkistan and the Fate of the Russian Empire*, London/New York 2003, Routledge Curzon.

Buchta, Wilfried, *Who Rules Iran? The Structure of Power in the Islamic Republic,* Washington 2000, Washington Institute for Near East Policy-Konrad Adenauer Stiftung.

Christopher, W., *The Turks of Central Asia*, London 1993, Praeger Publishers.

Constant, Antoine, *L'Azerbaïdjan*, Paris 2002, Karthala.

Faradov, Tair, "Religiosity in Post-Soviet Azerbaijan: A Sociological Survey", *ISIM Newsletter*, September 2001, p. 28.

Faradov, Tair, "Religiosity and Civic Culture in Post Soviet Azerbaijan: A Sociological Perspective", in A.B. Sajoo ed., *Civil Society in the Muslim World, Contemporary Perspectives*, London 2002, I. B. Tauris, pp. 194–213.

Geyushov, A., "Azerbaycanda Sovet Hakimiyyetinin Islam Münasibetde Yeritdiyi Dövlet Siyaseti" (Soviet politics towards Islam in Azerbaijan), in *Qütb* +, Bakou n° 1, 2004, p. 10.

Halbach, Uwe, "L'islam dans le Caucase du Nord", in *Archives de sciences sociales des religions*, 115, July-September 2001, pp. 93–110.

Halm, Heinz, *Shi'ism,* New York 2004, Columbia University Press.

Hasanov, R. M., "Islam v Obshhestvenno-Politicheskoi Zhizni Azerbaijana", *Socis,* vol. 1, Spring 2003. http://2001.isras.ru/SocIs/SocIsArticles/2003_03/GasanovRM.doc

Henze, Paul, *Islam in the North Caucasus: The Example of Chechnya*, Santa Monica 1995, Rand.

Keller, Ssoshana, *To Moscow, Not Mecca: The Soviet Campaign against Islam in Central Asia, 1917–1941*, Westport, CN/ London 2001, Praeger Publishers.

Kuru, Ahmet, "Globalization and Diversification of Islamic Movements: Three Turkish Cases", *Political Science Quarterly*, 120/2, 2005, pp. 253–74.

Mardin, Serif, *Religion and Social Change in Modern Turkey, the Case of Bediüzzaman Saïd Nursi*, New York 1989, University of New York Press.

Martin, R. C., "Conversion to Islam by Invitation, Proselytism and the Nego-ciation of Identity in Islam", in Witte, J., and Martin, R. C., eds., *Sharing the Book, Religious Perspectives on the Rights and Wrongs of Proselytism*, New York 1999, Orbis Books, pp. 95–117.

Mervin, Sabrina, "La quête de savoir à Najaf. Les études religieuses chez les chi'ites imâmites de la fin du XIXe siècle à 1960", in *Studica Islamica*, 81, June 1995, pp. 165–85.

Motika, Raoul, "Islam in Post-Soviet Azerbaijan", in *Archives de sciences sociales des religions*, 115, Summer 2001, pp. 111–24.

Ro'i, Yaacoy, *Islam in the Soviet Union, From the Second World War to Perestroika*, New York 2000, Columbia University Press.

Riaux, G., *Le nationalisme azéri en Iran*, unpublished Memoir for a DEA of Geopolitics, University Paris 8, 2004.

Shaffer, Brenda, *Borders and Brethren, Iran and the Challenge of the Azerbaijani Identity*, Cambridge, Mass. 2002, MIT Press.

Suny, Ronad G., ed., *Transcaucasia, Nationalism and Social Change: Essays in the History of Armenia, Azerbaijan and Georgia*, Ann Arbor 1996, The University of Michigan Press.

Swietochowski, Tadeusz, "Azerbaijan: The Hidden Faces of Islam", in *World Policy Journal*, 19/3, 2002, p. 69.

Swietochowski, Tadeusz *Russian Azerbaijan 1905–1920*, Cambridge 2004, Cambridge University Press.

Tohidi, Nayereh, "The Global-Local Intersection of Feminism in Muslim Soci-eties: The Cases of Iran and Azerbaijan", in *Social Research*, 69/3, 2002, pp. 853–4.

Valiyev, Anar, "The Rise of Salafi Islam in Azerbaijan", in *Terrorism Monitor*, 3/13, July 1, 2005, p. 6. http:// www.jamestown.org

Valiyev, Anar, "Azerbaijan, Islam in a Post-Soviet Republic", in *Middle East Review of International Affairs*, 9/4, December 2005. http://meria.idc.ac.il/journal

Yarlykapov, Ahmet, "Islamic Fundamentalism in the Northern Caucasus: Towards a Formulation of the Problem", in *Caucasian, Regional Studies*, 4/1, 1999. http://poli.vub.ac.be/publi/crs/eng/0401-02.html.

Yavuz, Hakan, "Search for a New Social Contract in Turkey: Fethullah Guelen, the Virtue Party and the Kurds", *SAIS Review*, 19/1, winter-spring 1999, pp. 114–43.

Yunus, A., *Azerbaycada Islam* (Islam in Azerbaijan), Baki 2005.

Main Internet sites
The website of Haji Ilgar Ibrahimoglu's Islamic Association for the Protection of Human Rights: http://www.humanrights-az.org

A publication of Haji Ilgar's community: www.deyerler.org

Among many sites dedicated to Said Nursi and his ideas, see: www.bediuzza-mansaidnursi.net as well as www.nur.org (in English) and www.nursistudies.org (multilingual).

On the *nakshibandi* movement of Osman Nuri Topbach, heir of Aziz Mahmut Hudayi, see: www.hudayivakfi.org

On the followers of Süleyman Hilmi Tunahan, see: www.beyan.com.tr and www.tunahan.org

The Directorate of Religious Affairs in Turkey (*Diyanet*): www.diyanet.gov.tr

General information on Islam in Azerbaijan: http://azerislam.com

The official website sponsored by the State Committee for Religious Affairs: http://www.islam-az.net/az

BORIS PÉTRIC

The Ironis in post-Soviet Uzbekistan: the Virtues of Mental Dissimulation (*taqiyya*) in a Context of Sunnitization

The collapse of the USSR more than a decade ago abruptly reminded the world of the wide and diverse range of population groups that made up the world's largest country. By withdrawing from Muslim Central Asia,[1] Moscow forced the elites of the five new states thus created[2] (paradoxically all leaders who originated in the former political system) to develop a political discourse to legitimize their newly found independence. When the First Secretary of the Communist Party, Islam Abdouganievich Karimov, became president of Uzbekistan,[3] he rapidly developed a national discourse that drew heavily on Sunnism. Within this newly imagined national identity, the recurrent evocation of the cities of Samarkand and Bukhara recalled Central Asia's contribution to the history of Islamic thought, notably through the constitution of the Hanafi law school. This discourse provides Sunni Islam with a new legitimacy in the political arena and in a society where Muslims coexist with non-Muslims

---

1. The Belovezha Accords signed by Russian president Yeltsin and his Byelorussian and Ukrainian counterparts put an end to the USSR, and Russia *de facto* abandoned the republics of Central Asia and the Soviet Caucasus.
2. "Soviet Central Asia" usually designates Kazakhstan, Kyrgyzstan, Uzbekistan, Tajikistan and Turkmenistan.
3. Uzbekistan has over 25 million inhabitants, the majority of whom are Sunnis.

(Christians, Jews, etc.) as well as non-Sunni Muslim groups such as the Ironi and Azeri communities, who are Shi'a. The current political situation is complex because religion in general and Islam especially are (re-) forged into essential identity markers – elements of social affirmation in the new Uzbek nation state. Yet the authorities simultaneously pursue a policy of repression against any movement aiming to politicize Islam. This new configuration of Sunnitization and Uzbekization forces the Ironi population, intimately associated with Shi'ism, to renegotiate its position in society. What is the attitude of the state and its institutions *vis-à-vis* this group? Which strategies do the Shi'a Ironis deploy to adapt to the new political context? Has the region's opening up after the collapse of USSR enabled the Ironis to renew contacts with the traditionally Shi'a regions of Iran or neighboring Turkmenistan and Azerbaijan? Can we observe the formation of a new relationship to ~~Iranian~~ society and the appearance of new religious, commercial and other networks?

A short history of Shi'ism in Uzbekistan

While Uzbek society is today considered to be mainly Sunni, there are nonetheless a variety of groups with ties to Shi'ism living on Uzbek territory. Moreover, the Shi'a of Uzbekistan do not constitute a single community, as there are no institutions capable of uniting them. Besides, the religious element in itself is not sufficient to create a shared sense of belonging. Lastly, although religion has taken on a new importance in political discourse, the construction of social differentiation in Uzbek society is achieved on the basis of other criteria, linked to the Soviet legacy. The different groups that made up the society of Soviet Uzbekistan were differentiated first and foremost via ethnic or national categories. Some of these can be associated to Shi'ism (the Ironis, the Persiyons, the Azeris and the Ismailis). However, while there is an important Azeri population,[1] which implanted itself in Uzbekistan's urban mesh after

---

1. A large part of this population has left Uzbekistan for the Russian Federation and Azerbaijan since independence. The Azeri population is officially set at 60,000.

World War II, as well as some Ismailis[1] and other small groups,[2] here we will study Shi'ism in Uzbekistan by taking a look at the current situation of a population that has been established in the region for several centuries: the Ironis.[3] The Ironis adhere to Imamite or Twelver Shi'ism, and have the specific peculiarity of having been cut off for decades from their Iranian source of reference.

The ethnonym "Ironi"

The ethnonym "Ironi" is an ethnic category used in Russian and later Soviet statistics to indicate the various Shi'a population groups who, in the course of the eighteenth and nineteenth centuries, migrated in important numbers from the north of Iran to the Emirate of Bukhara.[4] These population groups settled principally in the urbanized oases of Samarkand and Bukhara. The unclear beginnings of this migration are situated in a period of intense commercial and cultural relations between the various political spaces of the region. The first migrants, who settled in Turan,[5] were of various origins: traders and craftsmen from the region of Khorasan; and captives sold on the slave market originating from northeastern Iran and Azerbaijan or from Merv – currently Mary in Turkmenistan – another city that has played an instrumental role in Islamic history.

The colonial Russian administration chose to gather these different population groups under the same statistical category of "Ironis" when they took a census of Turkestan in 1897. The term refers to the memory of an original migration and to Shi'ism as a common identifying factor, but it groups populations from various regions who speak different languages. It is therefore a standardizing term imposed by the tsarist and later the Soviet administration, which hides diverse identities. This is

---

1. A few hundred Ismaili families live in Uzbekistan. A larger Ismaili community exists in Tajikistan.
2. We cannot cite them all here, but they include the Persiyons and some Kurdish groups.
3. Liuskevic, 1997.
4. The presence of Shi'a population groups and places of worship, however, predates this large migration.
5. In contrast to Iran, they were "the country of the Turks", the name used by Iranians when speaking about the Khanates of Khiva and Kokand and the Emirate of Bukhara.

evident even today in the continuing linguistic difference between the Ironis of Samarkand and those of Bukhara. Although most Ironis are bilingual or even trilingual, the Samarkandi mother tongue is a Turkic language,[1] while Bukharis are Tajik speakers. The denomination "Ironi" is therefore a social stigmatization rather than an identity affirmation of the groups' own making.

The Shi'a in the Uzbek khanates

Since the sixteenth century, when Shi'ism was closely associated with the political order of the Safavid dynasty who made it their official religion, the political spaces in Central Asia[2] self-defined by contrasting themselves with Iran. Since that time, Islam has also been a factor legitimizing authority in the Emirate of Bukhara, although this refers exclusively to the Sunni Islam adopted by the ancient Turkic tribes (*Turk*) who had conquered political power in the Özbek Khanates.[3] Important exchanges between these two spaces, however, continued and many Shi'a lived in the cities of Bukhara and Samarkand, a fact which has been attested by a Soviet Orientalist who studied the toponymy of places, neighborhood communities (*mahalla*) and mosques.[4]

The Emirate of Bukhara was thus made up of a very diverse population in terms of religion and identity. Özbek political power derived from the reference to an initial conquest and was connected to descendants from the great Mongolian conqueror Genghis Khan. The initially sedentary native population was predominantly Persian speaking, and retained a Sunni Islamic culture. Persian remained the language used at the court of Bukhara until the end of the nineteenth century. These were the two basic principles sustaining the social contract that allied the sovereign to a population of nomadic origin and a sedentary population. The Özbek

---

1. Which they call "Ironshi", the "language of the Ironis", and which is said to be different from Uzbek. On the other hand, Bukharis say they speak "Farsiyon" or Tajik. The great majority of them also speak Russian.
2. The Khanate of Khiva, the Emirate of Bukhara, and later the Khanate of Kokand.
3. The term "Özbek" refers to the dynasty that derives its political legitimacy from tribal genealogical references. The term "Uzbek" refers to the construction of nationality in the Soviet era.
4. Suhareva, 1976.

tribes thus essentially held political and military positions, while the *tat*[1] population occupied both political and religious posts. Other population groups within the emirate lived outside this social contract: captives, Jews, Hindus and others, including the Ironis. This social equilibrium was called into question when change began to affect Bukhari society, with the emergence of trade, the affirmation of a Turkish-speaking clergy and the attempts at autonomy of the Beks, who challenged the existing order.[2]

At the beginning of the twentieth century, a time of social unrest, the emir called on a population group excluded from this initial social contract to administer the emirate. To counter the erosion of his power, he appointed a large number of Ironis in his administration. In 1905, while the emirate was navigating its way through a political crisis, the emir nominated a new prime minister of Shi'a origin. The latter in his turn appointed a significant number of Shi'a in administrative functions. In 1910, the crisis deteriorated and the population rose up, not against the government as such, but against the Shi'a population that at that specific moment represented the emir's administration. A social crisis was thus transformed into an ethnic conflict in which many Shi'a were killed.

This episode in the history of Bukhara has not left any significant traces in the contemporary collective memory of the Ironi population, but it clearly shows that political participation by the Shi'a population was not considered legitimate in the existing system.

The establishment of Soviet power: the principle of "autochthonization"

The establishment of a Russian protectorate and the birth of a modernist reformist movement, Jadidism,[3] at the beginning of the twentieth century again put into question the principles underpinning the political system. Some of the Jadidists were fellow travelers of the Soviet power, which they saw as an instrument to abolish the emir's despotism. Next, since religion in general and the different Islamic currents in particular did not have access to the public space under the Soviet system, Islam sustained itself

---

1. Ethnonym used to indicate the Tajik population as opposed to the *Turks*.
2. Carrère d'Encausse, 1981.
3. Cf. Dudoignon, 1997.

in a so-called "parallel" or "traditional"[1] form so as to ensure the continuation of the rites of passage (male circumcisions, marriages, funerals, etc.), while the new power first and foremost promoted national affirmation as a social identity marker.

The influence of the scientific state: national categories, census and statistics

The establishment of Soviet power considerably changed the sources of political legitimacy. In the new Republic of Uzbekistan everyone was a Soviet citizen and the issues of social integration and access to power and the state were redefined. The new political system offered a very different interpretation of the sociological reality of this space, in a context of massive immigration of European population groups. The Soviet political system was structured around a new categorization of population groups and spaces as nationalities[2] and national republics. Soon, it became obligatory for a census[3] to show that a majority of Uzbeks populated Uzbekistan. The choice of the "Uzbek" national category was part of a policy of Uzbekization. "Uzbek" was an all-encompassing category and many small identity groups declared themselves – or were forced to declare themselves – Uzbek. Many Ironis, out of concern for their social integration, thus preferred to officially renounce their specific identity.

From this point onwards, administrative and statistical science played a considerable role in conferring sociological reality on the new administrative entities. While the census of the Tsarist administration had lent a very cosmopolitan face to the territory now called Uzbekistan, the first Soviet census constituted a formidable "scientific" weapon in presenting this republic as the main home of the Uzbek nationality. The new Soviet historians, in a parallel operation, applied themselves to describing the birth of the Uzbek nation. As promoters of Uzbek ethnogenesis, they considered the Uzbek nation to be the result of the evolutionary process of a small ethnic group eventually leading to the birth of a nation. They based their vision on a genealogical study of the different Turkic groups

---

1. Bennigsen, 1956. For a nuanced reappraisal of Bennigsen's model, see the article by B. Balci on Azerbaijan in this volume.
2. Bennigsen, 1960.
3. Rahimov, 1991.

which formed the skeleton of the Uzbek nation.[1] From this perspective, a number of population groups, the Ironis among them, were left out of the new vision of the nation's history. Other forms of belonging – such as *narodnost*,[2] which indicated membership of a group that did not have its own political space inside the Soviet Union – were recognized by the Soviet administrative apparatus. Ironis continued to be mentioned in statistics and official documents,[3] but their number diminished considerably over the course of several censuses. Indeed, the new social norm in matters of nationality led many Ironis to declare themselves Uzbeks, since membership of a nationality conferred huge advantages for social integration – access to work, education and political power.[4]

Nevertheless, we should not conclude from the aforementioned that the Ironis were particularly victimized by this identity policy. On the contrary, the "Uzbek" national category was an inclusive instrument for small groups, because it united them in an autochthonous national constellation which was distinguished from the European population groups. This policy of nationalities moreover contributed to an autochthonization of political power: power to the Uzbeks in Uzbekistan. The new "otherness" was formed specifically on the basis of autochthonous origins, and by declaring themselves Uzbeks, the Ironis could thus participate in power through the policy of *korenizatsia* (indigenization of the elites), contrary to the old system of the emirate. In this scheme, many Ironis (officially classified as Uzbeks) had access to political power or to the administration. From a cultural point of view, the power favored Russification and Uzbekization to the detriment of the Tajik language, although this was the majority language in Samarkand and Bukhara.[5]

The Ironis now experienced a certain degree of social ascent, incarnated by a leading politician in the 1980s, Ismaïl Djurabekov.[6] He was a central

---

1. Jakubovski, 194.7
2. This terminology refers to the concept of minority.
3. It is necessary to specify that the Soviet system made a distinction between (Soviet) citizenship and (Uzbek or other) nationality. Every citizen had a passport which mentioned his or her national membership.
4. Cf. Bennigsen, 1986.
5. It is indeed necessary to add that Samarkand and Bukhara have for a long time been Tajik-speaking cities and remain so today.
6. Djurabekov, former deputy prime minister, is a close adviser to President

figure in the power set up after perestroika and remains so today. Born in Samarkand, he was at the origin of the ascent, during the 1980s, of Islam Karimov, a young *apparatchik* who would end up as the First Secretary of the Uzbek Communist Party. Djurabekov is said to have family ties to President Karimov, who himself, or so goes the rumor, was born to an Ironi mother.[1] Popular opinion is that the president is an Ironi.[2]

Distortion between identity norms and practice: the underground expression of the Ironis' Shi'a identity

None of this means that the Ironis are very visible in the public space: it takes some familiarity with the society to discover their importance. In his book *The Sufi and the Commissioner*, Bennigsen wrote of the Ironis that they were "in the process of losing their specific Shi'a character and blending into the Sunni community." Indeed, if the Soviet census of 1989 is to be believed, there were practically no Ironis left by then.[3] Yet these official figures do not mean, as the great French expert believed, that the Shi'a Ironis had lost all their particularity and been assimilated. In spite of this apparent national homogeneity, the Soviet state has not been able to eliminate the diversity of identities. The system rapidly became affected by a distortion between the affirmation of a social norm and social realities.

Thus, while all religions were combated in Uzbekistan, the intensity of this operation varied in different periods.[4] When the frontal attacks on religion and the elimination of part of the elite in the purges of 1937 failed to root out religious practices, notably in the case of the Shi'a,[5] Stalin set up a different management system for religions in 1943. From 1941 onwards, the state took charge of religious affairs. Islam was institutionalized by means of the "Directorates of Spiritual Affairs of the Muslims"

Karimov.

1. Cf. Trofimov, 2001.
2. Abasin, 1999.
3. Cf. R. Caratini, 1990.
4. Peyrouse, 2003.
5. According to Bakinskij Rabocij, in "Là où les athéistes ont déposé les armes: la faiblesse de la propagande anti-musulmane dans le district de Kedabek et la participation des jeunes à la fête chiite de *muharram* ", 12 December 1958, a publication mentioned in Quelquejay, 1960.

(Nizarat),[1] organized on a geographical basis, with an affiliate in Tashkent covering the five Republics of Soviet Central Asia. The Directorate of Baku (Azerbaijan), which was also responsible for the Muslims in the Transcaucasus, was the only one to have a mixed competence (Sunnism and Shi'ism). The Directorate of Baku published works destined for all Shi'a in the USSR, some copies of which can still be found today in the library of the Shi'a mosque of Bukhara. However, contacts were very difficult during this period and the Shi'a of Uzbekistan organized their worship locally – although the mosques remained closed until 1986.

The Shi'a of Bukhara indirectly benefited from the presence of the only training institute for Muslim religious personnel in the Soviet space, the madrasa of Mir Arab. It seems that an Ironi notable, Ibrahim Kasimov, born in Mashhad in 1911, with no official function in this religious institution, regularly taught there. Very unofficially – since Shi'ism was not supposed to be taught at the madrasa – he thus managed to train Shi'a mullahs. The most distinguished of his students, Allahshukur Humatogli Pachazade (*sheikh al-islâm*), currently heads the Spiritual Directorate of Azerbaijan. Kasimov also contributed to the survival of Shi'a religious practices in Bukhara. Ibrahim Kasimov thus held an official position in the Soviet apparatus[2] while also being active in the religious domain. It is hardly possible to speak about an underground Islam, as his activities were widely known, but he did have to adopt a very discreet attitude. At the time of perestroika and the re-entry of religion into the public space, Ibrahim Kasimov imposed himself as the leader of Bukhara's Shi'a community and reopened the city's Shi'a mosque.

Religion did not constitute a central reference in the Soviet public space and the Ironi population was considered first and foremost as autochthonous. Ironis did not perceive themselves as a minority, and actively participated in power and in the activities of society as a whole. They were in a process of Uzbekization in an era when the distinction between Shi'a and Sunnis was less important than that between autochthonous and foreign (notably as a differentiation from the Russian population). They could therefore deploy a complex strategy which allowed them to

---

1. Indicated by the Russian acronym SADUM.
2. He was an accountant in a large construction society.

live their Ironi specificity while declaring themselves Uzbeks. They could easily practice mental dissimulation *(taqiyya)* in a social context hostile to any form of religion. The Shi'a *Nizarat* of Baku had little influence on the social life of the Shi'a in Uzbekistan, and the Ironi communities of Bukhara and Samarkand organized their daily worship locally in a context of international isolation.

In Soviet Uzbek society, social integration depended on membership of a regional faction. This form of spatial identity which structured the domestic playing field of the Republic of Uzbekistan was not based on religious or ethnic considerations. The majority of the Shi'a in Bukhara and Samarkand participated in social life as members of the regional *sambouh*[1] faction, which held power from the 1960s until the 1980s. Sharaf Rashidov,[2] a Samarkandi and First Secretary of the Uzbek Communist Party, greatly contributed to the integration of Ironis in the Soviet socio-political system. Come independence, the Ironis were also in a position of power *via* the reign of Karimov, himself a *sambouh*.

The Ironis in post-Soviet Uzbekistan

During the Soviet period, this urban population moved deeper into the Soviet Republic of Uzbekistan, so that today Ironis are found in the urban centers of Djizzakh, Guijduvan, Namangan, Marguilan and of course in the capital Tashkent,[3] although the two main Ironi communities are still Samarkand and Bukhara. Today, in Bukhara, this population group does not necessarily use the term "Ironi",[4] preferring "Djigari",[5] which means "the liver", "Ironi" rather being a name which others use to indicate them. The Ironis of Uzbekistan share a common sense of being Shi'a, although

1. *Sambouh* is formed from the first syllables of Samarkand and Bukhara, and indicates the regional faction which unites the administrative regions of Samarkand, Navoi and Bukhara.
2. Cf. Carlisle, 1986.
3. Note that Ironis have also emigrated – and still emigrate – to Moscow and St. Petersburg.
4. This article is based on ethnographic research done principally in Bukhara (1996–9).
5. The liver is a central organ in the representation of the body in the regional culture, comparable to the heart in European cultures.

they experience the new political situation in different ways. Beyond this religious difference, the population does not use phenotypical criteria[1] or physical appearances to distinguish Ironis from other local groups. Consequently, the distinction can be made only in a context of mutual knowledge. This example illustrates the difficulty, if not impossibility, of listing ethnic differences. A Russian ethnologist remarks: "According to the last census of 1989, the official figure for Persians (*Ironis*) officially registered in Uzbekistan is some 28,000."[2] But according to estimates by the same author, they would number 100,000 in Samarkand, and between 70,000 and 80,000 in Bukhara, which leads him to write that: "it is possible to estimate that there are about 200,000 to 250,000 Persians in the Republic."[3] Any objective count seems very difficult, considering the impossibility of establishing a simple classification. The Ironi identity cannot be reduced to its religious dimension.

The linguistic marker: Tajik speakers and Uzbek speakers

The linguistic difference[4] between the Ironis of Samarkand and those of Bukhara is important because it partly changes their relationship to the current process of Uzbekization and de-Russification. The Ironis of Samarkand speak Uzbek and therefore do not experience the difficulties confronting Tajik speakers. They consequently perceive the new political situation in a rather positive light. They feel close to the Uzbeks and want to differentiate themselves from the Tajik speakers in the population. The Bukhari Ironis, on the contrary, speak Tajik and therefore feel closer to Tajiks. They currently perceive themselves as penalized or even marginalized by the affirmation of the Uzbek language. This feeling is reinforced by the migration of a rural population of Uzbek speakers to Bukhara and Samarkand, where they have entered into social competition with the Tajik speakers. This phenomenon creates tensions in the urban societies.

---

1. Max Weber uses this notion to indicate clothes, hats, jewelry and other items used by some population groups to distinguish themselves from others. In the case of the Ironis, nothing permits to distinguish them from Tajiks or Uzbeks.
2. See Abasin, 1999.
3. Ibid.
4. Trofimov, 2001.

The new arrivals neatly fit into the newly imagined nationality and experience some social ascent. Thus, to the great displeasure of the local Ironis, the municipality chose a retired Uzbek teacher recently arrived from his village to service a predominantly Ironi neighborhood community.

The Ironis and the Tajik speakers of Bukhara thus experience the establishment of the new political order as a potential social marginalization in the making. Zamir, a young Bukhari student, states: "I decided to leave for Moscow, because it is going to become more and more difficult for us here. I do not speak Uzbek and people don't see me as an Uzbek." Depending on the circumstances, the linguistic marker can thus function to the benefit or the detriment of the Ironis.

The increasing importance of the religious marker

In the context of a developing Uzbek nation state, the issue of membership in society is redefined. The Uzbekization process that began in the Soviet era received new impetus after independence. It translates into a nationalist political discourse that defines new norms, which in turn have consequences for the social integration and political participation of population groups excluded from this definition of Uzbek identity. The religious marker thus becomes more relevant in social life.

Despite the differences between the Ironis of Bukhara and Samarkand, their Shi'a identity constitutes the fundamental marker differentiating both of them from the other autochthonous population groups, the Tajiks and Uzbeks, who are Sunnis. The identity markers of the Shi'a population groups are not very visible and identity is therefore negotiated in function of the context and the social situation. It is not unusual for Ironis to modify their identity depending on their interlocutor. Timur, a young Bukhari Ironi student at the diplomatic university, explains:

> I only became aware that I was different when I came to study in Tashkent. One day, I prayed with an Uzbek student and he told me that I had a different way of praying because I held my arms at my side during prayer, while he crossed them [...]. I also thought everybody in Uzbekistan celebrated Ashura [...] In fact, it is only recently that I realized we are Shi'a while the majority of the Uzbeks are Sunnis [...] In any case, in Tashkent the students knew that I was

from Bukhara, that was the important thing, and we Bukharis are not very good at Uzbek.

The importance placed on religion and language in the construction of the new political order tends to change the status of population groups such as the Ironis. As Sunni Islam becomes an unavoidable reference, the social situation of the Ironis becomes complicated, although they enjoy a relatively privileged position.

The Ironis are well integrated in the current social system and are generally part of the "local middle classes". Their participation in power is explained by their membership of the Samarkand faction, to which Islam Karimov, the current president, also belongs. It is not their specific identity as such that plays a role in this type of political alignment; rather it is their membership in a regional faction that determines political solidarity.

Marital and educational strategies

At the local level, we can observe a certain degree of ethnicization of social relationships. Nevertheless, marital alliances allow the development of a complex crucible of identities. The study of marital alliances[1] reveals a complex strategy: Ironi families from Bukhara forge alliances with each other or with Ironi families from Samarkand or Mary (in Turkmenistan), but also with locally well-established Uzbek families. Through both accepting and offering women, Ironi families ensure their collective membership in many groups. Although marital choices can contribute to maintaining a Shi'a identity, they also have a major effect in terms of expanding their solidarity networks beyond ethnic and religious considerations, thus ensuring better social integration. There is no religious endogamy between the Shi'a and the Sunnis.

As a part of the same strategy, many Bukhari Ironi families who used to send their children to Russian schools[2] in the Soviet era now decide to send them to Uzbek schools. Farida explains:

---

1. Cf. Pétric, 2002.
2. In the Soviet era, children could be sent to Russian, Tajik and Uzbek schools. The Soviet elite, whatever its national identity, always sent its children to Russian schools.

> My elder children went to a Russian school, because at the time it was important to know the Russian language, but we decided to send the youngest to an Uzbek school because in the future it will be very important for him to speak Uzbek [...] We will teach him Tajik and Russian at home.

Identities are renegotiated as a function of the social context. The reorientation of marital and educational strategies allows the Ironis to soften the effect of some social markers. The simultaneous affirmation of one's Uzbek and Ironi identities is not necessarily perceived as a contradiction. Nevertheless, the increasing importance of the religious marker reduces this willingness to blend in with the new social norm and creates a paradoxical situation, since the increasing visibility of religious practice tends to distinguish the Ironis more.

A renewed religious practice

Today, the acceleration of the Uzbekization process inevitably leads to the Sunnitization of the national identity. This forces non-Sunni groups to redefine their identity as a function of this new social context. The importance of the religious marker therefore entails a growing visibility for the Ironis. Perestroika liberated the religious field, which translated in the reopening of places of worship. Since that period, several Shi'a mosques have become active in Uzbekistan: two in Samarkand and two in Bukhara.[1]

Appointing a community leader

In the Soviet era, the Shi'a community had no leader, although as we have seen, a charismatic figure did ensure the survival of Shi'ism in Bukhara. In 1989, Ibrahim Qosimi Kasimov (1911–97) was chosen as the first leader of the Shi'a community of Bukhara. This man exercised a social influence extending well beyond the Shi'a community. He reopened the mosque and reorganized religious life. Soon a young

---

1. These "mosques" are actually *husayniyyas*. The Bukhari mosques currently active are Hodja Mirali in the *mahalla* Choukour and Tor-tor in the *mahalla* Tor-tor.

mullah, Naim, trained in the Mir Arab madrasa, became the mosque's full-time caretaker. He had contacts with other mullahs of Samarkand, but was closely watched by the authorities. After the attacks[1] of February 1998, while he was progressively setting up an informal education system, he was imprisoned for two years. The young mullah had a limited audience within the Shi'a community, and it is Kasimov, not properly speaking a religious figure, who was the leader of the community. After his death in 1997, the new leader of the community, Abdulaev Najaf, who himself died in 1999, was replaced with another *oqsoqol* (white beard).

Since 1990, there has been a clearly identified representative for the community in every city but no committee or organism uniting those leaders on the national level. The religious men's authority remains limited to the local space, in a paradoxical political situation that sees the return of religion accompanied by sometimes arbitrary political repression. In such a context, individuals do not attach undue importance to the religious differences between Muslims. The mullah of the Bukhara *husayniyya* Hodja Mirali explains: "We attract more and more believers since we reopened our mosque. It is frequented by Shi'a, but on Fridays half of the audience is Sunni ..."

The Shi'a worship mainly in the private sphere or in discreet places, which leads to the absence of visible religious differences in the public space. This favors social exchanges where the difference between Shi'a and Sunnis is not observable. Considering the close surveillance of religious affairs by the state, it is difficult for the mullahs to maintain relations outside their city. They claim to have no official links with any Iranian authorities of the *marja'iyya* type, although the hall of one mosque does sport the Ayatollah Khomeini's portrait. According to a Shi'a mullah, the Uzbek authorities try hard to make their movements within or outside the country particularly difficult.

However, the Shi'a mosques take on a particular importance at the time of the celebrations of *muharram* and Ashura.[2] These exclusively Shi'a

---

1. A series of attacks on symbols of the Uzbek government took place in the Uzbek capital.
2. Cf. Richard, on 1991, p. 132.

ceremonies have reclaimed their public character after being celebrated in the family sphere only in the Soviet era. They celebrate the cult of the dead and the martyrs, which occupies a central place in Ironi devotion. The memory of centuries of Sunni persecution of the Shi'a resonates particularly strongly with the Ironis of Uzbekistan, who live in an ever more hostile environment. It is a time when the memory of the dead is honored with pilgrimages to the tombs of the saints and their descendants.

Visits to the holy tombs (*ziyâra*) occupy a relatively small place in Shi'a religious life in Uzbekistan. This phenomenon can to a great extent be explained by the police's supervision of the religious sphere, which encourages believers to remain very discreet. The instant of empathy, in the month of *muharram,* with the persecution that has marked the destiny of Shi'ism is strictly controlled. The Shi'a processions, known worldwide for their ostentatious character, are forbidden by the Uzbek authorities and the Shi'a limit themselves to a meeting inside the mosque where the men devote themselves to laments – a relatively modest expression of faith in comparison with the flagellations and mutilations observed during recent commemorations in Najaf and Karbala.

There are local holy places, such as Mazar Hodja Baror or Maamat Bogir[1] in Bukhara, but the latter is not much frequented compared with the devotion witnessed at some holy places in Iraq and Iran. Two other holy places important to the Shi'a in Uzbekistan are Nurata[2] and Sharimirdan,[3] where it is said that footprints left by 'Alî can be seen in the clay (*Qadamgoh 'Alî*). Worship at these places is not, however, exclusive to the Shi'a: many Sunnis also visit them. Uzbekistan's independence has first and foremost allowed the Ironis to renew their acquaintance with the traditional places of Shi'ism, prominently among them Iran.

---

1. Not far from the Shi'a graveyard of *Imam Maamat Boril Djuïbor* in Bukhara.
2. A small city between Samarkand and Bukhara in the *viloyat* of Navoï.
3. An Uzbek enclave in the Kyrghyz Republic, in the Oblast of Osh in the Ferghana valley. This place is particularly difficult to access for Uzbek citizens.

The opening of the country and the birth of transnational networks with Iran

Iran occupies a key geostrategic position in the opening up of Central Asia, a fact that has allowed Tehran to break its isolation and urge the international community to recognize its role as a regional power and its strategic role, alleviating to some extent the boycott policy installed by the United States. For Tashkent and Ashgabat, the road through Iran forms a connection with Europe which bypasses Russia. There has been no direct clash between Uzbekistan and Iran over the role of Islam or Shi'ism in the region. Although the two countries had a disagreement over the settlement of the Tajik conflict,[1] Iran remains an inevitable transit country for Uzbekistan. Iranian governments have acted primarily in their own economic interest, as was apparent in the creation of the Eurasian Economic Cooperation Organization (ECO).[2] Tehran has never shown a desire to export the Islamic revolution to Central Asia or to adopt a specific policy regarding Uzbekistan's Shi'a. It has closer diplomatic relations with Tajikistan, but this is explained both by a shared language and by a shared interest with Russia, as Tajikistan is largely a Russian protectorate.

Although the Iranian presence in Uzbekistan is very discreet, many Ironi families travel regularly to Iran. Some even discovered or rediscovered family members there. In the early 1990s, the first road trips to Serah[3] and Mashhad also offered access to a consumer society where many products were available which did not make it to the Uzbek bazaars. For Ironis, the discovery of Mashhad held a particular fascination, because it is a holy city of Shi'ism; it houses the mausoleum of the eighth Imam 'Alî Ridâ (Rezâ). The travelers – the majority of them women – set up small retail businesses while also reconnecting to a centre of Shi'a pilgrimage. Farida recounts:

> The first time I went to the Rezâ's tomb, it was a big shock for me to see all these people, all this emotion … I think it changed something in me […] I feel closer to the Iranians, even if there are many things there which I do not like.

---

1. Mafinazem, 1999.
2. De Cordier, 1996.
3. A town on the border between Iran and Turkmenistan.

These trips allow the Ironis to tie commercial and affective links with the local population of Mashhad, which also houses one of the biggest religious foundations of the country, Âstân-e Qods Razavi, whose objective is to re-establish links with post-Soviet Central Asia. Both parties involved, however, prudently ensure that the practice of Shi'ism does not gain greater visibility in Samarkand and Bukhara, because repression is severe.

A strong affective link definitely exists between the Ironis of Uzbekistan and Iran. But this relationship does not automatically turn Iran into a social model for the Ironis to follow, because the "Uzbek" Ironis also have a very strong feeling of differentiation from the Iranian social system. It is necessary to stress here that the Soviet power's choice of the category "Ironi", which closely links religious practice and Iranian nationality, has reinforced the ambiguity surrounding the collusion between Shi'ism and the Iranian identity – historically, the two are not necessarily very closely linked.[1] Yet this collusion is a commonly held opinion and Iran appears to be the Shi'a space *par excellence* for most Ironis of Bukhara and Samarkand. On the other hand, this feeling of closeness to Iran is more complex for the Uzbek-speaking Ironis of Samarkand, who do not understand Persian. The importance of Persian in the practice of Shi'ism necessarily leads to a much stronger attachment to the language and culture of Shi'a Iran on the part of the Persian-speaking Ironis of Bukhara. Beyond these representations, we do not yet see any networks of marital alliances being woven between Bukhari and Mashhadi families to crystallize the emergence of new social ties. For many Uzbek Ironi families, this affective relation with Iran translates mainly into the discovery of a new spirituality and access to a more developed world.

A delicate overall situation: official Islam and the increasing power of Salafist movements

It is important to situate the resurgence of Shi'ism among the Ironis in Uzbekistan's current political context. The authoritarian Uzbek government intends to use Islam to distinguish itself from the Soviet experience, but simultaneously rejects the politicization of Islam in any form or shape.

---

1. Richard, 1991.

The organization of Islam in Uzbekistan follows the Soviet model to a great extent. The Spiritual Directorate no longer has a Central Asian vocation and now limits itself to the national territory. Islam is managed by state institutions charged with appointing and training religious cadres and supervising the opening of places of worship. At present, the Shi'a are not recognized as such by the Spiritual Directorate. While some Ironis strive for official recognition of their sect, they disagree on the way this should be achieved and remain very prudent in practicing their religion. While the Shi'a mullahs seek official recognition, the secular community leaders prefer to preserve a relative anonymity to avoid jeopardizing their social integration.

The Uzbek government has inaugurated an international school of Islamic studies that does not have a Shi'a section. The representatives for the different mosques therefore train future religious cadres informally, in a context of close surveillance. In the wake of the February 1998 attacks, the situation for the mullahs of small mosques deteriorated. The official in charge of the Mirali mosque in Bukhara was suspected of extremist activity and imprisoned for several months, despite protest from the community. He was later cleared of all charges and reinstated. It is not unlikely that following the attacks of 2004 the authorities again applied serious pressure on religious figures in the whole of the country.

The Shi'a also have to reckon with the growing influence of some Salafist movements. Hezb-e Tahrir, the most influential movement today in Central Asia, condemns Shi'ism as much as official Islam. One of its leaders recently declared: "We are much more opposed to the Shi'a and Shi'ism, which is not a current of Islam [than to Sufism]."[1] In this difficult context, Ironi groups try to preserve their privileged social status as best they can while resuming their religious practice. The virtues of the *taqiyya* (mental dissimulation) particular to Shi'ism prove their eminent value, faced with the vicissitudes of Uzbek history, in the fight against the enmity of the surrounding social world.

The Ironi identity is situational, contextual and manifold depending on the local and national climate. In these conditions, it is very difficult to determine the identity of the Ironi population through a constellation

---

1. Rashid, 2000.

of objective criteria such as language, religion or culture. The difficulty in categorizing and counting the Ironi population shows the limits of a social system which wants to lock identity into relationships of statistical forces. Whatever the number of Ironis in Uzbekistan, the official statistics do not reflect their influence and importance in the social and political life of post-Soviet Uzbekistan.

Although the current situation tends towards the recognition of Shi'ism, Ironi community leaders have no wish for religious figures to play a bigger role in social life.

Besides the case of the Ironis, the new political situation of Uzbekization and Sunnitization transforms the status of other groups which have never before looked on themselves as minorities. They may now perceive themselves and/or be perceived by others as belonging to a minority, which *de facto* threatens their privileged social position. However, the Ironi capacity for adaptation makes it possible to believe that they possess the cultural resources – notably by using *taqiyya* – to deal with a rather disadvantageous context. The perpetuation of transnational Shi'a networks may prove to be an unmined resource opening new horizons to the Ironi population of Uzbekistan.

Bibliography

Abasin, S. N., "O samocaznanii narodov Srednei Azii" (About the modes of belonging among the peoples of Central Asia), in *Vostok*, Moscow, n° 4, 1999.

Babadjanov, Bakhtiar, "Islam officiel contre islam politique en Ouzbékistan aujourd'hui : la direction des musulmans et les groupes non-hanafî", in *Revue comparative Est-Ouest*, 31/3, September 2000.

Bennigsen, Alexandre, "La littérature anti-religieuse dans les Républiques soviétiques musulmanes", in *Revue des études islamiques*, 1, 1958, pp. 73–81.

Bennigsen, Alexandre, "La famille musulmane en Union Soviétique", in *Cahiers du monde russe et soviétique*, 1/1, May 1959.

Bennigsen, Alexandre, "Le problème linguistique et l'évolution des nationalités musulmanes en URSS", in *Cahiers du monde russe et soviétique*, 1/3, April-June 1960.

Bennigsen, Alexandre, *Le soufi et le commissaire : les confréries musulmanes en URSS*, Paris 1986, Seuil.

Bennigsen, Alexandre, and Lemercier Quelquejay, Chantal, *L'islam en Union soviétique,* Paris 1968, Payot.

Caratini, R, *Dictionnaire des nationalités et des minorités en ex-URSS*, Paris 1990, Larousse.

Carlisle, Donald S., "The Uzbek Power Elite : Politburo and Secretariat (1938–1983)", in *Central Asian Survey*, 5/3–4, 1986.

Carrère d'Encausse, Hélène, *Réformes et révolutions chez les musulmans de l'empire russe*, Paris 1981, Presses de la FNSP.

De Cordier, Bruno, "The Economic Cooperation Organization: Towards a New Silk Road on the Ruins of the Cold War", in *Central Asian Survey*, 15/1, 1996.

Djalili, Mohammad-Reza, and Kellner, Thierry, *Géopolitique de la nouvelle Asie centrale : de la fin de l'URSS à l'après 11 septembre*, Paris/Geneva 2003, PUF/IUED.

Dudoignon, Stéphane, ed., *L'islam de Russie*, Paris 1997, Maisonneuve et Larose.

Jakubovski, Y. A., *Istoria narodov Uzbekistana : c dreVneisih vremen do nacala 19 veka* (History of the ancient peoples of Uzbekistan : from ancient times to the beginning of the 20ᵗʰ Century), Tashkent 1947, Uzfan.

Liuskevic, F. D., "Etnograficeskaja gruppa ironi : zaniatia I bit narodov srednei Azii" (The ethnic group of the Ironis : knowledge and customs among peoples of Central Asia), in *Trudy*, Moscow 1997, vol. 97.

Mafinazem, Ali, "Iran and Uzbekistan, Friends or Rivals ?", in *The Analyst*, 19 July 1999.

Mervin, Sabrina, "Les autorités religieuses dans le chiisme duodécimain contemporain", in *Archives de sciences sociales des religions*, 125, January-March 2004.

Pétric, Boris, *Pouvoir, don et réseaux en Ouzbékistan post-soviétique*, Paris 2002, PUF.

Peyrouse, Sébastien, *Des chrétiens entre athéisme et islam. Regards sur la question religieuse en Asie centrale soviétique et post-soviétique*, Paris 2003, Maisonneuve et Larose.

Planhol, Xavier de, *Minorités en islam : géographie politique et sociale*, Paris: Flammarion, 1997.

Quelquejay, Chantal, "Les sources de documentation sur la religion musulmane en URSS depuis 1945", *Les cahiers du monde russe et soviétique*, vol. 1, January-Marsh 1960.

Rahimov, R. R., "K voprosu o sovremennih tadjisko-uzbeskih meznatsionalnih otonoseijah" (The Question of Tadjiko-Uzbek Relations), in *Sovietskaja etnografia*, Moscow, 1991, pp. 13–24.

Rashid, A., "Interview with the Leader of Hizb-eTahrir", in *Central Asia-Caucasus analyst.org*, 22 November 2000.

Roy, O., "Islam et politique en Asie centrale", in *Archives de sciences sociales des religions*, 115, July-September 2001, pp. 49–62.

Suhareva, O. A., "K voprosu o Kul'te musul'manskih Svjatyh v Srednej Azii" (The question of the worship of Muslim saints in Central Asia), in *Materialy po archeologii I etnografii Uzbekistana*, vol. II, Tashkent 1950, Institute of History and Archaeology of the Academy of the SSR of Uzbekistan.

Suhareva, O. A., *Kvartalnaja obstina : pozdnefeodalnogo goroda buhari* (The community of vicinity in the town of Bukara during the late Middle Age), Moscow 1976, Naouka.

Trofimov, D., "Tachkent mezhdu Ankaroj I Tegeranom : uroki 90-x Perspektivi" (Tashkent between Ankara and Tehran : Lessons and Perspectives from the 1990s), in *Centralnaja Azia I Kavkaz*, 5/17, 2001.

Richard, Yann, *L'islam chi'ite*, Paris, 1991, Fayard.

MARA A. LEICHTMAN

Shi'a Lebanese Migrants and Senegalese Converts in Dakar[1]

Historians and anthropologists have recently begun to trace the expansion of Shi'a Islam from the center (Iran) to the periphery (the Middle East and Asia), yet very little has been written on the Shi'a of Africa. Rizvi and King[2] and Penrad[3] depict the Shi'a community in East Africa, who came from Arabia, the Persian Gulf, India and Pakistan, making the island of Zanzibar their headquarters as early as the 1830s. Shi'a migrants spread throughout East Africa, and their institutions can be found in Tanzania, Kenya, the Congo (ex-Zaire) and Uganda. In West Africa, Shi'a Islam is mentioned only with regard to the Islamic movement in Nigeria, whose leaders are regarded as Shi'a, although they do not necessarily identify themselves as such.[4] While there is a small but growing movement of Shi'a

---

1. Fieldwork in Senegal was funded by the J. William Fulbright Program, Population Council, the National Science Foundation, Brown University and Michigan State University. I would like to thank Mamadou Diouf, David Kertzer, Calvin Goldscheider, Bill Beeman, Phil Leis and Sabrina Mervin for their feedback on my writing. I am much obliged to the Lebanese of Senegal and Senegalese Shi'a converts for welcoming me into their community, sharing their religious experiences with me, and, above all, having faith in my research.
2. Rizvi and King (1974).
3. Penrad (1988).
4. Sulaiman (1993); Maier (2000); Umar (2001).

Islam throughout Africa, their presence remains unknown to scholars of Shiʻism and African Muslim intellectuals.

The case of Senegal is important in illuminating the impact of migration on religious change through examining the transformation of Lebanese ethnic identity. Secondly, the Senegalese example sheds light on missionary processes, evident in the influence of both Lebanese and Iranian religious leaders on attracting Senegalese to Shiʻa Islam. Like communities of Shiʻa in the Middle East and Asia, the Shiʻa in Senegal create their own spaces, both ethnic and religious. This paper explores relationships between Lebanese and Senegalese Shiʻa, the location of Shiʻa Islam in national and international religious networks, and the creation of an indigenous form of Shiʻism in Senegal. Incorporating West African cases into discussions about Shiʻism and global Islam highlights social, political and cultural change in relation to migration, ethnicity, proselytizing and Muslim networking.[1]

History of the Lebanese community of Senegal

The Lebanese first arrived in West Africa as the result of a colonial fluke. As early as the 1880s, and especially during the 1920s, emigrants left the region that is today known as Lebanon because of economic hardship, especially in the south, and to improve their local social rank.[2] Foreign influence was also a factor in emigration: the Ottoman Empire treated the Lebanese harshly and many emigrated to avoid conscription into the Ottoman army during World War I. The final blow for the Muslims came when modern Lebanon was established on 1 September 1920 by the French, who created a Christian state.[3] Emigrants went to Marseilles, the transportation hub at that time, from where they planned to continue on to the United States or South America.

According to the tale told by Senegal's Lebanese today, their ancestors

---

1. This chapter draws on more than two years of ethnographic fieldwork in Senegal between 2000 and 2008, including archival research in the *Archives Nationales du Sénégal, Institut Fondamental d'Afrique Noire* and *Centre d'Etudes Scientifiques et Techniques de l'Information* in Dakar.
2. Taraf (1994).
3. Hanf (1993).

boarded a ship heading for the Americas but they never reached their destination; the ship docked at Dakar, and the French colonial powers convinced the Lebanese to stay in West Africa to work as intermediaries between the French in the cities and the West Africans in the interior. Other sources state that health requirements for immigration to the United States were strict, and many Lebanese failed to satisfy these requirements because of trachoma. Furthermore, many emigrants spent most of their money in Marseilles while waiting for transport and did not have enough money to go to the Americas. The best solution to these difficulties was West Africa, where fares were cheap, health requirements lax, and French reports favorable.[1] The first migrants were temporary, and had the intention of returning to Lebanon to retire and reinstate their children in their country of origin. The nature of migration later changed, as the Lebanese civil war (1975–92) encouraged the Lebanese of West Africa to go instead to Europe or America or to remain in Africa.[2]

Currently, there are between 15,000 and 30,000 Lebanese in Senegal. The higher figure represents estimates by the Lebanese Embassy of Dakar which attempt to emphasize the importance of the population. The lower number is given by the Ministry of Emigrants in Beirut and is symbolic of the government deflating the flow of resources to the emigrant community in Senegal. Ninety-five to ninety-seven per cent of Lebanese migrants reside in Dakar, and the community is heavily concentrated near the city center. The first and second generations are traders and small businessmen. Lebanese shops range from small groceries to sellers of African cloth, imported European fabric and clothing, household items, shoes, furniture and cosmetics. The Lebanese also own numerous fast food, falafel and shawârma restaurants, and finer French-style bakeries and cafés that also offer Lebanese specialties. The second and third generations have begun to move into industry and the professions. They dominate the plastic, paper and cosmetics industries, and even hold a share in the African cloth industry, manufacturing some of their own textiles. Others are doctors, lawyers, dentists, pharmacists, tailors and mechanics.

---

1. Boumedouha (1987), pp. 45–6.
2. Labaki (1993); Hourani and Shehadi (1992).

The Development of a Lebanese Ethnic Identity

The French not only encouraged the Lebanese to come to West Africa; they were also instrumental in a formation of the Lebanese identity in Senegal. Seeing itself as a "Muslim power,"[1] that is an imperial power with Muslim subjects, France made a conscious effort to control the Islamic societies it ruled and to select their leaders. William Ponty, the civilian Lieutenant-Governor of the colony of Upper Senegal and Niger (1907–15), developed the French policy of ethnic particularism. He set about to erode the alliance of the marabouts, the local Senegalese religious leaders, and the community chiefs by ensuring that Muslims were not placed as chiefs over non-Muslim peoples. This became known as the *politique des races*, which was a central theme of colonial administration in West Africa until the World War II. Ethnic particularism was also applied to Islam, where "African Islam", or "Black Islam", which contained indigenous and pre-Islamic customs, was seen by the French as "inferior" to "Arab Islam."[2]

This policy directly affected the French colonial treatment of the Lebanese. Ponty, in a May 1911 circular, banned the use of Arabic in the colonies and also attempted to exercise greater control over the importation of engravings and publications in Arabic, especially those that had taken an anti-French position on the Moroccan colony.[3] The Lebanese were furthermore forbidden from entering Senegalese mosques or the *médersas,* Senegal's Islamic schools. From the 1930s on, the French exercised complete surveillance over Libano-Syrian[4] activities. The colonial archives report on individual Lebanese who were suspected of dispersing banned literature, conspiring against the French in their homes late at night, or being too political or pan-Islamic.[5] The French also followed with fear

---

1. Robinson (2000), p. 75.
2. Harrison (1988), p. 129.
3. Harrison (1988), pp. 51–52.
4. Before the end of World War I, the Ottoman Province of Syria contained all of present-day Lebanon and Syria. After the collapse of the Ottoman Empire in 1918, the former Province of Syria was divided by France in 1920 into two administrative units: Syria and Lebanon. While most emigrants in Africa were from Lebanon proper, the names "Syrians" and "Libano-Syrians" continued to be used in French West Africa as late as the 1950s in administrative reports and newspapers.
5. Archives Nationales du Sénégal (21G23(17)).

the reaction of the Lebanese in French West Africa to the independence of Lebanon and Syria in 1945. They record:

> In Black Africa, where the Arabic language and the Muslim religion constitute so many cultural and spiritual affinities between Blacks and Arabs, the presence of such a large number of Lebanese-Syrians harboring nationalist pride, enjoying an unbounded hospitality and possessing powerful financial means would be without a doubt a grave danger to which an expedient solution must be found, considering that it was with discreet exultation that the Levantines welcomed the different events that led in Syria to the ousting of the French by England.[1]

France's Libano-phobia existed on a number of levels. On the religious level, the French had a fear of Islam in general; in particular, they feared that the Lebanese "White Islam" would contaminate the African "Black Islam", which they were trying to mould to their own needs. Politically, they feared an outburst of pan-Arabism and pan-Islamism that would unite Arabs and Africans and undermine colonial authority in West Africa. Finally, on an economic level, they were aware of the ability of the Lebanese to compete with them and even to win their market share in West Africa. As a result of these concerns, the French chose not to differentiate between the Lebanese in Senegal nor did they give preferential treatment to the Christians, as they had in Lebanon. They classified all the Lebanese, even Christians, as the White Islamic, economically and politically powerful enemy.

Later, in independent Senegal, Lebanese migrants continued to be grouped together.[2] Seen as economically dominant, and therefore scapegoats for Senegal's post-colonial ills, the Lebanese were classified as *naar*, meaning "Arab" in Wolof. Second and third generation Lebanese in Senegal remained "Lebanese".[3] The community began to envision themselves as others defined them and to develop their beliefs and ideologies to conform

---

1. "Renseignements" (14 June, 1945, 21G8(1)). French to English translations of texts are by Meadow Dibble-Dieng and Noémi Tousignant. Mamadou Diouf helped me check the correctness of this work. Cassettes of interviews in French were transcribed by Birama Diagne, Mohamad Cama, and Patricia Pereiro.
2. Leichtman (2006), ch. 4.
3. Leichtman (2005).

to their categorization. Economic and political realities also encouraged them to come together as a community and look after themselves. In this period of change and uncertainty for Lebanese in Senegal, ethnic identity became central at the expense of religious identity.[1]

Religious accommodation through ethnic unity

Although religious differentiation has remained strong in Lebanon, my informants emphasized in the initial stages of my fieldwork (2000–03) that "there are no problems between Muslims and Christians in Senegal." The Lebanese of Senegal lived through the Lebanese civil war from a distance, and their religious differences even began to be accommodated by the religious institutions. Boundaries between "Muslim" and "Christian" melted away as inter-religious marriages became more frequent, children of different religions studied together in Christian or Muslim schools, and all community members, Muslim and Christian alike, celebrated weddings, funerals and even religious holidays together in mosques and churches. While there are both Shi'a and Sunnis in Senegal, most Lebanese Muslims did not distinguish between the two sects. Only when they visited Lebanon were they confronted with religious differences. One man born in Senegal visited a Shi'a friend's family in the south of Lebanon, where he was introduced as a Sunni, which disturbed him. Another man only learned that he was a Shi'a during a trip to Lebanon. Before that he identified himself as a Muslim.

This religious mingling among the Lebanese in Senegal is enforced by

---

1. Not all migrant communities are made into "ethnic communities." For example, Abner Cohen (1969) describes a "ritual community" of Hausa migrants from northern Nigeria to Yoruba towns in southern Nigeria. The migrants are influenced by a new type of Islam, which was practiced neither by the Yorubas of the south, nor by the Hausas of the north, but was introduced to Hausa migrants by a Senegalese religious figure of the Tijaniyya order. The religious distancing of migrants was necessary economically to continue the exclusivity of the Hausa trade network, but also politically for their acceptance in the community, as they were seen as religiously superior to the Yoruba. Furthermore, Hausa adoption of Tijaniyya Islam brought about a homogenization of the Hausa diaspora culture, blending different Hausa cultural practices brought by migrants from different parts of Hausaland into a new Hausa culture particular to the settlers.

changes in the Lebanese religious institutions in Senegal. The oldest is the Lebanese Maronite Church, *Notre Dame du Liban*, which was built in 1952. The Maronite church is the only Lebanese religious body representing the Lebanese Christian population of 1,200 in Senegal, 300–400 of whom are Maronites and most of the rest Greek Orthodox. It is therefore surprising that the primary Lebanese church institution is a Maronite church. This reflects the organization of the Maronite mission abroad, and perhaps some of its funding from Rome, while the Orthodox church is more locally established in Syria and lacks such a diplomatic presence outside the Levant. Nonetheless, the Maronite church in Senegal differs from the Maronite church in Lebanon in that it tends to accommodate all Christian denominations. The publication celebrating *Notre Dame du Liban*'s fiftieth anniversary in Senegal states: "The Parish *Notre Dame du Liban* looks after the spiritual life of all the Eastern Christian families disseminated throughout Senegal regardless of their order: Maronite, Melchite-Catholic, Orthodox, Armenian and Protestant."[1]

Not only does the church open its doors to all Christian denominations, it also recognizes the important role of the Muslims in the Lebanese community of Senegal. The church was established at the request of the entire Lebanese community, and it was financed by the community, Maronite and Orthodox Christians, as well as by many Muslims. The church publication acknowledges this fact:

> Thanks to the generosity of the Lebanese of Senegal, *both Christians and Muslims*, Father Sarkis had the great pleasure of witnessing the creation and development of the foundations of the first Lebanese Maronite Mission in Black Africa, and in Senegal in particular, contributing thus to *the diffusion of Arab culture and allowing Lebanon's spiritual and cultural life to shine.*[2]

In recognizing the Muslims, the Church publication stresses secular Arab and Lebanese culture. Such language is also the language of Arab unity, and leads to the idea of a "national" Lebanese church, the Maronite church. While such changes have occurred in the Lebanese diaspora, it is important to keep in mind that sectarian incorporation at the church

---

1. Cinquantenaire (1999), p. 6.
2. Cinquantenaire (1999), p. 3; emphasis added.

level differs from Lebanon, where each church has its own tradition and its own following.

The same is true for the Lebanese Muslim institution in Dakar. Ninety per cent of the Lebanese community in Senegal is Shi'a Muslim, with maybe one or two hundred Sunni Muslims and one Druze family. Founded in 1978 by Sheikh Abdul Monem el-Zein, *L'Institution Islamique Sociale* is mainly Shi'a. However, the vice president of the institute is a Sunni, and the sheikh addresses the Sunnis in the community as "our Sunni brothers." Most importantly, the sheikh understands the mentality of the community – he is everyone's sheikh, and does not take part in the village and clan politics that were so dominant among religious groups in Lebanon. In contrast to this religious coexistence, the colonial archives detail that the first generation of Lebanese in Senegal arrived as a religiously divided community.[1] Only over time, the selectiveness of the Maronite church and Shi'a mosque has expanded to include all Lebanese Christians and Muslims, regardless of religious sect. Like the French colonial power, religious organizations also played a role in the making of an ethnic Lebanese community in Senegal. The Lebanese valued their religious beliefs and practices enough to establish these institutions in Senegal; however, in their need to unite as a community, they did not maintain the sectarian divisions dominant in Lebanon. More recently, however, as a result of the 2006 Israel-Hezbollah war, growing sectarian divisions in Lebanon have begun to infiltrate Senegal's Lebanese community.

Return to Shi'a Islam

Sheikh Abdul Monem el-Zein was sent to Africa for the first time in 1969 to lead the Lebanese Shi'a community of Dakar. Born in 1945 in Yater, a small town in the south of Lebanon between Tyre and Bint Jubail, to Sheikh Ali el-Zein and Fatima Karim (a Sunni Muslim), Abdul Monem's education began in a Maronite Catholic primary school. He then moved to Beirut where he attended a branch of the prestigious Sunni Muslim al-Azhar University of Cairo. With this educational background from Catholic and Sunni Muslim institutions, he then began his formal Shi'a

---

1.   Leichtman (2006).

education in Najaf in Iraq, where he studied under a number of scholars, including Ayatollah Sayyid Abul Qasim al-Khu'i, who died in 1992. Abdul Monem el-Zein is a *wakil*, or authorized representative, for Ayatollah Sayyid Ali as-Sistani, Ayatollah al-Khu'i's successor.

Musa al-Sadr, the legendary religious leader who fought for equality for Lebanon's oppressed Shi'a,[1] traveled throughout Africa in 1967 instilling Shi'a pride in Lebanon's Muslim diaspora and gaining support for his cause. Representatives of the Lebanese community in Dakar, the oldest Lebanese community in Africa, asked him to establish the first Shi'a religious center in Africa. Later these representatives traveled to Lebanon to remind Sadr of their need. In turn, Sadr journeyed to Najaf in Iraq to find the right man for the job. There he met Abdul Monem and appointed him to go to Dakar.

Before Abdul Monem came to Senegal, the Lebanese embassy had chosen six religious men, who had made the pilgrimage to Mecca, to conduct weddings and divorces for Lebanese Muslims. However, these men were businessmen, and not formally educated in religion. Sheikh el-Zein writes in the introduction to his first book in 1973:

> The idea to write this book was born after my arrival in Senegal. The religious situation of the Lebanese community was disastrous with regard to a great void in religious culture and jurisprudence. This culminated in a lack of religious learning and ritual practices, where prayer, the most important, was not at all satisfactory. Young people rarely approached religious circles and did not worry about their legal obligations ... The majority of parents were not interested in these problems. Others ... were at too great a distance to learn the laws of religion and the rules of practice so that the symbols could be put to action and not only words.[2]

Through courtesy calls to family homes, the young sheikh and the community held discussions on different problems in society. For congregation members, these were largely the worries of emigrants, including economic concerns, lack of ties to the motherland and problems with integration in a new homeland where they became second-class citizens. The Lebanese

---

1. Ajami (1986); Halawi (1992).
2. El-Zein (2001), pp. 3–4.

are seen by the Senegalese as parasites who profit off Senegal and do not invest back in the land, as well as being racist and entertaining a superiority complex.[1] "It is not enough merely to take on the Senegalese nationality, speak Wolof, construct buildings, set up businesses and be buried in Senegalese soil in order to truly become Senegalese," one informant claimed. Marriage is the Senegalese solution to integration, and the rarity of mixed Lebanese-Senegalese marriages is a sore point for Senegalese, although Lebanese claim it has nothing to do with being racist, but with having a different culture.[2] Whereas the Lebanese community is marginalized by Senegalese society and is itself a closed community, they do maintain privileged networks to Senegalese decision-makers; this buys them protection in times of need.

For his part, Abdul Monem slowly succeeded in making the community more aware of religious affairs and obligations. At first Sheikh el-Zein worked from his home, where it took him years to learn the ways of Senegal, establish himself among the local religious leaders and encourage the Lebanese community to pay their religious taxes so he could carry out his work. In 1973 he was finally able to buy the first piece of land of what would in 1978 become the *Institution Islamique Sociale*. The Islamic Institute is a multi-purpose organization, which has been granted NGO status. The sheikh stresses that the Institute is an *Islamic* institution, not a *Shi'a* institution. Many Sunni Muslims attend Friday prayer at the Lebanese mosque because Abdul Monem is an influential man and many come to hear his *khutba* or Friday sermon. Also, the Islamic Institute houses the only mosque in Dakar where the Friday sermon is conducted in Arabic; Imams at other mosques preach mostly in Wolof. Senegalese, Moroccans, Mauritanians, Algerians and Lebanese Sunnis, among others, attend the Friday prayer with the Lebanese Shi'a community.

The institute consists of a large formal lecture hall on the ground floor, black and white tiled with separate entrances for men and women. On the first floor is the mosque, a rectangular room with green carpeting decorated with a motif of red arches and geometric designs. Administrative offices are found on the first and second floors, while the third floor

1. Thibault (1976).
2. See Leichtman (2006), ch. 4.

houses Abdul Monem's office. It is lined with bookcases filled with books: collections of Shi'a and Sunni law, *tafsír* (commentary) on the Qur'an, Islamic history, biographical dictionaries, and books on Christianity and Judaism. His office also contains a comfortable air-conditioned room with plush chairs and sofas, green furniture and carpeting, a red rug, chandeliers, and black Islamic decorations on the wall. In this room he holds religious classes for men and women. Attached to the building is a clinic that treats the poor free of charge and helps those in need to travel to France, Europe or Lebanon for specialized medical treatment that is not available in Senegal. The clinic treats approximately ten per cent Lebanese and 90 per cent Africans. There is also a kitchen and guest rooms, and the sheikh resides with his family on the upper levels of the institute.

In addition to the Islamic Institute, in 1979 Abdul Monem founded the *Collège Al Zahraa,* a primary and secondary school in Dakar that offers courses on Islam and the Arabic language in addition to the regular Senegalese curriculum. The school is a mix of religious sects: different Senegalese Sufi Muslim orders, such as Tijans and Murids, Shi'a, and even some Christians attend the "sheikh's school", as it is called. The student population is approximately 20 per cent Lebanese and 80 per cent African. More recently, in 1998, he founded the *Institut de Langue Arabe*, which offers instruction in the Arabic language for children and adults, and computer literacy classes taught in both French and Arabic.

Abdul Monem has written several books on Islam, which he sells to the community. The books are written in Arabic and translated or transliterated into French for the many Lebanese in Senegal who are not literate in the Arabic script. Subjects range from a collection of prayers to two volumes on the family of the Prophet, a book on Islamic law and doctrine, more specialized books on the meaning of the Ramadan fast, and the history of the battle of Karbala where Imam Husayn was martyred. He is working on a new manuscript that discusses various social vices including "mental and sexual deviancies", alcohol, drug use and abortion, and a second booklet comparing the veil in Islam to Judaism and Christianity.

Whereas Sheikh el-Zein claims to be running an *Islamic* establishment, his activities, writings, and lectures are clearly Shi'a. One of the most important events of the Institute are the *ta'ziyas,* or recitals of the suffering and martyrdom of Husayn, grandson of the Prophet Muhammad, during the first ten days of the Islamic lunar month of *muharram,* a mourning period known as Ashura.[1] During the ten days of Ashura, I attended the afternoon *ta'ziyas* for women. The lecture hall of the Islamic Institute was filled with a crowd of 300–400 Lebanese women and a few children, dressed all in black, the color of mourning. Outfits varied from the traditional Muslim women's *'abâya,* a loosely fitting long-sleeved gown, to tight fitting pants or skirts and sweaters. The room was decorated with black wall-hangings with colorful pictures and Arabic script illustrating the battle of Karbala and the martyrdom of Husayn, who was killed along with his family. A female *khatîba* is brought annually from Lebanon to recount the story of his death. Women went around with boxes of pastries and bags of doughnuts and biscuits flavored with anise and sesame seeds, and also passed around boxes of tissues for those who were eating and those who were crying. The audience was moved by the recitations, which at times became quite emotional, as if the *khatîba* was wailing in sorrow, and women cried, some passionately, dabbing their eyes red with tears, and convulsing in sobs. At various points in the recitations they beat their hearts in rhythm to the poetry. When the *khatîba* finished the day's segment of the story, the sheikh came in and lectured on various topics. Baskets were passed around to collect charity donations.

Lebanon plays a prominent role in the sheikh's teachings. He leads an annual *hajj* (pilgrimage) to Mecca following Ramadan, which is organized by a Lebanese travel agency, and takes Lebanese pilgrims from Senegal first to Lebanon, and then on to Mecca.[2] Sheikh el-Zein's influence as a Shi'a has spread beyond Senegal. He has strong ties to Lebanon, most famously exemplified by his role in negotiating the French hostage crisis of the 1980s. Abdou Diouf, past president of Senegal, personally called upon Abdul Monem to help free the French hostages taken by Hezbollah in Lebanon. From April 1987 until May 1988 he traveled between Paris, Beirut and Tehran, seeing to the release of the hostages.[3] Abdul Monem

---

1. Ashura technically signifies only the tenth day of the month of Muharram, but Lebanese in Senegal refer to the entire ten-day period as Ashura.
2. See Delaney (1990) for a comparison of *hajj* and return migration.
3. See Péan (2001).

has also been present at numerous international conferences and dialogues on Islam in Shi'a centers such as Detroit, London, Tehran, Qom and Mumbai. He is an important figure in local politics and met with Pope John Paul II during his visit to Dakar in 1992, when they discussed the Israeli occupation of South Lebanon.

Yet during the 2006 Israel-Hezbollah war the sheikh overstepped the boundaries he had carefully put in place several decades earlier, when he mixed religion with politics. On 20 July 2006 he led the Lebanese community in organizing a large protest, estimated at 3,000 people, which took place between Senegal's national television station and Dakar's Grand Mosque. Those in attendance waved Lebanese, Hezbollah and Senegalese flags in addition to signs denouncing the war and Israel, and thanking Senegal for its hospitality. The protest was followed by a march past the presidential palace and the American Embassy, ending at the Lebanese Islamic Institute. Afterwards there was a well-attended service at the institute, which included the Syrian and Iranian ambassadors and other dignitaries. I was told that the sheikh spoke more about politics on this occasion than during the usual religious ceremonies, and was full of praise for Sayyid Hasan Nasrallah, whereas before he had always been careful not to demonstrate any political attachment. In addition to the sheikh's leadership, the round-the-clock reporting of Hezbollah's channel *al-Manar*, which has been airing on cable television in Senegal for the past eight years, and the horrific images of death and destruction it displayed moved the Lebanese in Senegal to action for the first time.

On 3 August 2006, a silent vigil took place at Dakar's Independence Square where Lebanese and some Senegalese lit hundreds of candles commemorating the victims, who were pictured on placards signed by those in attendance as a gesture of solidarity. While previously the odd Lebanese individual in Senegal collected Hezbollah paraphernalia, posters of Nasrallah and other images of Lebanese Shi'a resistance were never so numerous or so prominently displayed in Dakar as during and after the 2006 war. This latest war in Lebanon has further altered the delicate balance between religion and secular ethnicity among members of the Lebanese diaspora in Senegal.[1]

---

1. See Leichtman (2010) for analysis of these events.

The Islamic Institute's celebration of Ashura, Sheikh el-Zein's political connections to the Shi'a of Lebanon and Iran and his outspokenness on Shi'a issues in international conferences demonstrate that the sheikh's activities, while Islamic, are distinctly Shi'a in nature. Shi'ism is one branch of Islam and its proponents believe it is the only true Islam. The sheikh's approach in using the language of "Islam" or "Shi'a Islam" varies with his audience. His strategy to unite Muslims as a Lebanese ethnic group is to refer to his Institute as *Islamic*. When dealing with Lebanon, where sectarian conflict is strong, he clearly identifies as a "Shi'a Muslim" and strives to be recognized as such by the international Shi'a community. With the Senegalese population, however, his politics vary.

Sheikh el-Zein's mission in Senegal

Originally Abdul Monem came to Senegal to serve the Lebanese community, but eventually his work spread to benefit Senegalese Muslims as well. While the Islamic Institute and its affiliated institutions in Dakar cater to both Lebanese and Senegalese, Abdul Monem has founded five mosques and approximately 130 *madâris* (Islamic schools) outside Dakar, all led by Senegalese religious men whom he trained.[1] The *madâris* range from larger schools to simple one-room learning facilities, and teach the Arabic language and the Qur'an to Senegalese villagers. This charitable work, too, is Shi'a in its approach.

The cover of the September/October 1994 *Noor Al Islam*, a bi-lingual Arabic-English Shi'a magazine printed in Lebanon, is titled "Senegal: Efforts to Strengthen its Deep-rooted Islam." The cover story describes Sheikh el-Zein's work among the Lebanese and Senegalese communities, highlighting the number of Senegalese students in his schools and the money he contributes to the building of mosques, schools and wells in (often Christian) villages in the south of Senegal. The dates and figures the journalist cites are as follows:

> During the last twenty-five years, a number of Senegalis [sic] began
> to adopt the Ahl el-Beit (A.S.) doctrine. Moreover all Muslims in
> Senegal respect Ahl el Beit Imams (A.S.). There are a few thousand

---

1. I have not verified these figures, which are cited in Aïdara (2003).

that have adopted the Ahl el-Beit doctrine, but we should add about 25,000 Lebanese immigrants who have been living in Senegal for decades.[1]

A second round of publicity for Sheikh el-Zein occurred more recently. In Islamic history, the death of the Prophet Muhammad divided Muslims into Sunnis and Shi'a according to which successor they followed. Starting with Abû Bakr, the Sunnis followed a series of caliphs who were the selected or elected successors of the Prophet in political and military leadership, but not in religious authority. In contrast, the Shi'a vested leadership of the Muslim community in an imam, who must be a direct descendant of the Prophet Muhammad and 'Ali, the first imam. The imam is both the political leader and the religious guide, and the final authoritative interpreter of God's will as formulated in Islamic law.

The French wished to sponsor a western (pro-French) caliphate that would act as a balance to the eastern caliphate of Mecca, which they saw as pan-Islamic.[2] Whereas in most of the Muslim world the title of caliph is no longer used, the French colonial administration in Senegal gave the title to the leaders it selected to head each Sufi order. The title of caliph continues to be passed down from father to son in the marabout families, the most influential of which are the Tijan, Murid and Qadir orders, where each caliph has power over his own followers and disciples. The Sufi leaders in Senegal play a very important role politically as well as religiously.[3] The Shi'a sheikh in Senegal wanted to be recognized as the leader of the Shi'a, so he recently accepted the title Caliph Ahl Al-Beit, even though the title caliph has traditionally been used for Sunni Muslim leaders.

An article in *Le Soleil*, Senegal's national newspaper, describes the 2002 Gamou celebrations for the Prophet's birthday in the Tijan order's center of Tivaouane:

Among the numerous delegations to the Gamou of Tivouane, the

---

1. Youssef (1994), p. 8.
2. Harrison (1988), p. 124.
3. Behrman (1970); Copans (1980); Cruise O'Brien (1971); Cruise O'Brien, Diop and Diouf (2002); Diop (1992); Diop and Diouf (1990); Kane and Triaud, (1998); Magassouba (1985); Piga (2002); Robinson and Triaud (1997); Triaud and Robinson (2002).

representatives from the Lebanese community distinguished them-selves in particular because the head of the delegation, Cheikh Abdoul Moneim Zein, was about to receive the title of Khalifatou Ahlou Baïty Rassoul (Caliph of the family of the Prophet Muhammad[1] – SAWS[2]) in Senegal. The title was conferred by three caliphs from the brotherhoods, Serigne Mouhamadou Mansour Sy [Tijaniyya], Cheikh Salihou Mbacké [Muridiyya] and Cheick Bou Mohamed Kounta of Ndiassane [Qadiriyya].[3]

This title, Caliph Ahl Al-Beit, is one the sheikh proudly uses and can be found after his signature on all written documents. Further publicity for the sheikh can be found on the front page of the 2 December 2003 issue of *Le Messager*, one of Senegal's myriad newspapers, which advertises "Sheikh Abdul Monem El Zein, A Charitable Soul." A follow-up article calls him "an atypical Shi'a sheikh in Senegal." Here, too, his title is cited:

> Consequently, the General Caliph Ahlul Beit is not only the spiritual guide of the Lebanese community in Senegal, but of all Ahlul Beit followers in Senegal, West Africa, North Africa and beyond. It is important to mention that this is the first time that a general Caliph Ahlul Beit is appointed for Africa and Senegal.[4]

The article thus declares Sheikh el-Zein to be not only the spiritual leader of the Lebanese community in Senegal, but of all Shi'a in Senegal, and in West and North Africa as a whole.[5] Furthermore, in discussing the meaning of this title with Senegal's "islamologues", scholars who study Islam or religious men who are also academics, it was revealed that this title has no meaning and does not exist elsewhere; and the three caliphs of the Tijan, Murid and Qadir orders never agree on anything. In fact,

1. This is a poor translation. The sheikh is not named caliph of the family of the Prophet Muhammad, but of the followers of the family of the Prophet Muhammad – the Shi'a.
2. "May God bless Him and give Him peace," a blessing said after referring to the Prophet.
3. Tall (2002).
4. Seck, Diop and Aïdara (2003).
5. One must keep in mind that the press in Senegal is referred to as a "*presse alimentaire*", where for a small fee journalists will publish any information.

as one Islamologue confirmed, the Lebanese sheikh himself created his title and asked the Senegalese caliphs to sign on to it.

Furthermore, the *Messenger* articles describe the Shi'a, in the sheikh's words, as the followers of the family of the Prophet, and stresses the similarities between Sunnism and Shi'ism, which share the fundamental principles of Islam: God, the Qur'an, the Prophet Muhammad, prayer, Ramadan, and pilgrimage to Mecca. This language is necessary in order to avoid tensions between the sheikh and the government and wider Senegalese community. In covering up the differences of the two schools of Islam, the sheikh also hopes to attract more Senegalese followers. Yet, in describing his charitable work in Senegal and in understanding the pains he took to establish himself as the leader of Ahl al-Beit of not only the Lebanese community, but of Senegal (and West/North Africa) as a whole, the sheikh stresses the Shi'a nature of his mission. This is further highlighted by the figures he gives for the number of Shi'a in Senegal:

> The sheikh estimates that the number of Shi'a Muslims in the country is approximately between 120,000 and 130,000. According to him, most of them have been trained in the schools he has opened in Dakar's suburbs and in the other regions of Senegal.[1]

From the few thousand Senegalese Shi'a mentioned ten years earlier, suddenly this number has increased exponentially. Sheikh el-Zein's title and these figures make him more credible to the Senegalese Shi'a community and heighten his and Senegal's importance in international religious networks. But the actual number of Shi'a, that is to say those who identify themselves as Shi'a, remains a mystery.

Senegalese conversion to Shi'a Islam

While Senegalese Shi'a do greatly respect Sheikh el-Zein, turn to his expertise to answer their questions about Shi'a Islam and appreciate what he has done for Shi'ism in Senegal, they claim it is not enough. Many of them do not credit the Lebanese for introducing them to the Shi'a

---

1.   Aïdara (2003). Not all of the students enrolled in the sheikh's schools are Shi'a.

school of thought. "You know, the Senegalese Shiʿa did not learn Shiʿism from the Lebanese," one informant emphasized. He explained that the Lebanese are not very religious, being merchants and not intellectuals, and sometimes do not even know that they are Shiʿa. He complained that Sheikh el-Zein's work is limited to the Lebanese community that brought him to Senegal and finances his institution. Because the Lebanese are a closed community, marry and do business among themselves, and have their own culture, there is an "invisible barrier" between the Lebanese and Senegalese communities. For these reasons, Senegalese Shiʿa see Sheikh el-Zein's leadership of their movement to be no more than symbolic, as his activities are limited not only by the Lebanese community but also by the Senegalese government, with whom he does not want relations to sour by accusations of spreading propaganda. Some Senegalese Shiʿa hope for the emergence of an African Shiʿa leader.

Although Lebanese Shiʿa first arrived in Senegal over a century ago, today's Senegalese Shiʿa movement is much more recent, brought about by two processes.[1] First, Iranian books in Arabic, French and English translation began to circulate in Senegal as early as 1971. Second, the Lebanese sheikh, despite allegations that he is not doing enough, began to teach Shiʿism to the Senegalese. These two developments are evident in people's conversion stories.[2] While I must protect the identity of my informants, including their occupations, the men cited here are leaders of the Senegalese Shiʿa movement, active in its institutions and organizations, and fluent in Arabic, many having enjoyed a university education in the Arab world. One man claims to have been the first Senegalese to learn about Shiʿism in 1985 when he worked at the library of the Senegalese-Turkish school, aged twenty-two.[3] There he discovered books on Shiʿism,

---

1. Methods include formal and informal interviews with a few dozen leaders and members of the Senegalese Shiʿa movement, visiting schools, mosques, and institutions, and participant observation and discourse analysis at meetings and Ashura conferences. I collected cassettes of radio programs, Friday prayer sermons and video recordings of holiday celebrations.

2. For a more in-depth discussion of Senegalese converts see Leichtman (2009).

3. This is a school operated by the Fethullah Gülen revivalist movement in Turkey, with the view that Islam, as it developed in Anatolia, has a global aim. This vision encompasses education for all and Turkish schools have been established

but was told by a librarian that the Shi'a were heretics and the books were not useful. Such comments only sparked his imagination more, as man is always curious about what is forbidden to him, and he began to read. The library closed at six p.m., and he would often stay until ten or eleven at night discussing Shi'a ideas with his friends.

Another man discovered Shi'ism as a result of the Iranian revolution. He followed the press coverage of Khomeini, and was disgusted by the way in which he was demonized by Western and Senegalese journalists, and Shi'a were accused of being blasphemous. "I finally realized that [Shi'a Islam] is Islam in its primordial form; authentic, sincere and loyal." He saw the Iranian revolution, which for him restored dignity to Islam and belief to Muslims, as the only successful revolution since the time of Muhammad. He became Shi'a in 1987 in his late twenties.

A third man adopted the Shi'a school of thought shortly after the end of the Iran-Iraq war in 1988 when he was thirty-three. He was of that generation of critical students who discovered Shi'ism because of Imam Khomeini.

> I became Shi'a ... mainly to tranquilize myself, in the sense that Shi'a Islam offers solutions to all the issues I have been grappling with and could not find solutions or answers to anywhere else, except in Shi'a Islam. I found there the adequate answers I needed to satisfy my thirst.

Becoming a Shi'a was a sudden spiritual awakening for one young woman. One night in 1993, when she was just eleven years old, she had a dream in her village in southern Senegal, in which Fatima Zahra, the daughter of the Prophet Muhammad, appeared to her and told her that if she continued on the path she had begun for herself, it would bring her happiness. She had just begun to read the Qur'an. After her dream she began to wear the veil, against the will of her family, and she learned Shi'ism from one of her school teachers, an active believer. What her teacher, who later became her husband, taught her about the religion corresponded to what she saw in her dream.

---

in more than eighty countries, including throughout Africa. http://en.fgulen.com.

Other leaders of the Senegalese Shi'a movement discovered Shi'ism outside of Senegal. One man was studying in Canada in 1988 when he was nineteen; reading books on Islam alone in the library he discovered the Shi'a school of thought. He was drawn first to the spiritual message of Shi'a Islam, the notion of the Imamate, and only later became convinced by the philosophical arguments and the uses of logic and reason by Shi'a scholars. Another student was studying in Tunisia in the late 1970s and heard that Imam Khomeini was in France. He started asking questions: "Who is this Imam Khomeini? He is a Shi'a. What, then is Shi'ism?" The further he searched for answers to his questions, the more convinced he became that Shi'a Islam was the path for him, and he became a Shi'a in 1988. A third student at the University Cheikh Anta Diop of Dakar was introduced to Shi'ism in 1987 through magazines from Iran which he found in the Arabic department. After graduating, he went to Sierra Leone from 1989 to 1990, where he studied Shar'ia and Islamic law in a Lebanese-and-Iranian run *hawza*. In 1991, he got a scholarship from the Iranians to study in Qom for two years. Still others learned about Shi'ism at a younger age, when they were recruited from Sunni religious schools by Sheikh el-Zein and given scholarships to study in the Lebanese *Collège al-Zahraa*.

Senegalese Shi'a converts are from all ethnic groups in Senegal, primarily from various Sunni Muslim orders. While many of them were Tijan before becoming Shi'a, others were Murid or Qadir. One man, from a prestigious religious family of the Qadiriyya order in Ndiassane, was only able to learn about Shi'a Islam by leaving Senegal and the strong religious traditions of his family. He was teaching Arabic in Burkina Faso and one of his students had a book by Muhammad al-Tijani al-Samawi, called *Thumma Ihtadaitu* (Then I Was Guided), about the Tunisian author's discovery of Shi'a Islam. This teacher told his student, who was given the book by an Iranian school in Ouagadougou, that the Shi'a do not believe in God. But once he started to read the book, he could not stop. He went to a Shi'a library in Ouagadougou to get more facts, and immediately converted in 1990.

Not all who became Shi'a knew at first that their new convictions were Shi'a beliefs. One woman began to learn about Islam from the leaders of the Senegalese Shi'a movement, but was never told that they were teaching her Shi'a Islam. She began to wear the veil in 1990 in her mid-thirties; in those days the few veiled women in Senegal befriended each other. She had a friend who was a member of Ibadu Rahman, a reformist Sunni Muslim group characterized by women wearing Iranian-style dress.[1] The friend tried to initiate her into this school of thought, bringing her to some of the Ibadu Rahman leaders, who called her a Shi'a. She had never heard this word before, and began to read about Shi'ism, praying at night that God would guide her to choose the right path, Sunni or Shi'a Islam. One night in 1993 her prayers were answered. It was the dry season in Senegal, and as she prayed to end her confusion, a heavy rain began to fall. She understood this to be a sign from God and was thus convinced to identify openly as a Shi'a.

Not every Senegalese who comes in contact with Shi'ism is as strong a believer in the Shi'a cause. One informant describes three attitudes towards Shi'ism in Senegal. First are the Shi'a themselves. Second are the sympathizers, people who are not Shi'a but come to Shi'a gatherings and accept many Shi'a theories and beliefs. However, while they philosophically accept Shi'ism, they continue to practice as Sunni Muslims. Third are the opponents of Shi'ism, who have never read a book about Shi'ism and accept the stereotypes that Shi'a believe in Ali, and not Muhammad as the Prophet. This informant, a committed Shi'a in both belief and practice, argues that ignorance is the reason people are opposed to Shi'ism, but that once they begin to listen to Shi'a ideas, they too will "cross the border" from the Sunni to the Shi'a school of thought.

The Iranian Embassy in Dakar

The Iranian embassy has played a subtle role in encouraging Shi'a Islam in Dakar. Iran has a history of economic cooperation with Senegal from the time of the Shah, but the embassy was closed in 1984 for encouraging Islamic propaganda:

> The Senegalese authorities, according to these sources, have accused the staff of the embassy of unlawful activities, in particular: circulating

---

1. See Augis (2002); Loimeier (2003).

"extremist propaganda" among Senegalese Muslim associations and among the Lebanese Muslim community in Senegal; financing Senegalese associations as well as newspapers;[1] reinforcing their infrastructures and staff without authorization; and organizing visits to Mecca for the Senegalese despite repeated warnings.[2]

The Iranian Embassy reopened in the early 1990s, employing some Senegalese Shiʻa, and has been careful to stress only its economic activities in Senegal. However, certain events continue to promote Shiʻa Islam in Senegal. The embassy holds annual receptions for prominent Lebanese and Senegalese Muslims at the anniversary of the Islamic Revolution, in addition to purchasing full-page ads in Senegal's major newspapers publicizing the meaning of the revolution and Iran's subsequent evolution. The embassy sponsors an *iftar*, the dinner to break the fast at nightfall, on Jerusalem Day, the last Friday of Ramadan, as decreed by Khomeini to show solidarity with the Palestinian people. Iran also finances the attendance of certain Senegalese intellectuals at an annual conference on Islam in Tehran. Other events that have enhanced ties between Senegal and Iran include: a friendship pact between the Iranian Red Crescent and Senegal's Red Cross in April 1990; the visit of Ayatollah Yazdi, president of the judiciary power, to Senegal in May 1991; Rafsanjani's presence at the Organisation of the Islamic Conference Summit meeting in Dakar in October 1991; and his visit to Touba, the important pilgrimage site for Senegal's Murid order. President Wade has visited Iran in 2003 and 2006. *Hauza Al-Rassoul Al-Akram* in Point E, not far from the University of Dakar, was recently built by an Iranian sheikh, but claims not to be affiliated with the Iranian embassy. The teachers are mainly Senegalese Shiʻa who received scholarships to study in Qom.

The Iranian Embassy has more contacts with Senegalese than with Lebanese. Sheikh el-Zein claims that he does not have good relations with the embassy. He describes his work in Senegal as being not political, but benevolent and educational in nature. Because he does not promote the Iranian revolution, the embassy criticized him and published their

---

1. Iran helped finance the newspaper *WalFadjri*. See Kepel (2000) and Niasse (2003).
2. Drame (1984).

denunciation in a newspaper in Iran. The Lebanese Shi'a do not believe in Khomeini's *wilâyat al-faqîh* and these different views on the role of Islam in politics cause tensions between Iranian and other Shi'a. Sheikh el-Zein does, however, have contacts in Tehran, as was demonstrated by his involvement in the French hostage crisis. He was also present at Beirut Airport to greet Khatami during his 2003 visit to Lebanon. The Lebanese community at large has practically no connection with the few Iranians in Dakar, although occasionally an Iranian sheikh is present at Islamic Institute events.

Senegalese Shi'a practices

Senegalese Shi'a stress that while they may be influenced by Iranian or Lebanese Shi'a, the Islam they practice is distinct from that of the Middle East or Asia. Three provisions of Shi'a Islam, the *marja'* system, *taqiyya*, and the commemoration of Ashura, will be examined through comparing Senegalese and Lebanese practices. Many Shi'a emulate a *marja'*, a religious scholar from Najaf or Qom who serves as their reference. While not all Lebanese or Senegalese Shi'a are knowledgeable about this fundamental of Shi'ism, many Lebanese claim to follow Ayatollah Ali Sistani in Najaf because Sheikh el-Zein follows his teachings, and a few of them adhere to Sayyid Muhammad Husayn Fadlallah in Lebanon, the ex-spiritual leader of Hezbollah, whose status as *marja'* is disputed. The Senegalese are influenced by many more Shi'a thinkers. While some of them choose the teachings of Ayatollah Ali Khamenei, Khomeini's successor in Iran, others abide by the authority of a combination of others, including Fadlallah, Sistani, and, before his death, Muhammad Shirazi of Iran, who is popular among the Shi'a of the Gulf.[1] This fusion of *marja'* distinguishes them from the Lebanese sheikh, who follows Sistani exclusively, and the Iranian Embassy, which officially carries out the work of Khamenei. One Senegalese informant explained that the *marja'* system resembles Senegal's medical system: when somebody needs surgery and the medical specialist for their particular ailment cannot be found in Senegal, they go to France or another country for the operation. The *marja'* system works

---

1. Louër, Mervin and Roy (2003).

in the same way; if there is an expert in Shi'a Islam in Senegal, they can approach him with questions, but given the lack of expertise they go to Iran or Iraq. Books written by some of these *marja'* can be found in Senegal in Arabic, French and English translation.

Taqiyya (dissimulation) is permitted when persecution is imminent. Senegal is not a country where people are oppressed; therefore, Senegalese Shi'a claim, they do not need *taqiyya*. However, many of them are not open about being Shi'a and do practice dissimulation. For example, when praying in Sunni mosques, they hide their Shi'a ways to avoid lengthy explanations to people who are unlearned, who may not have open minds, and who may think that the Shi'a are mistaken in their practice of Islam. *Taqiyya* allows them to strengthen the relationship with Senegal's *umma* (Muslim community). Differences in the practice of Sunni and Shi'a Islam include variations in ablutions and the Shi'a use of a small clay tablet made from the earth of Karbala (or other natural material) during prayer. Furthermore, a small number of Senegalese scholars earned the turban in Iran for their knowledge of Shi'ism. While some wear it openly, others do not, afraid of being targeted by the Wahhabi anti-Shi'a campaign.[1] One Senegalese Shi'a sheikh, who studied in Iran during the Iranian revolution, leaves off his turban when in Senegal so that he can continue to guide both Sunni and Shi'a Muslims. Well respected for his knowledge of Islamic jurisprudence, he is not only a *wakîl* for Khamenei, but also a *muqaddam,* the Sunni equivalent of *wakîl,* for the Tijan Caliph Mansour Sy. Senegalese use of *taqiyya* to move adeptly between the Sunni and Shi'a worlds gives them more liberty than the formal Lebanese and Iranian institutions allow them. As such, they are key in convincing other Senegalese that Shi'a Islam is the true path. Lebanese Shi'a in Senegal

---

1. The term "Wahhabi" refers to an Islamic movement that purports to be ortho-dox, named after its Saudi founder Muhammad ibn Abd al-Wahhâb (1703–92). This name is rarely used by members of the group today, and was first devised by their opponents. Also known as Salafism, the movement accepts the Qur'an and Hadith as fundamental texts and advocates a puritanical and legalistic theology in matters of faith and religious practice. Salafists envision their role as restorers of Islam from what is perceived to be innovations, superstitions, deviancies, heresies and idolatries. Wahhabi ideology has spread to Africa, and common targets are Sufi and Shi'a Islam.

have no use for *taqiyya* as they are already identifiable as an ethnic and racial minority.

Another difference between Lebanese and Senegalese Shi'a is in the commemoration of Ashura. As described earlier, the Shi'a bring a visiting storyteller from Lebanon for a full ten days of lectures, food and decorations. They conduct activities in the Lebanese dialect, which is foreign to most Senegalese Shi'a, who are fluent in standard Arabic. Senegalese Shi'a prefer to organize their own tribute to Husayn through public debates that cater to a Senegalese Sunni Muslim audience in a mixture of Wolof, Arabic and French. Conferences and television and radio appearances discuss whether Ashura is a celebration or a day of mourning and play up the closeness that African Sufis also feel towards the family of the Prophet.

In addition to educating Senegalese about the history of the battle of Karbala, talks also address the origins of the Senegalese holiday Tamkharit, whose carnival-like festivities conflict with the somber remembrance of tragic events of Ashura.[1] A Senegalese Shi'a sheikh told me that religious practices reflect a people's customs.

> Whereas in Iran the Shi'a practice self-flagellation and some die (until Khomeini and later Khamenei forbade the practice), in Senegal the situation is different from places such as Iran, India, Pakistan ... you know, the Senegalese are very calm, not agitated, very sensitive, even. So we give our lectures, we awaken people, because chest-beating is not something that is required by Islam. Our approach is cultural. So as Senegalese we also have our habits and customs to respect. For our part, as Shi'a, what we do is organize lectures, only lectures, nothing

---

1. Tamkharit, like Ashura, falls on the tenth day of the month of *Muharram*, but it is a joyful occasion resulting in a sort of Muslim Halloween where members of Sufi orders feast on couscous with beef, girls dress as boys and boys as girls, and women and children receive gifts to the rhythm of drums. Senegalese Muslims chant nocturnal evocations on the night of the ninth of *Muharram*, and the holiday also evokes the obligation to give in charity to help the most deprived. Tamkharit is believed to be a syncretism between Islamic rituals and pre-Islamic popular practices linked to the Lebou ethnic group's offerings to pagan divinities. Some believe that Tamkharit is a product of the Omayyads, and that Yazîd, the son of Mu'âwiya, was its promoter; others consider its pagan rituals very far from Islamic prescriptions.

more. It is an intellectual activity. What we want is to truly respect that, to adapt it to our reality, because Imam Husayn and those who were chest-beating were generally people who were redeeming themselves. They were confessing something.

Lebanese and Senegalese live Shi'ism in different ways, in their knowledge, practice, and application of the religion. Despite the formal and institutional interventions of the Lebanese sheikh and the Iranian Embassy, Senegalese have adapted Shi'a Islam to their own spiritual needs and in accordance to their financial means.

The development of the Senegalese Shi'a movement

Senegalese Shi'a perceive their calling as a mission – to spread the truth about Shi'ism and to encourage the growth of their movement. This is achieved through various means, most of which involve, in the words of one founder of a Shi'a association:

> Teaching. Teaching is crucial and organizing public lectures is one way to disseminate our ideas. We organize a lot of them because people are willing and ready to attend lectures, roundtables, study days, study nights, debates, discussions ... So that is how we were able to expand interest in the subject. That is how we were able to attract the attention, most notably of young people, towards Shi'a Islam.

Senegalese Shi'a, however, do not all share the same vision of how to make Islam understood to other Senegalese. Despite being a small minority movement, there are numerous Shi'a institutes, a testimony to the Senegalese insistence on doing things their own way. Some prefer teaching, while others are working towards establishing a formal Shi'a movement. Some encourage political involvement, while yet others spread the word through radio or television programs. Because they arrived at Shi'ism from various perspectives, usually after a Sufi, Salafist or French education, they envision their missionary work in different ways.

Building Islamic schools and institutions

Many Senegalese Shi'a schools and institutes were built in the 1990s, and they are hidden in Dakar's suburbs of Guediawaye, Parcelles and Yeumbeul, or in cities in the Casamance region of southern Senegal, such as Kolda and Ziguinchor. Built on the outskirts of villages or deep inside the residential maze of the suburbs, the quasi-invisibility of these institutes is another form of *taqiyya*. Hard to find and therefore hard to target, these institutions cater to those who are open to learning from them, Shi'a and Sunni Muslims alike. Senegalese and Lebanese Shi'a finance these institutes through the *khums*. Nonetheless, Senegalese are critical of both Lebanese and Iranians for not getting more involved in their activities and being more generous. One sheikh told me there are myriad institutions despite the small number of Shi'a because the founder of each new institute hopes for funding from the Iranians – unfortunately for them, to no avail.

Dakar's suburb of Guediawaye was chosen as the site for the *Ali Yacine (PSLF) Centre Islamique de Recherche et d'Information* because, as its founder told me, the neighborhood was full of dance and music, not religion and scholarship. The small institute was initially located in a rented building in the popular residential quarter with goats roped outside and laundry drying in the wind. It consisted of a small mosque, a table and chairs for classes, and a library with two old computers. A phone booth was built in the institute to help finance its activities, and a large television was installed to attract passers-by, to use the telephone or to discover Islam. The Islamic center in particular and Shi'a Islam in general were publicized by the distribution of a calendar containing colorful photos of the Iranian Ayatollahs Khomeini and Khamenei.[1]

These methods were successful and in February 2007 *Ali Yacine* moved to a larger building purchased by the Islamic center, which consists of a salon furnished with sofas and a computer room with newer facilities – two computers, several printers, scanners, a photocopier, and a large

---

1. Distributing calendars to clients at the start of each year to advertise a business or institute is a common practice in Senegal. Often calendars portray glossy photos of Sufi marabouts. Replacing such photos with Shi'a leaders is one adaptation of Shi'a Islam to a Senegalese custom.

hifi installation with fancy speakers, all donated by the wives of several ambassadors to Senegal. A library/prayer room is full of Shi'a books from Iran and Lebanon, and some that Sheikh el-Zein has published in Senegal. Most books are in Arabic, dealing with philosophy and Islam in general, with a few in French, especially contributions written by Ayatollah Musavi Lari of Qom.[1] Outside in the courtyard there was a tutoring session for a dozen high school students who were struggling with their math lessons. I was told that the center is a Franco-Islamic school, and lessons are both religious and secular in nature. Activities include Arabic classes for adults and children, and the sheikh who founded the center teaches a *tafsir* (Qur'anic commentary) class on Thursday nights and philosophy and *fiqh* (Islamic jurisprudence) on Saturdays. The institute hosts celebrations for Ramadan and *mawlud*, the Prophet's birthday, in addition to Ashura. If the center continues to grow, the plan is to add an additional floor to the house. Religious pictures of Mecca and Ayatollahs Khomeini and Khamenei decorate the walls, in addition to photographs of the center's founder with Sheikh el-Zein and various Iranian religious and political dignitaries.

Ali Yacine also expanded to become *Association Pour le Developpement Humain Durable*, with plans to apply for NGO status for its work with the environment, drugs, malaria, AIDS and famine. This includes an *Association Fatima Zahra*, a women's development organization that functions as a *tontine* (a Senegalese rotating credit association) and encourages the women to work, for example, selling powdered soap or vegetables in small quantities. The association also provides free medical consultations for the neighborhood and envisions itself as working to eradicate poverty. The founder of *Ali Yacine* told me that being merely an Islamic organization no longer suffices without also providing services to the people.

Madrasat Imam Al-Baqr in Yeumbeul is an Arabic-French school of 139 students (in 2003), led by a Shi'a sheikh who studied in Iran during the

---

1. Sayyid Mojtaba Musavi Lari established the Office for the Diffusion of Islamic Culture Abroad in Qom in 1980. This organization dispatches free copies of his translated works throughout the world and has printed copies of the Qur'an for free distribution among Muslim individuals, institutions and religious schools in Africa. (www.irib.ir/worldservice/Etrat/English/Nabi/Besat/seal1.htm)

revolution. The oldest students form a youth association called *Jama'at Ahl Al Beit,* with thirty-five active male and female members. The association helps the school with fundraisers and event planning. They distribute letters and invitations to people, set up tents and chairs for invitees and buy sheep for celebrations. Books come from a variety of places: the Qur'an from Saudi Arabia; Arabic grammar books from Lebanon; an Arabic math book from Nigeria; Maliki *fiqh* books from Tunisia; history books written by Sheikh el-Zein; and books with French lessons from Senegal. Whereas it is common for Islamic schools to acquire books from many places, in Senegal many Islamic schools do not have any books at all. The fact that the Shi'a schools make books available to their students attests to the importance that educators place on literacy. The school is financed through student fees and donations from the Lebanese community, Senegalese remittances from Gabon, America and France, and Shi'a in India, Lebanon and Iran, among other sources.

Schools in the Casamance region of Senegal are smaller and poorer. The school in Kolda is situated in the outskirts of the village, and few people know of its existence. The school comprises two classrooms, a small cement mosque with a tin roof, doors and window shutters, a farm with sheep, goats and chickens, a well and a satellite dish. The sheikh and his family reside in the school. In Ziguinchor, *Ecole al-Rassoul al-Islamiyatou as-Sahihatou* is located five kilometers outside of town, well hidden among agricultural fields. Part of the children's education includes manual labor in the fields, following the tradition of West African Sufi *madaris.*[1] Schools in the south of Senegal tend to be dominated by Senegalese sheikhs trained by Sheikh el-Zein, whereas the Senegalese sheikhs heading the institutions in Dakar and its suburbs were trained in Iran.

Media and publicity

The Shi'a took advantage of the popularity of radio in Senegal to spread knowledge about Shi'a Islam on the air. Radio Dunyaa was the first station to sponsor a program on Shi'a Islam, which started in 1994 and lasted a year and a half. Leaders of the Shi'a movement spoke on Wednesday nights from midnight to 6 a.m., and took questions from their audience. The show was

---

1. See Brenner (2001).

later moved to Friday evenings. The goal of the radio shows was to counter Wahhabi propaganda, and debates concerned differences between Sunnism and Shi'ism, and discussed monotheism, the Qur'an, the prophecy and Islamic history. Radio served as publicity for the Shi'a movement, helping Senegalese people to discover that Shi'ism is Islam, despite its portrayal by the Wahhabis. The program soon came to an end, however, as Radio Dunyaa's Wahhabi funders disagreed with the station's use of its airtime. Walfadjri Radio began where Radio Dunyaa left off, creating an Islamic radio show on Friday afternoons from 3:30 to 5 p.m., which was repeated later in the week. This show, which is only a few years old, chooses popular topics and invites speakers representing different Islamic schools to voice their opinions. One program paired Youssou N'dour, Senegal's most famous musician, with a Shi'a painter to discuss what Islam says about art. Senegalese Shi'a also publish articles on religious topics in Senegalese newspapers, and speak on Islamic television programs.

El Hadj Ibrahim Derwiche mosque

El Hadj Ibrahim Derwiche, a prominent Lebanese industrialist, built a large Shi'a mosque located next to his empire of sanitary, plumbing and kitchen appliances, Sheikh el-Zein's *al-Zahraa* school, and Dakar's main bus station. The mosque is headed by a Senegalese sheikh, dressed in full Shi'a robes and turban, and is the only Senegalese Shi'a institution in a central location. It is impressive, with high ceilings and a decorated plaster dome, and is packed with a few thousand devout Muslims during Friday prayer. Friday sermons are given in Wolof to a mixed group of Murid, Tijan, Qadir and a minority of Shi'a Muslims. The sheikh also teaches classes in a three-room school, constructed by Hadj Derwiche. Senegalese Shi'a pray in this mosque, as well as in Sheikh el-Zein's mosque.

Senegalese Shi'a associations

Various associations exist for Senegalese Shi'a, the largest of which, *Ansar Muhammad*, was created in 1999. The temporary headquarters of this association were located outside the residence of one of its members, on a cement platform at the top of a staircase. The members could not afford chairs or electricity, so their Friday evening meetings were lit by moonlight.

The objectives of the movement were "to contribute to the development of our country (...) the principal vocation (...): to use Islam to serve the Senegalese people by making them understand Islam, and to teach them Shiʻa Islam, and use it as the medium to realize these objectives." The movement was active in organizing debates on Islam in various locations throughout Senegal, and in sponsoring dinners and celebrations of the major Islamic holidays. Other smaller associations met regularly for prayer and study meetings in various locations in and around Dakar. One group met every Sunday night in a lovely little mosque on the corniche.[1] They studied together and lectured one another on Shiʻism with the sound of the waves crashing in the background.

I was surprised to find that many of these fledgling associations had disbanded when I returned to Senegal in 2007. Some – although not all – of those involved in the earlier movements had joined a larger institute, well financed (some say by the Iranians), which had suddenly emerged on the Senegalese Shiʻa scene (although press releases claim the idea for the institute was first initiated in 2000). Mozdahir International, founded by a Senegalese *sherif* (one who claims descent from the Prophet Muhammad) of Mauritanian origin from Kolda, and who published a book on the Succession of the Prophet Muhammad, is located near Dakar's airport and consists of offices, a large salon and library, a prayer room and classrooms. The institute's goals are the promotion of education, health and agro-pastoral development. It runs agricultural projects in Kolda with the aim of teaching workers how to farm banana plantations and share the profits, in the hope of keeping young farmers rooted in Senegal and helping to prevent illegal immigration, a growing problem in Africa. Like *Ali Yacine*, Mozdahir International uses Shiʻa Islam, and the teaching of the Prophet Muhammad to "work in this world as if you will live forever, and for the next world as if you will die tomorrow" to carry out development activities in the name of religion.[2] Mozdahir International also sponsored a large colloquium on 27 January 2007 on "Ashura: A Day of Celebration or a Day of Mourning?", the first of its kind in Senegal

---

1. Despite the protests of community members, this mosque has since been demolished in a large construction project to "modernize" Dakar for the 2008 Organization of the Islamic Conference summit.
2. See Tall (2006).

(and possibly in Africa), and published conference papers in a French volume, with an Arabic translation forthcoming, in addition to producing a DVD of the event. Their 12 January 2008 "annual conference" was titled "The Role of the Imams of Ahl al-Bayt (may peace be upon them) in the Preservation of Islam and the Unity of Muslims." Some converts believe that the founder of Mozdahir International is the African Shi'a leader they had been waiting for.

A small but growing movement, Senegalese Shi'a are spread over various locations, and rely on different public followings and financial networks, some depending entirely on funding from wealthier non-Senegalese Shi'a, others accepting donations but also creating means to become financially independent. They know each other and speak highly of the others' work, but the movement's leaders tend to work independently in their native neighborhoods or in areas that they think are ripe for change. Leaders specialize in different aspects of Shi'a Islam. Some are trained sheikhs whose expertise ranges from Islamic jurisprudence to Sunni and Shi'a philosophy; others are laymen who are artists, government employees, bankers, teachers and students. Coming together occasionally for certain meetings and holidays, the Senegalese Shi'a follow a theory of divide and conquer, despite their small and generally unknown presence, to reach out to as many people as possible.

Conclusion

Whereas the Iranian revolution has succeeded in drawing Senegalese Muslims to Shi'a Islam, it has not achieved its goal of Muslim unity worldwide, or even Shi'a unity in Senegal. Despite belonging to a minority religion in Senegal, Lebanese and Senegalese Shi'a form two distinct ethnic, racial and socio-economic communities. Both are part of a global Shi'a movement, but in different ways and through different networks. The Lebanese community provides an example of the changing role of ethnicity in the imagining of a migrant community and its impact on religious identity. Although part of the economic elite, many Lebanese do not have a formal university or Islamic education, and many cannot read or write the Arabic language. Shi'a identity is synonymous with having origins in South Lebanon, and Hezbollah's *al-Manar* television channel informs the Lebanese in Senegal of the struggles of their brothers in the motherland. While many Lebanese Shi'a are not religious, others follow the lead of Sheikh el-Zein and learn from his lectures, often pronounced in the Lebanese dialect for their benefit. They partake in elaborate celebrations of Muslim holidays and organize fancy fundraising dinners for their Islamic charity institutions. A closed community, the Lebanese of Senegal do not seek to proselytize their religion to include Senegalese Muslims. Instead, they identify themselves ethnically as Lebanese, and Muslims and Christians unite for the common needs of Lebanese merchants.

The Lebanese sheikh has different goals from the Lebanese community. Brought to Senegal at the request of the Lebanese Shi'a, and initially focusing his work on the Lebanese community, his objective as a religious leader is to increase his following. As there is a limited and decreasing number of Lebanese in Senegal, the sheikh has begun to include the Senegalese population in his efforts as well. Changing his discourse depending on his audience, referring either to an exclusive Shi'ism or to a more global Islam, the sheikh is a man of politics as much as he is a man of religion. In acquiring the title Caliph Ahl al-Beit, placing him at the same level as the heads of Senegal's marabout families, the sheikh has been nationally recognized as the leader of the Shi'a in Senegal, expanding his influence beyond the Lebanese community.

However, the sheikh's inclusion of the Senegalese population is recent, perhaps competitively encouraged by the influence of the Iranian revolution on the religious and political ideologies of Senegalese Muslims. While the Iranian Embassy has had a turbulent history in Senegal and has avoided the public proclamation of religion after reopening, its activities, carried out under the guise of economic development, continue to be Islamic. In addition, the role of non-governmental Iranian institutions and individuals in spreading knowledge of Shi'ism by sending books to Senegal, bringing Senegalese to Iran, or building a *hawza* in Dakar cannot be ignored.

Awakened to the existence of Shi'a Islam through these two independent transnational Shi'a networks, one Lebanese (Arab) and the other Iranian (Persian), the Senegalese continued to discover Shi'a Islam on their own. Fluent in the Arabic language, many have university degrees from the Arab world and pride themselves in their knowledge of both Sunni and Shi'a schools of thought. Drawn to the religion for many reasons – political, spiritual, philosophical, financial, or because Shi'a scholars convincingly answered their questions about Islam – their mission is to convince others. They spread knowledge of Shi'a Islam in Wolof or other local languages, first to their friends and families, and eventually to a larger population through teaching, conferences, holiday celebrations and media publicity.

Depending on the Lebanese sheikh and prominent community members to help finance their institutions and activities, Senegalese Shi'a also hope for more tangible rewards from Iran for their faith. Forming a network of missionaries, where each intellectual reigns over his village or neighborhood, they support each other's work while respecting each other's domains. Most importantly, while influenced by the *marja'* of Iran, Iraq, and Lebanon, they emphasize that their Shi'ism is *Senegalese* (African). Indeed, through keeping their feet in both Sunni and Shi'a worlds, the Senegalese Shi'a hope to find their place in the country's politics of religion. Religious transformation and adhesion can thus be understood through historical and political contexts: despite global and transnational influences of Shi'a Islam in Senegal, sharing the religion theologically or culturally does not imply connections to believers' ethnic, racial, socioeconomic or national identities.

Bibliography

Aïdara, Abdel Karim, "Trente-Quatre Années au Service de l'Islam au Sénégal: Cheikh Abdul Monem El Zein, un Atypique Cheikh Chiite au Sénégal ...", in *Le Messager*, 84, Tuesday 2 December 2003, p. 4.

Ajami, Fouad, *The Vanished Imam: Musa al Sadr and the Shia of Lebanon*, Ithaca 1986, Cornell University Press.

Augis, Erin Joanna, *Dakar's Sunnite Women: The Politics of Person*, PhD Thesis, Department of Sociology, The University of Chicago, December 2002.

Behrman, Lucy C., *Muslim Brotherhoods and Politics in Senegal*, Cambridge, MA 1970 (1999), Harvard University Press.

Boumedouha, Said, *The Lebanese in Senegal: A History of the Relationship Between an Immigrant Community and its French and African Rulers*, PhD Thesis, Center of West African Studies, University of Birmingham, October 1987.

Brenner, L., *Controlling Knowledge: Religion, Power and Schooling in a West African Muslim Society,* Bloomington 2001, Indiana University Press.

Cinquantenaire, *Cinquantenaire de la Paroisse Notre-Dame du Liban,* Dakar 1999, Paroisse Notre-Dame du Liban.

Cohen, Abner, *Custom and Politics in Urban Africa: A Study of Hausa Migrants in Yoruba Towns,* Berkeley 1969, University of California Press.

Copans, J., *Les Marabouts de l'arachide: la confrérie mouride et les paysans du Sénégal,* Paris 1980, Le Sycomore.

Cruise O'Brien, Donal B., *The Mourides of Senegal: The Political and Economic Organization of an Islamic Brotherhood,* Oxford 1971, Clarendon Press.

Cruise O'Brien, Donal B., Diop, M. C., and Diouf, M., eds, *La construction de l'État au Sénégal,* Paris 2002, Karthala.

Delaney, Carol, "The Hajj: Sacred and Secular", in *American Ethnologist,* 17/3 1990, pp. 513–30.

Diop, M. C., *Sénégal : trajectoires d'un État,* Dakar 1992, CODESRIA.

Diop, M. C., and Diouf, M., *Le Sénégal sous Abdou Diouf : État et Société,* Paris 1990, Karthala.

Drame, Alioune, "Fermeture de l'ambassade d'Iran : Coup d'arrêt", in *Le Soleil,* 6 February 1984.

Halawi, Majid, *A Lebanon Defied: Musa al-Sadr and the Shia Community,* Boulder 1992, Westview Press.

Hanf, Theodor, *Coexistence in Wartime Lebanon: Decline of a State and Rise of a Nation,* London 1993, I.B. Tauris & Co Ltd.

Harrison, Christopher, *France and Islam in West Africa, 1860–1960,* Cambridge, MA 1988, Cambridge University Press.

Hourani, Albert, and Shehadi, Nadim, eds., *The Lebanese in the World: A Century of Emigration,* London 1992, I.B. Tauris & Co Ltd.

Kane, O., and Triaud, J. L., eds., *Islam et islamismes au sud du Sahara,* Paris 1998, Karthala.

Kepel, G., *Jihad : expansion et déclin de l'islamisme,* Paris 2000, Gallimard.

Labaki, Boutros, "L'émigration libanaise en Afrique occidentale sud-saharienne", in *Revue Européenne des Migrations Internationales,* 9/2 1993, pp. 91–112.

Leichtman, M., "The Legacy of Transnational Lives: Beyond the First Generation of Lebanese in Senegal", in *Ethnic and Racial Studies,* 28(4) 2005, pp. 663–686.

Leichtman, M., *A Tale of Two Shi'isms: Lebanese Migrants and Senegalese Converts in Dakar,* PhD Dissertation, Department of Anthropology, Brown University, May 2006.

Leichtman, M. "Revolution, Modernity and (Trans)National Shi'i Islam: Rethinking Religious Conversion in Senegal," in *Journal of Religion in Africa* 39(3) 2009, pp. 319–351.

Leichtman, M. "Migration, War and the Making of a Transnational Lebanese

Shi'i Community in Senegal," in *International Journal of Middle East Studies* 42(2) 2010, pp. 269–290.

Loimeier, Roman, "Patterns and Peculiarities of Islamic Reform in Africa", in *Journal of Religion in Africa* 33(3) 2003, pp. 237–62.

Louër, Laurence, Mervin, Sabrina, and Roy, Olivier, "Les chiites d'Irak : renaissance à Najaf" round table, in *Esprit*, 296, 2003, pp. 82–97.

Magassouba, Moriba, *L'islam au Sénégal. Demain les mullahs?*, Paris 1985, Karthala.

Maier, Karl, *This House Has Fallen: Midnight in Nigeria*, New York 2000, BBS Public Affairs.

Niasse, S. L., *Un arabisant entre presse et pouvoir*, Dakar 2003, Éditions Groupe Wal Fadjri.

Pean, Pierre, *Manipulations Africaines*, Paris 2001, Plon.

Penrad, Jean-Claude, "'Sauti Ya Bilal', ou les Transformations de l'Islam Shia Missionnaire en Afrique Orientale", in *Islam et Sociétés au Sud du Sahara*, 2, 1988, pp. 17–33.

Piga, Adriana, *Dakar et les Ordres Soufis. Processus socioculturels et développement Urbain au Sénégal Contemporain*, Paris 2002, L'Harmattan.

Rizvi, Seyyid Saeed Akhtar, and King, Noel Q., "The Khoja Shia Ithna-Asheriya Community in East Africa (1840–1967)", in *The Muslim World*, LXIV/3 1974, pp. 194–204.

Robinson, David, *Paths of Accommodation: Muslim Societies and French Colonial Authorities in Senegal and Mauritania, 1880–1920*, Athens, OH 2000, Ohio University Press.

Robinson, D., and Triaud, J. L., eds.,*Le temps des marabouts : itinéraires et stratégies islamiques en Afrique occidentale française v. 1880–1960*, Paris 1997, Karthala.

Al-Samawi, Muhammad al-Tijani, *Then I Was Guided,* Kuwait, Committee Ahl Al-Bait Charity.

Seck, Ndiougou W., Diop, Idrissa, & Aïdara, Abdel K., "...Cheikh Abdul Monem El Zein: Des réalisations pour soigner l'âme et corps', in *Le Messager*, 84, Tuesday 2 December 2003, p. 4.

Sulaiman, Muhammad Dahiru, "Shiism and the Islamic Movement in Nigeria 1979-1991", in *Islam et Sociétés au Sud du Sahara*, 7, 1993, pp. 5–16.

Tall, Al Hadj Khaly, "Cheikh Abdoul Moneim Zein khalife de la famille du Prophète au Sénégal", in *Le Soleil*, Tuesday 28 May 2002, p. 5.

Tall, Al Hadj Khaly, "Organisations Islamiques au Service du Développement: Les Exemples de 'Mozdahir'," in *Le Soleil,* July 14 2006 http://www.lesoleil.sn/imprimertout.php3?id_rubrique=355.

Taraf, Souha, *L'espace en mouvement. Dynamiques migratoires et territorialisation des familles Libanaises au Sénégal* (Doctorate), Tours 1994, Université de Tours.

Thibault, Jean, "Les Libanais en Afrique: Parasites ou Agents de Développement?", in *Voix d'Afrique*, 24, 4–17 October 1976.

Triaud, J. L., and Robinson, D., eds., *La Tijâniyya : une confrérie musulmane à la conquête de l'Afrique*, Paris 2002, Karthala.

Umar, Muhammad Sani, "Education and Islamic Trends in Northern Nigeria: 1970s–1990s," in *Africa Today* 48(2) 2001, pp. 127–50.

Youssef, Jihad, "Senegal: Efforts to Strengthen its Deeprooted Islam", in *Noor Al Islam: Islamic Cultural Magazine*, 51–52 1994, pp. 3–14.

El-Zein, Cheikh Abdul Monem, *L'Islam: Ma Doctrine et Ma Loi* (5eme edition). Dakar 2001, l'Institution Islamique Sociale.

Archives Nationales du Sénégal, Dakar: Renseignements (50 – Source Indigène – Bonne)," 14 June 1945, 21G8(1); 21G23(17).

PART THREE

Which Iranian Model?

PIERRE-JEAN LUIZARD

The Sadrists in Iraq: Challenging the United States, the *Marja'iyya* and Iran

Muqtadâ al-Sadr arrived on the scene shortly after the US troops' forced march across Iraq. In a radio interview on 18 February 2003, Paul Wolfowitz stated: "The Iraqis are mostly secularized. In majority Shi'a, they do not give the impression of being aware that they have holy cities on their territory." On 7 April 2003, two days before the official fall of Baghdad, al-Sadr's supporters sprang into action, attacking police stations, taking over arms depots and establishing control over the huge disinherited quarter of Madînat Saddâm, which the communists still call *al-Thawra* (the revolution). They renamed it Madînat al-Sadr (Sadr City for the international media). With over two million inhabitants, almost half of the population of Baghdad, the quarter came under the control of a movement that was then practically unknown, and which the US specifically had been largely unaware of. Madînat al-Sadr thus became the first part of Iraqi territory to experience the power of local militias and, with the exception of Kurdistan, has remained the only enclave where this situation continues uninterrupted. From the first days of the occupation, Jamâ'at al-Sadr al-Thânî (named after Ayatollah Muhammad Sâdiq al-Sadr, Muqtadâ's father) installed a new local power, ensured public order, regulated the life of the inhabitants, and instituted its own police force and a justice system based on sharia.

Muqtadâ: between Shi'a puritanism and Iraqi tribalism

So who is Muqtadâ al-Sadr? He is the survivor of a massacre perpetrated on his family on the orders of Saddam Hussein's regime in February 1999. The regime killed his father, Ayatollah Muhammad Sâdiq al-Sadr, and two of his brothers. His age is not known with any certainty: his biography[1] states that he was born in 1974 but he is more likely to be between twenty-five and thirty years old at the time of writing (2006). His father was not a great *marja'* and had little in common with the "first Sadr", Ayatollah Muhammad Bâqir al-Sadr, who was also executed by Saddam Hussein's regime when the Iran-Iraq war started in 1980. Whereas the first Sadr, Muqtadâ's cousin and father-in-law, was an accomplished intellectual and a prolific author, whose ambition was to formulate an Islamic response to the questions of the age (he was a direct inspiration for the constitution of the Islamic Republic of Iran), the "second Sadr", Muqtadâ's father, whose life was dominated by decades of Ba'athist dictatorship and a besieging of the *marja'iyya* by a ruthless power, left a very limited literary output. In the late 1960s, he published two books, *al-Islâm wa al-mîthâq al-'âlamiyya li-huqûq al-insân* (Islam and the Iinternational Treaty of Human Rights) and *Mâ warâ' al-fiqh* (What lies behind the fiqh), which can purchased anywhere on Baghdad's streets today. Compared to the ample oeuvre of the first Sadr, it is a pittance.

Ayatollah Muhammad Bâqir al-Sadr was torn from anonymity by his confrontation with Saddam Hussein's regime. In 1992, Grand Ayatollah Abû al-Qâsim al-Khû'î had recently died and the question of succession promised to be difficult. The *marja'iyya* of Najaf was caught between incessant repression from Baghdad and an Islamic Republic of Iran that had turned the entire Shi'a world upside down and undermined the foundations of religious authority.

After the Shi'a intifada of February and March 1991, Saddam Hussein tried to reestablish his hold over the Shi'a community by "retribalizing" its power networks. The sheikhs of some tribes were encouraged to exercise control on behalf of the government in their regions, while the Iraqi authorities legitimized tribal practices, notably at the expense of women.

---

1. The "official" biography of Muqtadâ al-Sadr can be consulted on http://www.muqtada.com

By promoting tribal identities, the Iraqi regime hoped to get some leverage over a society that it had harshly oppressed, and additionally to bypass Najaf. (Historically, relations between Shi'a tribes and the Shi'a religious establishment have always consisted of a mix of reverence and incomprehension. The tribal world, imbued with Bedouin values, remains distant from the elitist, erudite and cosmopolitan world of the *hawza*.)

Tribal customs do not always agree with sharia as the *mujtahid* see it. The regime's new tribal policy could work. However, it was still missing a religious seal of approval; the regime would find this in the person of Muhammad Sâdiq al-Sadr. As an Arab, he was opposed to the "Persian ayatollahs", and he subsequently conferred Islamic justification on a number of tribal rulings, which are laid out in his *Fiqh al-'ashâ'ir* (The Fiqh of the Tribes) and which today enjoy widespread distribution in Madînat al-Sadr and the cities of the Iraqi south. In this controversial work, al-Sadr attempted to reconcile sharia with tribal customs, notably giving tribal leaders the right to apply Islamic law.

After the deaths of Sabzavâri and Golpâyegâni, the recognized successor to Khû'î seemed to be Ayatollah Sîstânî. It was in opposition to Sîstânî, therefore, that Baghdad put forward the *marja'iyya* of Muhammad Sâdiq al-Sadr. For a while, Muhammad Sâdiq al-Sadr fulfilled the function of "official Ayatollah" for Saddam Hussein's regime, and was denounced for this by every Shi'a authority. From 1997 onwards, however, al-Sadr claimed the right to lead the Friday prayer. (In Iran the authorities are considered to be "Shi'a", and the *emâm-e jom'a* [Friday Imams] are traditionally appointed by the government to pronounce the Friday sermon in the important mosques, In Iraq, the *marja'* expressed their rejection of a "foreign" and/or Sunni power by refusing to pronounce Friday sermons; to do so would have been to legitimize the regime. The Friday sermon had been reinstated by Ayatollah Mahdî al-Khâlisî in the 1920s, as a demonstration of anti-British mobilization, and was seen by the Iraqi powers as a direct challenge – rightly so, since it was pronounced in the name of the *marja'* without mentioning the name of the president.) In the same year, al-Sadr began to oppose the government openly, issuing a *fatwa* demanding the release of 106 Shi'a clerics imprisoned since the intifada of 1991. Actions such as these, combined with his work to increase tribal rights, made him a rallying figure for Iraqi Shiʿa; suddenly the regime's puppet was becoming a serious threat. Although warned in 1999 that Saddam Hussein was losing patience with his actions, he was defiant; on the day he was assassinated he was wearing his death shroud, to symbolize the Shiʿa refusal to be intimidated.

After the death of his father, Muqtadâ went into hiding. Muhammad Sâdiq al-Sadr had left instructions to his supporters: he called on his followers to refer to Ayatollah Kâzim al-Husaynî al-Hâʾirî, who lives in Qom. This cleric, who was born in Iran but spent the major part of his life in Iraq, where he was a co-founder of the al-Daʿwa party in the 1950s, had been forced to flee to Iran in the 1970s because his political activities had put his life in jeopardy. As a proponent of *wilâyat al-faqîh*, Kâzim al-Hâʾirî today recognizes the *marjaʿiyya* of Khamenei, whom he serves as a close adviser. Muhammad Sâdiq al-Sadr specified: "Let my emulators follow Ayatollah Kâzim al-Husaynî al-Hâʾirî until one of my students becomes a *marjaʿ*." From that point on, Kâzim al-Hâʾirî was considered the successor to Ayatollah Muhammad Sâdiq al-Sadr, as well as the religious reference for his son Muqtadâ, who does not have any proper religious authority himself. (Although Muqtadâ's biography describes him as a *mujtahid*, most students of the *hawza* of Najaf doubt that he took even a minimum of religious courses and claim never to have seen him attending the seminars of the great *marjaʿ*.) On 8 April 2003 Kâzim al-Hâʾirî issued a *fatwa* calling on his supporters to obey Muqtadâ and to ignore the American occupation, inviting the Shiʿa to fill the power void. This is exactly what the Sadrists have done in Madînat al-Sadr.

First confrontation with the *marjaʿiyya* and the coalition forces

After coming to power in the largest quarter of Baghdad, the Sadrists rapidly entered into violent confrontation with the Shiʿa establishment. On 3 April 2003, while the American, British and Polish troops were still in the south of Iraq on their way to Baghdad, ʿAbd al-Majîd al-Khûʾî, the elder son of the late ayatollah, returned to Iraq. After the crushing of the 1991 Shiʿa uprising and the subsequent repression, which affected a number of clerics, ʿAbd al-Majîd had taken refuge in London, where he led the Khoei Foundation, an extension of his father's *marja'iyya* that was active not only in Iraq, but throughout Asia and Africa. Arriving in Najaf ahead of the coalition forces, he succeeded in meeting with Ayatollah Sîstânî along with two of his aides, before he was killed by a mob in front of the mausoleum of Imam 'Alî. Almost all the people in the crowd were Muqtadâ al-Sadr's followers. Three days later, one hundred members of the Jamâ'at al-Sadr al-Thânî surrounded Ayatollah Sîstânî's residence in Najaf, ordering him to return to Iran within forty-eight hours. The siege was lifted only after Sîstânî called in 1,500 tribesmen from the surrounding countryside, who managed to disperse the menacing crowd.

Representatives of the *hawza* subsequently carried out an inquiry and declared Muqtadâ responsible for the murder of Khû'î. They passed the result of their inquiry to a US Marine officer, who transmitted it to his superiors, but the coalition authority took no immediate measures. The war was still ongoing and the time had not yet come to bring people to justice, which would look like interference in the internal affairs of the Shi'a community. Shortly after, the *kalîdâr* (guardian) of the mausoleum of Imam 'Alî was also assassinated, again apparently by supporters of Muqtadâ. Haydar al-Rufây'î knew the secret location of the entrance to a basement where the mausoleum treasures were kept: the Sadrists were later accused of looting these treasures when their troops barricaded themselves inside the mausoleum in 2004.

The confrontation between Muqtadâ and the *marja'iyya* thus began with bloodshed. The Sadrists reproached 'Abd al-Majîd for returning from exile in the tanks of the American army, whereas they themselves claimed to represent a "national and patriotic Shi'ism". They also accused him of attempting to persuade Ayatollah Sîstânî to collaborate with the coalition forces. They denounced the *kalîdâr* for his connection to Saddam, and Ayatollah Sîstânî both for being "Iranian" and for failing to oppose the occupation overtly. On 11 April 2003, Muqtadâ gave his first sermon in the mosque of Kûfa, which would function as his platform from then onwards.

Friction between the Sadrists and the inhabitants of the holy cities did not end there. Several Najafis were arrested by Muqtadâ's militia and brought before religious courts instituted in his name, where some were subsequently sentenced to death. At the same time, private property was stolen in the name of religion. These excesses led the inhabitants of Karbala to declare Muqtadâ "worse than Saddam". Muqtadâ's challenge also entailed economic consequences: the disturbances prevented the *hawza* from collecting large sums of money from pilgrims and rich donors. On 15 October 2003, Muqtadâ's militiamen tried to invade the mausoleums of Imams Husayn and 'Abbâs in Karbala. The resulting armed confrontation with the supporters of Sîstânî left dozens dead. In Najaf, the Sadrists managed to occupy the mausoleum of Imam 'Alî, causing bloody conflict with the Badr militias of the Supreme Council for the Islamic Revolution in Iraq (SCIRI),[1] which controlled the mausoleum and its Friday sermon with the consent of the *marja'iyya*.

The *hawza* was not blind to the threat posed by Muqtadâ's newly created Mahdî Army *(jaysh al-mahdî)*. On 26 July 2003 the clerics of Najaf issued a statement:

> This army is made up of suspicious elements, including individuals from the deposed regime, members of its former security services and of the Ba'ath party, who have donned white and black turbans to deceive the people into believing that they are men of religion, while in truth they are demons ... We do not need your army, which you have falsely and blasphemously called the Mahdî Army. The hidden Imâm does not need an army of criminals, thieves and depraved deviants run by a one-eyed charlatan.

Muqtadâ also manifested himself by his rejection of the occupation. He was the first in Iraq to express such a refusal and remains the only Shi'a leader to have declared the occupation illegitimate. From his first sermons onwards, he hammers home this point: "We do not recognize the occupation, either directly nor indirectly, since it is contrary to the wishes of the Iraqi people, whose political and religious leadership completely rejects it." In fact, the *grand marja'* had not issued any calls to fight the advance of

---

1. The Supreme Council for the Islamic Revolution in Iraq (SCIRI) was founded in Iran in 1982 in the wake of the Islamic revolution. Initially intended as an umbrella organization for all Iraqi Shi'a Islamist parties opposed to Saddam Hussein's regime, it was soon reduced to the supporters of Muhammad Bâqir al-Hakîm, who had become the privileged discussion partner of the Iranian leaders within the Iraqi opposition.

the coalition forces, and had even asked Iraqis not to take sides. However, Muqtadâ called for peaceful resistance, condemning blind violence.

During the negotiations to form the Interim Iraqi Governing Council (IGC) in May 2003, the American proconsul Paul Bremer approached al-Daʿwa and SCIRI but ignored Muqtadâ. The Americans were well acquainted with the highly organized parties of the former opposition-in-exile to Saddam Hussein's regime, whose conferences they had often sponsored, but they were as yet unaware of what the informal movement of Muqtadâ held in store for them. Would he have joined in the political process if he had been invited in the same capacity as the other Shiʿa forces? That is hard to determine, but the fact remains that finding himself excluded, Muqtadâ immediately challenged the legitimacy of the IGC, before engaging in all-out opposition to the institutions created by the Coalition Provisional Authority (CPA). On 18 July 2003, in an incendiary sermon given in front of thousands of Shiʿa in Kûfa, Muqtadâ rejected the twenty-five member IGC appointed by the United States, qualifying them as "unbelievers".

Interviewed on al-Jazeera, he declared that the IGC was "a toy of the Americans'" and condemned its ministers, maintaining that they had been chosen "on a sectarian basis and not for their competence". He went on: "The current government is the result of an illegitimate decision taken by the Interim Governing Council, which is itself illegitimate because it was appointed by an illegitimate occupation force." Muqtadâ then announced that he would form his own government and found a religious army, the Mahdî Army, while calling for "a general mobilization to fight the American and British occupiers". This army would fight with peaceful means, he added, before denouncing the suicide attacks against the coalition troops. On 10 October 2003, in a direct challenge to the IGC, Muqtadâ appointed a parallel government. Speaking in Kûfa, he declared: "I have formed a government comprising Ministries of Justice, Finance, Information, Interior and Foreign Affairs."

Until then, the Americans had largely ignored Muqtadâ, even allowing him to impose his power and his conception of an Islamic order in Madînat al-Sadr. The Sadrists had taken over the quarter from their bases in the network of mosques and *husayniyya* that they already had under their control. After the war, the *al-Hikma* mosque became the central base for the Sadrists in the quarter. In an office building annexed to the mosque, Muqtadâ's administration formed twelve committees, each consisting of fifteen or twenty persons; they were responsible for the Friday prayer, the health services, the media, the application of religious law, the courts, justice, electricity, telecommunications, and of course the discouragement of vice and the encouragement of virtue.

In the name of Muqtadâ, Muhammad al-Fartûsî imposed strict religious laws. Women were forced to wear the veil, while acts of violence against alcohol traders, some of whom were killed or publicly flogged, increased. Cinemas were closed, as were video stores. In Madînat al-Sadr, as in the holy cities, the Sadrists granted substantial autonomy to local leaders, most of whom were barely over twenty years of age, hence their regular clashes with other clerics. However, despite his incendiary speeches, Muqtadâ was careful not to provoke the Americans, aware that his hold on Madînat al-Sadr depended on a tacit agreement with them. In order to avoid clashes with the Americans at a time when the violence of his Islamic law enforcement was terrorizing the quarter of 'Adnân al-Shamhânî, the Sadrist spokesman maintained that these acts "are not the result of instructions from our offices, but of the actions of pious youths acting on their own initiative." "We have some Imams who say that women should be beaten in the street when their hair shows under the veil and that alcohol shops must be burned down," al-Fartûsî declared to Associated Press, "but we think that this is not necessary: friendly advice or a simple tap on the shoulder should be enough." These statements had the desired effect; a certain degree of relaxation in the enforcement behavior of the quarter's vice police was felt subsequently. Then, on 12 March 2004, the gipsy village of Qawliyya near Dîwâniyya, reputed for its musicians and dancers, was razed to the ground by a hostile crowd led by the Mahdî Army: the militiamen qualified the small village and its inhabitants as a "nest of corruption and prostitution".

The Sadrist insurrections of April and August 2004

The Interim Constitution, written by American experts and made public in February 2004, provoked a general hardening of attitudes among the

Shi'a. Ayatollah Sîstânî broke his relative silence to maintain that the Constitution was unacceptable, because it had set Iraq on an authoritarian course by neglecting to consult the people. Free elections on the basis of universal suffrage, which would legitimize the "right of the majority" (that is to say, the right of the Shi'a), had by then in effect become the *Leitmotiv* of the *marja'iyya*.

Muqtadâ did not hesitate to denounce the "occupier's constitution" either. In sermon after sermon, he vituperated against the text, which he considered to be "a declaration of war on the Iraqi people". The Coalition Provisional Authority had by that time only clamped down on one newspaper (*al-Mustaqilla*), which it closed on account of its presumed support for the Sunni resistance. Muqtadâ's weekly, *al-hawza al-nâtiqa* (The Eloquent *Hawza*, as opposed to the so-called silent *hawza* of Sîstânî and the grand *marja'*), was shut down on 28 March 2004. On 3 April, Muqtadâ's representative Mustafâ al-Ya'qûbî was arrested by the Americans for the murder of 'Abd al-Majîd al-Khû'î. On 4 April, an arrest warrant was issued for Muqtadâ for the same reason. Subsequent peaceful demonstrations came under fire from American troops and the Iraqi police. Several bodies were counted.

Shortly afterwards, Muqtadâ declared that "peaceful protests have now become useless" and calls on his supporters "to terrorize their enemies". In a sermon, he invoked both ancient and recent history: "The memory of the Revolution of 1920 and of the *intifâda sha'bâniyya* (the Shi'a uprising of 1991) is still fresh." His words were acted upon in his strongholds of Madînat al-Sadr, Kût and Nâsiriyya. Some disturbances also occured in Basra. But elsewhere, nothing happened. The coalition, however, was unable to control the uprising quickly and Muqtadâ gained in popularity and audacity – an audacity that would manifest itself once more at Sîstânî's *hawza*. The Sadrists went so far as to block the streets leading to the residences of Sîstânî and Ishâq al-Fayyâd – two of the four *marja'* of Najaf – and the two holy cities of Najaf and Karbala now fell under their control. (The mausoleums would ultimately be used as shelters, as the Sadrists were convinced that coalition forces would not violate their sacred walls.) Tribunals were set up to judge opponents of the movement, notably SCIRI members.

Facing what appeared to be a violent coup, the highest authorities of the *hawza* condemned Muqtadâ's *fatwa* calling on his supporters to sacrifice themselves if the coalition forces were to enter Najaf and Karbala to pursue the Mahdî militiamen entrenched there. In a press release, the *marja'* denied that Muqtadâ had the qualifications required to issue such a *fatwa* and also rejected any notion of giving permission to use suicide attacks against the coalition forces.

On 11 April 2004, the CPA submitted a proposal to Muqtadâ al-Sadr to resolve the conflict, demanding he meet three conditions: he must disperse his militia, respect government institutions and withdraw his armed men from all public spaces.

The al-Da'wa party's Jawâd al-Mâlikî, who would subsequently be named Prime Minister, served as the intermediary. Muqtadâ answered by posing his own conditions: the coalition forces must leave Najaf, Karbala and Kûfa.

Mediation followed mediation and each time Muqtadâ's answer was to insist that the demands come from an illegitimate government. According to the newspaper *al-Zamân*, "Muqtadâ will accept no agreement as long as he is excluded from the political process". Whatever the ulterior motives of the Sadrist leader may have been at this instant, Paul Bremer increased the pressure by maintaining that Muqtadâ must either be captured or killed. But he would be neither killed nor captured. Instead, the CPA issued a decree barring Muqtadâ from any political activity for three years. But even that turned out to be a hollow threat, since after the transfer of sovereignty in June 2004 – which Muqtadâ denounced as a farce – the Iraqi government urged Muqtadâ to join the political process for the reconstruction of the country.

However, faithful to his refusal of any form of government not elected by the people, Muqtadâ denounced Iyâd 'Allâwî's transitional government, swearing that he would have nothing to do with him "until the day of the Last Judgment". In sermons pronounced in June, Muqtadâ maintained that he would "support the government if it demonstrated a greater concern for Iraqi public opinion than for the interests of the occupiers." He also denounced Ghâzî al-Yâwir, the Sunni president of Iraq, for shaking hands with Bush.

After weeks of mediations, American troops attacked Muqtadâ's position in Najaf, Karbala and Kûfa, killing hundreds of his supporters and confiscating their weapons and ammunitions, which were mostly hidden in mosques. On what had now become hostile ground for them, the militias, undisciplined and inexperienced, had trouble resisting the joint attacks of the coalition forces and the Iraqi National Guard.

In desperation, Muqtadâ called on the *hawza* to assist him by denouncing the American incursion into the holy cities. His calls went unanswered; the *hawza* was satisfied to see Muqtadâ defeated, or at least expelled from the holy cities. The stream of pilgrims had been interrupted and the traders of religious articles, on which the economy of the holy cities is based, were now the most fervent opponents of Muqtadâ's militia. On 27 May 2004, Muqtadâ and the coalition forces agree to a ceasefire that stipulated the withdrawal of the Sadrist militias from Najaf. Initially, Muqtadâ appeared to comply with the agreement, calling on the fighters of the Mahdî Army "who sacrificed their bodies and souls to please God and their people" to return to their provinces. But it quickly became obvious that this was only a smokescreen, as he retained control of the mausoleums. In mid-August, Muqtadâ threatened to destroy the pipelines and set fire to the oil wells if he was attacked within the sacred surrounding walls of the mausoleum of Imam ʿAlî, while Wâdî al-Salâm, the big necropolis of Najaf, was covered in blood.

The Iraqi government then decided on an ultimatum: Muqtadâ's militia must lay down its weapons, evacuate the holy city and accept publicly the terms of the ceasefire, or expose itself to military force. In typical fashion, Muqtadâ first rejected the ultimatum, then promised to accept it and to return the keys of the mausoleum to the officials of the *hawza*. On 19 August 2004, when it became clear that he had again reneged on his commitment, the Iraqi police, the National Guard and the American forces launched the attack. Hundreds of civilians were killed. Muqtadâ's forces, cut off inside the mausoleum, sustained huge losses, but military action failed to force them out or to get Muqtadâ to hand over the keys to the mausoleum until Ayatollah Sîstânî agreed a ceasefire, which took effect on 27 August. Under a secret agreement with the government, the Mahdî Army was then allowed to leave with its weapons.

Sîstânî had been in London for a month to be treated for a cardiac failure. The return of the ayatollah to Iraq on 25 August 2004 was greeted with relief by all the Shi'a, a good many of whom took to the streets to head for Najaf (the date coincides with the birthday of Imam 'Alî, one of the rare occasions when the Shi'a celebrate a happy event). Like an honor guard, a peaceful march of truly epic and historic proportions "in defense of the Holy places" accompanied the *marja'* from Basra to the holy city. A similar invitation to defend the holy places against the Americans, issued two weeks earlier by Muqtadâ, had largely been ignored. The triumphal arrival of the ayatollah in Najaf seemed to consecrate the victory of the *marja'iyya* and the defeat of the Sadrists. However, the "heroic" resistance of the militiamen of the Mahdî Army to the combined Iraqi and American forces has lent Muqtadâ an amount of prestige that transcended the Shi'a community.

From now on, Muqtadâ was the most popular Shi'a among the Sunnis. "There can be no politics under occupation, no freedom under occupation, no democracy under occupation," he stated after evacuating Najaf. In an opinion poll taken in June 2004 by the CPA, 81 per cent of Iraqis stated that their opinion of Muqtadâ was now "higher" or "much higher" than before the insurrection; 92 per cent per cent considered the American army to be an occupation force, while only 2 per cent saw them as liberators; and 55 per cent wanted them to leave immediately. Only the holy cities, where people were busy repairing the terrible damage inflicted by the battle, persisted in their hostility towards the Sadrists.

Muqtadâ al-Sadr and Iran

The Sadrist insurrection of 2004 provoked many questions. Were Muqtadâ and a part of the Shi'a community moving towards a jihadist tendency? Was it the irrational reflex of a young leader still traumatized by the anxieties of a regime that had been overthrown but remained in people's minds? Was it an Iranian intervention? While the Americans were quick to point an accusing finger at Tehran, we should nevertheless examine the relations between Muqtadâ and the neighboring Islamic Republic.

Muqtadâ is said to have visited Iran on 4 June 2003 to take part in ceremonies commemorating the fourteenth anniversary of Khomeini's death. Apparently, he spent a week there meeting with Iranian leaders including Khamenei, Mahmud Hâshemi Shahrudi, the leader of the Iranian judicial institutions and a former leader of SCIRI, and Qâsem Sulaymâni, commander of the Qods Force (a special force within the Pasdaran and the Iranian intelligence services). His visit was heavily criticized at the time by the *hawza* in Iraq as well as reformers in Iran, as he was then already accused of the assassination of ʿAbd al-Majîd al-Khûʾî. Khatami's supporters especially judged his visit inopportune, not only because of the arrest warrant against him, but also because in their eyes he represented a repulsive form of "Shiʿa Talibanism".

The Americans maintain that Muqtadâ became a supporter of the Islamic Republic after his visit to Iran. Washington accuses Iran of playing a double game in Iraq, by supporting the Iraqi government in place dominated by the Shiʿa, the *marjaʿiyya* of Sîstânî and the troublemaker Muqtadâ. They believe the Iranian conservatives were behind Muqtadâ's decision to engage in a confrontational policy, forming the Mahdî Army as he did immediately after his return to Iraq. According to them, the Mahdî Army's transformation into a well-trained and well-equipped militia was not achieved in Iraq, but across the border in Iran, where the Qods Force of the Revolutionary Guards had opened three training camps in Qasr-e Shirin, Ilam and Hamid.

An Iranian official is said to have claimed that Iran trained 800 to 1,200 Sadrists and that the Iranian embassy in Baghdad distributed 400 satellite phones to Muqtadâ's forces and to clerics in Madînat al-Sadr and Najaf; moreover, that eighty million dollars was paid directly to the movement. Whatever the reality of these accusations, we may assume that the Islamic Republic, anxious to contain the influence of Najaf, does have an interest in weakening a religious leadership not under its control.

Support for Muqtadâ was criticized in Iran itself, where it became a stake in the struggle for influence and specifically a weapon wielded by the conservatives close to Khamenei and, later, to Ahmadinedjad. Yet Muqtadâ himself denied any link with Iran, claiming that these allegations were being spread to disqualify him. A sign of Sîstânî's success can be seen in the new line taken by the conservatives in Iran, who had secretly supported Muqtadâ and implicitly criticized Sîstânî for his tacit partnership with the Americans in Iraq. They "rectified" their line immediately when the *marja'iyya* and the holy places of Iraq seemed directly threatened by the siege of Najaf in August 2004.Thus, *Kayhân* and *Jomhuri-ye eslâmi* – two newspapers reputedly linked with the conservatives – criticized Sîstânî's trip to London for medical reasons at a time when Najaf was under the bombs, and accused the circles of the *marja'* of collaborating with the Americans. But the same two newspapers later unconditionally supported the demonstrations in honor of Sîstânî's return to Iraq. The Iranian authorities officially invited the Iranians to join the huge stream of people that was forming. President Khatami always maintained that Iran supported Sîstânî and the SCIRI, and he was joined in this by the deposed successor of Khomeini. In an interview granted to *Time Magazine* on 9 April 2004 in Qom, Ayatollah Montazeri declared:

> The supporters of Sadr chose the name of the Mahdî for their militia, but how could the Imâm al-Mahdî ever be content to be the origin of dissension, division and factionalism in his name? It is logical for a stable government in Iraq to be established under the leadership of Ayatollah Sîstânî and under the banner of the union of Shi'a, Sunnis and Kurds, who are all Muslims.

Yet on the same day, during his Friday sermon, Rasfanjani praised Muqtadâ and qualified the Mahdî Army and Muqtadâ as "young, passionate and heroic people who contribute to the security of the nation". After his election, President Ahmadinejad placed his actions under the banner of the imminent return of Imâm al-Mahdî. Many Sadrists, too, believe that they are living in the last days before the return of the Messiah. In Iran, as in Iraq, the mystical reference to the Mahdî seems to provide a means to bypass the *marja'iyya* – a sign that religious leadership is beginning to escape from the hold of the religious authorities.

The patronage of Ayatollah Kâzim al-Hâ'irî

As an aside in this discussion of Muqtadâ's relations with Iran, we must examine the link between Muqtadâ and Ayatollah Kâzim al-Hâ'irî, which was highlighted on the occasion of Muqtadâ's first visit to Iran when Muqtadâ went to see "his" *marja'* in Qom. As an adviser to Khamenei,

Kâzim al-Hâ'irî wanted to work out a strategy with Muqtadâ to bypass the *marja'iyya* of Sîstânî. But while Muqtadâ accepted Iranian money and assistance, he broke with his mentor. Kâzim al-Hâ'irî demanded that Muqtadâ co-ordinate his activities with al-Hâ'irî's office in Najaf. But it could not be denied that ever since he was chosen as the successor to Muhammad Sâdiq al-Sadr, Ayatollah al-Hâ'irî has been incapable of fulfilling his role. Indeed, he has maintained his own network of representatives and preachers in Iraq, and these are often in competition with Muqtadâ's, to the point where the two sides sometimes fight each other for control over a mosque or a Friday prayer.

Ayatollah al-Hâ'irî did of course issue *fatwas* against the American occupation and on 5 April 2004 he told AFP: "We warn the Americans against any irrational action and any attempt to undermine the dignity of the Iraqis and the *hawza* students." He decreed three days of mourning in Qom to support Muqtadâ and Madînat al-Sadr, where fifty-three Shi'a had been killed by the Americans during a demonstration against the ban of the newspaper *al-Hawza al-nâtiqa* and the arrest of Muqtadâ's representative Mustafa al-Ya'qûbî. But he publicly criticized Muqtadâ for leading his insurrection against the Americans in al-Hâ'irî's name. Most supporters of Muqtadâ today say that they continue to emulate Muhammad Sâdiq al-Sadr rather than al-Hâ'irî. Muqtadâ's spokesmen maintain that al-Hâ'irî himself said that it was possible to continue to refer to the deceased Muhammad Sâdiq al-Sadr, except for newly arisen issues or issues he had never dealt with. In these cases, it would be necessary to refer to Muqtadâ. Although some of Muqtadâ's offices continue to display portraits of Ayatollah al-Hâ'irî, his influence on the Sadrists seems weak.

Muqtadâ and the legacy of the "second Sadr"

Although he does not possess the required religious qualifications, Muqtadâ has appropriated his father's legacy. In Madînat al-Sadr, portraits of Ayatollah Muhammad Sâdiq al-Sadr, shown alone or with Muqtadâ, have largely disappeared and been replaced by portraits of Muqtadâ alone. However, he is no longer the only one in Iraq to claim this legacy. In 2003 one of his father's closest companions, Muhammad al-Ya'qûbî, proclaimed himself *marja'* in Najaf, where he resides. He bases his legitimacy on the fact that Muhammad Sâdiq al-Sadr had indicated Ayatollah al-Hâ'irî as his successor only until one of his own students would attain the rank of *marja'*, and he certainly has the advantage over Muqtadâ in religious terms. (A video broadcast on www.yaqoobi.com shows Ayatollah Muhammad Sâdiq al-Sadr explicitly indicating Sheikh Muhammad al-Ya'qûbî as his heir. This was one form of proof that Muqtadâ could not refute.) As a consequence, there was a schism within the Sadrist movement. This led to the creation of *hizb al-fadîla al-islâmiyya* (The Party of Islamic Virtue, or the Virtue Party for short), which today controls the provincial council of Basra, the biggest Shi'a city in the south, and holds majorities in several other provincial councils in the south and centre of the country.

The supporters of Muhammad al-Ya'qûbî also founded the Imam al-Mahdi Center for Islamic Studies in Basra. It is known for its intensive high-quality publishing activities, notably in reproducing the writings of Ayatollah Muhammad Sâdiq al-Sadr and Ya'qûbî in Arabic as well as in English. The Virtue Party is the only party today to benefit from the direct auspices of a *marja'*, whose position is similar to that occupied not so long ago by Sayyed Fadlallâh in Lebanon with regard to Hezbollah. Sheikh al-Ya'qûbî, who maintains cordial relations with Fadlallâh, is the only *marja'* in Najaf who adheres to the theory of *wilâyat al-faqîh*. Open to the outside world and to modern science (he studied engineering before dedicating himself to religious studies), Sheikh al-Ya'qûbî picked up on Muhammad Bâqir al-Sadr's concept of a *marja'iyya rashîda*, where every *marja'* would have a specialization in a particular area. Muqtadâ's latent anti-clericalism, as well as his frequent and confusing changes of opinion, provide the new Ayatollah al-Ya'qûbî with a comfortable margin of action, the more so because the image of the Mahdî Army continues to be tainted by the undisciplined character of its fighters, whose behavior sometimes makes it look rather more like an ordinary street gang than an Islamic militia. In Karbala, meanwhile, another schism has taken place: Mahmûd al-Hasanî, reputed as much for his anti-Americanism as for his hostility towards Iran, has in his turn declared himself ayatollah and heir of Muhammad Sâdiq al-Sadr, attracting his share of deserters.

Muqtadâ and the outbreak of anti-Shi'ism

The rise of sectarian tensions between Shi'a and Sunnis has had a greater impact on the Sadrists, who had intended to maintain a united Islamic front of Shi'a and Sunnis against the occupation. This desire manifested itself in their close ties to the Sunni Association of Muslim Scholars and in Muqtadâ's public display of solidarity with the "martyrs of Fallûja". But the outbreak of anti-Shi'a terrorism affected the most disinherited section of the Shi'a population, which happens to be the Sadrists' social base.

On 1 September 2005, Muqtadâ announced that he would consult Sîstânî on the issue of sectarian violence. Some days before, supporters of Muqtadâ in Kûfa had addressed a letter to him asking his opinion "in the name of the supporters of the Sadrist line especially, and the Shi'a in general" on Zarqâwî's declaration that the Shi'a were unbelievers. Zarqâwî's statement – published only later, on 14 September 2005, as a voice message on a jihadist website – was made "in retaliation for the massacres of Tall 'Afar". It was followed by bloody attacks against the Shi'a. Muqtadâ, who is the most popular Shi'a among the Sunni Arabs – and who is often accused by some Shi'a, notably SCIRI members, of collaborating with "the enemies of the Shi'a" – did not wish to take responsibility for stating that the Shi'a had to refrain from retaliation in the face of these attacks. His answer consisted of three points:

1) Refer for this question to your noble *marja'*, who are, as is well known, Sayyid Sîstânî (may God grant him a long life) and Sayyid al-Hâ'irî (may God grant him a long life). They must be consulted first. If they do not intervene, return to me for a new response;

2) Publish books and educational material against the occupation and its consequences, the Wahhabi criminals, the *takfîrî* (excommunicators – the name that the Shi'a give to the supporters of Zarqâwî) and the Ba'athists;

3) Call on the Imams to declare them unbelievers in their Friday sermons. May God curse them, these apostates!

In conclusion, he called upon all to preserve the unity of Islam and the unity of the Shi'a, "which is their best weapon" against "the criminals and their masters and against the Ba'athists." Only days after his call to fight the Shi'a, Zarqâwî made an exception for the Sadrists, who were to be spared for having fought the occupation. Muqtadâ's reaction was immediate: "This is a pathetic maneuver to divide the Shi'a. If he falls into our hands, we will smash him to bits."

Sistânî answered through an official statement published in Arabic on his website:

> Those who want to divide the Iraqis and push them towards civil war serve the objective of preventing Iraq from recovering its sovereignty and its security. The Iraqis must not fall into this trap, whatever horrors are inflicted on them. The Shi'a must refrain from reacting and collaborate with the official services for their protection in the region where they live. In any circumstances, and specifically in their sermons, Iraqis as a whole must call to resist these depraved deviates. The Iraqi government must ensure security to all Iraqis, whatever their religion or their ethnic identity.

The social and regional base of the Sadrists and their ideology

The Sadrist social base is strangely reminiscent of the Iraqi Communist Party's "democratic organizations" at the end of the 1950s. Today, only Muqtadâ can mobilize the disinherited Shi'a who suffered under Saddam and whose situation did not improve under the occupation. This force constitutes a tremendous electoral base under any circumstances; as yet, Muqtadâ has no serious competition in Madînat al-Sadr. This quarter, constructed in the 1950s to absorb the Shi'a population of the south, has held on to its tribal identity, which sets it apart from the rest of the city. Its inhabitants' tribal ties make the province of 'Amâra another stronghold of the movement. Sadrists suffer from their isolation from the *hawza*: Muqtadâ, who pronounces his sermons in the Iraqi dialect, is scorned by the grand *marja'*. The Sadrists have little presence in Karbala, where the Iranians are influential. In Najaf, they had some credit, which they squandered with the murder of Khû'î, the attacks against Sîstânî's person, and especially with the ravages caused in the holy city during the 2004 battles.

Despite the desertion of Muhammad al-Ya'qûbî, whose strongest base is in Basra, and of al-Sharqî in Karbala, Muqtadâ still controls the mosques of Madînat al-Sadr, 'Amâra and Kûfa, and several Friday mosques in Basra. The Sadrists took over several Sunni mosques in Basra and have regular standoffs with SCIRI over the control of mosques in Karbala. The Sadrist base is strongly marked by a majority representation of the lowest social levels, as well as by a strong local and regional identity. This explains why the intensity of the Sadrist insurrections of April-May and again of August 2004 considerably varied from one city to another.

Sadrists do not have a distinct ideology. Muqtadâ uses his Friday sermons to announce important political moves. While he was answering the questions of journalists on the names of the various ministers, those nominated for the jobs were fighting the supporters of Sîstânî in Karbala, battling the Americans in Madînat al-Sadr, or holding demonstrations in Basra.

What does Muqtadâ want? The immediate departure of the American troops, and for any foreign troops remaining in Iraq to be placed under UN command (he also refuses troops sent by the Arab League, which he accuses of having supported the regime of Saddam Hussein); the re-establishment of a strong central Iraqi government, albeit one without any link to the Ba'athists; a united Iraq – which leads him to denounce the claims of the Kurds and to support the Turkmen Shi'a of Kirkuk in the face of Kurdish attempts to annex the city; and an Iraqi Shi'ism that affirms its identity separately from Iran. While he sometimes speaks about democracy for post-occupation Iraq, he probably means a regime in which his militias impose a puritanical moral order by force.

Other than rejecting the Iranian model, he has never put forward a real long-term vision of an Islamic government. The Sadrists denounce Western consumerism and American globalization, but it is in their street-level activism that they define themselves most clearly – this is largely marked by the localized nature of their implantation. In Madînat al-Sadr and in the cities of the south under their control, Sadrists appointed clerics to mosques, kept the hospitals open, organized garbage collection, took care of the orphans and provided access to the minimal necessities of life for the poorest Iraqis.

One foot out, one foot in: towards integration of the Sadrists in the political process?

Even when he was driven to armed resistance against the occupation, Muqtadâ has always drawn lines: he continued to condemn attacks and assassinations and in that capacity, he denounced the August 2003 attack on the UN headquarters in Baghdad. Later he called on his militia not to attack the Iraqi security forces – which in any case included many of his supporters – and he is equally opposed to the taking hostage of journalists, some of whom he managed to free. As for the practices of jihadists, he states: "There is no religion or religious law that prescribes decapitation as a punishment. Yes, they are your enemies and occupiers, but that does not justify cutting off their heads." Muqtadâ has never called for a jihad against the coalition forces.

On the ground, Madînat al-Sadr perfectly represents the attitude of Sadrists. They have developed a true politico-military strategy to turn the quarter into a permanent autonomous zone. This strategy consisted of expelling the American forces from their domain. Muqtadâ's followers only attack the American forces from Madînat al-Sadr when they are attacked on their home ground. Within their domain, they are attempting to build up a government that is parallel to the one in the "green zone". They maintain public order using the Mahdî Army, controlled by their shadow government, which is led by tribal leaders and clerics. The militiamen of the Mahdî Army cooperate with the Iraqi police in the fight against terror, that is to say against the Wahhabis. Foreign combatants arrested by Muqtadâ's militiamen and suspected of wanting to carry out anti-Shi'a attacks are handed over to the authorities. The Mahdî Army has met with growing success in having its fighters co-opted by the Iraqi police. And what they do in Madînat al-Sadr, they also do in the cities of the south, as we have seen in August 2005 during the crisis that pitted the local Iraqi police, supported by the Virtue Party and the Sadrists, against British troops accused of opening fire on the faithful in Basra. The line between the Iraqi police force and the militias has never looked so thin.

One foot out and one foot in. This also seems to have been Muqtadâ's policy regarding the political process, which he continued to vilify. On 12 July 2005 he announced that he had collected over a million signatures demanding an immediate end to the occupation. However, in the legislative elections of 30 January 2005, which he rejected because of the occupation and its institutionalization of sectarianism, he had allowed some of his supporters to join the Shi'a list of the United Iraqi Alliance, which had the blessing of Ayatollah Sîstânî. Most of these were elected, and as a result the Sadrists, who had only participated in the elections in a marginal way, were now playing in the national league as a part of the most important group of elected representatives. In the provinces of Maysân and Basra, Sadrists or their allies emerged as the winners and now control the provincial councils. The Virtue Party won twenty-one out of forty-one seats on the provincial council of Basra. In the new parliament, Muqtadâ will be able to count on some twenty deputies and he will have three ministers in the government (including the Minister of Health). Muqtadâ left his supporters free to vote as they saw fit in the referendum on the Constitution of 15 October 2005, although he denounced the referendum. Voters, he said, must refer to their *marja*': most emulators of Muhammad Sâdiq al-Sadr follow the opinions of Sîstânî, Kâzim al-Hâ'irî, Ishâq al-Fayyâd or Muhammad al-Ya'qûbî in this matter.

October also saw sectarian clashes becoming more frequent. In the region of Nahrawân, east of Baghdad, Badr Brigades were for the first time seen helping the Mahdî Army fight the Sunni guerilla. The sectarian dynamic swiftly gained the upper hand: on 28 October, faced with the latent war between Sunni and Shi'a, which was making more and more victims, Muqtadâ finally announced that he would participate in the general election scheduled for 15 December 2005 as part of the Shi'a United Iraqi Alliance. Muqtadâ's supporters were thus included on the UIA list: as a precondition, they insisted on parity with SCIRI and "no recognition of the Zionist entity", a "red line that cannot under any pretext be crossed". Under the name Kutlat al-Sadr (al-Sadr Bloc), the Sadrists hoped to win between thirty-two and forty seats, thus attaining a dominant position in Baghdad, 'Amâra, Kût, Hilla, Dîwâniyya and Samâwa. In some places, they formed alliances with al-Da'wa-Iraq ('Abd al-Karîm al-Anzî) or Islamic Da'wa (the party of Prime Minister Ibrâhîm al-Ja'farî).

Iraq's first political party

The Sadrists thus went to the 15 December 2005 elections under three flags: beside Kutlat al-Sadr, there was the Virtue Party, which dominates Basra and the south, and finally the Risâliyyûn (the Upholders of the Message), a list of Sadrists opposed to the United Iraqi Alliance and specifically to SCIRI. The list was headed by Sheikh 'Abd al-Hâdî al-Darrâjî, one of Muqtadâ's collaborators, whose base is in Madînat al-Sadr. It seems that this independent list was created to recuperate the votes of those among the Sadrists who were reluctant to vote for a list containing SCIRI.

The elections gave a simple majority to the United Iraqi Alliance (128 seats of 275). The fact that their majority was smaller than in the previous legislative elections can be explained by the massive participation of Sunni Arabs this time around. Once again, the mobilization of the Shi'a community is strong. Within the United Iraqi Alliance (UIA), the Sadrist Bloc was the biggest force, with thirty-two seats, to which must be added the fifteen seats won by the Virtue Party in Basra, i.e. forty-seven seats in all. As for the Risâliyyûn, it won only 1.8 per cent of the vote in Baghdad, as opposed to 58.5 per cent for the UIA. In Basra, another Sadrist stronghold, this non-UIA list received only 0.5 per cent of the vote compared with 77.5 per cent for the UIA. Its biggest win was in Najaf, with 4 per cent of the vote against 82 per cent for the UIA. This shows that the huge majority of Sadrists voted for the Shi'a community house represented by the UIA – a consequence of sectarian polarization, in which Muqtadâ's supporters have been the main victims of the anti-Shi'a attacks. As Sîstânî recommended the list, there was no dispersion of Shi'a votes going to small lists. On the national level, the Risâliyyûn list wins two seats, which brings the number of Sadrist seats to forty-nine, much more than SCIRI or either of the two branches of al-Da'wa. For a movement that only a year earlier was besieged in the mausoleum of Imam 'Alî in Najaf and unanimously condemned by the *hawza*, it was a most gratifying revenge.

Henceforth, Sadrists agreed to participate in the government, although they refused to hold important positions that would force them to have contact with the Americans. Instead they demanded posts "in the service of the Iraqis", such as the ministries of electricity and health. After the election, four UIA candidates were in the running for the post of prime minister: the incumbent head of government Ibrâhîm al-Ja'farî of al-Da'wa; 'Âdil 'Abd al-Mahdî, vice-president and representative of SCIRI; Nadîm al-Jâbirî, secretary general of the Virtue Party; and Husayn Shahrestânî, an independent candidate. The two branches of the Sadrist movement disagreed over the question of the prime minister. The Virtue Party, sponsored by Muhammad al-Ya'qûbî, chose 'Âdil 'Abd el-Mahdî, while the Sadrist Bloc preferred Ibrâhîm al-Ja'farî. In Tehran, the conservatives seemed to prefer to 'Âdil 'Abd al-Mahdî (cf. the editorials of *Baztab*).

'Âdil 'Abd al-Mahdî had spent twenty-three years in exile in France. He has successively adhered to Marxism, Ba'athism and Shi'a Islamism; today, he presents himself as a supporter of the free market, which also makes him a favorite with the Americans. Nadîm al-Jâbirî and Husayn Shahrestânî having stood down before the vote, the final battle played out between 'Âdil 'Abd al-Mahdî and Ibrâhîm al-Ja'farî. It was the outgoing Prime Minister Ibrâhîm al-Ja'farî who was elected as the new prime minister by way of a secret internal ballot within the UIA, with both Risâliyyûn deputies authorized to participate. In a very tight win, al-Ja'farî received sixty-four votes and 'Âdil 'Abd al-Mahdî sixty-three.

On 31 December 2005, Muqtadâ called for an alliance of Sunni and Shi'a Arabs against the Kurds. We must remember here that most of Kirkuk's Turkmens are Shi'a who supported Muqtadâ, who had already demonstrated his solidarity with them in the face of a SCIRI suspected of wanting to sell out the Shi'a of Kirkuk to the Kurds in exchange for a purely Shi'a zone in the south. Muqtadâ then proceeded to brush up his regional image. In January 2006 he paid a second visit to Iran, where he called for solidarity with the Islamic Republic in the event of an American attack. Once again, he emphasized his closeness to Ahmadinejad . The visit was the start of a regional tour meant to appease the fears of Sunni Arab countries that were uneasy to see the Shi'a coming to power in Iraq. The tour took him from Syria to Jordan and finally, after a pilgrimage to Mecca, to Lebanon. In Damascus, where he arrived on 5 February, he swore loyalty to Syria in the face of Israel, Great Britain and the United States. In an interview with Al-Jazeera in Amman on 18 February 2006, Muqtadâ announced: "We are ready to attack the Americans if they attack Iran or Syria."

From the Syrian capital, while calling on the Sunnis to clean Iraq of al-Qaeda and Zarqâwî, Muqtadâ calls for the unity of Sunnis and Shi 'a in the affair of the Danish caricatures of the Prophet. On 10 February 2006, he spoke with Reuters on this subject: "This is a Western crusade and a campaign against Islam." He was happy to compare himself to Hasan Nasrallâh of Hezbollah, and declared himself close to Hamas in Palestine: "Our ideas are similar, since we are confronted with the same oppression and occupation, as well as with the corruption which the West wants to spread in the region and in the Muslim countries."

At the same time, the Sadrists continued to defend their strongholds through armed opposition to the Americans. They also upheld the Islamic moral order and the struggle against blasphemy; more than 5000 demonstrators marched against Denmark in Kût. The newspaper *al-Hawza* asked the Pope to condemn the caricatures, while the Sadrists positioned themselves as protectors of the Christians in Iraq following attacks on the churches of Baghdad. In Basra, the Sadrist-dominated provincial council broke with the British command, demanding the departure of the Danish contingent but also denouncing the British troops' mistreatment of young Iraqis, video images of which had recently been revealed. The provincial council of Maysân, also under Sadrist control, followed suit some days later.

In the current Iraqi government, the Sadrists are the only group to have attempted military resistance to the occupation. Although Muqtadâ admits that it has failed, it lends him a halo of prestige that other personalities of the Iraqi political class sorely lack. On the other hand, the outbreak of anti-Shi'ism seems to have got the better of his will to represent a patriotic and pan-Islamic movement representing both Shi'a and Sunnis. By joining under a Shi'a flag in a political process that he condemned not so long ago, at a time when this process is hampered by ever-growing obstacles, one could wonder if Muqtadâ does not risk losing what his "one foot out, one foot in" strategy has allowed him to achieve.

In that case, other Sadrist actors such as Ayatollah al-Yaʿqûbî, who have deputies in parliament but refused, after some hesitancy, to enter the government, could prove to be formidable rivals for his authority over the Sadrist current.

Bibliography

Today, there is no academic work or research study available on the Sadrists in Iraq. The Sadrist phenomenon is a recent one and access to Iraq is difficult. Added to this is an ever-burning relevance to current affairs that makes it hard for the researcher to remain detached, as well as the Sadrists' mode of communication, which for a long time was very chaotic, due as much to the nature of the movement and the personality of its leader as to ongoing events. The media (written press, TV, radio, Internet) and especially blogs, are an integral part of the sources for this article. The author's own sources, often oral and acquired on the ground, supplement these. (March, 2006)

Internet
In terms of blogs, the one written by American researcher Juan Cole is best informed: http://www.juancole.com
For the Sadrists' own websites, see: www.muqtada.com and http://www.alsader. com

Newspapers
In the Iraqi written press, the newspaper *al-Zamân* has been my main source for the sermons Muqtadâ pronounced in Kûfa:
"Najaf assault turns allies against US" (13 August 2004, Reuters)
"Al-Sadr: Allawi team worse than Saddam" (14 August 2004, Al-Jazira)
"U.S. vs. Sadr: A saga of missed opportunities" (14 August 2004, *The Philadelphia Inquirer*)
"Najaf standoff ends" (27 August 2004, Al-Jazîra)
"Najaf standoff ends: Al Sistani and Al Sadr Bring Peace to Najaf" (26 August 2004, Al-Jazira)
"Ready to attack the Americans if they Attack Iran or Syria. In a Democratic Iraq, Kurds will not need Own Region," 18 February 2006, interview of Muqtadâ al-Sadr on Al-Jazira.

Articles
Cole, Juan, "The Iraqi Shiites', in *The Boston Review,* October-November 2003.
Feiser, Jonathan, "Moqtada al-Sadr: Islamic Revolutionary or Political Catalyst?", in *Power and Interest News Report*, 26 August 2004.

Frankel, Glenn, and Boustany, Nora, "Mob kills 2 Clerics at Shiite Shrine. Identity, Motives of Assailants unknown", in *Washington Post*, 11 April 2003.

McCarthy, Rory, "Son of the Hidden Imam preaches rebellion to his army of men in black", in *The Guardian*, 6 April 2004. http://www.guardian.co.uk/Iraq/Story/0,2763,1186535,00.html

Murphy, Dan, "Sadr the Agitator: like father, like son", in *Christian Science Monitor*, 27 April 2004. http://www.csmonitor.com/2004/0427/p01s03-woiq.html

Raphaeli, Nimrod, "Muqtadâ al-Sadr not supported by other Iraqi Leaders", in MEMRI, 9 April 2004. http://www.memri.org/bin/latestnews.cgi?ID=IA17004

Raphaeli, Nimrod, "Understanding Muqtada al-Sadr", in *Middle East Quarterly*, Fall 2004.

Recknagel, Charles, "Symbol of Insurgency", in *Asia Times*, 9 April 2004. http://www.atimes.com/atimes/Middle_East/FD09Ak03.html

Rosen, Nir, "Muqtadâ's powerful push for prominence", in *Asia Times*, 18 March 2004. http://www.atimes.com/atimes/Middle_East/FC18Ak01.html

Rosen, Nir, "US newspaper ban plays into cleric's hands", in *Asia Times*, 31 March 2004. http://www.atimes.com/atimes/Middle_East/FC31Ak01.html

Rosen, Nir, "Muqtadâ's Shi'ites raise the stakes", in *Asia Times*, 6 April 2004. http://www.atimes.com/atimes/Middle_East/FD06Ak02.html

Rubin, Michael, "Learning from Sadr", in *National Review*, 8 April 2004. http://www.nationalreview.com/comment/rubin200404080818.asp

Schwartz, Michael, "You thought Fallujah was Tough? Guerilla War in Sadr City", in *Against The Current*, 114, volume XIX, n° 6, January-February 2005.

Shadid, Anthony, "An Iraqi call: Get on the Bus. Weekly Pilgrimage Mixes Politics, Piety", in *Washington Post*, 31 October 2003. http://www.washingtonpost.com/wp-dyn/articles/A44403-2003Oct30.html

Vincent, Steven, "The ungovernable Shiites. It's their tradition", in *National Review*, 8 April 2004. http://www.nationalreview.com/comment/vincent200404081542.asp

PETER HARLING & HAMID YASSIN NASSER

The Sadrist Trend:
Class Struggle, Millenarianism and *fitna*

Little was known about the phenomenon that we now call "Sadrism",
which originated in the movement created by Ayatollah Muhammad
al-Sadr[1] during the 1990s, until the emergence on the Iraqi political
stage of the ayatollah's son Muqtadâ al-Sadr shortly after the fall of
Saddam Hussein's regime. The extreme polysemy of the phenomenon
complicates our understanding of it. It is not based on the principle of
marja'iyya – Muqtadâ neither possessing the legitimacy nor controlling
the institutional apparatus on which the *marja'iyya* is founded – and it
does not conform to the notion of a party, as it lacks both a programmatic
ideology and formalized structures of decision-making and hierarchic
integration. Rather, it is characterized by a charismatic figure employing
a combination of heterogeneous forms of legitimization, which include:
lineage, mobilization of popular millenarian sentiments, traditional forms
of populism, clientelist techniques, and a set of oppositions (to Persia, to
the politicians returned from exile, to the quietist *marja'*, to the occupying
forces and their collaborators, to the *saddâmiyyîn*, *takfîriyîn* and *nawâsib*[2]).

---

1. In fact, his complete name is Muhammad Muhammad Sâdiq al-Sadr (Muham-
    mad Sâdiq being the composite first name of his father), which is commonly
    reduced to Muhammad al-Sadr.
2. The fall of the regime saw the emergence in Iraq of a new semantic field
    particular to the current situation. The terms *saddâmiyyîn* and *takfîriyîn*
    etymologically indicate the faithful of Saddam and the Salafists practicing

Around this figurehead orbits a constellation of "Sadrists", whose actions often seem to contradict the words of their *qâ'id* (declared leader).

From one perspective, the Sadrist phenomenon follows a continuous and rational trajectory, moving from verbally denouncing the occupation to armed confrontation followed by a subtle juxtaposition of different registers (virulent sermons, unclaimed attacks, and measured participation in the political process and in the government). Yet this transformation does not give rise to a political vision but rather appears to be the ongoing refinement of a strategy that is solidly anchored in the present. The illegibility of this strategy leads the movement to invent itself first and foremost through its own dynamics. Incidentally, the gradual transition from violence directed against the coalition to massive sectarian violence contradicts two pillars of the Sadrist discourse, Arab identity and Iraqi unity. On the whole, no evolution is observed in terms of overcoming these contradictions, which make sense to the degree in which they ensure, in the present situation, the cohesion and durability of the movement.

We will therefore talk here of the Sadrist trend, which we define as a group whose coordination is determined not so much by formal ideological or organizational structures as by a rather loose frame of reference that will have to be defined. The challenge thus consists of "solidifying" the Sadrist phenomenon by uncovering the foundations of its cohesion.[1] This approach immediately confronts us with the limits of any analysis done in purely organizational or structural terms, although that is the approach observers have often intuitively chosen. For some, the rapid rise of the phenomenon is explained by the "apparatus" built by his father, which Muqtadâ supposedly inherited; an apparatus incorrectly presumed to have continued working clandestinely up to the fall of regime, although

---

"excommunication" of the Shi'a (*takfîr*), but both are widely used by Sadrists to qualify the Sunni generally. The term *nawâsib*, which refers to the notion of hostility, is used by Sadrists to indicate "those who detest the Twelver imams" and "those who are hostile to the *ahl al-Bayt*", that is to say the descendants of Husayn. It is a response to the term *rawâfid* which the Sunnis use against those (i.e. the Shi'a) who challenge the legitimacy of first three caliphs (Abû Bakr, 'Umar and 'Uthmân).

1. This chapter leans on the results of preliminary efforts that have been made in this direction. Cf. Yasin, 2005, and International Crisis Group, 2006.

its destruction prior to that time is established fact.[1] Muqtadâ's financial resources have equally been the object of exaggerated attention. Finally, a quest for "advisers in the shadows" – invoking the device of an unfathomable strategy – has sometimes been substituted for the necessary examination of the fluidity and the fundamentally unresolved contradictions that characterize the Sadrist trend.

In order to historicize the phenomenon, it is useful to approach it from several quite different angles. Firstly, we must re-situate the phenomenon in the context of a theological debate that has evolved progressively from appraising the role of the *marja'* to challenging the social order incarnated and perpetuated by the *hawza*. Secondly, it is necessary to underline the coherence of the Sadrist social base, which constitutes a real class, as a key factor of cohesion. Thirdly, the emergence of Sadrism is connected to a specific opportunity structure; the fluctuating and dynamic field of Sadrist contestation is engaged in a dialectical relationship with other fields, including a wider, more complex and itself largely undetermined Middle Eastern Shi'a space. Finally, the question of resources will be shown to present a strange parallel with the phenomenon of the *Fidâ'iyû Saddam*,[2] thus revealing the significance of the dynamics of the social disintegration which started under the former regime.

A word of caution is nevertheless warranted. Combining these various frames of analysis has the advantage that it makes sense of the Sadrist trend by clarifying its origins and the processes of its formation; but the fact remains that such a phenomenon invents itself in the uncertainty of an indivinable future and in constant interaction with an environment that is itself ever-shifting. Rationalizing Sadrism should not obscure the indecisiveness of politicians, and making sense of the Sadrist phenomenon at a specific moment in time in no way allows us to foretell its implication in the long term. Historicizing the implications of the ephemeral

---

1. Cf. the official biography of Muqtadâ, published on the site www.muqtada. com. The document is credible on this point in as much as the Sadrists rather tend to exaggerate their underground activities in the period between the assassination of Muhammad al-Sadr and the fall of the regime.

2. A paramilitary force formed in the first half of the 1990s through various initiatives to mobilize an urban youth harshly hit by the economic sanctions imposed on Iraq following the invasion of Kuwait.

mobilization triggered by Muqtadâ's father can really only be attempted today. The pitfalls of instant analysis of ongoing phenomena must therefore be borne in mind.

The theological background

The opposition that has arisen between, on the one hand, the so-called "quietist" or "traditional" school *(al-madrasa al-taqlîdiyya)*, represented by the *marja'* of Najaf ('Alî al-Sîstânî, Muhammad Ishâq al-Fayyâd, Muhammad Sâ'îd al-Hakîm and Bashîr al-Najafî) and, on the other, the Sadrist trend derives from a theological debate on the powers legitimately held by the *mujtahid* while the Imâm al-Mahdî remains occulted; more specifically, on issues related to collecting religious taxes, leading the Friday prayer, declaring jihad and so on. This debate, which is highly complex and has been drawn out over a long period of time, cannot be elaborated on here in any meaningful way; moreover it affects the opposition between Sadrists and quietists only in an extremely simplified form. In practice, it is mostly a product of the controversy engendered in the late 1960s by the work done by Ayatollah Muhammad Bâqir al-Sadr, great-uncle of Muqtadâ, and Ayatollah Khomeini on the concept of *wilâyat al-faqîh*, which deeply structures and divides the Shi'a theological field today. While their work was intimately connected with the rich historical debate mentioned above, at the level of popular representations it has mostly resulted in a binary opposition between the quietist, essentially invisible, *marja'* and the Islamist activism embodied by Muhammad Bâqir al-Sadr.[1]

For this analysis, the latter's line of thought can be brought down to its doubly revolutionary nature. On the one hand, he advocates the rejection of oppression, which constitutes a remarkable break with the long Shi'a tradition of acceptance and adaptation, notably through *taqi-yya* (the principle of dissimulation). The development of elites and their organization into a party apparatus along the lines of the communist and

---

1. While Khomeini remains an icon for the Sadrist tendency, it is the heritage of Muhammad Bâqir that it claims as its own. Sadrists maintain that Muhammad Bâqir al-Sadr is the true creator of the Islamic Republic of Iran, the foundations of which he is supposed to have set out in his work *Islam guides life* before conceding leadership to Khomeini.

Ba'athist paradigms makes it possible to overthrow the political system by mobilizing the masses, as expressed in the famous slogan "the masses are stronger than the oppressors".[1] His thinking is also revolutionary in the sense that it radically transforms the status and functions of the *marja'*.[2]

Asserting the principle of *wilâyat al-faqîh* first led to a schism within the *hawza* of Najaf,[3] and later to a stark divergence in the trajectories followed by the Iraqi and the Iranian Shi'a. While the Islamist republic model bloomed in Iran, Saddam Hussein's systematic suppression of Shi'a Islamism in any form or shape reduced the Iraqi theological field to the quietist dimension, even as it exacerbated its traditional characteristics, particularly the detachment of the *marja'* from the wider population. A shift in policy at the beginning of the 1990s enabled the revival in Iraq of an activist current of thought, largely inspired by the works of Muhammad Bâqir and carried by Muqtadâ's father.[4] Ayatollah Muhammad al-Sadr introduced three important innovations, however, the examination of which is necessary to understand the Sadrist phenomenon.

---

1. Extract from Muhammad Bâqir al-Sadr's sermons, published in the newspaper *al-Istiqâma* on the occasion of the twenty-fifth anniversary of his death (number 68, 11 April, 2005).
2. See notably Al-Hâ'irî, 1979; al-Kharsân, 2004; Ra'ûf, 2000; Ra'ûf, 2001; al-Miyâhî, 2001; Jabar, 2003.
3. Jabar A., 2003. An anecdote perfectly illustrates the antagonism between quietists and the proponents of Shi'a Islamism: directly following the Iranian revolution, the supreme *marja'* from Najaf, Abû al-Qâsim al-Khû'î, sent a "congratulatory" message to Khomeini in which he addressed him as *hujjat al-islâm*, thereby denying him the status of ayatollah and treating him as a vulgar *hawza* student – and particularly as an usurper, as theoretically the principle of *wilâyat al-faqîh* can only be exercised by the supreme *marja'*. The assassination of Muhammad Bâqir al-Sadr by the regime of Saddam Hussein elicited no reaction from the quietist *marja'* of Najaf, a silence for which the Sadrists bitterly reproach them.
4. On the policy change of the regime and its possible interpretations, cf. International Crisis Group, 2006.

A nationalist anchoring

While Muhammad al-Sadr certainly appropriated the principle of *wilâyat al-faqîh*, as well as the Khomeinist claim to a state of *'irfân* (gnosis) that establishes a hermeneutical communication with the eclipsed imam, he reinterpreted to his advantage the distinction between *wilâya 'âmma* (applying to all believers) and *wilâya khâssa* (applying only to a given territory). He proclaimed his own *wilâyat alfaqîh* over Iraq, which enabled him to inscribe his own action in a nationalist perspective by defying both the temporal authority of Saddam Hussein and the spiritual authority of the successor to Khomeini, Ayatollah Khamenei. The break with Iran translated into the immediate expulsion of his representatives from the holy places in Iran. His falling out of favor with the Iraqi regime, which had initially supported him, was rather more progressive, but the end result was his assassination in 1999.[1] He reached the point of no return in his relations with the Iraqi authorities with the reintroduction of what Sâdiq al-Sadr called *al-fatwâ al-mu'attala* (the suspended fatwa), that is to say the *khutba* (politico-religious Friday sermon).[2]

Subversion of the *hawza*

The confrontation between Muhammad al-Sadr and the other ayatollahs of the *hawza* of Najaf was based on the opposition he construed between a *hawza sâmita* or *sâkita* (dumb, silent) and a *hawza nâtiqa* (active, eloquent).[3] He charged the ayatollahs of the *hawza sâmita* with having retreated into an ivory tower, limiting their activities to devising obscure

---

1. International Crisis Group, 2006.
2. The question of the Friday sermon of is one of the bones of contention between the Sadrists and the *marja'* of Najaf. The latter refused its reintroduction on the pretext that it demands the presence of a "just prince" (*hâkim 'âdil*) ruling the state. Muhammad al-Sadr resolved this problem by proclaiming himself *hâkim 'âdil*, at the risk of his own life. When the regime fell, the *marja'* from Najaf resumed the practice of the *khutba*, even though power was then in the hands of Paul Bremer, which led the Sadrists to accuse them of cowardice, hypocrisy and opportunism.
3. In this way, Muhammad al-Sadr tacitly reminded the *marja'* of their duty to express themselves and to explain a Qur'an which remains *sâmit* without them.

rulings on trivial religious rituals,[1] and consequently not only leaving the Shi'a population ignorant of the foundations of its own religion, but contributing to its oppression through a tacit complicity with the regime. This accusation undercut the very bases of the ayatollahs' legitimacy, notably the principles of invisibility, erudition and co-option. Muhammad al-Sadr construed the invisibility of the ayatollahs – whose silence and inaccessibility inspired respect in believers whilst maintaining the myth of their infallibility – as a form of cowardice, weakness and even corruption.[2] For al-Sadr, erudition, according to tradition the *conditio sine qua non* to become a *marja'*, needed to be combined with or even relegated behind other criteria, specifically Arab identity and activism.[3] Finally, while the legitimacy of a *marja'* had until then been a product of co-option among peers, al-Sadr did not hesitate to proclaim himself supreme *marja'* and *walî faqîh*. He then instituted a testamentary system designed to prevent his supporters from turning to a *marja'* belonging to the *hawza sâmita* upon his death.[4]

A form of populism

Muhammad al-Sadr strove to establish a direct connection with the Shi'a population, based on the *marja's* accessibility,[5] the institution of *al-fatwâ al-mu'attala* and a discourse that addressed the concerns of the masses and resonated with popular feelings. This resulted in a combination of respect for tribal traditions (notably in his famous work *Fiqh al-'ashâ'ir*)

---

1. International Crisis Group, 2006.
2. "People have an idealized image of the *hawza*, thinking that all *ulemas* are infallible and sacred and that a spirit of brotherhood reigns within the *hawza*. They do not know that the quietist *ulemas* construct grand palaces with the money of the underprivileged, to perpetuate their empire that is Najaf." Al-Miyâhî, 2001, p.44.
3. Muhammad al-Sadr was reputed to recruit his adherents and representatives (*wukalâ'*) less in view of their academic qualities than for their courage, boldness and "qualities of the heart".
4. International Crisis Group, 2006.
5. An anecdote often told by Sadrists describes the exhaustive and considered answer Muhammad al-Sadr gave to a visitor enquiring about the price of tomatoes. This parable serves to show that he intimately knew and shared the fate of his fellow citizens. Cf. International Crisis Group, 2006.

and popular religious practices;[1] an all-out denunciation of the forms and forces of oppression (virulent anti-Zionism and anti-imperialism, audacious criticism of Saddam Hussein's regime, rejection of Iranian domination, etc.); and a millenarist promise of eschatological fulfillment, which underlies many of his writings.[2] At stake is no longer the foundation of an alternative Islamist regime; rather he is laying the groundwork for the return of the Mahdî through the immediate – i.e. without the mediation of any elite – edification of the grass roots. This vision is a novelty in twentieth-century Middle Eastern revolutionary traditions: the overthrow of the existing order does not aim at opening a new era, but at closing history by preparing for the last judgment. His claim to a gnostic state of consciousness implied moreover that he himself was worthy of identification with the Imâm al-Mahdî, which generated widespread rumors that he was careful not to deny. This Mahdist discourse specifically addressed the element of Iraq's Shiʿa population likely to be most sensitive to it. He thus opened the doors of the *hawza* to youngsters who were previously excluded from it: his representative in Basra, for example, ʿAbd al-Sattâr al-Bahâdilî, had been a popular singer before entering the circle of his students.[3]

These innovations in part explain the theological liberties later indulged in by the Sadrists, notably the emphasis on militancy and millenarianism as principles of legitimization, to the detriment of the *marjaʿiyya* as an institution. From them also flows the partial respect for the designated successor to Muqtadâ's father, Ayatollah Kâzim al-Hâʾirî, who is based in Qom. While he allows the movement to cultivate a measure of continuity with al-Sadr, he is not seen as a leader by the Sadrists, who only apply those of his fatwas which suit them, such as his 2003 *fatwa* legalizing the assassination of Baʿathists.[4]

---

1. Among these, the pilgrimages on foot at the occasion of the *Arbaʾîn* are notable.
2. Al-Sadr (Muhammad Sâdiq), 1992; 2006.
3. Interviews by one of the authors in Iraq, August 2006.
4. Fatwa of 10 *al-Râbiʿ al-Thânî*, 1424 h.

The sociology of a social movement

In his efforts to build up his grass roots, Muhammad al-Sadr focused overtly on specific regions. His discourse notably attached particular importance to the inhabitants of the huge Shi'a district of *al-Thawra* or "Saddam City" in Baghdad, as well as those of the governorate of *Maysân* (also called *al-'Amâra*, after the name of its biggest city). He appropriated the famous slogan of Muhammad Bâqir, "The revolution starts in *al-Thawra*". In his *Encyclopedia of the Imâm al-Mahdî*, he points out that most of the supporters of the awaited Mahdî would be descendants of the tribes of al-'Amâra, which in fact provided the largest contingents of the population of Saddam City – renamed Sadr City after the fall of the regime. Today these are the two Sadrist power bases, Maysân being the only governorate where the Sadrists have won a majority in the local elections of early 2005.

From a sociological point of view, the geography of the Sadrist phenomenon partly coincides with a fundamental divide within the Iraqi Shi'a population, which in a quasi-Marxist analysis can be described in terms of a class struggle. The divide is between the conservative Shi'a constituencies – an alliance formed by the religious elite of Najaf, the commercial middle classes thriving on pilgrimage to the holy places, the tribes historically linked to the *hawza* by a high level of interrelation (geographical nearness, participation in the pilgrimage trade, etc.) and finally a privileged category made up of descendants of the prophet or *sâda*[1] – and the oppressed. It is useful at this point to qualify the collective experience of the latter group and describe its composition.

The tribes of al-'Amâra, and more generally all the tribes living in the south-eastern marshes of Iraq, have over time developed a very specific identity[2] as a result of their way of life, their "remoteness", and the way in which they are perceived by other segments of the Iraqi population. Insulated from the institutions in the holy sanctuaries, which radiated an orthodox and highly theorized Shi'ism, they cultivated popular forms of religiosity that gave precedence to rituals such as *Ashura* or *Arba'în* over

---

1. *The sâda (sing. sayyid)* occupy an important place in society, their status authorizing them to receive a part of the *khums*.
2. Al-Sudânî, 1990; al-Jawibrâwî, 1990.

some of the "pillars of Islam", notably the five daily prayers and Ramadan.[1] These divergences naturally provoked the ire and contempt of the religious authorities in Najaf. Adding to these prejudices were the negative perceptions attached to their "archaic" way of life[2] and, more importantly, the subordinate position to which they were confined in the traditional tribal hierarchy. In early twentieth-century Iraq a hierarchic classification on the basis of "nobility" still predominated, ranking Bedouin tribes at the top, followed in descending order by semi-nomadic sheep breeders, settled farmers, and finally buffalo breeders dwelling in the marshes. The low status of the marsh tribes translated in the nationalist era into a recurrent questioning of their Arab identity (they were often accused of being of Persian or even Indian origin), which explains the al-Sadrs' insistence on their Arab identity.

At the end of the Ottoman era and the beginning of the monarchy that replaced it, Iraq saw a spectacular transformation of the tribal world, marked by the emergence of a tribal elite and the introduction of land-based capitalism, which plunged subsistence farmers and breeders into a state of impoverishment and servitude.[3] This in turn brought about a rural exodus that particularly affected the tribes of al-'Amâra, whose clansmen flocked to large shanty towns at the periphery of big cities, in particular Baghdad. By keeping their inhabitants in an economically deprived and socially inferior position, the sarâyif[4] merely generated an urban version of the deprivation these tribes endured in the countryside. Moreover, they locked their inhabitants into cultivating their cultural specificities, with each tribe concentrated in a particular quarter. Finally, the short distance separating these shanty towns from the centers of power and the habitats of the ruling elites, combined with their chaotic fabric, caused the elites to perceive them as hotbeds of volatile dissension. In that sense,

1. Jabar A., 2003; Luizard, 1991.
2. This way of life inspired an entire literature of the folklore type, extolling its "purity". "Fulanayn", 1928; Maxwell, 1957; Thesiger, 1964; Fernea, 1965; Young, 1977.
3. Cf. notably Batatu, 1960; Fernea R. A., 1991.
4. Luizard, 1994. The habitats in these quarters initially took the form of light buildings similar to those in the marshes. The name of one of two main sections of Sadr City, al-Tshwâdir, is derived from the word used in the dialect of Maysân for the traditional homes of woven reed in the marshes.

they formed spaces of political and social exclusion, as well as incubators for a specific urban identity that came to be known under the derogatory term of *shrûgi*.[1]

From 1958 onwards, the urbanization of the *sarâyifs* under the republican regime of General Qâsim – designed mostly to facilitate control by restructuring the shanties into inhabitable quarters separated by broad arteries – produced the belt of popular neighborhoods that now surround the centre of Baghdad. This reorganization did little, however, to alter their insular character, isolated as they were from the rest of Baghdadi society. The official street names, for example, never replaced the local practice of naming quarters after the tribes that moved into them. In the 1970s and 1980s, the process of national construction initiated by Saddam Hussein's regime certainly contributed to a relative opening up of the marshes and the former *sarâyif* – again for purposes of control, of course, but this time complemented by a considerable effort at development and social integration. This drive, however, came up against a tradition of defiance toward the central government that dates back to the Ottoman era. The marshes and al-Thawra became havens for deserters and all who refused conscription, notably during the war against Iran. It miscarried as the national construction project itself was abandoned, to be replaced by a process of anomization of Iraqi society[2] and the disposal, in the late 1980s, of the welfare state model of social organization.[3]

Another factor to keep in mind is the destruction of all non-state organizational structures within Iraq's Shi'a population. The systematic suppression of Shi'a Islamism inspired by Muhammad Bâqir and the *hawza's* retreat from public life left the Shi'a population to its own devices. This phenomenon was particularly acute among remote tribes and in underprivileged urban circles. Supporters of the Sadrist trend, whether they were tribe leaders in al-'Amâra or inhabitants of al-Thawra, readily admitted being unfamiliar with the concepts of *hawza* and *marja'iyya*

---

1. The *shrûg* (alternative plurals *sharâgawa* and *shrûgiyya*) are the descendants of rural immigrants, refugees from the south and more particularly from Maysân, living in the *sarâyif* and dismissed as thieves, liars and thugs in the longstanding urbanized milieus.
2. Darle, 2003.
3. On this last point, cf. Harling, 2007. See also Baran, 2004.

until the advent of Muhammad al-Sadr, who in the 1990s managed to restore the link between Najaf and those who would form his grass roots. Besides, the silence of the so-called quietist ayatollahs in the face of the eradication of the Shi'a Islamist movement after the Iranian revolution, and again during the bloody suppression of the 1991 uprisings, contributed to a decisive collective experience that was grounded in the rejection of those perceived to have turned their backs on the sufferings of the Shi'a. Symptomatically, the riots that followed Operation Desert Storm mobilized a young generation of underprivileged Shi'a urbanites, whose incoherent behavior can be explained to a great extent by this absence of organizational structures.

Finally, the mutation of the regime around the 1991 war from a model verging on totalitarianism to a system whose far narrower ambition was to manage social dynamics with the single objective of maintaining power[1] gave the above-mentioned groups far greater autonomy. The regime's hold on the territory was reduced to its most coercive forms, aimed at countering any decisive threat to the security of the power structure. At the same time, the regime accommodated the resurgence of tribal traditions and tolerated acts of insubordination as long as they did not undermine its vital interests. A particularly vigorous shadow culture developed in Saddam City.[2]

The mobilization inspired by al-Sadr in the1990s can therefore be understood in terms of a political opportunity structure: potential for mobilization existed within a context that enabled al-Sadr to exploit it adroitly. His Mahdism served as a means of rehabilitating a widely denigrated popular identity and tie it to the promise of eschatological fulfillment. The ayatollah's discourse also resonated with tribal origins and bonds. His efforts to establish a social link between the *hawza* and the Shi'a population could not but have an immediate appeal in this context of deep anomies. Finally, in the absence of any Islamist mobilizing structures, forthright confrontation with oppressors of all shapes and forms – be it imperialist America, Israel, Iran, the regime or even the *de facto* complicity between quietists and tyrant – asserted itself as the new

1. Harling, 2007.
2. Rigaud, 2003.

modality of political expression. This point is extremely important, given that the specific modalities of al-Sadr's defiance towards the regime were an essential element of his popularity.[1]

The nature of the repression suffered by Muhammad al-Sadr's entourage in 1998 and 1999 was yet another factor in the subsequent emergence of the Sadrist trend. Unlike in the case of the Islamist movements of the 1970s and early 1980s, there was no militant base for the regime to eradicate; repercussions took the form of the decapitation of the movement and the dispersion of its supporters. The grass roots movement therefore remained intact. One last factor remains to be analyzed hereafter, namely the generational dimension of the Sadrist trend, which is essentially confined to a generation of young, underprivileged, urbanized Shi'a.

An analysis in terms of social arenas

The existence of this rallying potential hardly suffices to explain either the emergence of Muqtadâ or the particular form taken by the Sadrist phenomenon. The continuity between Muhammad al-Sadr and Muqtadâ was in no way self-evident, given the son's weak qualifications in terms of the traditional requirements for a leading religious role in the Shi'a world. Lineage did not in itself constitute a sufficient source of legitimacy, although in Muqtadâ's case, it was a *conditio sine qua non*. Muqtadâ's resources differ from those of his father, who followed the *marja'iyya* template. Contrary to popular belief, he did not inherit a turn-key network of charitable institutions, as these had been dismantled under the former regime. Finally, the *khums* paid to Muhammad al-Sadr could not be directly transferred to Muqtadâ, who had to negotiate an arrangement with Ayatollah al-Hâ'irî after failing to reach an agreement with Ayatollah Muhammad Ishâq al-Fayyâd, a *marja'* from Najaf.[2]

The circumstances in which this new mobilization began were in any case profoundly different from Muhammad al-Sadr's. The latter had filled a void in terms of the Iraqi Shi'a population's social recognition, political

---

1. Aware that he was condemned to assassination by the regime, Muhammad al-Sadr appeared during the Friday prayer draped in a shroud, a symbol that has been vigorously expropriated by Muqtadâ.
2. Interviews in Iraq by one of the authors, January 2006.

representation and religious leadership. In contrast, the period following the collapse of Saddam Hussein's regime was marked by multiple and vigorous forms of representation of a Shi'a population that had finally been made visible to itself and to the rest of the world. The *hawza* emerged from the shelter of invisibility, while Islamist parties returning from exile ostensibly squatted the scene. Iran was free to expand its influence overtly. Lastly, Muqtadâ had to face competition from his father's other self-styled "heirs" such as Mahmûd al-Hasanî and Muhammad al-Ya'qûbî,[1] as well as a proliferation of rival Mahdist movements, the *Sulûkîn* being but one example.[2]

In assessing the conditions that made a new mobilization of the grass roots possible after the fall of the regime, it is fruitful to resort to an analysis in terms of social arenas, the Sadrist "arena" being defined as a fluctuating and dynamic space of dissension, which interacts with other arenas and is structured around the tradition established by Muqtadâ's father, the strategies of other Shi'a actors, and Sunni forms of dissension. The issue is thus to describe how the Sadrist field gelled around the figure of Muqtadâ, in dialectical correlation with these other fields.

More precisely, the pivotal role of Muqtadâ can be understood in terms of his "positional charisma",[3] an expression that characterizes a man devoid of any particular qualities, but whose centrality derives both from the symbols that he epitomizes and, more importantly, from the configuration of the movement he heads at a given point in time. On the one hand, Muqtadâ has found strength in his very weaknesses. The removal of Muhammad al-Sadr's entourage having left no obvious successor, Muqtadâ was in a position to stress the issue of descent without thereby destroying the ambitions of other possible contenders. While he incarnates a tangible connection to Muhammad Bâqir and Muhammad al-Sadr through the notion of Sadrist lineage, his illegitimacy in other

---

1. Unlike Muqtadâ and Mahmûd Sarkhî, Muhammad al-Ya'qûbî obtained certificates of *ijtihâd* from several Iranian ayatollahs, which placed him in a relatively stronger position on the level of religious qualifications.

2. The *Sulûkîn* are mostly former supporters or students of Muhammad al-Sadr whose erratic and sacrilegious behavior aims to precipitate the return of the Mahdî by contributing to the chaos that will precede the return of the hidden Imam. They are also said to pray nude and break various sexual taboos.

3. Dobry, 1992

respects paradoxically allowed him to rally many of his father's intimates and supporters around him. He thus formed expedient alliances with al-Hâ'irî and al-Hasanî, who could accommodate his presence in the pursuit of their own objectives,[1] and further surrounded himself with an entire generation of *hawza* students who opted for politics over erudition – a choice validated by the trajectory and discourse of Muqtadâ himself.

The principle of *hawza nâtiqa*, formulated by his father and on which he based his own leading role, now changed; it was no longer designated a reformed *hawza* but an alternative, conceptual *hawza,* detached from Najaf and from any didactic project. Only the element of activism remained, offering a framework of remarkable flexibility to all those dissatisfied with the traditional system. The very fluidity of the movement proved an essential precondition for its overall cohesion and for the central position of Muqtadâ, who remains a reference and an instrument of legitimization for many Sadrists who are otherwise reluctant to bow to his authority.[2] Further room for Sadrist dissension was made by the condescension with which Muqtadâ was initially disregarded by the *marja'* of Najaf, formerly exiled Shi'a politicians and the coalition forces, as well as Iran. At the same time, the Sadrists received immediate attention from the media; the magnifying lens of Western journalists strongly contributed to the field's formation by making it visible to itself, by lending it a degree of structure, coherence and popularity that it had not yet achieved, and by overly personifying the movement, a phenomenon that benefited Muqtadâ.

A final important point here is Muqtadâ's identification with the grass roots, for whom he serves both as a mirror and as a model. Young, in a subordinate position within his own family, relatively uneducated and a substandard orator, he has nevertheless been able to turn his stigmata into the emblems of a revolutionary class which he truly represents. His

---

1. Although it is out of the question to place Ayatollah al-Hâ'irî, a *marja'* respected for his theological competences, on the same footing as Mahmûd al-Hasanî, a minor figure whose influence is limited to rather small circles in Karbala and Diwâniyya.
2. On the many contradictions that characterize the tendency and its embrace of personalities theoretically "repudiated" by Muqtadâ, cf. International Crisis Group, 2006.

rejection by the coalition and by conservative Shi'a circles resonates with the rejection that his supporters experience on a daily basis. At the same time, the fear – or the respect, or at least recognition – that he now arouses makes him the champion of their aspirations. Precisely because it contrasts with his apparent mediocrity, this fact lends a certain depth to his character, a Mahdist dimension in which many of his supporters readily believe.

On the other hand, the Sadrist trend is the product of surrounding dynamics set in motion by the overthrow of the former regime. The nature of the political process sponsored by the United States certainly deserves attention: it translated into a sudden opening of the field of Shi'a representation, both politically and in terms of religious leadership, but in doing so revealed, extended and exacerbated the fundamental rift between conservatives and revolutionaries. By instituting an arbitrary dichotomy between "moderate" Shi'a representatives (Sîstânî, Husayn al-Sadr, Muhammad Bâqir al-Hakîm, Ibrahîm al-Ja'farî, etc.) and "extremists", the coalition barred any political participation by the Sadrists. The collusion of occupier and conservatives, which on a symbolic level echoed the "alliance of oppressors" denounced by Muhammad al-Sadr, spurred the radicalization of the Sadrists by providing excuses for ever more violent repertoires of discourse and action.

More generally, the opening of the field led to a struggle over the foundations of Shi'a representation, in terms of legitimacy, symbols, means and resources. The selective mobilization of two icons, Imâm al-Mahdî and Imâm Husayn, came to draw the line between the imagined communities of revolutionaries on one side and conservatives on the other. Competition over symbols delved into key events and figures in the contemporary history of Iraqi Shi'a, notably the 1991 insurrection[1] and the legacy of Muhammad Bâqir al-Sadr. Out of political calculation, and in contradiction of well-established religious principles, the Sadrists appropriated the right to issue *fatwas*, while under Paul Bremer the *marja'* reintroduced the *khutba*, which they had declared illegitimate under

---

1. Thus, the uprisings of 1991 are presented by members of the Supreme Council for the Islamic Revolution in Iraq as feats of arms illustrating their heroism, while the Sadrists use the latter's subsequent flight to Iran in the face of the repression of the regime as proof of their cowardice and treason.

Saddam Hussein. The conditions and limits structuring participation in the political arena, along with recourse to violence, were also the object of pragmatic redefinitions catering to the prevailing context. Islamist parties reneged upon any aspiration to establish an Islamic republic and adjusted to elections that disavowed the concept of *wilâyat al-faqîh*.[1] Sîstânî gave his *de facto* consent to the increasing politicization and instrumentalization of his authority so as not to undermine it. Via the ceasefire reached with the coalition forces in 2004, Muqtadâ opted for revising his resistance repertoire, moving away from armed confrontation toward a reluctant and measured political participation. This competition between different Shi'a figures,[2] although initially explosive, progressively structured the field of Shi'a representation, ultimately leading to a fairly clear distribution of roles and resources. These by no means eliminated the remaining disputes, notably the question of the seat of the Sadr family in Najaf.[3]

But the fault line dividing conservatives and revolutionaries did "stabilize" in a way.

Sadrist violence now follows the lines of rather localized power struggles.[4] Most importantly, this violence shifted from a nationalist repertoire (national liberation struggle, rejection of Iranian influence, support – or at least lip service – of the armed opposition) to that of *fitna*, which Muqtadâ simultaneously denounces and tolerates.

An analysis of the Sadrist movement that leans too heavily towards the *inherited* elements of mobilization is therefore insufficient to understand a phenomenon that is deeply anchored in the post-Saddam context.

---

1. During a meeting with 'Abd al-'Azîz al-Hakîm, Muqtadâ underlined this contradiction, to the embarrassment of his interlocutor, by asking him what was "lawful proof" (*dalîl shar'î*) authorizing him to take part in elections in the absence of the *hâkim 'âdil*, since Iran had abandoned demanding the *wilâya* over Iraq. DVD of the visit of 'Abd al-'Aziz al-Hakîm to Muqtadâ al-Sadr, Najaf, October 2005.
2. Cf. the chapter by Pierre-Jean Luizard in this volume.
3. International Crisis Group, 2006.
4. The battles between the Army of the Mahdî and the Faylaq Badr militia of the Supreme Council for Islamic Revolution in Iraq (SCIRI) in October 2006, for example, were confined to the city of al-'Amâra, while Sadrists and members of SCIRI in Basra remained allied against their common enemy, the Hizb al-Fadîla (a party formed by Muhammad al-Ya'qûbî, a former student of Muhammad al-Sadr).

The issue of Sadrist resources is commonly formulated in terms of the symbolic capital bestowed on Muqtadâ by his father, and then converted into numerous resources of different kinds. This logic deserves to be revisited.

Sadrist resources

Muqtadâ's resources, like his father's, are broadly derived from the recognition of aspirations particular to the grass roots, from their desire for social recognition, to satisfaction of their material needs, to the appeal of Mahdism as a promise of restored justice in this world. As the most obvious resources of the Sadrist trend have been amply dwelled upon elsewhere,[1] the focus here will be on the uncharted category of "trivial resources"; treated as a taboo on the political stage, ignored by observers and yet essential to the survival of an organization such as the Mahdî Army. For the most part, the members of this army, recruited among the economically most deprived, receive no wages. To understand their motivation, therefore, it is necessary to consider the array of benefits that they derive from their activities. The narcissist gains linked to the use of violence, notably the petty power of intimidation conferred by carrying a weapon and belonging to a militia, figure prominently among them. The same is true of the prestige by proxy conferred by the mere evocation of the movement's symbolic figures, namely Muqtadâ, his martyred ancestors and the Imâm al-Mahdî. These references are the actual foundation of the coercion – or at any rate the symbolic violence – exercised by the Sadrists over the Shi'a population itself. The cause pursued, construed as noble by virtue of the double discourse and pretences that conceal its more ambiguous reality, is another important factor. Serving in the Mahdî Army also grants immediate social recognition through attribution of recognized status, social competence (rendering services, performing tasks reminiscent of the police, mobilizing connections to "get things done"), as well as social ascent in the form of progress within the hierarchy. For a marginalized urban youth, the stake is a way out of anomie – and anonymity – augmented by the thrilling experience of virile social

1. International Crisis Group, 2006.

interaction between comrades-in-arms. Finally, militiamen secure access to state resources (for example through paid protection of ministries controlled by the Sadrist trend) and, more importantly, to an expansive black economy (misappropriation of state resources, oil smuggling, racketeering, expropriation of victims labeled as *takfîriyîn* and *saddâmiyîn*).

These concerns closely match those of the organization called the Fidâ'iyû Saddam, which recruits in very similar circles.[1] The parallel could even be extended to the eschatological expectation shared by Sadrists and Fidâ'iyûn, which amounts simultaneously to the promise of an afterlife and that of the advent of justice in this world, forever delayed by an oppressor who must be fought here and now. These two rallying cries are built around the longing for fulfillment felt by an urban generation that has been denied any future in Iraqi society as it stands. The Fidâ'iyûn fought the 2003 American invasion with a resolve unequalled by conventional units of the Iraqi armed forces, not out of a fanatic love of Saddam (many of them have since joined the Mahdî Army) but out of nihilism. In short, they sought fulfillment via and within a state of violence. A similar orgy of pointless sacrifice defined the 2004 confrontation between the Sadrists and the coalition forces. The generational gap revealed by the Sadrist phenomenon, which generally repels the parents of Mahdî Army members, can only be understood with reference to age groups that are more or less predisposed to militant mobilization. The armed Sunni opposition, by contrast, is transgenerational. It is necessary to bear in mind the collective identity of this young revolutionary class, which is devoid of a past as much as a future outside of the Sadrist trend.

Conclusion

In view of these different frames of analysis, it would be delusional to treat the Sadrist current as an ephemeral and superficial phenomenon. As an object of research, it is as deserving of in-depth study and perhaps as important to the contemporary history of Iraq as the political awakening of the officers and small town shopkeepers who filled out the ranks of the Ba'ath party in the 1950s and 1960s, or the Islamist mobilization

---

1. Baran, 2004.

of the 1960s and 1970s. It nevertheless remains surprisingly neglected in academia. The fancy that the Sadrist movement is mired in contradictions does not justify researchers' lack of interest. The potential for stricter organization is present, notably if the civil war should intensify. At this point, however, the movement is not attempting to institutionalize itself any more than it is, nor does it strive to overcome its contradictions, because these make sense as elements in processes in which the phenomenon as a whole is inscribed.

Faced with a movement that it could not easily control because of its ideological foundations and its weak institutional integration, Iran opted for a policy of containment whilst never alienating the Sadrists unnecessarily. On the one hand, the Islamic republic has blocked Ayatollah al-Hâ'irî's return to Najaf, as well as his efforts to correspond with his representatives and other Shi'a actors in Iraq. Likewise, Iran has never catered to the material needs of the Sadrists to any meaningful extent. Until recently, at any rate, the Sadrists were not invited to participate in the talks organized by Tehran to discuss the future of Iraq, the implication being that they were not seen as political actors worthy of consultation.[1] On the other hand, Iran has clearly tried to avoid any confrontation; more precisely, it has attempted to construct a relationship flexible enough to evolve in function of the prevailing context. Muqtadâ and his representatives have occasionally been received with respect in Tehran. Minimal financial and logistical support was given to the Mahdî Army within the framework of resistance to the occupation forces,[2] which apparently allowed the Iranian intelligence services to lay the foundations for closer collaboration in case the threat of an American military intervention against Iran's nuclear program should become a reality. This position is part of a strategy designed to facilitate the expansion of Iran's sphere of influence through numerous channels, recognizing simultaneously the diversity of the Iraqi Shi'a world and the necessity to prepare for a multitude of

---

1. For more details, cf. International Crisis Group, 2006.

2. This support does not seem to exceed beyond moderate sums (of the order of a few thousand dollars) and equipment granted occasionally to groups of Sadrist fighters, mostly in Basra. Interviews in Iraq by one of the authors, August 2006. It is unclear whether this is an effective state policy or mere private initiatives.

possible scenarios on the strategic level.[1] Relations between Iran and the Sadrists are therefore likely to evolve, as the deepening conflict within Iraq will exacerbate the fluctuation of alliances between internal actors and foreign sponsors.

Bibliography

Baran, David, *Vivre la tyrannie et lui survivre. L'Irak en transition*, Paris 2004, Mille et Une Nuits.

Batatu, Hanna, *The Shaikh and the Peasant in Iraq. 1919–1958*, PhD dissertation, University of Harvard, 1960.

Darle, Pierre, *Saddam Hussein maître des mots. Du langage de la tyrannie à la tyrannie du langage*, Paris 2003, L'Harmattan.

Dobry, Michel, *Sociologie des crises politiques*, Paris 1992, Presses de la Fondation nationale des sciences politiques.

Jabar A., Faleh, *The Shi'ite Movement in Iraq*, London: Saqi Books, 2003.

Fernea, Elizabeth W., *Guests of the Sheikh*, New York 1965, Doubleday.

Fernea, Robert, A., "State and Tribe in Southern Iraq: The Struggle for Hegemony before the 1958 Revolution", in Fernea, Robert A., and Louis, William, R., *The Iraqi Revolution of 1958: The Old Social Classes Revisited*, London 1991, I. B. Tauris.

Fulanayn (pseudonym), *The Marsh Arab: HajjiRikkan*, Philadelphia 1928, J.B. Lippincott.

Al-Hâ'irî, Kh., *Asâs al-hukûma al-islâmiyya* (The Bases of the Islamic government), Beirut 1979, Nil.

Harling, Peter "Saddam Hussein et la débâcle triomphante. Ressources insoupçonnées de Umm al-Ma'ârik", in *Revue des mondes musulmans et de la Méditerranée*, no 117–118, *L'Irak en perspective,* July 2007, pp. 157–178. http://remmm.revues.org/index3401.htm

Harling, Peter, and Yasin, Hamid, "L'Unité de façade des shiites irakiens", in *Le Monde Diplomatique*, September 2006.

International Crisis Group, "Iraq's Muqtada al-Sadr: Spoiler or Stabilizer?", in *Middle East Report* 55, 11 July 2006.

Al-Jawibrâwî, J. A., *Tarîkh Maysân wa 'ashâ'ir al-'Amâra* (History of Maysân and thel-'Amâra Tribes), Baghdad 1990.

Al-Kharsân, S., *Muhammad Bâqir al-Sadr fî zakirât al-'Irâq* (Muhammad Bâqir al-Sadr in the memory of Iraq, Baghdad 2004.

Luizard, Pierre-Jean, *La formation de l'Irak contemporain*, Paris 1991, CNRS Éditions.

Luizard, Pierre-Jean, "Bagdad : une métropole moderne et tribale, siège de

---

1. Harling and Yasin, 2006.

gouvernements assiégés', in *Maghreb-Machrek*, special issue, 1994, pp. 225–242.

Malik, Jamal, *Colonialization of Islam: Dissolution of traditional institutions in Pakistan*, New Delhi, 1996, Manohar.

Maxwell, Gavin, *People of the Reeds*, New York 1957, Harper.

Al-Miyâhî, A., *al-safîr al-khâmis* (The Sixth Ambassador), Beirut 2001, Publications Muhammad Sâdiq al-Sadr.

Ra'ûf, 'Adil, *al-'amal al-islâmî fil-'Irâq bayn al-marja'iyya wal-hizbiyya* (Islamic action between the *marja'iyya* and political parties in Iraq), Damascus 2000, al-Markaz al-'irâqî lil-dirâsât.

Ra'ûf, 'Adil, *al-Sadr bayn diktatûriyayn* (al-Sadr Between two Dictatorships), Damascus 2001, al-Markaz al-'irâqî lil-dirâsât.

Rigaud, F., 'Irak : l'impossible mouvement de l'intérieur?' in Bennani-Chraïbi, Mounia, and Fillieule, Olivier, eds., *Résistances et protestations dans les sociétés musulmanes*, Paris 2003, Presses de la Fondation nationale des sciences politiques, pp. 197–217.

Al-Sadr, Muhammad Sâdiq, *Mawsû'ât al-imâm al-Mahdî* (Encyclopaedia of the Imâm al-Mahdî), Beirut 1992, Dâr al-Ta'âruf.

Al-Sadr, Muhammad Sâdiq, *Mata Azhar al-imâm al-Mahdî ?* (When will the Imâm al-Mahdî appear?), Beirut 2006, al-Bâqir.

Al-Sudânî,. Al-Hâjj A. H, *al-'Adât wal-taqâlid al-'ashâ'iriyya fil-'Amâra* (The Customs and Tribal Traditions of al-'Amâra), Baghdad 1990, matbâ'at al-Jâhiz.

Thesiger, Wilfred *The Marsh Arabs*, New York 1964, Dutton.

Yasin, Hamid, *Les processus du courant sadriste de père en fils*, unpublished memoir for a DEA (under the direction of Gilles Kepel), Paris 2005, Institut d'études politiques.

Young, Gavin, *Return to the Marshes: Life With the Marsh Arabs of Iraq*, London 1977, Collins.

MARIAM ABOU ZAHAB

Between Pakistan and Qom: Shi'a Women's Madrasas and New Transnational Networks

The Iranian revolution has had a major effect on the presence of Islam in the Pakistani public sphere. Indirectly, it has contributed to the flourishing of various Sunni Muslim institutions and movements, including some radical ones. Both local and foreign sponsors, especially from the Arabian peninsula, have resorted to supporting the radical strain in Sunni Islam in an effort to counter the revolutionary messages radiating from Iran. But more directly the revolution has galvanized the Pakistani Shi'a communities, as it did Shi'a communities all over the world, setting in motion a strong movement of religious intensification and purification, and creating or reinforcing transnational networks that connected Pakistani Shi'a with their co-religionaries in Iran and elsewhere. This paper deals with one particular aspect of the resurgence of Pakistani Shi'ism: the emergence of women's madrasas and the subsequent advanced studies undertaken by some of their best graduates in Qom in Iran.[1]

---

1. This chapter presents the preliminary findings of a research project that is still in progress. It is based on fieldwork done in Pakistan (July 2001, December 2004 and September 2005) and Qom (November 2004). In Pakistan, I visited three madrasas: Jami'at Khadijat al-Kubra in Pakki Shah Mardan (Mianwali), Rajoa Sadat (Chiniot) and Jami'at al-Muntazar (Lahore). In Qom, I visited Jami'at al-Zahra, a madrasa for foreign female students, where roughly one third of the students were from Pakistan. A first English version of this article

Shi'ism, in its various forms, has had a long presence in the regions that make up present Pakistan. Currently, the Shi'a are believed to constitute 15 to 20 per cent of the population.[1] Most are Twelver (*ithna 'ashari*) Shi'a, but there is also a certain presence of Ismailis, especially in Karachi and in the northern territories. According to local tradition, the presence of Shi'ism here goes back to the first centuries of Islam, when members of the Ahl al-Bait, the Prophet's family, fled east from Sunni persecution and found a safe haven on the banks of the Indus. The genealogies of the Pakistani *sayyids* (descendants of the Prophet) trace their family origins all the way back to the seventh century and believe their ancestors settled here soon after Husain's martyrdom at Karbala and the persecution of his descendants. Most *sayyids* in Pakistan are Shi'a.

However, the majority of Pakistani Shi'a are the descendants of Hindus who were converted to Islam by *dâ'i* (Ismaili missionaries), whose presence in the region is attested from the tenth century onwards.[2] The state of Multan in fact actually adopted Ismailism as the state religion for a brief period in the tenth century, under an independent dynasty allied with the Qarmatis, until its conquest and incorporation into the Sunni Ghaznavid Empire under Sultan Mahmud of Ghazna in 1010.[3] Another wave of conversions, this time to Twelver Shi'ism, took place in the Safavid period (1505–1722), when Ismaili shrines in the Punjab and the present Northwest Frontier Province were taken over by Twelver Shi'a. Conversions to Shi'ism did not come to an end after the Safavid period but have continued to this day. A number of well-known Shi'a *ulemas* and preachers today are converts from Sunni Islam.

The Shi'a population is highly fragmented and heterogeneous, divided into numerous ethnic, linguistic and social communities, with rituals and practices showing great variety from region to region and

---

was published in Farish A. Noor, Yoginder Sikand, and Martin van Bruinessen (eds), *The Madrasa in Asia: Political Activism and Transnational Linkages*, Amsterdam 2008.

1. No actual statistics exist, but these figures are commonly given in official Pakistani publications. At 25 to 30 million, this is the second largest Shi'a community after Iran

2. See Maclean, 1989.

3. Cf. "Multan" and "Karmati", Bearman et al, 1960–2005.

even from one city to the other. The *azadari* (mourning rituals) are particularly rich and complex, with apparent borrowings from Hindu rituals, and rather different from the more austere rituals observed in Lebanon, Iraq and Iran.[1]

In terms of gender relations, in the Indian subcontinent Shi'ism is commonly considered more liberal than Sunnism, giving a more important position to women in social life. Shi'a women have access to the religious public space whereas Sunni women, apart from visits to the shrines, do not participate in public religious activities. Moreover, Shi'a religious law is more favorable to women than the Hanafi *mazhab*, especially in matters of marriage, divorce and inheritance.

Juan Cole has shown that women in urban circles in the Shi'a principality of Awadh (1722–1856) enjoyed a high degree of independence *vis-à-vis* men. This, together with the practice of gender segregation, "contributed to the development of a specifically feminine Shi'a religious discourse that was [...] more syncretic and innovative than the scripturalism of literate males."[2] Cole adds that these women believed in astrology and were heavily influenced by Hindu rituals. All this contributed to the elaboration of a distinct female Shi'a culture that is still very much alive among the *sayyid* families who settled as *muhajir* (refugees) in Multan, Lahore and Karachi after the Partition of British India.

One remarkable result of the relatively independent position of women and strict gender separation in Shi'a communities is the existence of a class of female informal religious experts. Many daughters of poorer *sayyid* families remained unmarried, because they were not allowed to marry commoners and their families could not afford the high dowries demanded by the better-off *sayyid* families.[3] These women were trained as religious teachers and preachers. They would teach the Qur'an to the daughters of the aristocracy and during the month of Muharram they would lead women's *majlis* (gatherings) and recite the mournful stories of the martyrdom of Husain and the suffering of the other Imams. The female religious

---

1. Schubel 1990, Pinault 1992. Pinault, 2001.
2. See "Women and the making of Shi'ism" in Cole 2002, pp. 138–60. The quoted passage is at pp. 150–1.
3. As elsewhere, South Asian *sayyid* families have a strict code of status maintenance that forbids women to marry non-*sayyids*.

experts constituted a widespread network of learning, independent of the male *ulema* networks. In contemporary Pakistan, however, such celibate *sayyidas* are not the only class of educated women among the Shi'a. The Pakistani Shi'a, especially the Urdu-speaking Muhajirs, have long given more weight to girls' education than the Sunnis. Before the 1980s, this mainly concerned secular education. Due to their relatively high educational achievements, Shi'a women were over-represented in the media (on television and in the English-language press) as well as in the professions (lawyers, doctors, academics) and in literature and the arts.

The Iranian revolution and its apparently empowering effect on women's social roles had a pervasive effect on the self-perception and ideals of South Asian Shi'a women, who took Iranian women as their role models. It was especially in the field of religious education and in the increased visibility of women in the religious space that the Iranian influence made itself felt. A number of girls' madrasas were established, initially with financial support from Iran. During Khatami's presidency, exporting the revolution gave way to the support of educational institutions as an instrument of foreign policy. Consequently, the number of women seeking a religious education or taking courses in such a madrasa while continuing their secular studies has increased tremendously. Moreover, since the mid-1980s, a growing number of Pakistani women has been going to Iran for advanced study in the seminaries of Qom.

The remainder of this chapter discusses three of these new women's madrasas in Pakistan and the seminary for foreign female students in Qom, the Jami'at al-Zahra, where some of the best graduates of these madrasas have gone to continue their studies. The madrasas are located in very different geographical and social settings, were established with different purposes, and serve different constituencies. One is an urban elite institution in Lahore that is highly "Persianized"; another is a school in a Shi'a village with a largely *sayyid* population; and the third, with which I begin, is located in an isolated rural district, where Shi'ism is deeply anchored in local tradition and culture.

The Jami'at Khadijat al-Kubra

One of Pakistan's largest madrasas for girls is the Jami'at Khadijat al-Kubra in Pakki Shah Mardan, a remote Shi'a village about forty kilometers from Mianwali in a socially conservative area where the women's literacy rate is particularly low. The founder of this madrasa is Sayyid Iftikhar Hussain Naqvi, a Shi'a *'alim* born in 1951 in Multan district. Upon return from his studies in Iraq in the 1970s, Naqvi became a close associate of Allama Arif Hussain al-Hussaini, the most prominent leader of the reformist group among Pakistani Shi'a clerics, and got actively involved in politics.[1] His first venture into education was in 1982 when he founded the Madrasa Imam Khomeini for boys in Marri Indus, near Mianwali. The Jami'at Khadijat al-Kubra began its activities in 1993 in a small house next to the boys' madrasa. Land was later acquired in Pakki Shah Mardan, where the madrasa was inaugurated in September 1996. In the first year, forty girls received admission; currently the number of students is close to two hundred, and the school has some sixty full-time and part-time teachers, twenty of whom are men.[2] At the time of my last visit, in December 2004, a new dormitory was under construction, indicating that expansion continued. The madrasa attracts students from far afield, but the complex also includes two institutions catering to the needs of the local community: a training centre, where local girls are taught practical skills such as sewing and embroidery but also computer skills, and a dispensary. The current director of the madrasa is Iftikhar Naqvi's daughter, Wajiha Naqvi, one of the early Pakistani graduates from the Jami'at al-Zahra in Qom.

Some of the students belong to *ruhani* (clerical families), and could be said to be stepping into a known though previously male domain. They

---

1.   Allama Hussaini, a Pashtun *'alim* from Parachinar, who studied in Najaf and Qom, was the wakil (representative) of Khomeini in Pakistan. He was the leader of the Shi'a political movement Tahrik-i Nifaz-i Fiqh-i Ja'fariya (later renamed Tahrik-i Ja'fariya Pakistan) from 1984 until August 1988, when he was assassinated. He transformed this originally religious movement into a political party and became an inspiration for the Shi'a students' movement and the leader of the "Iranianized" group among the Pakistani Shi'a clergy. He was succeeded as the leader of the Tahrik by Allama Sajid Ali Naqvi.

2.   These numbers are based on observations made during my visit in December 2004.

are a minority however. The other girls have chosen to study in a madrasa either out of personal interest in religion, or because they perceived these studies as a way to social advancement. Quite a few students are from the northern areas (Gilgit, Baltistan), although this region has many madrasas supported by Iran. I also met a number of British Pakistani girls, who had enrolled in the madrasa in order both to receive a religious education and to get better acquainted with their own culture.

The madrasa offers courses of four types, each designed for a different audience. The curriculum follows the prescribed curriculum developed by the Wifaq al-Madaris al-Shi'a (Union of Shi'a madrasas), the body in charge of religious studies that organizes exams and issues degrees.[1] Courses are taught in Urdu, and many of the prescribed books are translations from Persian textbooks, published in Lahore in cooperation with Iranian publishers.

The first course, *fahm-i din*, which lasts three months, is a basic course intended especially for girls who study in government schools or who are living abroad. It consists of basic knowledge of Islam: *'aqa'id* (the articles of faith) and *akhlaq* (morality); the girls are taught from the Qur'an and the *Sirat Fatima* (the life of the Prophet's daughter Fatima – the ultimate role model for Shi'a women); they learn the correct form of the rituals and memorize numerous *salawat* (invocations) that are recited daily.

Wajiha Naqvi explains that the objectives of this course are that the basic knowledge imparted should enable the girls to develop their personalities and give spirituality a proper place in their lives. It should also give them a better understanding of Shi'ism and correct the negative image of madrasas in Pakistani society. Students are formally required to have obtained their matriculation exam, i.e. have successfully completed ten years of general education, before they can apply for admission. In exceptional cases, girls who have only completed the intermediate (8th grade) or even primary levels (5th grade) can be admitted if they have the required intellectual capacities and motivation; the course is then adapted to their level.

---

1. Pakistan has similar umbrella organizations responsible for maintaining standards of education in the madrasas of each of the major denominations: Deobandis, Barelwis, Ahl-i Hadith, Jama'at-i Islami and Shi'a. See Malik 1996.

Wajiha Naqvi argues that there are good reasons for offering this type of basic religious education in a school context instead of at home, as was common in the past. The family, she claims, is not the best environment to provide even this basic disciplining; a more structured learning environment is needed. With more systematic disciplining, even those girls who do not continue their education after this course will contribute to spreading the faith as "silent preachers": through performing the daily prayers regularly and wearing the hijab, they act as role models for children and attract them towards religion.

Over the ten years that this course has been offered, about 500 girls have followed it. The madrasa attempts to stay in touch with the former students and has thus gradually been building up a network of pious, committed young women.

The second course, which takes a full year, is meant to train girls as *muballigha* (female preachers) and *zakira* (the ritual experts who lead the *majlis*, the gatherings where the suffering and martyrdom of the Imams is commemorated). The teaching focuses on memorization and the practical aspects of the *majlis*. Students memorize Qur'anic verses together with their Urdu translation; learn about the life of the Prophet and of the Imams; and study the foundations of Arabic (in order to pronounce the Qur'anic verses correctly), *tafsir* (exegesis) and *fiqh* (jurisprudence). They memorize *marsiyas, nohas, qasidas* and *musaddas*, which are sung during the *majlis*. The courses focus on performance techniques: the students view videocassettes of famous (male) *zakir*s and *wa'iz* (preachers)[1] and learn how to prepare sermons in Urdu and in Siraiki (the local language) for different types of audiences. They also acquire the technique of reciting the *faza'il* (meritorious qualities) of the Imams and the *masa'ib* (misfortunes) of the Ahl-i Bait. A good *zakira* must have a strong voice, and she must be able to arouse emotion among the participants and make them cry.

The madrasa expressly intends to produce a new type of *zakira*, different from the traditional *zakira*s, who, lacking any formal religious education, had learned their skills from their mothers or from experienced

---

1. The video cassettes in circulation are exclusively of male preachers and *zakir*s, because the public visibility of women to male audiences is a controversial matter in pious circles. There do exist, however, audio cassettes of female preachers and *zakira*s.

zakiras. The traditional religious ideas mediated by the old-style *zakiras* often bordered on the heterodox. The training of better qualified (and more orthodox) *zakiras* continues an earlier movement of reform of the *majlis* and rationalization of ritual that was launched as early as the mid-1960s by Maulana Mohammad Hussain Dhakku. Dhakku's initiative provoked hostile reactions from more traditional elements, who called him a Wahhabi intent on destroying religion. The revolution in Iran, however, gave a strong boost to the reformist effort to purify belief. As a part of their training, the students are required to do textual research in preparation of their recital of one of the episodes of the Imams' lives. Their teachers make them compare the written texts with popular oral versions told by traditional *zakiras* and denounce the latter as erroneous and heterodox.

Wajiha Naqvi considers the *majlis* an excellent occasion for *tabligh* (predication), but unfortunately, these are mostly organized and led by men. Women do attend the *majlis*, but they usually return home after listening to the *faza'il* and *masa'ib*, without acquiring any religious knowledge. Therefore educated women have had to take charge and organize separate women's *majlis* as a vehicle for the transmission of religious knowledge that is both accessible to rural women and adapted to their specific needs.[1]

In rural areas, where women are not highly educated and indeed are often illiterate, the graduates of this one-year course can make a significant impact on society because of their access to the women. Especially during the months of Ramadan and Muharram, *muballighas* travel from village to village, delivering pious homilies, teaching about the Qur'an, and leading invocations.

This second course has so far been completed by 120 students; some of them have opened schools in their own village or neighborhood. They act as role models; many of the current students say that they joined the madrasa because they were influenced by these *muballighas*. After completing this course, the students who wish to do so have the right to

1. On women's *majlis* in Pashawar, see Hegland, 1998a; and Hegland 1998b.

take part, as external candidates, in the final exams of the secular higher secondary school.[1]

The third course, which lasts two years, is a proper madrasa curriculum that prepares the students for the degrees of *fazil-i Arabi* and *sultan al-afazil*. The holders of the latter degree can obtain a statement that is equivalent to an M.A. in Arabic or Islamic Studies from the University of Punjab.[2] After passing an examination of their didactic abilities at the Allama Iqbal Open University, they are also allowed to teach these subjects in government schools. During the past decade, 140 students have obtained the degree of *sultan al-afazil*, and many of them have in fact become teachers.

The course is traditional in content: it is based on the *dars-i nizami*, which constituted the standard curriculum of South Asian madrasas since the mid-eighteenth century, along with some specifically Shi'a texts prescribed by the Sh'ia madrasa board (Wifaq al-Madaris al-Shi'a).[3] The students must also acquire a solid if only passive mastery of Arabic; this language is taught by a Lebanese woman married to a Pakistani cleric who lived in Syria for seventeen years, studying at the Imam Khomeini madrasa in Damascus. The language teaching too is traditional and consists of the memorization of textbooks of *nahw* (morphology) and *sarf* (syntax). Persian is also taught, using more modern textbooks published in Iran, but the students do not acquire more than a passive knowledge of this language either.

The fourth course, which lasts another two years, leads to the degree of *'alima*. The program of study includes methods of *tabligh*, teaching and research, with an emphasis on *munazara* (theological debate). This course is primarily for students who wish to continue to higher studies

---

1. This concerns the F.A. and F.Sc. exams (arts and sciences, respectively) taken at the end of the twelfth year.
2. The madrasa reform proposed by the government of Pakistan in 1980 entailed among other things a rule of equivalence that gave the highest degrees of madrasa education parity with the M.A. degree in Islamic or Arabic studies at one of the universities. Most universities, incidentally, rejected this idea of equivalence. See Malik, 1996, pp. 140–1.
3. The *dars-i nizami* owes its name to the scholar Maulana Nizamuddin Sihalvi of Lucknow. It has remained, with some revisions, the standard curriculum not only of Sunni, but also of Shi'a madrasas in India and Pakistan.

in Iran. It prepares them for the entrance exam of the Jami'at al-Zahra in Qom, where they will study for at least another two years. In the past decade, thirty-eight graduates of this course have gained admission in Qom; twenty-two of them have returned to Pakistan after completing their studies. Some of them are directors of madrasas in Pakistan now; the majority have become well-known preachers, whose *majlis* attract large crowds. They have experienced a definite rise in social status and prestige as a result of their stay in Qom.

Rajoa Sadat

Rajoa Sadat is a Shi'a village in Punjab, situated close to the road linking Faisalabad to Chiniot and built around the shrine of a local Shi'a saint, Shah Daulat Bukhari. As the name of the village indicates (*sadat* being the Arabic plural of *sayyid*), the majority of the inhabitants are *sayyid*s, and most of these *sayyid* families are large landowners, whose land is cultivated by peasants who live in the same and surrounding villages. These landlord families have strong connections with Iran, where many of the men have gone for religious studies; some have been commuting between Iran and their village for the last twelve to fifteen years.

In September 2005, I visited a girls' madrasa here that was founded in 2002 by a young university-educated member of one of these landowning families. The madrasa then had 125 students, who were living in two large but dilapidated houses donated by one of the *sayyid* families, and the school appeared to be run on a very modest budget. However, a huge new building was under construction at the entrance of the village on a piece of land donated by another feudal family. According to the director of the madrasa, once this building is completed it will accommodate 1,500 students. He claimed that the demand for the type of education the school provides is very high; at present many prospective students have to be rejected for lack of space. Currently, the staff of the madrasa consists of only two female teachers and the (male) director. Both teachers are married to clerics, and both spent over ten years studying in Qom. They are assisted by the more advanced students, who instruct the younger ones. For subjects such as *hifz* (memorization of the Qur'an) and *tajwid* (its proper articulation) they also use video and audio cassettes.

The madrasa is located in a rural environment, although less isolated than Pakki Shah Mardan, and the girls who get admission after completing their matriculation are from rural backgrounds, mostly from villages of South and Central Punjab. Only a small proportion of them belong to religious families; many say that they were influenced by *muballighas* who had come to their village to preach during Ramadan and Muharram.

Contrary to Pakki Shah Mardan, this madrasa does not aim at training *zakiras* or preparing girls for higher studies in Qom, but rather at giving a basic religious education and promoting values. There is a section for *hifz* and a short course for *muballighas*. As the director stated, most girls are unlikely to complete five years of madrasa education, and for them *tarbiyat* (moral disciplining and training to be good wives and mothers) is more important than *ta'alim* (textbook learning). Girls study for one or two years before wedding; a girl who has studied in a madrasa has more value on the marriage market.

The madrasa has no fixed syllabus and no exams. Its objective, in the director's words, is to enable the girls to develop their capacities (how to pray, recite the Qur'an and perhaps lead a *majlis*) and to change their personalities so that after returning to their villages they will be "vehicles of silent *tabligh*" and by their examples bring about social revolution in their environments. In his view it is more important to teach the girls how to bring up their children and how to solve conflicts with their mothers-in-law rather than to immerse them in *fiqh* or complex Arabic grammar, which will be of little use to them in their daily lives. Education should be relevant to the students' lives, and the students are expected to spend their lives within limited horizons.

Jami'at al-Muntazar

My third women's madrasa is the section for girls in the Jami'at al-Muntazar in Lahore, the most prestigious Shi'a madrasa of Pakistan. This is the major intellectual centre of Pakistan's Shi'a community, and the Wifaq al-Madaris al-Shi'a, the institution in charge of religious studies which organizes exams and issues degrees, is based here. Unlike the earlier two, this madrasa recruits primarily students of urban background, and modernizing Iranian influences make themselves even more strongly felt here.

The girls' section was established in 1988, by Safdar Hussain Najafi. Originally based in another Lahore neighborhood, it was recently moved to the main campus in Model Town for security reasons. At the time of my visit in September 2005 there were thirty-eight students, who had been admitted after completing their matriculation or intermediate levels. Only about a quarter of them were from Lahore, two were from Northern Pakistan (Gilgit), and the remainder were from Central and South Punjab, Jhang and Multan being especially well-represented. For some of the students, the madrasa diploma is an aim in itself but many have academic ambitions. Several of the girls were, besides their religious studies at the madrasa, preparing to take the state F.A. or B.A. exams as external candidates; one of them in fact had just passed her M.A.

The atmosphere in the Jami'at al-Muntazar is strikingly different from the other two madrasas I visited. This is an elite institution, more strongly "Iranianized" than the others, and catering to an urban middle-class public. The girls wear neat uniforms consisting of white shalwar-qameez with dupattas of different colors for each grade. The syllabus is very similar to that of the seminary in Qom, with an emphasis on Arabic language. Unlike the other madrasas, *hifz* is not taught here, nor is there a section for training *muballighat*.[1] The basic four-month course offered here, which is similar to successful courses elsewhere, does not attract any students – another indication that this madrasa serves a different type of public, with more academic ambitions.

Most of the girls dream of continuing their studies in Qom, which together with Najaf is the main centre of Shi'a learning. Every year a committee from Qom comes and visits Pakistan's best madrasas to select students; however, the number invited to Qom is not high, just two each year from this madrasa. Those fortunate enough to be selected join a remarkable transnational scholarly network that brings them into contact with colleagues from all over the world.

---

1. *Hifz* is only in demand in rural areas. Students interested in *hifz* would not apply for admission at the Jami'at al-Muntazar. The training of *muballighat* is not considered an academic discipline here; one of the teachers told me that this is not a skill which can be imparted through formal teaching, as it takes much more than one year of on-the-job training to become a *muballigha*.

Iran: the Jami'at al-Zahra in Qom

Jami'at al-Zahra in Qom, the first women's madrasa there, was inaugurated in 1984 and the section for foreign students started its activities two years later.[1] In February 2004, the madrasa moved to more spacious premises in a new campus which is still being enlarged. At the time of my visit in November 2004, there were some 200 girls studying in this madrasa, from around forty countries. Pakistanis, numbering some sixty, made up the largest contingent among them; twenty to twenty-five were Indian Shi'a, and a smaller number were British Muslims of Pakistani background, many of them Gujaratis. Another conspicuous group consisted of some ten French-speaking *ithna 'ashari* Khojas from Madagascar.[2] More surprising was the presence of Sunni students, notably from China, Tajikistan and various African countries. The director of the madrasa told me that demand from China is overwhelming and there would be many more Chinese students if the admission policies were less restrictive. The same is true of Pakistanis: many more capable students are eager to study in Qom than the school can accommodate.

The Pakistani students at the Jami'at al-Zahra hailed mainly from the Punjab (Lahore and Islamabad/Rawalpindi) or from Karachi and many belonged to *ruhani* families. Most had completed four years of study in a Pakistani madrasa before coming to Qom. I found a few students among them whom I had first met in Pakki Shah Mardan, three years before. There were also a number of students who had grown up in well-to-do, secular-minded urban families. They were the first in their families to receive a higher religious education, and some of them had to struggle hard to overcome their parents' reluctance to let them follow this path.

The students at the Jami'at al-Zahra are not the first Pakistani women

---

1. There is another madrasa for foreign women in Qom, named Bint al-Huda, where the emphasis is more on Arabic language. According to Pakistani sources, about twenty-five Pakistani students were studying at the Bint al-Huda in 2005. Most of the students in this madrasa were Iraqis and many of them appear to have returned to Iraq after the fall of Saddam Hussain.

2. Most Khojas are Nizari Ismailis, but in the early nineteenth century part of the community converted to Twelver Shi'ism. Both in South Asia and in the diaspora (East Africa, Europe) there are sizeable *ithna 'ashari* Khoja communities.

to study at Qom. Several had done so before the madrasa was established. One of them (whom I also met in Qom) had even acquired the title of *mujtahida*, meaning she had completed the highest level of education available. This woman, from a *muhajir* family in Karachi, had first arrived in Qom in 1982, following her marriage to a Pakistani cleric who was then studying in Qom (currently, he is an influential Shiʻa personality in Karachi, where he directs a cultural centre with close links to Iran, and a part-time resident of Qom, where he leads a research institute). At that time, there was no madrasa for girls, so for nine years she followed a very heavy traditional program of studies, being tutored in her teachers' private homes. In her memory, the relationship between the (female) teachers and students was very warm and close, and the students highly motivated. Several of the Pakistani women who studied in Iran in those early days, she claims, established their own women's madrasas in Pakistan upon their return, and many others have become madrasa teachers. None of those who have completed their studies in Qom have become housewives only; they are all active in public life. They enjoy prestige and most earn considerable incomes.

The Jamiʻat al-Zahra has set itself the task of producing a Shiʻa female elite in a competitive environment, and it is very selective in recruiting foreign students. Those who are selected, however, do not have to pay anything. They should be aged between seventeen and twenty-five, unmarried, and have at least the equivalent of a Pakistani F.A. or F.Sc. diploma.[1] In fact, the girls I spoke with found the level of teaching so demanding that they thought a B.A. degree would be a better preparation. The complete course for foreign students takes five years, divided into an introductory year and two higher levels. The students are evaluated at the end of each year: admission to the second level is not automatic even for those who have passed their exams; only the best students are allowed to proceed with their studies. Foreign students begin with preparatory coursework, the first four months of which are used to acquire a working knowledge of Persian. For Urdu speakers this appears to be sufficient; to my surprise the Pakistani girls were even speaking Persian among themselves. Those

---

1. For long-term foreign residents of Qom other rules apply. Married women up to the age of thirty-five can be admitted; the madrasa even offers a day-care centre for their young children.

who did not study in a madrasa in their own country before coming to Qom have to follow this up with an intensive basic course in religious subjects that takes another six months. The other students take exams and, if successful, are directly admitted to the first level of the general course (*dawra-i umumi*).

The curriculum has been revised and modernized during the last two years, following the appointment of Sheikh Mohammad Ali Shomali as the director of the madrasa. Shomali graduated in Western philosophy at Tehran University alongside his religious studies in Qom and went on to obtain a PhD degree in philosophy from Manchester University. The most important subjects are *fiqh*, philosophy, pedagogy and the theory and practice of education. The textbooks used here are mostly modern texts, unlike what is common in Pakistan. The works of Ayatollah Mutahhari, especially, have pride of place in the syllabus.[1] There is also a strong emphasis on Arabic (twenty credits out of seventy-seven for the first level), which appears to present the greatest difficulty for many students. They express their frustration at not being able to speak the language in spite of the amount of teaching devoted to it. (Some of the Pakistani women living in Qom have arranged to be tutored in spoken Arabic by Iraqi women at home.)

At the second level, comprising the final two years of the five-year course, the emphasis is on the methodology of critical textual studies. The students can choose between two types of education at this level: knowledge of Shi'a doctrine or ethics and Islamic teaching. They have to write more than a dozen research papers and a dissertation to obtain the concluding degree. After this, they are expected to return to their home countries. The madrasa does not aim to produce Islamic scholars who will stay in Qom but rather highly qualified teachers who will go back to their country of origin and become agents of *tabligh*. Some of the most successful students, who are still below the age of twenty-three when they pass the *tahsilat-i takmili* exams, are allowed to continue to an M.A. level advanced course. Two advanced course programs have recently been introduced, specializing in Islamic spirituality and Shi'a studies (the

---

1. The curriculum lists numerous works by Ayatollah Murtaza Mutahhari on philosophy and the fundamentals of Shi'ism.

history and sociology of Shi'ism). Most of the students in these programs are, however, semi-permanent residents of Qom, who live there with their husbands or parents.

Besides the five-year course, the Jami'at al-Zahra also offers summer courses of three to six weeks that are very popular with students from Pakistan and the Pakistani diaspora. A six-week course in 2004 was attended by thirty-four girls from Karachi. There are also teacher-training courses, and a basic course that takes a single year. Knowledge of Persian is not required for these shorter courses; the lectures are given in English, Arabic, or even in French, depending on the audience. Unlike the five-year course, however, these short courses are not offered free of charge.

The madrasa offers Pakistani students a cosmopolitan environment and a relative freedom which contrast starkly with the situation at home. Their stay in Qom means a temporary escape from the stifling control of families and neighbors. Many also commented on the freedom of movement which women enjoy in Iran, which is very unlike Pakistan. Moreover, coming from a country where Shi'a feel constantly threatened, have to keep a low profile and sometimes even hide their religious affiliation, it is a liberating experience for them to live in a Shi'a environment. One would expect that the cosmopolitan composition of the student population would be conducive to the strengthening of transnational connections, but as the largest national group, constituting a third of the students, the Pakistanis tend to keep to themselves and do not mix much with the other students – notably not with the Indians. The students whom I interviewed did not even have an idea of how many Indian students there were in the madrasa.[1] Yet the years spent at the Jami'at al-Zahra have a profound effect on the world view and attitude of the students, who return to their homes as changed persons, eager to reform their own communities.

The Jami'at al-Zahra and its relationships with the growing number of Shi'a women's madrasas outside Iran exemplify the new pragmatic policy adopted by Iran under the reformist presidency of Mohammad Khatami (1997–2005). Iran's previous policy of attempting to export the revolution

---

1. This is true for the students at the madrasa. The Pakistanis who have settled in Qom as long-time residents, however, have developed wide-ranging contacts with Shi'a residents of Indian origin, and the shared Shi'a and Urdu identity appears to be overriding national affiliations.

had proved counter-productive and led to widespread sectarian violence, in Pakistan as well as elsewhere. The reformist policy consists of attempting to create in the madrasas of Qom a transnational Shi'a elite and stimulating the development of networks among the graduates. The Pakistani women graduating from Qom are part of this new elite, a self-consciously new type of Shi'a women. They have adopted the Iranian-style dress (a long raincoat and headscarf) that has become a symbol of modernity among young urban Shi'a women in Pakistan. Their studies have earned them considerable prestige, and a religious authority that is recognized by their male counterparts. To a certain extent, these female scholars moreover represent a form of Islamic feminism, based on a deconstruction of the Qur'an and of the *hadith* with a view to improving women's rights. Islam as they preach it is not a religion of fear, strict rules and severe punishments, but one of simple principles of belief and behavior in everyday life. In their public talks they explain points of belief but also address the practical and mundane matters faced by women in their daily lives, from health and child care to the psychology of education.

The moderately reformist trend that these women *ulemas* represent is often seen as a threat to the cultural specificities of popular South Asian Shi'ism and they are sometimes branded Wahhabis who want to destroy the very foundation of Shi'ism as it has developed over the centuries in South Asia. Some of them have understood that Shi'ism can only exist if it is rooted in a particular culture and they have developed a hybrid style of *majlis* in which the sermon uses rationalistic language and spreads a reformist message, whereas the part dealing with *masa'ib* remains very traditional. This moderate reformism can at times provoke violent reactions. In February 2005, a reformist *zakira* originally from Pakistan but resident in Kenya, who had been invited to Bombay for Muharram, was expelled after she criticized some of the local traditions before an audience of 400 women, inviting them to turn away from "deviant" practices.

The new madrasas for women are the vectors of transmission of reformed practices and a tool for women's empowerment and social advancement. The preliminary observations we made both in Pakistan and in Qom raise several questions that still need to be addressed: the relationship between social class and religious practices; the resources that the traditional clergy can mobilize to counter the reformist trend; the role of the transnational networks and of the Pakistani clerics who commute between Iran and Karachi; and finally, the core question. What is Iran's real aim in training this new elite, and how and why did Iran respond so efficiently to the demand coming from Pakistan?

Bibliography

Bard, Amy, "Value and Vitality in a Literary Tradition: Female Poets and the Urdu Marsiya", in *Annual of Urdu Studies*, 15, University of Wisconsin, 2000, pp. 323–335.

Bearman, P. J., Bianquis, T., Bosworth, C. E., van Donzel, E., and Heinrichs, W. P., *Encyclopaedia of Islam*, 2nd Edition, Leiden 1960–2005, Brill

Blanchy, Sophie, *Karana et Banians. Les communautés commerçantes d'origine indienne à Madagascar*, Paris 1995, L'Harmattan.

Cole, Juan, *Sacred Space and Holy War. The Politics, Culture and History of Shi'ite Islam*, London 2002, I. B. Tauris.

Hegland, Mary Elaine, "The Power Paradox in Muslim Women's Majales: North West Pakistani Mourning Rituals as Sites of Contestation over Religious Politics, Ethnicity, and Gender", in *SIGNS. Journal of Women in Culture and Society*, 23/2, 1998, pp. 391–428.

Hegland, Mary Elaine, "Flagellation and Fundamentalism. (Trans)forming Meaning, Identity, and Gender through Pakistani Women's Rituals of Mourning", in *American Ethnologist*, 25/2, 1998, pp. 240–266.

Howarth, Toby, *The Twelver Shi'a as a Muslim Minority in India. Pulpit of Tears*, London 2005, Routledge.

Maclean, Derryl, *Religion and Society in Arab Sind*, Leiden 1989, E. J. Brill.

Mohamed-Arif, Amina, *Salam America. L'islam indien en diaspora*, Paris 2000, CNRS Éditions.

Pinault, David, *The Shiites. Ritual and Popular Piety in a Muslim Community*, London 1992, I. B. Tauris.

Pinault, David, *Horse of Karbala. Muslim Devotional Life in India*, New York 2001, Palgrave.

Schubel, Vernon James, *Religious Performance in Contemporary Islam. Shi'i Devotional Rituals in South Asia*, Columbia 1990, University of South Carolina Press.

SABRINA MERVIN

Transnational Intellectual Debates

Iranian intellectual debates resonate far beyond Iran. An elite composed of Shi'a clerics, religious intellectuals and militants carefully pays attention to what is said, thought and written in Qom, Tehran and Mashhad. The Islamic sphere in which they move has no borders; it exists wherever individuals meet, exchange information and news picked up elsewhere, reminisce, discuss and debate. Students of the religious sciences from all corners of the Shi'a worlds visit Qom for a while, then leave again, taking with them knowledge and a certain idea of Islamic modernity which they will transmit to others. For several years they study together, then they lose sight of each other only to meet again by chance during a pilgrimage, a pious visit or any other voyage, in the *majlis* of a sheikh, the offices of a magazine or publishing house, a research centre, a library, an Islamic foundation ... The connections are closest among men who have been circulating for a long time between Persian and Arabic Shi'ism, between Iran, Iraq, Lebanon and the Gulf states, especially Saudi Arabia.

Many members of this elite have passed through the *hawza*, while others have studied at universities and those who completed a double education are increasingly numerous. Some are autodidacts, others are teachers or students; and among them are also women, whose numbers and importance are growing. All share the same references to a religious Shi'a culture, a corpus of classical texts and the founding texts of the Shi'a Islamic movement but also of Sunnism. Nevertheless, they do not necessarily hold the same opinions, each using these shared references to develop a personal point of view, always prone to nuances, re-examinations and pragmatic readjustments in accordance with new events and theories.

Should we see in this a characteristic of Shi'ism, where the ultimate aim of religious studies is to practice *ijtihâd*, to forge one's own opinion and defend it, and where the individual, the *mujtahid*, prevails over the institution? Nothing is more difficult than tracking currents and tendencies, constructing categories that enable us to develop a structured representation of this Islamic sphere. Actors and observers distinguish between Islamists and liberals, activists and quietists, supporters of the regime and its opponents.[1]

Meanwhile, the fault lines are sometimes subtle and difficult to determine. Supporters of the Iranian Islamic regime have also been influenced by the arguments of reformists, if only to refute them. A good example is the philosophy of Soroush, which everybody knows directly or indirectly. While he was the leading religious intellectual in the Islamic Republic at the time of the reformists, preaching for the individualization of the faith, more recently Shari'ati has become an authority even within the Islamic movements by advocating the declericalization of society. These are not contradictions in an otherwise coherent system, but phenomena proper to the Islamic sphere, which is to be understood as a dynamic field in constant movement, crisscrossed by subtle divisions which resist systematic categorization. Thus, the Shi'a Islamic sphere in Beirut includes milieus that are more or less close to Hezbollah and others that overtly distance themselves from the party. Each side has its own ties to Iran, depending on the positions it takes. They are distributed over both sides of the *khatt al-imâm* (line of the Imam), which Hezbollah adheres to and which is mainly based on the theory of *wilâyat al-faqîh* as conceived by Khomeini. But here too, there are nuances; a distinction is made between the theory and its application after the Revolution, and there are many who cherish the dream of a return to the purity of Khomeini's intentions – seen as diluted through the exercise of power – in order to reconnect with the ideal which remains the Islamic utopia.

1. The term "quietist" is to be understood here in the sense given to it by Keddie, namely "withdrawn from political engagement". Cf. Richard, 2006, p. 258, note 13. About the neo-conservatives, see Khosrokhavar, 2001.

Common History, Shared References

The "mechanical solidarities" that link the clerical milieus and specifically the elites are still operative today, although newcomers not belonging to the great families "of science" have transformed the landscape. Organic ties, moreover, connect the militants of political parties and other politico-religious formations. But the Islamic sphere also includes individuals with disparate profiles and individual intellectual trajectories who are not affiliated to any established group. The factor that preserves internal cohesion and ensures that each person can recognize the other as an interlocutor is the common history of the Shi'a movement, which has produced the references each and every one of them shares.

This history has deep-seated roots and spans a centuries-long elaboration of the religious doctrine, with its division between Usûlism and Akhbârism and the victory of the former over the latter. More recent are the premises of the Islamic constitutional movement in Iran (1906–11) and the debates between the great Shi'a *mujtahids* of Qom and Najaf.[1] This is the history of the Shi'a movement, which began in the late fifties and early sixties as a reaction to the revolution of the Free Officers and General Qâsim in Iraq in 1958 and the white revolution of Mohammad Reza Shah in Iran in 1963. Agricultural reforms and the elaboration of a new family code particularly affected the *ulemas*, whose position had already been undermined by the secularization of the institutions, the decrease of their income and the slow decline of their religious schools. Moreover, students were tempted by the Marxist ideas that were spreading through the holy cities; many arrived to study religious sciences but left without a turban, instead becoming communists.[2] In answer to these threats, the clerics, the *marja'* at their head, emerged from their wait-and-see attitude and threw themselves into this worldly battle. In Iran, they had until then opted for a policy of accommodation with the Shah, whereas in Iraq they had remained silent in the mid-1920s, except for Mahdî al-Khâlisî.[3]

Borujerdi (1875–1961) reorganized the *hozeh* of Qom and attempted

---

1. Hairi 1977, Martin 1989.
2. Naef, 2001.
3. For his biography in French, see Luizard, 2005.

to consolidate the religious institutions, which he did so well that the number of students increased even more.[1] Muhsin al-Hakîm (deceased in 1970) pursued the same objectives in Najaf and gave an impulse to the creation of the Association of Ulemas in 1960 – this brought together clerics of different generations and nationalities.[2] However, the two grand *marja'* were soon overtaken by younger, more active clerics, less fearful of participating in politics, with whom they had an ambiguous relationship. In Qom there was Ruhollah Khomeini, and later his disciple Mortazâ Motahhari and in Najaf Muhammad Bâqir al-Sadr, surrounded by some others.[3] They became the pillars and ideologues of the Shi'a movement, for which their works are still the main references.

Muhammad Bâqir al-Sadr was in the first place a *faqîh*. Teaching at the *hawza*, he engaged in the reform of Islamic jurisprudence, more specifically the *usûl*, in order to make it more accessible to his students. His publications on the matter are today widely used manuals.[4] He is moreover known for two books that aim at countering Western philosophy and Marxism and thus introduced these subjects into the domain of the *hawza*; *Our Philosophy* and *Our Economy*[5] became important reference works in Islamic circles. However, he was not the only one to try to lay the foundation of an Islamic economy as a third way next to socialism and capitalism. As far back as the 1940s, Sayyid Qutb had dealt with the question of social justice in Islam, and on the Shi'a side Mahmud Taleqâni had studied the issue of property. But with his knowledge of Marxist terminology, al-Sadr initiated a new way of dealing with Western materialism, which he believed needed to be better known so as to be

---

1. Martin, 2003, pp. 50–56.
2. Abdul-Jabar 2003, , pp. 110–3.
3. Such as Muhammad Bahr al-'Ulûm, Murtadâ al-'Askarî, Muhammad Bâqir al-Hakîm, who later founded SCIRI, Muhammad al-Sadr (father of Muqtadâ.) and two Lebanese, Muhammad Husayn Fadlallâh and Muhammad Mahdî Shams al-Dîn.
4. Notably *al-Ma'âlim al-jadîda*, a very clear introduction to the *usûl*, and *Durûs fî 'ilm al-usûl*, a more difficult work translated into English by Roy Mottahedeh. Cf. al-Sadr, 2003.
5. *Falsafatunâ* (1959) and *Iqtisâdunâ* (1961) are regularly reprinted in Arabic and at least partially translated by Islamic publishers. About these works, see Mallat, 1993; and Donohue, 1988.

more efficiently refuted. His influence in this matter first spread to his close companions and his contemporaries, starting with his cousin Mûsâ al-Sadr, who wrote articles on economy in the journal *Maktab-e eslâm*, published in Qom, focusing on the question of redistribution, a subject given much attention by Muhammad Bâqir.[1] Note that Mûsâ al-Sadr was also in contact with Mohammad Beheshti, who published on Islamic economy and particularly on the banking system.[2]

On the political level, Muhammad Bâqir al-Sadr developed an original conception of the Islamic state, a conception that evolved significantly between the 1960s and the late 1970s. His theory is different from Khomeini's; he advocates militancy and the institutionalization of the clergy, but also the separation of power between the nation and the clergy, with both remaining subject to the constitution and the law. It can thus be considered a liberal hierocracy or a semi-liberal populist system.[3] Al-Sadr, who was a prolific author, also published a journal, *al-Adwâ'* (The Lights) in close collaboration with the young Lebanese clerics Muhammad Husayn Fadlallâh and Muhammad Mahdî Shams al-Dîn.[4] Furthermore, he played a role in the Islamic movement as an inspiration to the al-Da'wa party, although up to the present moment little is known about his exact relationship with the party. Shortly after the Iranian revolution, Muhammad Bâqir al-Sadr had become too dangerous in the eyes of the Ba'athist regime. He was executed in April 1980 and members of al-Da'wa were prosecuted. This caused them to disperse geographically and diverge in their political choices, leading to a ramification of the party into different branches. Nevertheless, the experience of al-Da'wa

---

1. Abdul-Jabar, 2003, pp. 296–305, gives an overview of the theory of Muhammad Bâqir al-Sadr on redistribution. See also Chehabi, 2006, p. 148.

2. See Beheshti, 1997, pp. 36–7. Beheshti, a student of Khomeini, later played a major role in the establishment of the Islamic Republic. He died in a bomb explosion at the headquarters of the Party of the Islamic Republic in Tehran in June 1981. Cf. Digard, Hourcade and Richard, 1996, p. 184.

3. Terms used by Faleh Abdul-Jabar in *The Shi'ite movement in Iraq*, p. 281, in his presentation of the political theory of Muhammad Bâqir al-Sadr. See also pp. 280–7. In his study of theories on the state in Shi'a jurisprudence, the Iranian philosopher Mohsen Kadivar classifies al-Sadr's ideas under the theories of the intikhâbi (elected) Islamic state. Cf. Kadivar, 2004, p. 185.

4. Abdul-Jabar, 2003, p. 114 and following.

and the ideas of Muhammad Bâqir al-Sadr constitute the basis of current movements, especially for the Arab Shi'a. Almost every party refers to him in some fashion or another.

The doctrines of Ruhollah Khomeini are another element of these foundations. He partly fits into the tradition of Islamic utopias that also includes Farabî, Ibn 'Arabî and Mollâ Sadrâ Shirâzî, who themselves were inspired by the concept of the virtuous wise man who governs the *polis* in Plato's *Republic*. Indeed, Khomeini was not only a famous Islamic law expert and politician, he was also a gnostic, which is reflected in his writings on Islamic government.[1] He taught mystic philosophy in Qom from 1940 onwards, at a time when this was frowned upon in clerical circles. Today he is credited for the reintroduction of this discipline in the *hozeh*. Khomeini's principal contribution therefore lies in the way he combined mystical philosophy, *feqh* and his political vision to create his theories of Islamic government and *velâyat-e faqih*. He propagated these theories during his exile in Najaf, conferring the powers of the hidden Imam on the theologian-jurist and thus elevating him to the position of guide of the community on the spiritual but also on the political level. This theory, in an adapted version, would later form the basis for the Islamic regime of Iran – as well as a subject of debate among the *ulemas*.

While Khomeini was a mystic theorist who would turn into a pragmatic politician when he came to power, his disciple Motahhari was the real ideologue of the Islamic regime, which would honor him with the title *mo'allem-e enqelâb* (Teacher of the Revolution). Today, his assassination is commemorated annually.[2] Motahhari developed the thought system which the regime drew on to define, organize and mobilize society. Like his master, he was a theosophist who shared with him a certain vision of the world. However, he was more interested in social issues and was more of a reformist cleric than a revolutionary militant. He vilified the conservative clerics, specifically for their reluctance to engage in politics, and his ambition was to modernize religious institutions.[3] In his readiness

---

1. Martin, 1989, pp. 31–47. For the gnostic aspects of Khomeini's ideas, see also Bonaud, 1997.
2. Nikpey, 2001, p. 221. Motahhari was killed in May 1979 by a member of the Forqan group.
3. About his reform programme for the clerical institutions, cf. Walbridge, 2001,

to change society in order to make it more just, Motahhari was competing with those in 1970s Iran who were influenced by Leninism and anti-
colonialism – that is, the ideas imported from the West that Motahhari
wanted to ban. He therefore engaged in a systematic criticism of Marxism,
although only after studying it attentively, and of the Islamic socialism of
Shari'ati, which he vehemently resisted. Any movement towards secularization, or any attempt to integrate foreign concepts into Islamic doctrines,
was in his eyes a conspiracy against Islam. His ideology, like Muhammad
Bâqir al-Sadr's, aimed to be an alternative and a barrier to the influence
of Western materialist thought. Nevertheless, and again like al-Sadr and
other Islamic thinkers, Motahhari ended up constructing a hybrid system
influenced by the ideas which he opposed. He was a prolific author who
left many varied and often reprinted works.[1]

Today, Muhammad Bâqir al-Sadr and Mortazâ Motahhari are often
named by players in the Islamic sphere as the founding fathers of Shi'a
Islamic ideology. What is particular to Shi'ism is that its ideologues, with
the exception of some Iranian "religious intellectuals" such as Shari'ati, are
all high-ranking clerics. The ideologies they construct aim in the first place
to reject the process of secularization affecting Islamic societies, as well as
the Western influence that is perceived as an effect of imperialism. Thus
they devote major efforts to the modernization of their institutions (*marjayat* and *hozeh*) and struggle to overcome the inertia of clerical milieus.
They fulminate against materialist philosophies, countering them with
Shi'a messianism and a mixture of rationalist, reformist, modernist and
even mystical theories, reconsidered in the light of anti-colonial ideals.
For them, Islam should be turned into an all-encompassing system able
to respond to all social problems. The quietist attitude, the *taqiyya* of old,
should be rejected and replaced by activism rather than passively waiting
for the return of the Mahdî.

These imperatives were taken from the Qur'an. The fight between good
and evil, between the oppressed and the oppressor, was thus described

---

pp. 161–182, which includes Motahhari's text "The fundamental problem in
the Clerical Establishment", with an introduction by Hamid Dabashi.

1. Martin, 2003, Chapter IV: "Motahhari: Towards an Islamic Ideology and the
Battle for Control of Political Islam"; Nikpey, 2001 pp. 218–30. About the
attacks against Shari'ati, see Rahnema, 2000, chapters XVI and XVII.

in terms which opposed the *mustad'afûn* (downtrodden)[1] to the *mustak-barûn* (arrogant of this world). The masses are mobilized during religious celebrations, particularly Ashura, with slogans that are chanted every year again without losing their evocative power. Thus, during the celebrations following the July war against Israel, the Lebanese Hezbollah proclaimed *intisâr al-mazlûm* (the victory of the oppressed), referring to the paradigm of Husayn, the martyr of Karbala. In doing this, the party gave a new sense to the paradigm, since it was no longer a symbolic or moral victory that they claimed but a real one.

While the concepts of traditional Shi'ism underwent an ideological reinterpretation, the organizational methods characteristic of Leninist parties, such as a pyramidal structure and a cult of secrecy, were freely borrowed to enhance the efficiency of activism. Yet both the concepts that were developed and the forms and methods of mobilization used always had the aim of producing and promoting an ideology that would uphold Islamic modernity. Since the end of the nineteenth century, Islamic societies and their clerics, confronted with a form of modernity imposed by a conquering and hegemonic West, have been searching for an appropriate response.[2] The "revolutionary" Shi'a movements, with Iran at their head since 1979, have also offered their versions.

Nevertheless, a more discreet current, which predates the revolution, has evolved, offering alternative answers, unfolding a vision of Islam that is more humanist than political, without the wholesale rejection of either the ideas imported from Europe or the secularization affecting Muslim societies. Two different types of players, clerics and religious intellectuals, spread this movement, which is often qualified as reformist. Here, we must again note the difficulty of classifying people and their ideas. The clerics involved in this movement became better informed about worldly affairs and a small elite among them was well versed in the profane sci-

---

1. In Lebanon, Mûsâ al-Sadr used the term *mahrûm*, traditionally translated as "disinherited": he was the initiator of the Harakat al-mahrumîn, the Movement of the Disinherited.

2. The representations in the media of a "retrograde" or "medieval" Iranian regime have wiped out the notion that the regime resulted from a rupture with the classic doctrines and an attempt to construct an endogenous modernity. On this point see the chapter "The Modernity of Theocracy" in Cole, 2002.

ences as well as Christian theology. A good example can be found in Mohammad Mojtahed Shabestari, who directed the Islamic Centre in Hamburg, founded in 1969 on Borujerdi's initiative. "Doctor Ayatollah Beheshti" was his predecessor in this position and Mohammad Khatami his successor.[1] Shabestari stayed in Hamburg for almost a decade studying Christian philosophy and theology, returning to Tehran just before the Revolution, by which time he spoke Arabic, English and German.[2] Similarly, many intellectuals, most of them with university degrees in various specializations, studied the religious sciences, following Soroush's example. And just as academics taught at the *hozeh*, especially in reformed schools, religious clerics offered courses at universities, mostly in the philosophy departments (as for example Shabestari and Kadivar). Some of them, like Malekian, never wore the turban even though they were integrated into the *hozeh* system.

While this phenomenon can today be observed throughout the *hâla islâmiyya,* notably in Iraq and Lebanon, it is still less common there than in Iran, where it was generalized by the *enqelâb-e farhangi* (Cultural Revolution). After the closure of the universities in 1980, Khomeini established several organs charged with integrating the *hozeh* and the universities, bringing together intellectuals and men of religion. After months of discussing and introducing certain "Islamized" subjects into their curriculums, certain university functionaries participating in the reform project considered that they could not go any further.[3] Others, on the contrary, wanted to proceed towards a complete Islamization of the social sciences and establish a system of lasting crossovers connecting the university with the *hozeh*, and they continued their efforts in this direction with the support of the government. Sheikh Mohammad Taqi Mesbâh Yazdi, for example, organized exchanges within the framework of the Hozeh o Daneshgâh (*hozeh* and university) Committee, sponsoring the initiation of about a hundred academics in the Islamic sciences

1. In the 1960s Beheshti, who read German and English, was an exception. The large majority of clerics hadn't completed their secondary education. Richard, 1983, p. 14. Note that his companion Mûsâ al-Sadr, who established himself in Lebanon, had also enjoyed a double education.
2. Amirpur, 2000, p. 315.
3. Interview with Gholamabbas Tavasoli, University of Teheran, 7 April 2004.

with the objective of bringing them to criticize the social sciences from an Islamic perspective. Upon their return to the university, they were supposed to become the pillars of the Cultural Revolution. This particular project was never implemented, but the radical sheikh continued to push for co-operation between the two institutions and the adoption of an Islamic point of view in the social sciences, both in his writings and in the educational institution in Qom which he directed.[1] The activities of the Hozeh o Daneshgâh Committee have become more important over the last ten years, especially through the publication of books aiming to Islamicize the social sciences.[2]

The Iranian experience in the matter is often considered a model, as in Lebanon where the *hawza* milieus wish to establish links with the universities in order to obtain equivalent diplomas for their students. Nevertheless, the same experience is also criticized inside and outside Iran, not only by intellectuals but also by reformist clerics. Schematically speaking, the matter comes down to the question of whether one wants to Islamicize modernity or modernize Islam. The proponents of the latter option tend to draw upon the social sciences, accepted as universal, in order to develop their comprehension of the doctrines.

A New Theology

In reformist circles in the Persian and Arabic worlds, scholars talk about a new or modern theology, which is distinguished from the ancient science of *kalâm* in both its methods and its object. New questions are asked and the tools used to answer them transcend the Islamic sciences to incorporate human sciences as they are practiced today. Furthermore, this new theology does not aim to defend religion but rather to understand it. In Iran, the cleric best representing this current, having become the main name in the field, is Mohammad Mojtahed Shabestari. For some, he has become a

---

1. Interview with Mohammad Taqi Mesbâh Yazdi, Qom, 19 August 2003. An illustration of his method can be found in his work *Usûl al-ma'ârif al-insâniyya*, which presents in Arabic the lectures he has given in Beirut.
2. Interview with Sayyed 'Arabi, Qom, 1 January 2004. Information can be found on the website of this institution, which later became a research centre affiliated to the *hozeh* of Qom in 1990: http://www.hawzeh.ac.ir

model, others have attacked him, but like Soroush he is now part of the cognitive landscape and those who are interested in the subject cannot ignore him. He has written relatively little, as he prefers to concentrate on teaching and on his research for an Islamic encyclopedia,[1] but he has marked an entire generation. His status as a cleric and his education at the *hozeh* of Qom, where he studied from 1950 until 1968, also give him credibility in religious circles. He was close to Beheshti and part of the editorial board of *Maktab-e eslâm*, a journal on social and political issues. Shabestari also has substantial knowledge of Catholic and Protestant theological matters, acquired during his decade-long stay in Hamburg. He is both *mojtahed* and doctor in philosophy and the influence he exerts clearly shows this fact.

Shabestari bases himself on the writings of 'Allâma Tabâtabâ'i (d. 1981), meaning that he refers to the Islamic philosophical tradition in its most contemporary forms. Tabâtabâ'i was not only a famous exegete; he also popularized the ideas of Mollâ Sadrâ Shirâzî, which he introduced to the *hozeh,* teaching from the *Book of four journeys*.[2] For Shabestari, the spiritual journey does not lead to annihilation in God, as is the case for the ideologues Motahhari, Khomeini and even Shari'ati, but to the consciousness of self and the affirmation of man and his freedom. That is to say he has a different approach to the *'erfân,* which he does not associate with Islam as an all-encompassing system capable of providing the answer to all the problems posed by modernity.[3] Moreover, when Shabestari takes up his metaphysical hypotheses, he notes the inability of classic philosophies, such as the *feqh*, to renew our comprehension of the world. It is therefore necessary to draw on modern sciences to build up those sciences that are missing in Islam, like the philosophy of law, morality, politics and economics.[4]

The contribution of Shabestari lies in his demonstration of the fact that religious knowledge, even though it is declared to be eternal, is limited and changing. It is therefore the task of thinkers to adapt to the age and develop an adequate approach and a critical apparatus, which is

---

1. *Da'erat-e bozorg-e eslami*, in Teheran.
2. Cf. Dabashi, 1993, chapter V and Ridgeon, 2005, chapter VIII.
3. Vahdat, 2000 , pp. 41–3.
4. Ibid. p. 39 and Sadri, 2001, p. 261.

something he applied himself to in his *Hermeneutics of the Qur'an and the Sunna* (1996), one of his main works, together with his work on freedom and faith and his *Critique of the Official Reading of Religion* (2000). Shabestari also took part in the public debate in Iran by writing articles for different journals.

The ideas of Shabestari and other Iranian thinkers travelled beyond the Iranian borders. In 1995, the journal *al-Muntalaq* (The Point of Departure) published an interview with him, in which, after explaining that this new theology was still in its infancy, he announced with pride the existence of a "nucleus" and expressed his hope to see an increase in contributions and debates.[1] *Al-Muntalaq* is the archetypal magazine of the Lebanese Islamic sphere, whose history has partly been written in its own pages over the years. It was created in Beirut in September 1977 by the Lebanese Union of Muslim Students, an organization sponsored by Muhammad Husayn Fadlallâh, who made the magazine his forum in the 1980s.[2] It subsequently opened its pages to the debates taking place within the Lebanese Shi'a movement. From the second half of the 1990s onwards, its editor-in-chief Hasan Jâbir used it to spread the ideas of Iranian thinkers. In 1998 he published a special issue on the renewal of theology, with four articles translated from Persian offering different perspectives on the matter.[3] For several years, a kind of euphoria reigned: this new approach opened fields that had not received attention in classic Shi'ism and allowed the discussion of issues grounded in reality and experience, including the experience of Islamic government in Iran and its limits. "Before, we would think about the relations between God and his servant, now we think about the problems of man in society, and about politics (*shûrâ* and democracy), and this implies an accommodation and renewal in all religious sciences."[4] Jâbir himself prefers to reflect on the philosophy of *fiqh* and is interested in the values underlying the norms.[5]

---

1. Jâbir, 2001b, p. 46.
2. Sankari, 2005.
3. *Al-Muntalaq*, nr 119, Autumn-Winter 1997–8.
4. Interview with Hasan Jâbir, Beirut, 28 December 2001.
5. Jâbir, 2001a.

Today he continues in this direction and, as a university graduate, has started to teach the new theology in a *hawza*.[1]

Enthusiasm for the new theology quickly spread;[2] in Qom, it reached the circles of non-Iranian students and teachers at the *hozeh* who had access to the Persian texts. Iraqi, Lebanese and Gulf Shi'a joined in informal discussion circles. In 1994 one of them, 'Abd al-Jabbâr al-Rifâ'î, founded a journal that would form a true bridge between the intellectual fields of Iran and the Arab world and, even more, a transnational forum for Shi'a and Sunni thinkers: *Qadâyâ islâmiyya mu'âsira* (Contemporary Islamic Issues).[3]

'Abd al-Jabbâr al-Rifâ'î was a prolific writer, and his intellectual trajectory deserves a closer look. He was born in a peasant family in a village close to Nâsiriyya and attended the primary school that was opened there after the revolution of 1958. Then he started a journey that brought him first to Baghdad, where he completed a course in agronomy, and then to the *hawza* of Najaf, where he studied from 1978 until 1980. The regime's repression forced him to leave Iraq and in 1984 he arrived in Qom. He describes himself as always "in search of science", and to this day he teaches at the *hozeh* and the university. Although he does not wear the turban, he is a "sheikh". He received a classic education and tried out all the possibilities offered by the freedom of choice that characterizes education at the *hozeh*, before formulating his critique of the system in order to "modernize it and open it to the century".

Qadâyâ ... and her sisters

His project entailed a real reconstruction of the religious sciences and the representation of the divine. This was the topic of his journal, which also gave a platform to a group of students and clerics at the *hozeh* who, as Rifâ'î puts it, "had no voice before".[4] Virtually without assistance, 'Abd al-Jabbâr al-Rifâ'î published in Arabic not only philosophers like Shayegan

---

1. Interview in Beirut, 13 April 2003.
2. Interview with 'Abd al-Jabbâr al-Rifâ'î, Qom, 28 August 2003.
3. The journal first carried the name *Qadâyâ Islâmiyya*, under which the first five issues were published from 1994 till 1998.
4. Interview with 'Abd al-Jabbâr al-Rifâ'î, Qom, 28 August 2003.

and reformist thinkers like Soroush, Shabestari or Malekiân, but also authors that opposed their ideas.

"*Qadâyâ* did not try to establish a certain position as the right line, but to expose the reader to various opinions," Rifâ'i explains. "What is important is opening breaches to trigger reflection, and this can only be done by raising questions, because the history of thought is the history of raising important questions."[1]

The articles published therefore sometimes sharply contrast with each other, although as is common in this type of publication, the tone and certain formulations soften the discourse. Some *ulemas* from Qom have written in *Qadâyâ*, such as Mohammad Taqi Mesbâh Yazdi, Ja'far Sobhâni and Nâser Makârem Shirâzi. Lebanese reformists including Muhammad Mahdî Shams al-Dîn, Muhammad Husayn Fadlallâh, Muhammad Hasan al-Amîn and Hânî Fahs have encouraged the publisher of *Qadâyâ*, which is printed in Beirut and distributed throughout the Arab world, especially in Egypt and Morocco, where it has found a wide audience. It also publishes texts by the Egyptian Hasan Hanafî, "discussing ideology rather than epistemology,"[2] and by Maghrebi authors. 'Abd al-Jabbâr al-Rifâ'i states that contrary to the Iranians, thinkers from the Maghreb are outside of the Islamic sphere, but stresses the closeness of their thought, mentioning Mohammed Talbi, 'Abd al-Majid Charfi, Abdou Filali-Ansary, and most of all Mohammed Arkoun, whom he considers the most remarkable among them.

Apart from publishing these articles and interviews translated from Persian to Arabic, *Qadâyâ* also offers reports on the debates and round tables that it organizes itself or takes over from Persian journals such as *Naqd o nazar*, which is connected to the *hozeh* of Qom. Its publisher grasps every opportunity to bring thinkers together and record their exchanges. The themes broached by *Qadâyâ islâmiyya mu'âsira* since 1998 are a good illustration of the evolution of the questions that are debated today. There are special issues on Shi'a political thought (nos. 1 and 2, 1998); contemporary Islamic thought and its new orientations (no. 5,

---

1. Interview with 'Abd al-Jabbâr al-Rifâ'i published in the newspaper *al-Ayyâm* (Bahrain), 26 January 2004, available on www.islamonline.net/Arabic/arts/2004/01/article17.shtml.
2. In the words of 'Abd al-Jabbâr al-Rifâ'i.

1999); Qur'anic exegesis (no. 4, 1998), which includes the translation of Shabestari's work on hermeneutics (nr. 6, 1999); the philosophy of Islamic jurisprudence and a new interpretation of the approach of the *maqâsid* (nos. 7 and 8, 1999; nr. 13, 2000); the doctrine of Muhammad Bâqir al-Sadr (nos. 11 and 12, 2000); the new theology (no. 14, 2001); liberalism (no. 24–25, 2003); tolerance (nos. 27 and 28–29, 2004); and "living together" and religious and cultural pluralism (no. 31–32, 2006). The latter issue publishes authors representing various currents, including Daryush Shayegan and Mojtahed Shabestari and a debate between John Hick and Hossein Nasr in Istanbul. The table of contents shows that the journal is sensitive to the questions raised by the current political situation in the region, notably in Iraq, where since 2003 the editor has been trying to re-establish himself; this explains the irregularity of its publication.

Although he lives in Qom most of the time, 'Abd al-Jabbâr al-Rifâ'î has founded a centre in Baghdad, the Centre for the Study of the Philosophy of Religion and the New Theology, which co-publishes books about scientific approaches to Islam, such as a collective volume on the anthropology of Islam[1] and a work by 'Abd al-Jabbâr al-Rifâ'î in which he exposes in a very didactic way what modern theology is and which important questions it has dealt with since the time of Jamâl al-Dîn al-Afghânî.[2] Its journal is moreover reprinted in Damascus and Beirut in the form of volumes that form several series.[3] We will take a closer look at two of the publications that directly concern new theology. The first, *Theological Ijtihâd*, contains several interviews with the Egyptians Hasan Hanafî and Muhammad Imâra and the Iranians Mojtahed Shabestari, Mostafâ Malekiân and Ahad Qaramelki, as well as Sâdiq Lârijani, who is renowned for offering the best conservative critique of Soroush. The second, *New Theology and the Philosophy of Religions*, contains interviews with several of the same authors as well as others, and includes moreover the texts of a round table on religious rationality and theology attended by Iranian

---

1. Bâqâdir, 2005. This volume contains Arabic translations of articles by Jacques Waardenburg, Eric Wolf and Cliford Geertz.
2. Rifâ'î, 2005a.
3. In Damascus, the books are published by Dâr al-Fikr and in Beirut by Dâr al-hâdî and Dar al-Fikr al-Mu'âsir.

clerics and philosophers.[1] We observe both a variety of perspectives and opinions and a diversity of authors, offering a glimpse on the richness of the Iranian intellectual arena.

The journal *Qadâyâ islâmiyya mu'âsira* has contributed a wealth of reflections on the modernization of Islam by giving a voice to authors ranging from the most reformist to the most conservative. It brings together actors from the *hozeh* and from the university, including Shi'a from Iran, Lebanon, Iraq and the Gulf as well as Sunnis, in particular the leading figures of various magazines published in Beirut and of the *Prologues* in Casablanca. This small world can gather and debate the issues during the pilgrimage to Mecca as well as at a conference in Rabat. *Qadâyâ Islâmiyya* is today the best known journal in its field and the most widely distributed, but it is not the only one published in Shi'a circles who consider themselves enlightened.

In Damascus a disciple of Rifâ'î publishes *al-wa'î al-mu'âsir* (Modern Consciousness). In Beirut, *al-Muntalaq al-jadîd* (The New Point of Departure) succeeds *al-Muntalaq* and continues in the same current under the direction of a woman, Zaynab Shurba. *Al-Kalima* (The Word) has been published since the 1990s by a Saudi Shi'a cleric, Zakî al-Mîlâd, who is the author of a dozen of books on contemporary Shi'a thought.[2] He is one of the new "Islamo-liberal" reformists[3] who, after returning to Saudi Arabia and rejecting their revolutionary ideals, want to make their voices heard in a dialogue with the political constituents of the country. Two other journals of a similar type are published at educational institutions. *Al-Hayât al-tayyiba* is published by the *hawza* Ma'had Rasûl al-Akram, which we will meet again later in this essay, and whose chief editor is the *hawza's* former director, the Iranian cleric Najafali Mirzâ'i. The journal, created in 1998, mainly focuses on the modernization of religious education and has gradually become an eclectic debating forum, as much because of the choice of authors as through the selection of themes. This pluralism is also reflected in the composition of its editing board[4] and shows that there

---

1. Rifâ'î, 2002a and 2002b.
2. Al-Mîlâd, 2001.
3. Lacroix, 2004, pp. 12–13.
4. Including clerics who are known as broad-minded, such as Muhammad Hasan al-Amîn and the "neo-conservative" Mohammad Taqi Mesbâh Yazdi, clerics

is room for maneuver even for institutions that depend on the Iranian clerical establishment: the journal and the *hawza* are both financed by the organ that co-ordinates Iranian schools abroad. It also confirms the importance of the individual in relation to the institution; in this case, because it is the chief editor who sets the tone. *Al-Mahajja* is a journal published by an institute that offers courses in Islamic philosophy in the southern suburbs of Beirut. Its focus is therefore on philosophical questions but in many ways it also resembles the other journals mentioned, often publishing the same authors and sometimes even the same articles. The particularity of *al-Mahajja* lies in the fact that it also publishes articles by Christian theologians and Lebanese authors such as philosopher and theologian Paul Khoury who are in touch with the institute, whose director is also editor-in-chief of the journal.

More recently, *Nusûs muʿâsira* (Contemporary Texts) was established; its offices are in Beirut but those in charge of it reside more often in Qom or in the Gulf. Published by a Centre for Contemporary Research (Markaz al-buhûth al-muʿâsira), the journal claims to specialize in "the translation of texts that deal with women's issues, modernity, dialogue, openness towards the other, philosophy of *fiqh*, modern theology, the plurality of interpretations, etc." To this purpose, it affirms its willingness to "benefit from the contemporary intellectual experience of the Iranian cultural arena" and offers texts that are of interest to the Islamic sphere in Arabic translation. Its objectives are clearly stated in its electronic version.[1] *Nusûs muʿâsira* offers the same type of debates as are published in *Qadâyâ*, such as a new translation of *Qazb va bast* by Soroush. This is justified with the argument that the previous translation was marred by omissions and lack of precision, and that the text and the polemics it incited are too important not to remedy this situation.[2] As for reformist options, although *Nusûs muʿâsira* offers more conservative analyses, its articles do often deal with reform and renewal, like the other journals. Not all authors attach the

---

and intellectuals, Shiʿa and Sunnis (for example Ridwân al-Sayyid, founder of the journal *al-Ijtihâd*, and today leading the journal *al-Tasâmuh*).

1. www.nosos.net – see notably 'Li-mâdhâ Nusûs muʿâsira?' (Why *Nusûs muʿâsira*?), by Haydar Hubb Allah, chief editor of the journal.
2. Cf. *Nusûs muʿâsira*, 5, Winter 2006, p. 136.

same importance to these notions, but the aim remains to find modalities to accommodate Islamic thought in the modern world.

Meanwhile, we should not forget that these journals only interest a small elite. Najafali Mirzâ'i, the Iranian cultural consul, estimates that some journals sell only 500 copies per issue; their readership is very limited in Lebanon, although it is larger in Morocco and Egypt.'[1] *Qadâyâ islâmiyya muʿâsira* has the largest readership, as it is the oldest journal and definitely the one most in touch with reformist debates.

A Predilection for Philosophy

If we are to draw a distinction between Arab and Persian Shiʿism, the predilection of the latter for mysticism, gnosis and philosophy must definitely be mentioned. This was also the view of Henry Corbin, who describes the phenomenon very well.[2] We find in Persia mystic orders that are absent in Arab Shiʿism and theosophists who are unparalleled there. Although the *hawza* of Najaf has started teaching philosophy again, it is far more closely identified with Qom. It is in the arena of philosophy that the opposing camps – conservative supporters of the regime on one side and reformists on the other – paradoxically meet each other, even if they do not understand the subject in the same manner. For the former, gnosis and philosophy serve a worldview that proposes an all-encompassing Islam, an Islamic utopia, while for the latter the same elements are the vectors for the individualization of religion.

In Lebanon, a generation of clerics trained after the revolution have returned imbued with a knowledge that was not shared by their elders, who were molded by the ideas current in 1960s Najaf. They in turn transmitted these ideas to others. Thus, in 1999 Sheikh Shafîq Jarâdeh founded the Institute of Theosophy for Religious and Philosophical Studies in the southern suburbs of Beirut. The evening courses there are organized in two sections: one is reserved for enrolled students who are required to succeed in a certain number of philosophy courses – *ʿirfân*, fundamental beliefs (*ʿaqîda*), theology, morality – to obtain their degree,

---

1. Interview at the Iranian Cultural Centre in Beirut (Bir Hasan), 21 December 2006.

2. Corbin, 1971–2.

which is not recognized by the state. The other, open to all, offers courses of methodology, Sufism and *'irfân*. The aim is not so much to educate specialists but to broaden the cultural horizon of *hawza* or university students in these disciplines and guide their researches by offering them a method. The registration fee is relatively modest, aiming mostly to sift out non-serious applicants, since the institute is financially supported by the *'marja'iyya khums'*, that is by 'Ali Khamenei.

Shafîq Jarâdeh originally started out by teaching a classic work of *'irfân*[1] as well as the work of 'Allâma Tabâtabâ'i, who is considered to be the founding father of the philosophical milieu in Qom.[2] Later he widened his interests, notably including the history of philosophy and Christian theology. "John Hick has influenced Iranian thought and I think he should be read like other Christian theologians, to benefit from their experience," he declares. Moreover, Muslims and Christians regularly gather at the institute for debates where all share their views on issues faced by all religions. Thus, the institute maintains a permanent dialogue with Paul Khoury, "who plays the role of John Hick in Lebanon," Bishop Georges Khodr and Father Mouchir Aoun, from the Université du Saint-Esprit in Kaslik.[3] "If we don't discuss the questions that affect us in a religious framework transcending Islam, we will not develop," considers Shafîq Jarâdeh. "And if God is for all of us, how can I monopolize Him? We need to have a dialogue and consider the points on which we agree and acknowledge those on which we differ."[4]

This discourse resonates with an audience in the southern suburbs, where the youth are demanding a new approach to Shi'ism, one that is different from the daily worship with its rules, and sometimes even

---

1. Muhammad Bahr al-'Ulûm, *al-Sayr wa al-sulûk*. This is a treaty of practical gnosis, describing methods for the adoration of God (*dhikr*, contemplation, etc.).
2. Rifâ'î, 2005b, chapter IV.
3. Paul Khoury is a theologian and philosopher at the Institut Saint-Paul de Philosophie et de Théologie in Harissa. Georges Khodr is the bishop of the Greek Orthodox Church for Mount Lebanon and has been very engaged in the renewal of the Church. Mouchir Aoun teaches philosophy and intercultural dialogue at the faculty of theology at the Université du Saint-Esprit in Kaslik.
4. Interview with Shafîq Jarâdeh, Beirut, 16 May 2006.

from spirituality. Philosophy and *'irfan* also attract militant students or sympathizers of Hezbollah; they find here an intellectual content to sustain their commitment. Besides, Shafiq Jaradeh is known to be close to the party. Women are also present at the institute and are even in the majority at the Institute of Oriental Philosophy directed by the cleric Muhammad al-Hâjj, a kind of cultural centre also located in the southern suburbs, where people come in the evenings to submerge themselves in metaphysics and theosophy.

The transcendental philosophy of Mollâ Sadrâ Shirâzî has also made its way into the Lebanese *hawza*, like other newly formed disciplines aiming at the modernization of education in the religious sciences. These schools are in fact reformed institutes that do not follow the system of the classic "free" *hawza*, where every student can choose his teachers and his courses, instead following the university model.[1] In Lebanon, the most modernist among them are directed by young clerics and placed under the religious authority of either Muhammad Husayn Fadlallâh or 'Ali Khamenei.[2] In addition to the secular social sciences (sociology, psychology, pedagogy), new disciplines of the Islamic religious sciences have been introduced. While it has become common to offer courses in Islamic jurisprudence with a comparative approach between the Shi'a and Sunni schools, it is a more recent phenomenon to have courses relating Islamic law to positive law. The general subject of *fiqh* has various branches: its history and practice, its social aspects, the norms and the *fatwas*, etc. are studied in separate courses. The philosophy of *fiqh*, a discipline that first appeared in journals, has made its entry in educational programs, as has the new theology. Eventually, debates between *ulemas* and religious intellectuals find their practical application in the introduction of new programs.

The institute al-Rasûl al-Akram and its female branch, al-Zahrâ', are considered to be in the vanguard of religious schools in the Islamic sphere. Its voluminous 2003–04 catalogue,[3] which lists the courses year by year, reveals a concern with a new categorization of disciplines, willingness to structure teaching and openness to social science literature produced

---

1. About the reform of the *hawza*, see Sabrina Mervin, 2003.
2. Namely *al-Ma'had al-shar'î al-Islâmî* and *Ma'had al-rasûl al-akram*, both situated in the southern suburbs of Beirut. Mervin, 2003
3. *Dalîl Ma'had al-rasûl al-akram*, 2003–04.

abroad. All of it is presented in a clear and elegant form. The director, well informed about the issues that occupy the religious circles, explains his objective in the introduction: to modernize the *hawza* without taking away its depth.[1] We could be tempted to see this as the influence of Iran, with its experience in founding and administrating this type of establishment, especially since the school follows the *marja'iyya* of 'Ali Khamenei. But in fact it should also be seen as the marks of individual initiatives. The institute is directed by Najafali Mirzâ'i, a cleric who is very taken by contemporary debates and publicizes them in the journal *al-Hayât al-tayyiba*, of which he is editor-in-chief.[2] He has also founded a research institute in Beirut, where efforts are directed towards introducing the Arabic and Iranian civilizations to each other, and which focuses mainly on the different currents in contemporary thinking.[3]

The Iranian Fingerprint?

When we ask him whether his taste for philosophy and new theology is an effect of the Iranian influence, Najafali Mirzâ'i seems to think it is not. "People study Mollâ Sadrâ Shirâzî because he is a Shi'a, not because he is Iranian." He goes even further: "Great thinkers are universal. Ibn 'Arabî, for example, wasn't 'Sunni and Arabic', he belonged to everybody.[4] The same is true today for Soroush or Shayegan, they are not Iranian thinkers ..." To the same question, Muhammad al-Hâjj answers rather humorously: "Our association does not follow Iran, it follows the ideas of Shiraz. Here we are not interested in ideology but in metaphysics."[5] Shafîq Jarâdeh declares that, as the history of philosophy wasn't being taught, he tried to teach it the "Iranian way", although adding Arabic authors.

---

1. Ibid., pp. 10–11.
2. Meanwhile he has founded a research centre in Qom and has returned to Lebanon as cultural counsellor.
3. The centre translates books into both languages on subjects ranging from contemporary poetry to the philosophy of *fiqh*, women's rights and the theoretical foundations of the Islamic Republic. Interview, Beirut, 21 December 2006.
4. Note that Ibn 'Arabî occupies an important position in the theoretical Shi'a *'erfan* because his theories have been adopted by Mollâ Sadrâ, which shows the pertinence of the example.
5. Interview, Beirut, January 2002.

With regard to the "new theology", it is not that new, according to some commentators. Its critics consider, albeit slightly in bad faith, that it is an ancient discipline in a new jacket and that only the formulation has changed. Its proponents, for their part, write its history. 'Abd al-Jabbâr al-Rifâ'î traces its origin back to the Indian scholar Shibli No'mani (d. 1914), author of a work titled *The New Theology*. He further mentions the famous Egyptian reformist Muhammad 'Abduh (d. 1905) and his *Risâlat al-tawhîd* (Treaty of Oneness) and finally Mohammad Iqbâl (d. 1938) who, more than the above-mentioned, truly nourished the project of the reconstruction of religious sciences in Islam.[1] The next step is found in the writings of Mohammad Hosein Tabâtabâ'i, his disciple Mortazâ Motahhari and Muhammad Bâqir al-Sadr.[2] Thereafter, Iran's strength lay, for him, in the production of intellectuals who were not only trained in the classic system of the *hozeh*, but also enjoyed a modern, scientific academic education.[3] They were therefore able to think about Islam with the intellectual tools of their time. Many proponents of the new theology draw a parallel between the openness of contemporary thinkers towards western social sciences and the movement to translate Greek philosophy in the ninth century, which was the origin of the development of the *falsafa*. "However," Shabestari adds, "in the time of Ma'mûn, Muslims dominated the world and translated, while now they borrow ideas that they think are universal."

Modern Islamic theology may be the outcome of a historical process, but it is not limited to Iran. The existence of the Islamic Republic certainly raised questions that encouraged its development but according to Shabestari, it has also been developed elsewhere in the Muslim world. He thinks that the writings of the Egyptian Nasr Abu Zayd, for example, or the Syrian Muhammad Shahrûr, also belong to the new theology even if they are part of Qur'anic exegesis, because they promote a new vision of Islam. He considers Mohammed Arkoun and Mohammad 'Abed al-Jâbiri

---

1. Cf. M. Iqbal, *The Reconstruction of Religious Thought in Islam*. The book is available in English on : www.allamaiqbal.com/works/prose/english/reconstruction/.

2. Cf. Rifâ'î's introduction to Shabestari, 2000, pp. 7–8. See also the comparison he draws between Abduh and Iqbâl in Rifâ'î, 2006.

3. Interview in Qom, 28 August 2003.

as modern theologists too.[1] Hasan Jâbir agrees, mentioning the same names and adding the Lebanese 'Alî Harb. The historicity of the sacred text has been studied by Arab authors before Soroush; "his reading was therefore a shock for the Iranians but not for us," he states.[2] If some years ago, one could hear remarks such as "we do as in Qom" or "this comes from Iran", this is no longer so prevalent today. More than a merely political reason, we should see in this the effect of a habit and an expression of attachment to Arabic culture. Furthermore, the reformist thinkers who claim to be open to the world are also open to the Islamic worlds and are consciously attempting to transcend identity constructions of "belonging", taking only intellectual affinities into consideration. Finally, let us not forget the personalities on the local religious and intellectual scenes, who do not refer to Iran and do not consider themselves influenced by its thinkers, even if they read them. This holds true for the Lebanese Muhammad Husayn Fadlallâh, who follows his own road as *marja'* and applies a reformism that is more practical than theoretical, as well as for another Lebanese, Muhammad Hasan al-Amîn, who is rooted in his society and in local Arabic Shi'ism.[3]

Bibliography

Abdul-Jabar, Faleh, *The Shi'ite movement in Iraq*, London 2003, Saqi Books.

Al-Amin, Muhammad Hasan, *al-Ijtima' al-'arabî al-islamî. Murâja'ât fî al-ta'addudiyya wa al-nahda wa al-tanwîr* (Arabic Islamic Society. Studies on Pluralism, Revival and Enlightenment), Beirut 2003, Dâr al-hâdî.

Amirpur, Katajun, Mohammad Mojtahed Shabestari, in *Orient,* 41/1, 2000, pp. 14–17.

Baqâdir, Abû Bakr Ahmad, ed., *Anthrubûlûjiya al-islâm* (Anthropology of Islam), Beirut 2005, Dâr al-hâdî.

Beheshti, Muhammad, *al-Iqtisâd al-islâmî,* (The Islamic Economy), Tehran 1997, Râbitat al-thaqâfa wa al-'alâqât al-islâmiyya.

Bonaud, Yahya Christian, *L'Imam Khomeiny, un gnostique méconnu du XXe siècle: Métaphysique et théologie dans les œuvres philosophiques et spirituelles de l'Imam Khomeiny,* Beirut 1997, al-Bouraq.

---

1. Interview in Teheran, 16 August 2003.
2. Interview in Beirut, 3 January 2007.
3. On Muhammad Husayn Fadlallâh see his website: www.bayynat.org; for Muhammad Hasan al-Amîn, we refer to al-Amîn 2003.

Chehabi, Houchang E., ed., *Distant relations. Iran and Lebanon in the last 500 years*, London 2006, Centre for Lebanese Studies and I. B. Tauris.

Cole, Juan, *Sacred space and Holy War. The Politics, Culture and History of Shi'ite Islam*, London 2002, I.B. Tauris.

Corbin, Henry, *En Islam iranien, aspects spirituels et philosophiques*, Paris 1971–2, Gallimard.

Dabashi, Hamid, *Theology of Discontent*, New York 1993, New York University Press.

Dalîl Ma'had al-rasûl al-akram al-'âlî li-l-sharî'a wa al-dirâsât al-islâmiyya, Beirut, 2003–04

Digard, Jean-Pierre, Hourcade, Bernard, and Richard, Yann, *L'Iran au XXe siècle*, Paris 1996, Fayard.

Donohue, John J., "Notre économie", in *Cahiers de l'Orient*, 8–9, 1988, pp. 179–202.

Fischer, Michael M. J., *Iran from Religious Dispute to Revolution*, Cambridge and London 1980, Harvard University Press.

Hairi, Abdul-Hadi, *Shi'ism and Constitutionalism in Iran. A Study in the Role Played by the Persian Residents of Iraq in Iranian Politics*, Leiden 1977, E. J. Brill.

Jâbir, Hasan, *al-Maqâsid al-kulliyya wa al-ijtihâd al-mu'âsir* (The *maqâsid* and modern *ijtihâd*), Beirut 2001a, Dâr al-Hiwâr.

Jâbir, Hasan, "al-Tajdîd wa al-taqlîd fî al-fikr al-îrânî al-mu'âsir" (Renewal and tradition in Iranian contemporary thought), in *Shu'ûn al-sharq al-awsat*, 103, summer 2001b, pp. 38–47.

Kadivar, Muhsin, *Nazariyyât al-dawla fî al-fiqh al-shî'î* (Theories of State in Islamic Shi'a law), Beirut 2004, Dâr al-hâdî.

Keddie, Nikki R., *Religion and Politics in Iran. Shi'ism from Quietism to Revolution*, New Haven and London 1983, Yale University Press.

Khosrokhavar, Farhad, "Neo-conservative Intellectuals in Iran", in *Critique*, 19, fall, 2001, pp. 5–30.

Lacroix, Stéphane, "Between Islamists and Liberals : Saudi Arabia's new 'Islamo-Liberal' Reformists", in *The Middle East Journal*, 58/3, Summer, 2004, pp. 345–65.

Luizard, Pierre-Jean, *La vie de l'ayatollah Mahdi al-Khalisi par son fils* (introduction, annotation and translation by Pierre-Jean Luizard), Paris 2005, La Martinière.

Mallat, Chibli, *The renewal of Islamic law. Muhammad Baqer as-Sadr, Najaf and the Shi'i International*, Cambridge 1993, Cambridge University Press.

Martin, Vanessa, *Islam and Modernism: the Iranian Revolution of 1906*, London 1989, I.B. Tauris.

Martin, Vanessa, *Creating an Islamic State. Khomeini and the Making of a New Iran*, London and New York 2003, I.B. Tauris.

Merat, Zarir, "Les revues intellectuelles. L'embryon d'une agora", in *Les cahiers de l'Orient*, 49, 1998, pp. 87–102.

Mervin, Sabrina, "La *hawza* à l'épreuve du siècle: la réforme de l'enseignement religieux supérieur chiite de 1909 à nos jours", in al-Charif, Maher, and al-Kawakibi, Salam. eds,, *Le courant réformiste musulman et sa réception dans les sociétés arabes,* Damascus 2003, IFPO, pp. 69–84.

Misbâh, Yazdî, M. T. *Usûl al-ma'ârif al-insâniyya* (The foundations of human knowledge), Beirut 2004, Mu'assasat Umm al-qurâ.

Al-Mîlâd, Zakî, *al-Fikr al-islâmî, tatawwurâtuhu wa masâratuhu al-fikriyya* (The Islamic thought, its developments and its intellectual path), Beirut 2001, Dâr al-hâdî.

Naef, Silvia, "Shi'i-shuyu'i or: How to become a Communist in a Holy City", in Ende, Werner, and Brunner, Rainer, eds., *The Twelver Shi'a in Modern Times. Religious Culture and Political History,* Leiden 2001, E. J. Brill, pp. 255–67.

Nikpey, Amir, *Politique et religion en Iran contemporain. Naissance d'une institution,* Paris 2001, l'Harmattan.

Rahnema, Ali, *An Islamic Utopian. A political Biography of Ali Shari'ati*, London 2000, I. B. Tauris.

Richard, Yann, "Le rôle du clergé : tendances contradictoires du chi'isme iranien contemporain", in *Archives des sciences sociales des religions,* 55/1, 1983, pp. 5–27.

Richard, Yann, *L'Iran. Naissance d'une république Islamique,* Paris 2006, La Martinière.

Ridgeon, Lloyd, *Religion and Politics in Modern Iran. A Reader,* London: I. B. Tauris, 2005.

Rifâ'î, 'Abd al-Jabbâr, ed.,*'Ilm al-kalâm al-jadîd wa falsafat al-dîn* (Modern theology and philosophy of religion), Beirut 2002, Dâr al-hâdî.

Rifâ'î, 'Abd al-Jabbâr, *al-Ijtihâd al-kalâmî. Manâhij wa ru'â mutanawwi'a fî al-kalâm al-jadîd* (The theological *ijtihâd*. Methods and various views on the new theology), Beirut 2002, Dâr al-hâdî.

Rifâ'î, 'Abd al-Jabbâr, *Muqaddima fî al-sû'âl al-lâhûtî al-jadîd* (Introduction to the modern theological question), Beirut 2005, Dâr al-Hâdî.

Rifâ'î, 'Abd al-Jabbâr, *Tatawwur al-dars al-falsafî fî al-hawza al-'ilmiyya* (The development of the teaching of philosophy in the hawza), Beirut 2005, Dâr al-Hâdî: Qadâyâ islâmiyya mu'âsira.

Rifâ'î, 'Abd al-Jabbâr, "Muhammad 'Abduh wa Muhammad Iqbâl, ru'yatân fi tahdîth al-tafkîr al-dînî" (Muhammad 'Abduh and Muhammad Iqbâl, two visions of modernization and religious thought), in Charif, Maher, and Mervin, Sabrina. eds, *Hadâthât islâmiyya/Modernités Islamiques*, Damascus 2006, IFPO, pp. 99–114.

al-Sadr, Muhamamd Bâqir, *Lessons in Islamic Jurisprudence* (translation by Roy Mottahedeh), Oxford 2003, Oneworld Publications.

Sadri, Mahmood, "Sacral Defense of Secularism: The Political Theologies of Soroush, Shabestari and Kadivar", in *International Journal of Politics, Culture and Society,* 15/2, 2001, pp. 257–70.

Sankari, Jamal, *Fadlallah. The Making of a Radical Shi'ite Leader,* London 2005, Saqi Books.

Shabestari, Mohammad Mojtahed, *Madkhal ilâ 'ilm al-kalâm al-jadîd,* Beirut 2000, Dâr al-Hâdî.

Group of *ulema, Sîra wa hayât al-shahîd Bihishtî* (Biography of martyr Beheshti), Beirut 2000, Dâr al-Hâdî.

Farzin, Vahdat, "Post-revolutionary Discourse of Mohammad Mojtahed Shabestari and Mohsen Kadivar: Reconciling the Terms of Mediated Subjectivity. Part I: Mojtahed Shabestari", in *Critique,* 16, 2000, pp. 31–54.

Vahdat, Farzin, "Post-revolutionary Discourse of Mohammad Mojtahed Shabestari and Mohsen Kadivar: Reconciling the Terms of Mediated Subjectivity. Part II: Mohsen Kadivar", in *Critique,* 17, 2000, pp. 135-157.

Walbridge, Linda, ed., *The most Learned of the Shi'a. The Institution of the Marja' Taqlid,* New York 2001, Oxford University Press.

Wâsifî, Muhammad Ridâ, *al-Fikr al-Islamî al-mu'âsir fi Irân. Jadaliyyat al-taqlîd wa al-tajdîd* (Islamic contemporary thought in Iran. Controversies about the tradition and the renewal), Beirut: Dâr al-Jadîd, 2001.

Glossary

Where two terms are given, the first is Arabic and the second Persian.

Ahl al-bayt:
: "the people of the house", refers to descendants of the prophet Muhammad.

Akhbârism:
: a current in Twelver Shi'ism which favours a literal reading of the sayings of the Imams. Today, only a minority of clerics follow it, as most adhere to the usûlî school.

Âkhund:
: a title for clerics, which can have neutral, negative or positive connotations depending on time, place and circumstance.

Ashura:
: tenth day of the month of *muharram*, in which the martyrdom of Imam Husayn in Karbala in 680AD/61AH is commemorated.

Ayatollah:
: "sign of god", title indicating a cleric who has finished studies to the level of *ijtihâd*.

Fatwa:
: non-binding advice given by an expert in Islamic law in answer to the question of a believer.

Fiqh/Feqh:
: Islamic law.

Hawza/Hozeh:
: religious school of the Twelver Shi'a. By extension the name given to a group of schools, the teaching system, or even the

clerical milieus which form around the schools, students and teachers.

Hujjat al-islâm: title given to a middle-ranking cleric who did not reach the level of *ijtihâd*.

Husayniyya/Hoseyniya: Shi'a place of worship where the *majlis husaynî* are held during the *muharram* commemorations, as well as lectures and funeral services.

Ijâza/Ejâze: certificate given by a master to a student, authorising the latter to transmit the knowledge which his master has imparted on him or to exercise *ijtihâd*.

Ijtihâd/Ejtehâd: the process of deriving norms from the four "sources" of Islamic law (the Qur'ân, the Sunna, consensus and reason) using a precise methodology.

Imam: a very polysemic term, literally "he who is in front". In Shi'ism, the Imam is the successor to the prophet Muhammad (akin to the caliph of the Sunnis), and therefore the temporal and spiritual leader of the community. By extension, the title is also bestowed on certain important clerics (such as Khomeini or Mûsâ al-Sadr). More generally, it designates the person who leads the assembly in prayer in the mosque.

Imami Shi'ism: another name for Twelver Shi'ism.

'Irfân/'Erfân: mystic philosophy, gnosis.

Ismailism: branch of Shi'ism also known as Sevener Shi'ism, itself divided into several groups including the *nizâri*, who follow the Aga Khan.

Ja'farî: the law school of the Twelver Shi'a, named

after its founder *Ja'far al-Sâdiq*, the sixth Imam.

Madhhab: doctrine, religious sect, law school.

Madrasa: school.

Majlis husaynî: a mourning sequence in which the tragic events in the story of the *ahl al-bayt* are recounted, specifically the battle of Karbala and the martyrdom of Husayn. Synonyms are *majlis al-'azâ'*.

Marja': the source of emulation whose prescripts believers follow in religious matters, and thus the supreme religious authority. The *marja'* must be the *mujtahid* who is considered the most learned by his peers for him to become a source of reference and to attract emulators who will follow his prescripts and pay their religious taxes to him.

Marj'iyya/Marjayat: the institution of the *marja'* – a term referring both to his religious authority and to the organization or apparatus built around his person.

Mawkib husaynî: public procession organised to commemorate the martyrdom of Husayn.

Muharram: first month of the year in the hijra calendar. The first ten days of the month (culminating in Ashura) are devoted to the commemoration of Husayn's martyrdom.

Mujtahid: a cleric competent to exercise *ijtihâd*.

Muqallid: cf. *taqlîd*.

Rahbar (Persian): guide of the Islamic regime (Khomeini until his death in 1989, Khamenei ever since).

Rahbariat (Persian): the institution which developed around the guide.

Risâla ʿamaliyya/Resâla: a work written by a *marjaʿ* setting out religious prescripts for his emulators to follow.

Ruhâni (Persian): cleric.

Sayyid/Sayyed: title used for descendants of the prophet, whether they are clerics or not. If they are clerics, they wear a black turban as opposed to the white turbans worn by ordinary sheikhs.

Shiʿism: a branch of Islam founded by those who supported ʿAli b. Abî Tâlib as the successor to the prophet Muhammad, and which has split into three main groups: Twelver Shiʿism, Zaydi Shiʿism and Ismailism. Each of these has developed its own doctrines, specifically concerning the imamate.

Talabeh: students in the religious sciences.

Taqiyya: the practice of prudential dissimulation. When the life or property of believers are threatened, they are permitted to hide their faith or to pretend to adhere to a different one.

Taqlîd: literally "imitation", often "emulation". The process whereby a believer (who thereby becomes a *muqallid*) conforms to the prescripts of a specific *marjaʿ* (who thereby becomes a *muqallad*).

Twelver Shiʿism: a branch of Shiʿism that recognizes a line of twelve imams, the last of whom was the *Mahdî* or "hidden Imam", whose return has been awaited since his "great occultation" in 941AD/329AH.

Umma: the community of believers.

Usûl al-fiqh/Osul-e feqh:	a discipline of Islamic law that describes the methods to develop norms.
Usûlism:	current of Twelver Shi'ism that favors the use of the *usûl* and of *ijtihâd* to derive religious norms from the four sources of Islamic law: the Qur'an, the Sunna, consensus and reason. Cf. also Akhbârism.
Wahhabism:	the strict neo-Hanbalite and Salafist Sunni doctrine developed by Muhammad b. 'Abd al-Wahhâb in Saudi Arabia in the eighteenth century.
Wakîl/Vakil:	local agent of a *marja'* who represents him and collects the religious taxes for him.
Walî al-faqîh/Vali-ye faqih:	the jurist-theologian leading the community.
Waqf:	legacy or estate administered as a religious endowment.
Wilâyat al-faqîh/Velâyat-e faqih:	leadership of the jurist-theologian. According to Khomeini's theory, this leadership or guidance applies to every spiritual and temporal domain.
Zaydism:	a branch of Shi'ism that follows Zayd, one of the sons of the fourth Imam, and which has developed rationalist doctrines that are close to Twelver Shi'ism.
Ziyâra:	pious visit to the mausoleum of a holy figure in Shi'ism, usually an imam or a descendant of the prophet.

Index

Index

Golpayegani, Ayatollah Mohammad Reza 40, 257
Gölpinarli, Abdülbaki 157, 158
Gordlevski, Vladimir 141
Guide of the Islamic Republic 18, 29, 39, 40, 42, 49, 174, 349
Gülen, Fethullah 187–8
Gulf, Organization for the Islamic Revolution in the 35, 41, 65, 75

Hâfez 128
al-Hâ'irî, Kâzim al-Husaynî, Ayatollah 258, 268–9, 269, 270, 271, 275, 288, 293, 295, 300
al-Hâjj, Muhammad 340, 341
al-Hakîm, Muhammad Bâqir 37, 296
al-Hakîm, Muhammad Sa'îd 284
al-Hakîm, Muhsin, Grand Ayatollah 37, 65, 324
al-Hakîm, Sayyid Mahdî 65
Hamas 34, 42, 278
Hamburg 329, 331
Hamedani, Sabri 149
Hanafî, Hasan 334, 335
Harakat-e Enqelâb 33
Harakat-e eslami (Islamic Movement) 57
Harb, 'Alî 343
Harb, Sheikh Râghib 116
Harling, Peter 22, 281–301
Harpviken, K.B. 53
Hasan b. 'Alî (2nd Imam) 12, 155
al-Hasanî, Mahmûd 270, 294, 295
Hâshemi, Mahdi 75, 78
Hatemi, Hüseyin 155
Hazarajat 52–3, 54
Hazaras 32, 45–7, 50–1, 59–60
Hekmatyar, Gulbuddin 33
Herat 32, 46, 57
Hezb-e Tahrir 211
Hezb-e Wahdat (Islamic Unity Party) 40, 42, 47, 56, 59
'Hezbollah' (Gulf monarchies) 78–9, 81, 82, 83
Hezbollah (Lebanese) 10, 19, 22, 23, 34, 37, 41, 42, 43, 89–112passim, 115–34passim, 222, 226, 227, 237, 246, 270, 278, 322, 328, 339
Hezbollah (Turkish) 30, 148
Hick, John 335, 339
Hindustani, Muhammadjan 170

Husayn b. 'Alî (3rd Imam) 12, 49, 123, 128, 140, 155, 177, 179–80, 225, 226, 239, 240, 260, 296, 304, 305, 328, 349
Huseyinzade, 'Ali Bey 169
Huseyni, Allama Arif 35
al-Hussaini, Allama Arif Hussain 307
Hussein, Saddam 10, 15, 28, 31, 40, 41, 80, 255–61passim, 272, 273, 281, 285, 286, 288, 291, 297, 299, 315

Ibn 'Abd al-Wahhâb, Muhammad 6
Ibn 'Arabî 326, 341
Ibrahimoglu, Haji Ilgar 173, 176–7, 177
IGC (Interim Iraqi Governing Council) 261
Iğdir 139, 142, 144, 145, 150, 151, 153, 155, 174
Imamiyya Student's Organization 38
Imâra, Muhammad 335
Iqbâl, Mohammad 342
Iran, Islamic Republic of 9, 11, 15, 18, 21, 74, 84, 90, 174, 181, 256, 300, 326
Iranian Charity Foundation 141, 143, 144, 146
Iranian Revolution 10, 15, 21, 29–31, 36, 39–41, 68, 140, 233, 246, 306, 322, 329
Iraq 30, 34, 87, 255–79passim, 321, 323, 329, 335, 336
Ironi Shi'a 11, 22, 194–212passim
ISI (Inter-Services Intelligence) 32
Islamic Action Organization 75, 77
Islamic Amal 37
Islamic Jihad 91
Ismaïl, Shâh 168, 184
Ismailis 304
Istanbul 139, 140–3, 144, 145, 146–51, 153, 154, 155, 158, 159, 169, 187, 335

Jabal 'Âmil 20, 69, 105
Jâbir, Hasan 332–3, 343
al-Jâbirî, Mohammad 'Abed 342
al-Jâbirî, Nadîm 277
al-Ja'farî, Ibrâhîm 276, 277, 296
Jamâ'at al-Sadr al-Thânî 255, 259
Jama'at-e eslami 31
Jami'at al-Muntazar 313–14
Jami'at al-Zahra 306, 307, 312, 315–19
Jami'at Khadijat al-Kubra 307–12
al-Jamrî, Mansûr 79
al-Jamrî, Sheikh 'Abd al-Amîr 65, 72

The Shi'a Worlds and Iran

Qaramelki, Ahad 335
Qâsim, General 291, 323
Qâsim, Sheikh 'Isâ 65
Qâsim, Sheikh Na'îm 23, 98, 107
Qasîr, Ahmad 126, 131–2
Qazvin 177
al-Qazwînî, Sheikh Murtadâ 67
Qods Force 267
Qom 13–15, 17, 18, 19, 23, 37, 38, 77, 84–5, 149,
    151, 167, 173, 174, 181, 182, 227, 234, 236, 237,
    242, 258, 268, 269, 288, 303, 306, 307, 312,
    314–19passim, 321, 323–4, 324, 326, 330, 331,
    333, 334, 335, 337–9passim, 341, 343
Qur'an 95, 96, 98, 100, 102, 103, 109, 127, 153,
    233, 305, 308, 310, 312, 319, 327
Qutb, Sayyid 324

Rabat 336
Rafsanjani, Akbar Hâshemi 41, 76, 236,
    268
Rahime Hanim, (daughter of 7th Imam)
    171, 179
Rashidov, Sharaf 202
Reza Shah, Mohammad 21, 49, 323
Ridâ (8th Imam) 12 see also 'Alî Ridâ
al-Rifâ'î, 'Abd al-Jabbâr 333–4, 335, 342
Rizvi, Seyyid Saeed Akhtar 215
Roy, Olivier 22, 29–44, 47, 48, 50
al-Rufây'î, Haydar 259

Şefizade, Haci Mehmet Naki 144
al-Sabah family 69, 70, 81
Sabiği, Ismail 149
Sabzavâri, Ayatollah 257
Saddam City see Madînat Saddâm
Sadr City see Madînat al-Sadr
Sadr family 20, 38, 297
al-Sadr, Husayn 296
al-Sadr, Muhammad Bâqir, Ayatollah 16, 31,
    65, 83, 256, 284, 289, 291, 294, 296, 324–
    7passim, 335, 342
al-Sadr, Muhammad Sâdiq, Ayatollah 255–
    8passim, 269, 270, 275, 281, 282, 283, 285–9,
    292, 292–3, 294, 296
al-Sadr, Muqtadâ 20, 22, 87, 151, 255, 256, 258,
    259, 260–78passim, 281, 293, 294–7
al-Sadr, Mûsa, Imam 20, 21, 35, 37, 38, 89–90,
    109, 116, 132, 223, 325, 328, 329, 348

SADUM (Soviet Spiritual Administrations)
    170, 200–1
al-Saffâr, Sheikh Hasan 67, 75, 82, 86
Salafists 31, 32, 33, 41, 42, 43, 83, 154, 211
Saleh, Fouad 'Ali 30
Samarkand 193, 195, 196, 199, 202, 203, 205,
    206, 210
Samarra 13
al-Samawi, Muhammad al-Tijani 234
Saudi Arabia 68, 69, 73, 76, 80–1, 86, 321
al-Sayyid, Sayyid Ibrâhîm Amîn 94
Sayyida Zaynab 15, 33, 79
Sâzman-e Nasr (Victory Organization) 55,
    56, 57
SCIRI (Supreme Council of the Islamic
    Revolution in Iraq) 38, 41, 77, 260, 261,
    263, 267, 268, 271, 273, 275–7passim
Senegal 216–48passim
Sepâh-e Mohammad 38
Sepâh-e pâsdâran (Army of Guardians) 55,
    56, 57
Serah 209
Seyidzade, Qazi Haci Mireziz 773
Sha'ban, Sheikh 33
Shabestari, Mohammad Mojtahed 329, 330–1,
    334, 335, 342
Shahrestânî, Husayn 277
Shahrudi, Mahmud Hâshemi 267
Shahrûr, Muhammad 342
Shams al-Dîn, Sheikh Muhammad Mahdî
    37, 39, 324, 325, 334
Sharaf al-Dîn, 'Abd al-Husayn 21
Sharaf al-Dîn (Sadr family) 20
Sharâra, Waddâh 103–4
Shari'at-Madâri 40
Shari'ati, Ali 322, 327, 331
Sharimirdan 208
Sharja 65
al-Sharqî 273
Shayegan, Daryush 335, 341
Shihab, President Fuad 21
Shirâzi family 20, 38, 66
al-Shirâzi, Hasan, Ayatollah 33, 79
Shirâzî, Mollâ Sadrâ 326, 331, 340, 341
al-Shirâzi, Muhammad, Ayatollah 37, 65, 66,
    67, 74, 77–8, 83, 84, 237
Shirâzi, Nâser Makârem 334
Shirâzi, Sâdiq 74, 84, 85
Shirâziyyin 66, 67, 68, 73, 74, 80, 82

358

Index